Advances in Semantic Media Adaptation and Personalization

Volume 2

Edited by
Marios C. Angelides
Phivos Mylonas
Manolis Wallace

CRC Press
Taylor & Francis Group
Boca Raton   London   New York

CRC Press is an imprint of the
Taylor & Francis Group, an **informa** business
AN AUERBACH BOOK

Auerbach Publications
Taylor & Francis Group
6000 Broken Sound Parkway NW, Suite 300
Boca Raton, FL 33487-2742

© 2009 by Taylor & Francis Group, LLC
Auerbach is an imprint of Taylor & Francis Group, an Informa business

No claim to original U.S. Government works
Printed in the United States of America on acid-free paper
10 9 8 7 6 5 4 3 2 1

International Standard Book Number-13: 978-1-4200-7664-6 (Hardcover)

Visit the Taylor & Francis Web site at
http://www.taylorandfrancis.com

and the Auerbach Web site at
http://www.auerbach-publications.com

Contents

Preface

It is becoming harder to access, manage, and transmit multimedia content according to the meaning it embodies. As text-based search engines give way to content- and context-aware engines, which personalize not only searching and delivery but also the content format, advanced network infrastructures are emerging that are capable of end-to-end ubiquitous transmission of multimedia content to any device (fixed or mobile) on any network (wired or wireless) at any time. This has opened up new markets for content and service providers who, recognizing the value of individual users, are investing in technologies that adapt and personalize content. In response, organizations have released new standards, such as MPEG-7, MPEG-21, and VC-1, which enable propagation of content adaptation and personalization. Consequently, a broad range of applications are emerging across many industry sectors, including music, film, games, television, and sports, to name but a few.

Personalizing and adapting content to the preferences and needs of users require processing of content, on the one hand, and recognizing patterns in users' behavior, on the other. The former involves stages such as extraction and analysis of content semantics and structure, modeling of the resulting content metadata, filtering of content metadata through user profiles, and adaptation of the content to suit the usage environment (i.e., the user, the client, the network, and the natural environment) or adaptation of the usage environment to suit the content. Recognizing user behavior requires the construction of user models that record usage history and user preferences for types of content, browser, and interface modalities in order to tailor content to cater to these preferences and to predict future usage behavior without too much stereotyping of the user.

Personalizing and adapting the semantic content of multimedia enable applications to make just-in-time intelligent decisions regarding this content, which in turn makes interaction with the multimedia content an individual and individually rewarding experience.

The Semantic Media Adaptation and Personalization (SMAP) Initiative was founded during the summer of 2006, in an effort to bring together researchers and practitioners working in this area to discuss the state of the art, recent advances, and future outlooks for semantic media adaptation. The first international workshop on

Semantic Media Adaptation and Personalization (SMAP 2006), held in December 2006, in Athens, was the first SMAP meeting. It outgrew all initial expectations and thus had to be extended from a one-day to a two-day event. The second workshop, SMAP 2007, held in December 2007 in London, saw a similar growth that resulted in the event having to be held over three days and the inclusion of a doctoral consortium. As a result of the overwhelming and continuing interest and support for the first two SMAP events, SMAP has become an annual event.

This edited book comprises extended versions of 18 papers originally presented at SMAP 2007, which have successfully made it through two additional rounds of reviews. The selection process was particularly difficult because a very high number of quality contributions presented during SMAP 2007 were up for consideration. We have made no effort to select papers of matching content; rather, we selected papers that are representative of the work presented at the workshop and that promote an understanding of the wider problems and issues pursued by researchers and practitioners working in the field. However, in arranging the order of the papers within the book, we have tried to position related topics together and to give an overall flow of topics within the papers, starting with those that address broader issues to those with more specific foci.

This book would have never come this far in so little time without the support and commitment of the review team, led by Dr. Harry Agius from Brunel University, who managed the entire review process from start to finish, and without the support and commitment of Richard O'Hanley, the publisher, and Amy Blalock, the project coordinator, of Taylor & Francis, who are two of the most efficient people working in the publishing industry at present. We therefore extend our deep gratitude to them.

Professor Marios C. Angelides
Dr. Phivos Mylonas
Dr. Manolis Wallace

Contributors

Harry Agius
Brunel University
Uxbridge, United Kingdom

Aydin A. Alatan
Middle East Technical University
Ankara, Turkey

M. C. Angelides
Brunel University
Uxbridge, United Kingdom

Ahmed Azough
France Telecom
Issy-les-Moulineaux, France

Mario Belk
University of Cyprus
Nicosia, Cyprus

Mária Bieliková
Slovak University of Technology
Bratislava, Slovakia

Laszlo Böszörmenyi
Klagenfurt University
Klagenfurt, Austria

Krishna Chandramouli
Queen Mary University of London
London, United Kingdom

Francisco Chávez-Gutiérrez
Parlamento de Canarias
Tenerife, Spain

Yolanda Cobos
Visual Communication Technologies
    VICOMTech
San Sebastian, Spain

Karin Coninx
Hasselt University
Diepenbeek, Belgium

Alexandre Delteil
France Telecom
Issy-les-Moulineaux, France

Fabien De Marchi
Claude Bernard Lyon University
Villeurbanne, France

Feng Dong
Bedfordshire University
Luton, United Kingdom

Nikolaos Ersotelos
Brunel University
Uxbridge, United Kingdom

Ander García
Visual Communication Technologies
    VICOMTech
San Sebastian, Spain

Panagiotis Germanakos
National and Kapodistrian University
of Athens
Athens, Hellas

Mohand-Saïd Hacid
Claude Bernard Lyon University
Villeurbanne, France

Mieke Haesen
Hasselt University
Diepenbeek, Belgium

Hermann Hellwagner
Klagenfurt University
Klagenfurt, Austria

Frank Hopfgartner
University of Glasgow
Glasgow, United Kingdom

Ebroul Izquierdo
Queen Mary University of London
London, United Kingdom

Joemon M. Jose
University of Glasgow
Glasgow, United Kingdom

Frank Kappe
Graz University of Technology
Graz, Austria

Sébastien Laborie
INRIA Rhône-Alpes
Grenoble, France

Janine Lachner
Klagenfurt University
Klagenfurt, Austria

Zacharias Lekkas
National and Kapodistrian University
of Athens
Athens, Hellas

María Teresa Linaza
Visual Communication Technologies
VICOMTech
San Sebastian, Spain

Hao Liu
Technische Universiteit Eindhoven
Eindhoven, the Netherlands

Andreas Lorenz
Fraunhofer Institute for Applied
Information Technology
Sankt Augustin, Germany

Kris Luyten
Hasselt University
Diepenbeek, Belgium

Jan Meskens
Hasselt University
Diepenbeek, Belgium

Constantinos Mourlas
National and Kapodistrian University
of Athens
Athens, Hellas

Özgür Deniz Önür
Middle East Technical University
Ankara, Turkey

M. J. Parmar
Brunel University
Uxbridge, United Kingdom

António M. G. Pinheiro
Universidade da Beira Interior
Covilhã, Portugal

Matthias Rauterberg
Technische Universiteit Eindhoven
Eindhoven, the Netherlands

Bernhard Reiterer
Klagenfurt University
Klagenfurt, Austria

Christian Safran
Graz University of Technology
Graz, Austria

Ben Salem
Technische Universiteit Eindhoven
Eindhoven, the Netherlands

George Samaras
University of Cyprus
Nicosia, Cyprus

Elena Sánchez-Nielsen
Universidad de La Laguna
La Laguna, Spain

Cristina Sarasua
Visual Communication Technologies
    VICOMTech
San Sebastian, Spain

Klaus Schöffmann
Klagenfurt University
Klagenfurt, Austria

Isabel Torre
Visual Communication Technologies
    VICOMTech
San Sebastian, Spain

Nikos Tsianos
National and Kapodistrian University
    of Athens
Athens, Hellas

Michal Tvarožek
Slovak University of Technology
Bratislava, Slovakia

Damon Daylamani Zad
Brunel University
Uxbridge, United Kingdom

Bilal Zaka
Graz University of Technology
Graz, Austria

Andreas Zimmermann
Fraunhofer Institute for Applied
    Information Technology
Sankt Augustin, Germany

Antoine Zimmermann
INRIA Rhône-Alpes
Grenoble, France

Chapter 1

Multimedia Metadata 2.0: Challenges of Collaborative Content Modeling

Damon Daylamani Zad and Harry Agius

1.1 Introduction

Web 2.0 refers to second-generation services available on the World Wide Web that enable users to collaborate and share information. Web 2.0 gives users an experience much closer to desktop applications than traditional static Web pages, harnessing the power of user contribution, collective intelligence, and network effects (O'Reilly 2006). Social networks and online communities lie at the heart of Web 2.0, and with their growth has come an increase in the sharing of multimedia content. In particular, sites such as YouTube and Flickr have given rise to multimedia communities by providing their users with the ability to attach metadata to multimedia content, such as videos and photos, in the form of tags.

In this chapter, we consider the next stage in multimedia metadata: multimedia content within Web 2.0 environments where users will both model and share multimedia content metadata collaboratively, which we refer to as *Multimedia Metadata 2.0* (MM 2.0). Creating metadata is a time-consuming process when undertaken

1

by a single individual. However, effort can be greatly reduced by harnessing the power of Web communities to create, update, and maintain content models for multimedia resources. Services based on wikis, which allow the pages of a Web site to be modified by anyone at any time, have proven that global communities of users are not only able to work together effectively to create detailed, useful content, even minutiae, for the benefit of others, but do so voluntarily and without solicitation (Bryant, Forte, and Bruckman 2005).

In order to enable an MM 2.0 environment, four key components are required, which are illustrated in Figure 1.1. The *resources* component facilitates population of the environment with the raw multimedia content in the form of video and audio streams, images, and so forth. The *modeling* component enables the creation and maintenance of metadata for the multimedia content contained within the resources component. The metadata is related to the multimedia content within the resources component through spatiotemporal decompositions of the content (i.e., demarcations of the streams in time and/or space). The *retrieval* component enables the retrieval of multimedia content based on queries regarding the content metadata and queries regarding the user community. Finally, the *community interaction and*

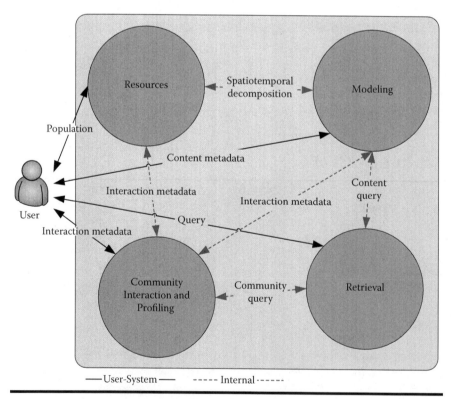

Figure 1.1   Typical MM 2.0 architecture.

profiling component facilitates user interactions within the community, such as instant messaging between users; and user profiling, such as user preferences and usage histories. Interaction metadata from this component enables community interactions and profiles to be related to content metadata.

In the next section, we examine the key challenges in realizing the above architecture for collaborative multimedia content modeling. Section 1.3 then considers the suitability of MPEG-7, the leading multimedia metadata standard, for overcoming these challenges. Section 1.4 summarizes and concludes this chapter.

1.2 Challenges of MM 2.0

MM 2.0 encompasses a broad range of topics of interest to the research community from which the following key challenge areas may be identified:

- *Standardization*, which concerns challenges regarding the technologies used to develop the MM 2.0 architecture, including the metadata representation format
- *Folksonomies*, which concerns challenges regarding the organization of the generated metadata
- *Awareness*, which concerns challenges regarding how to make users aware of both themselves and others through the communication of activities, emotions, and so on
- *Community*, which focuses on challenges regarding the engendering of community feeling and interaction, including issues regarding user intercommunication

These areas are interrelated: for example, standardization challenges impact upon folksonomy issues because they may restrict or enhance the metadata organization; awareness issues because they may restrict or enhance the types of awareness that may be represented and their level of detail; and community issues because they may restrict or enhance the level of communication. Table 1.1 provides an overview of the areas and the challenges, as well as typical solutions that are currently available. These challenges will be examined in detail.

1.2.1 Standardization

Standardization challenges concern technological issues at the heart of a multimedia collaborative system. The combination of heterogeneous devices and platforms used over the Internet engenders *interoperability* challenges. Consequently, collaborative multimedia systems need to be designed and developed using standards that can function across different component technologies so that group members are not excluded. The simplest examples of successful interoperability can be found in search engines and personal collaborative frameworks such as Digg.com that

Table 1.1 Principal Challenges of MM 2.0

Areas	Challenges	Existing Example Solutions
Standardization	Interoperability	Open metadata standards (e.g., XML); open Web development approaches (e.g., AJAX)
	Referential tractability	Subtitle annotations; XML (e.g., Flash CS3 Timed Text Caption)
Folksonomies	Synonym control	Semantic lexicons (e.g., WordNet)
	Tag expressiveness	
	Connectedness	
	Pattern stability	Suggested/mandatory fields
	Metadata propagation	Shared tagging
	Tag-based ranking	Tag-based retrieval systems
Awareness	Semantic awareness	Logging; revision control
	Identity awareness	Responsibility visualization (e.g., Palantir)
	Emotional awareness	Cameras, sensors, and icons
	Interreferential awareness	Verbal references; physical body gestures; office annotation tools (e.g., in Microsoft Office and Adobe Acrobat)
Community	Presence-enriched communications	Forums; IMs; live audiovisual streams
	Community profiling	Relational fuzzy approaches; topic taxonomy adaptations; ontological user profiles

are platform independent. The use of XML and JavaScript has helped to greatly improve platform independence, for example, through the increasingly popular use of RSS and Atom for content syndication. AJAX (Asynchronous JavaScript and XML) technology is a more recent development for creating interactive Web applications that are platform-free and compatible with different Web development technologies (Tapiador et al. 2006). Ultimately, any collaborative environment should be able to function identically on any platform and across all devices. However, while front-end interfaces are reasonably interoperable, underlying layers are less so and are the cause of current incompatibility issues (Carreras and Skarmeta 2006). Therefore, a multilayered architecture with AJAX interfaces but alternative underlying technologies may offer a solution.

Regarding multimedia content, a key standardization challenge is being able to exploit multimedia content metadata in the same way that HTML (HyperText Markup Language) is exploited by browsers. HTML is completely text-based and uses closed HTML tags to structure the display of the Web page. HTML has enabled the creation of user-based content within Web sites such as Wikipedia, where users create their own text and reference it in HTML in such a way that it is readable and searchable by others. Users may also incorporate multimedia content into the HTML by using URIs (Uniform Resource Identifiers). In a community where multimedia metadata is created collaboratively such that it may be searched and referenced, technologies are required that allow the metadata to be created and altered as easily as HTML so that it is nonproblematic to access and edit specific elements of the metadata. At the same time, the metadata should be organized in a way that permits referencing to any precise spatiotemporal location within the media stream, and it should be organized nonexclusively so that overlapping content features may be modeled. For video in particular, modeling, so that a feature starts and ends at a specific time in the stream is crucial (Pea, Lindgren, and Rosen 2006). The difficulty in reconciling such precision with easy flexibility is referred to as the *referential tractability* challenge. One approach has been proposed whereby a subtitle text is added to the video stream as an annotation, and a video editor is created to treat these annotation tracks as a "handle" by which to restructure playback (Blankinship and Mikhak 2007). An example of this approach is used in children's storybooks where the text in the subtitle is used to refer to the media time location. Children can search for keywords in the subtitles and thereby access exact moments in the video stream. The subtitle text is not easy to modify, however, nor is it possible to synchronize new annotations with those defined beforehand. Another approach is to use an XML-based solution for the multimedia metadata. The Caption Component of Adobe's Flash CS3 enables XML metadata to be connected to it. This approach is easier because modeling features and updating the metadata (to edit a feature or its temporal location) only require modifying the associated XML (Green 2007). However, the Caption Component is intended for video streams, and there is no option for specifying spatial locations of content features.

1.2.2 Folksonomies

These challenges deal with the format of the collaboratively generated metadata. The social networks and collaborative environments based on Web 2.0 generate an enormous amount of data. In collaborative multimedia systems, the most popular method for modeling is tagging, where tags are used to identify content features, such as objects and events, within the multimedia stream. Folksonomies are user-generated taxonomies in which tags are collaboratively created and managed to annotate and categorize content. In contrast to traditional subject indexing, metadata is generated not only by experts but also by creators and consumers of the content. Usually, freely chosen keywords instead of a controlled vocabulary are used (Voss 2007). Consequently, the tags are highly individualistic, and different users use a variety of terms to describe the same concept (Lee and Yong 2007). Such a lack of *synonym control* makes searching problematic because users may search for only one synonym but require results for the entire group of synonyms.

At the same time, tagging is so widely used now that users have become comfortable with it and therefore do not pay much attention to the clarity, structure, and subsequent usability of the tags (Lee and Yong 2007). Consequently, *tag expressiveness* is a nontrivial challenge. For example, unstructured text in tags results in having many tags that are difficult to interpret and relate to other tags by anyone other than the tag author (Golder and Huberman 2006). Similarly, incorrectly spelled keywords within the tags can cause retrieval problems and lead to orphaned content that is never able to be retrieved unless the query also happens to contain the misspelled tags. Acronyms also prove to be problematic and can reduce the usability of the tags. Acronyms are widely used in tags but often are chosen by the content author without being widely used elsewhere. Consequently, users may not search for different acronyms, or they may search for the full phrase instead.

Exploiting the full *connectedness* of the tags is a further challenge. The relationships between tags that make sense to human beings are difficult to develop within tag-based systems and thus are often not implemented—for example, searching for "swimming" and including all concepts related to swimming within the results, not just synonyms, but also concepts such as medals and Olympic events in which the word "swimming" may not be used within the tags.

Language tools to identify synonyms, acronyms, and relationships have sought to address these issues. One of the most popular tools used is WordNet (Fellbaum 1998), which is a semantic lexicon for the English language developed by the members of the Cognitive Science Laboratory at Princeton University. WordNet groups English words into sets of synonyms, provides general definitions and acronyms, and records the various semantic relations between terms. It has been used to solve tagging issues and develop retrieval systems that utilize folksonomies. One such retrieval system is TagPlus (Lee and Yong 2007), which retrieves from Flickr using WordNet to correct, identify, and group tags generated by users to improve the relevance of the results presented to the user.

The identification of patterns found within the tags created by the users can further enhance the retrieval process. For example, for a photo, users tend to specify the date the picture was taken, the location featured in the picture, and the people or landmarks visible in the picture. Research has shown that although users demonstrate great variety in the keywords and phrases they use within tags, including the frequency of certain keywords, stable patterns are emerging that can be used to help structure the tagging process (Golder and Huberman 2006). Recognizing such *pattern stability* and encouraging users to conform to these patterns through, for example, suggested or mandatory fields, can help in making the tagging process more goal directed and subsequently well formed, thereby improving the usability of the tags, although at the cost of some loss of creativity and comprehensiveness in the content modeling process.

Another challenge is that of *metadata propagation*. Often, multiple related media streams require tagging, which may be done simultaneously or sequentially. Frequently, such streams share many common content features, and thus tagging all streams with the same tags is a very repetitive process involving a lot of redundancy. This problem becomes even more apparent in collaborative modeling systems where multiple users perform the tagging. For example, photos of a certain occasion are often taken by many users who were present. These photos share information such as the people in them and the location. If the metadata could be propagated or inherited by all of the related photos once a single user had tagged them, user effort would be greatly reduced, and the consistency of the tags would be greatly improved (William 2006).

A final key challenge is how to use the tags to improve the ranking of retrieved results by, for example, making them more personalized to individual users. Studies show that *tag-based rankings* produce more relevant results than traditional rankings and clusterings (Firan, Nejdl, and Paiu 2007), as demonstrated by the recommendations of online music sites and communities such as Yahoo Launch and Last.fm.

1.2.3 Awareness

Providing various types of awareness has become important to improving the usability of collaborative systems. There are four types of awareness that are important to collaborative content modeling systems: semantic, identity, emotional, and interreferential.

When different users work collaboratively to model the same content, different versions of the same content model may be generated. It is important for the users to be informed about the type of changes that have been made to the metadata between revisions and which elements of the metadata have been authored by which users (Papadopoulou et al. 2006) so that they can correct the metadata, continue their own content modeling, or rethink their own decisions and modeling approach if necessary (Shen and Sun 2005). In collaborative content modeling systems, the changes made to a content model are not limited to just changes in phrases and keywords but, more importantly, relate to full semantic content features such as modeling different objects or changing a relationship between objects or events. To help provide *semantic awareness*, many logging- and revision-control approaches have been proposed, such as IceCube (Kermarrec et al. 2001), which enables general-purpose log-based reconciliation in which logs of alterations are combined into a single merged log and, by observing object and application semantics, are ordered in such a way that conflicts are minimized.

Different users adopt different perspectives on how multimedia content should be modeled. Consequently, to understand which users have authored or updated specific elements of the metadata, to know which users are presently active, or to be able to simply contact users, *identity awareness* is also required (including self-identity awareness so that authors may identify their own changes and activity). Patterns and profiles can be used to both raise awareness about users and increase collaboration standards between users (Gombotz et al. 2006). Several community configuration management tools have been developed recently. For example, Palantir (Sarma, Noroozi, and van der Hoek 2003) is a workspace awareness tool that informs a user of which other users have changed artifacts, calculates the severity of the changes, and graphically displays the information in a configurable and generally unobtrusive manner.

Emotion plays an important role in all human interaction (Money and Agius 2008) in terms of the user's own emotional state and his perception of that of others with whom he collaborates. In a collaborative system, a great deal of communication takes place among users, particularly those who are working on the same document or model, and therefore emotions influence how users collaborate with each other. Consequently, users should be aware not only of other users but of the emotions of other users; thus providing *emotional awareness* within collaborative multimedia systems is an important challenge. Research has shown that people are generally more comfortable, sometimes up to 70% more, using emotionally aware collaborative online systems than in face-to-face collaborations (Garcia, Favela, and Machorro 1999). Different approaches have been taken to increase emotional awareness, but most include the use of webcams and sensors to determine the users' emotional statuses and communicate them to others through images or symbolic icons.

The final awareness challenge, *interreferential awareness*, concerns how a user may refer to specific elements of the content or associated metadata during collaborative communication with others such that the reference may be understood by them (Chastine, Zhu, and Preston 2006) in both asynchronous and synchronous environments. While verbal references may be sufficiently effective, though inefficient, for metadata references, they are less suitable for references to content within the media stream because users may be attracted to the wrong features during playback, or they may become engrossed in an event and fail to notice certain objects (Pea, Lindgren, and Rosen 2006). In the physical world, looks, nods, and hand gestures serve to focus attention effectively, and thus we would expect suitable surrogates to be available within a collaborative environment. Both Microsoft Office and Adobe Acrobat enable users to add annotations to their work so that users can draw the attention of other users, and similar tools for using audiovisual files in collaborative environments would be invaluable.

1.2.4 Community

This final set of challenges relates to supporting the user community that develops around a collaborative content modeling system. One of the main challenges here is *presence-enriched communications* within the community. Forums and private and instant messaging have served as the backbone of collaborative systems for many years, reflecting the importance of communication between community members. In an asynchronous environment, one of the most challenging obstacles is how to promote a sense of presence and community among communicating users (Dringus and Ellis 2004), which can shape user behavior and affect how they ultimately participate within the community (Jung 2008; Yoo, Suh, and Lee 2002). For example, when a user senses many active users within a community, her behavior toward that community changes: she may spend more time and energy contributing to the community because she believes it to be worthwhile, or she may feel overwhelmed and be less likely to contribute. Consequently, this challenge bears strong relationships with the challenges of identity and emotional awareness discussed in the previous sections. Different types of communities have attempted to cope with this challenge, most prominently online learning communities consisting of students and teachers, where a sense of presence is vital to the teaching and learning process. In such communities, virtual classrooms that incorporate audiovisual communications, as well as regular text-based communications, so that all parties are able to see and hear each other, have proved to be beneficial in some cases. However, users often turn off these options after a short period either due to their low quality or because they find it distracting in conjunction with carrying out their tasks (Hung 2003).

Finally, there is the challenge of *community profiling*. Members of virtual communities tend to share similar interests, experiences, expertise, and so forth, and thus by grouping users according to their profiles, it is possible to bring similar users together (Tang et al. 2008). These users are likely to have much richer interactions and are also likely to be content modeling on similar multimedia streams, thereby improving collaboration. Systems have been proposed for multimedia communities that enable collaboration of preferences and recommendations. Instant, concurrent sharing of tags and other metadata enables users to feel the presence of other users while they retrieve their multimedia content and browse their metadata, hence improving the sense of community (Errico and Sezan 2006). Profiling also helps in search and retrieval tasks, and many approaches have been proposed for profiling users and clustering them into suitable groups based on their profiles, including relational fuzzy approaches (Castellano, Fanelli, and Torsello 2007), topic taxonomy adaptations (Tang et al. 2008), and ontological representations of user profiles (Sieg, Mobasher, and Burke 2007).

1.3 Suitability of MPEG-7 in Meeting the Challenges

The previous section reviewed the challenges in MM 2.0. This section considers the suitability of the MPEG-7 standard, particularly the Multimedia Description Schemes (ISO/IEC 2003), in meeting these challenges. MPEG-7 provides a standardized set of XML schemas for describing multimedia content richly and in a structured fashion. It addresses a broad spectrum of multimedia applications and requirements by providing a metadata system for describing the features of multimedia content. The building blocks of the standard are as follows:

- *Description schemes (DSs)*, which describe entities or relationships pertaining to multimedia content; DSs specify the structure and semantics of their components, which may be other DSs, descriptors, or datatypes
- *Descriptors (Ds)*, which describe features, attributes, or groups of attributes of multimedia content
- *Datatypes*, which are the basic reusable datatypes employed by DSs and Ds
- *Systems tools*, which support the delivery of descriptions, multiplexing of descriptions with multimedia content, synchronization, file format, and so forth

Each of these challenges may be met to differing extents by the various description tools provided by the standard, which are discussed in the following subsections. Table 1.2 summarizes the MPEG-7 tools that are available to meet each challenge.

1.3.1 Meeting Standardization Challenges

As mentioned previously, the metadata generated by a collaborative multimedia content modeling system must be in a format that is compatible across multiple platforms without loss of functionality, while at the same time remaining dynamic. XML has been identified as a valuable technology for meeting interoperability challenges, and MPEG-7 is based on XML. Consequently, conventional XML parsers, which are available for many different platforms, can be adapted to parse MPEG-7 metadata. In terms of referential intractability, MPEG-7 supports a range of description tools for modeling multimedia content. The various segment decomposition tools such as the VideoSegmentTemporalDecomposition DS, the StillRegionSpatialDecomposition DS, and the MovingRegionSpatioTemporalDecomposition DS enable the media stream to be precisely decomposed in time and space. In this way, it is possible to reflect the temporal start and end points of content features, such as events, or the bounding areas of onscreen content features, such as objects. However, as is typical of XML-based representations, modifications may be made to the MPEG-7 metadata efficiently without causing disruption to other elements.

Table 1.2   MPEG-7 Tools to Meet MM 2.0 Challenges

Areas	Challenges	MPEG-7 Tools
Standardization	Interoperability	Open source XML format
	Referential tractability	Segment decomposition tools (e.g., VideoSegmentTemporalDecomposition DS, StillRegionSpatialDecomposition DS, MovingRegionSpatioTemporal-Decomposition DS)
Folksonomies	Synonym control	Classification schemes; TermDefinition DS
	Tag expressiveness	StructuredAnnotation; KeywordAnnotation
	Connectedness	Relationship description tools (e.g., Graph DS); term description tools
	Pattern stability	Well-defined and organized description tools; StructuredAnnotation; KeywordAnnotation
	Metadata propagation	Content organization tools (e.g., ContentCollection DS, StructuredCollection DS)
	Tag-based ranking	preferenceValue; relation strength; MPQF
Awareness	Semantic awareness	Per-user, per-stream descriptions; creation and production description tools (e.g., Creation DS); revisions as MPEG-7 descriptions (e.g., Event DS, UsageHistory DS)
	Identity awareness	AgentObject DS; UsageHistory DS
	Emotional awareness	Affective DS; FreeTextAnnotation; StructuredAnnotation
	Interreferential awareness	Segment decomposition tools (e.g., VideoSegmentTemporalDecomposition DS, StillRegionSpatialDecomposition DS, MovingRegionSpatioTemporal-Decomposition DS); structural relation classification schemes (i.e., TemporalRelation CS and SpatialRelation CS); Reference datatype

(Continued)

Table 1.2   MPEG-7 Tools to Meet MM 2.0 Challenges (*Continued*)

Areas	Challenges	MPEG-7 Tools
Community	Presence-enriched communications	FreeTextAnnotation
	Community profiling	UserPreferences DS; UsageHistory DS; AgentObject DS

1.3.2 Meeting Folksonomic Challenges

A number of challenges were identified previously regarding folksonomies. In terms of synonym control, MPEG-7's TermDefinition DS enables the definition of terms used during content modeling within a classification scheme (CS). This DS incorporates an identifier for a term, its textual definition, and a set of human-readable names. Also, by using the termRelationQualifierType, one can define the relationships among different terms. The options that may be specified by the termRelationQualifierType are as follows:

- BT, to signify a broader term, such that the related term is more general in meaning than the current term
- NT, to signify a narrower term, such that the related term is more specific in meaning than the current term
- US, to signify "use instead" when the related term is (nearly) synonymous with the current term but the related term is preferred to the current term
- UF for "use for," to indicate that the related term is (nearly) synonymous with the current term but the current term is preferred to the related term
- RT, to signify a related term, which is not a synonym, quasi-synonym, or broader or narrower term, but is associated with the current term

Consequently, these options enable synonyms and related terms to be defined and new terms to be created and updated collaboratively by the user community.

Because MPEG-7 provides a scheme whereby description tools are defined for specific uses and may be combined and related to each other as required, the content model exhibits a well-defined structure in terms of tag expressiveness and connectedness. Defined structures can be enforced to ensure pattern stability across the community so that tags are not entered freely. Figure 1.2 illustrates the structure of the key semantic description tools within MPEG-7 and how they relate to the narrative of the multimedia stream. The Semantic DS is the basis of semantic descriptions within an MPEG-7 content model. It consists of the SemanticBag DS, which is an abstract base tool for describing collections of semantic entities and their relations. The SemanticBase DS, an abstract tool, is the basis for the tools that describe semantic entities, and the specialized semantic entity description tools extend the SemanticBase DS to describe specific types of semantic entities, such as objects, agent objects, events, concepts, states, places, and times. The SemanticBase DS can also contain SemanticRelation CSs, which describe semantic relations among entities, such as the relationship between events and/or objects in a narrative or the relationship of an object to the multimedia content that depicts that object. These can be used, for example, within the Graph DS to form a network of relationships. In addition, the text annotation description tools that are used mainly in the various content entity types (e.g., MultimediaContent, Image, Video, Audio, AudioVisual, Multimedia) support the use of both unstructured (free text) and structured textual annotations, with the latter helping to improve pattern stability. For example, the StructuredAnnotation datatype incorporates fields such as Who, WhatObject, WhatAction, Where, When, Why, and How, while the KeywordAnnotation datatype enables annotations to be expressed as a set of single words or phrases, each of which may be specified as primary, secondary, or "other" to denote its importance. In this way, the KeywordAnnotation datatype proves helpful in specifying acronyms. Using the MPEG-7 description tools in this way, as defined in the standard, enables users to comprehend the structure of multimedia content models that they have not participated in creating, since all MPEG-7 multimedia content models exhibit a core central structure reflected by the description tools. For example, all objects are defined using the Object DS with which the user defines an object name, definition, location, and spatiotemporal link to the media stream. Consequently, a great deal of pattern

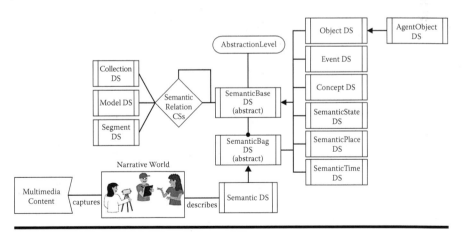

Figure 1.2 Relationships of the tools for describing the semantics of multimedia content. (Adapted from International Organization for Standardization/ International Electrotechnical Commission, Information Technology–Multimedia Content Description Interface, Part 5: Multimedia Description Schemes. International Standard 15938-5, Geneva, Switzerland.)

stability is exhibited, but because elements of the description tools are optional, a great deal of flexibility is also possible. In this way, models are readily understandable and thus broadly useful, while also making reuse feasible. Moreover, while MPEG-7 does not provide spell-checking tools, since it specifies the metadata representation only, there are many external tools that will spell-check the text of the tags and can be easily deployed in conjunction, thereby further improving tag expressiveness.

MPEG-7 can be used to group multimedia streams and multimedia content models through the use of collections and models, thereby enabling metadata propagation. The content organization tools describe the organization and modeling of multimedia content. For example, the ContentCollection DS describes collections of multimedia data, such as images, videos, and audio tracks, providing the basic functionality for describing a grouping of multimedia content, including aggregated audio and visual features, into an unordered, unbounded, nested collection. Similarly, the SegmentCollection DS is used for describing collections of segments; the DescriptorCollection DS is used for describing collections of descriptors of multimedia content; the ConceptCollection DS is used for describing a collection of semantic concepts related to multimedia content (e.g., objects and events); and the MixedCollection DS is used for describing mixed collections of multimedia content, descriptors, and semantic concepts related to multimedia content. The StructuredCollection DS is used to describe association relationships among collections. These content organization tools can be used to specify metadata common to a group of multimedia streams. For example, if a group of photos taken at a birthday party are being modeled, the Collection DS can include various features such as the people, locations, and events, which can then be inherited by all or a subset of photos. The metadata for each photo may then define spatial, temporal, and semantic relationships among these features.

A large body of research tackles various aspects of MPEG-7-based retrieval, such as image retrieval (Hejazi and Ho 2007), video retrieval (Tjondronegoro and Chen 2002), and video object extraction (Lu and Li 2008). Using MPEG-7 element attributes such as preferenceValue and relation strength can help to provide tag-based rankings (Mallik et al. 2007) when used in conjunction with the MPEG-7 Query Format (MPQF) specified in Part 12 of the standard (ISO/IEC 2007). The MPQF provides a standardized interface for multimedia content retrieval systems that enables users to describe their search criteria with a set of precise input parameters and also allows the specification of a set of preferred output parameters to depict the return result sets. Furthermore, query management tools are provided to support service discovery and service capability querying and description (ISO/IEC 2007). Various query types are defined, such as QueryByFeatureRange, which is a query based on given descriptions denoting start and end ranges; and a Join operation is specified, which enables filtering conditions to be defined over multiple sets of multimedia objects. In this way, separate filtered sets may be retrieved and then combined.

1.3.3 Meeting Awareness Challenges

While description tools for tracking content model revisions are not explicitly provided within the MPEG-7 standard to improve semantic awareness, MPEG-7 descriptions are effectively text files, and therefore current logging and revision control approaches can be used. Separate MPEG-7 descriptions can be created on a per-user, per-stream basis and then aggregated with the creation and production description tools used to describe the creation and production of the multimedia content, including title, creator, classification, purpose of the creation, and so forth. In particular, the Creation DS contains description tools for author-generated information about the creation process, including places, dates, actions, materials, staff, and organizations involved. Revisions could feasibly be described as MPEG-7 descriptions by exploiting the standard's ability to reference full and part descriptions in combination with the use of semantic description tools to refer to the revisions, such as the Event DS to describe the actions taken and the AgentObject DS to describe users, thereby facilitating identity awareness and enabling patterns and profiles to be developed. The UsageHistory DS from the user interaction tools could be used to describe selected revisions as user actions.

Regarding emotional awareness, the Affective DS describes a user's affective (emotional, mood, or analytical) response to multimedia content. The Affective DS attaches a numeric score to each member of a group of description tool instances; the score represents the relative (within the group of instances) intensity of a user's affective response (e.g., excitement, happiness, anger) to those instances (Agius, Crockford, and Money 2006). Using this DS to describe the user's general affective state can help promote general emotional awareness among users within the community. Other description tools—such as the FreeTextAnnotation datatype, which is incorporated as an element in many of the MPEG-7 description tools and enables free text input; and the StructuredAnnotation datatype, which incorporates fields such as Who, WhatObject, WhatAction, Where, When, Why and How—could allow users to denote their emotional status.

Interreferential awareness may be supported by the segment decomposition tools as described in Section 1.3.1, which can be used to refer to specific points within the media. These tools can incorporate multiple masks in space and/or time, which are not necessarily connected in space or time to group-related but nonsequential content. The TemporalMask D, SpatialMask D, and SpatioTemporalMask D allow the boundaries and composition of the segments to be described. Segments may be temporally connected to form a contiguous segment over a temporal interval, spatially connected to form a contiguous spatial region, or spatiotemporally connected to form a spatiotemporal segment that appears in a temporally connected segment and is formed from spatially connected segments at each time instant. In addition, structural relation classification schemes allow relationships to be defined in time and space to provide relative references to content. The TemporalRelation CS defines binary relations such as precedes, contains, and starts, and *n*-ary relations such as sequential and overlapping; the SpatialRelation CS specifies binary relations such as south, left, and below. In addition, the Reference datatype within the description tools allows users to reference part of a description—that is, an instance of a D or DS—where the references are expressed as URIs, IDs, or XPath expressions. Consequently, references to whole or part MPEG-7 descriptions may be made, thereby supporting interreferential awareness of the metadata.

1.3.4 Meeting Community Challenges

The use of the MPEG-7 description tools to promote awareness within the community helps to engender some sense of user activity, but without presence-enriched communication between users, this activity cannot thrive within a community. Instant messagers, such as Windows Live Messenger, often archive conversation logs in an XML format, and similarly, communications such as instant messages and forum posts can be represented as MPEG-7 descriptions and linked with user descriptions. For example, the FreeTextAnnotation datatype can be used to record extensive text or to incorporate comments into MPEG-7 descriptions.

User preference descriptions encapsulated in the UserPreferences DS can be correlated with content descriptions and descriptions of users found within the AgentObjectDS and then aggregated across users to enable community profiling. Preferences are described by description tools such as the CreationPreferences DS, ClassificationPreferences DS, and SourcePreferences DS and can be used to infer user preferences for modeling content. The UsageHistory DS can further help with profiling by maintaining a record of user actions taken while modeling or viewing content. Combining the UserPreferences DS and UsageHistory DS enables rich user profiles to be built; users can then be clustered on the basis of their interests, experience, and expertise (Agius and Angelides 2007). For example, expertise may be recorded in the AgentObject DS as well as inferred from activities within the UsageHistory DS (e.g., repeated modeling of certain types of content) or preferences specified within the UserPreferences DS.

1.4 Conclusion

Modeling multimedia content collaboratively may be seen as the second generation of multimedia metadata in which Web 2.0 environments are exploited so that users can model and share multimedia content metadata within online communities. This chapter considers the key challenges to Multimedia Metadata 2.0 (MM 2.0): standardization, folksonomies, awareness, and community. It then considers the ability of MPEG-7, the leading multimedia metadata standard, to meet these challenges. The reduced effort per user that MM 2.0 enables has the potential to yield more comprehensive content models, particularly with regard to high-level semantic content, enabling next-generation multimedia applications that can utilize multimedia streams more effectively.

Acknowledgment

This research is supported by the U.K. Engineering and Physical Sciences Research Council, grant no. EP/E034578/1.

Damon Daylamani Zad is an EPSRC research fellow and a doctoral candidate in information systems and computing at Brunel University, United Kingdom. He holds an MSc in multimedia computing (2006) from Brunel University. His research interests include image processing, collaborative content modeling, and the application of MPEG standards. He has widely published his research findings in journals, edited books, and presented his work at several conferences including several hosted by IEEE. He is a member of the British Computer Society, the ACM, and the IEEE Computer Society.

Harry Agius is a senior lecturer in computing at Brunel University, United Kingdom, and a member of the British Computer Society. His research interests are in the area of multimedia content management, with a focus on the MPEG-7 standard, on which he has published in various journals and books and presented at a range of conferences. He is currently the principal investigator on the EPSRC-funded national project MC², which is developing collaborative MPEG-7-based content modeling within online communities. He also serves as the doctoral chair of the IEEE Semantic Media Adaptation and Personalization (SMAP) group. He holds a BSc, MSc, and PhD from the LSE.

References

Agius, H., and Angelides, M. 2007. Closing the content-user gap in MPEG-7: The hanging basket model. *Multimedia Systems* 13(2): 155–172.

Agius, H., Crockford, C., and Money, A. 2006. Emotion and multimedia content. In *Encyclopedia of Multimedia*, ed. B. Furht, 222–223. New York: Springer.

Blankinship, E., and Mikhak, B. 2007. Video-Wikis and media fluency. In *Proceedings of the 6th International Conference on Interaction Design and Children*, Aalborg, Denmark, June 6–8, pp. 175–176.

Bryant, S. L., Forte, A., and Bruckman, A. 2005. Becoming Wikipedian: Transformation of participation in a collaborative online encyclopedia. In *Proceedings of the International ACM SIGGROUP Conference on Supporting Group Work*, Sanibel Island, FL, November 1–10, pp. 6–9.

Carreras, M. A. M., and Skarmeta, A. F. G. 2006. Towards interoperability in collaborative environments. In *Proceedings of the International Conference on Collaborative Computing: Networking, Applications and Worksharing (CollaborateCom 2006)*, Atlanta, GA, November 17–20.

Castellano, G., Fanelli, A. M., and Torsello, M. A. 2007. Relational fuzzy approach for mining user profiles. In *Proceedings of the 8th WSEAS International Conference on Fuzzy Systems*, Vol. 8, Vancouver, Canada, June 19–21, pp. 175–179.

Chastine, J. W., Zhu, Y., and Preston, J. A. 2006. A framework for inter-referential awareness in collaborative environments. In *Proceedings of the International Conference on Collaborative Computing: Networking, Applications and Worksharing (CollaborateCom 2006)*, Atlanta, GA, November 17–20.

Dringus, L. P., and Ellis, T. J. 2004. Building the SCAFFOLD for evaluating threaded discussion forum activity: Describing and categorizing contributions. In *Proceedings of the 34th Annual Frontiers in Education (FIE 2004)*, Vol. 1, Savannah, GA, October 20–23, pp. 7–12.

Errico, J. H., and Sezan, I. 2006. Presence-based collaborative recommender for networked audiovisual displays. In *Proceedings of the 11th International Conference on Intelligent User Interfaces*, Sydney, Australia, January 29–February 1, pp. 297–299.

Fellbaum, C. (1998). *WordNet: An Electronic Lexical Database*. Cambridge, MA: MIT Press.

Firan, C. S., Nejdl, W., and Paiu, R. 2007. The benefit of using tag-based profiles. In *Proceedings of the Latin American Web Congress (LA-WEB 2007)*, Santiago, Chile, October 31–November 2, pp. 32–41.

Garcia, O., Favela, J., and Machorro, R. 1999. Emotional awareness in collaborative systems. In *Proceedings of the String Processing and Information Retrieval Symposium and International Workshop on Groupware*, Cancun, Mexico, September 21–24, pp. 296–303.

Golder, S., and Huberman, B. A. 2006. The structure of collaborative tagging systems. *Journal of Information Science* 32(2), 198–208.

Gombotz, R., Schall, D., Dorn, C., and Dustdar, S. 2006. Relevance-based context sharing through interaction patterns. In *Proceedings of the International Conference on Collaborative Computing: Networking, Applications and Worksharing (CollaborateCom 2006)*, Atlanta, GA, November 17–20.

Green, T. 2007. Captions for video with Flash CS3. *Digital Web Magazine* (June 4), http://www.digital-web.com/articles/captions_flash_video/.

Hejazi, M. R., and Ho, Y.-S. 2007. An efficient approach to texture-based image retrieval. *International Journal of Imaging Systems and Technology* 17(5): 295–302.

Hung, W. 2003. Building learning communities by enhancing social presence: Implementing blended instructional delivery methods. *ACM SIGGROUP Bulletin* 24(3): 79–84.

ISO/IEC. 2003. Information technology–multimedia content description interface, Part 5: Multimedia description schemes. International Standard 15938-5, Geneva, Switzerland.

ISO/IEC. 2007. Information technology–multimedia content description interface, Part 12: Query format. Final Committee Draft 15938-12, Shenzhen, China.

Jung, Y. 2008. Influence of sense of presence on intention to participate in a virtual community. In *Proceedings of the 41st Annual Hawaii International Conference on System Sciences*, Waikoloa, HI, January 7–10, p. 325.

Kermarrec, A.-M., Rowstron, A., Shapiro, M., and Druschel, P. 2001. The IceCube approach to the reconciliation of divergent replicas. In *Proceedings of the 20th Annual ACM Symposium on Principles of Distributed Computing*, Newport, RI, pp. 210–218.

Lee, S.-S., and Yong, H.-S. 2007. TagPlus: A retrieval system using Synonym Tag in Folksonomy. In *Proceedings of the International Conference on Multimedia and Ubiquitous Engineering (MUE '07)*, Seoul, Korea, April 26–28, pp. 294–298.

Lu, Y., and Li, Z.-N. 2008. Automatic object extraction and reconstruction in active video. *Pattern Recognition* 41(3): 1159–1172.

Mallik, A., Chaudhury, S., Jain, A., Matela, M., and Poornachander, P. 2007. Content-based re-ranking scheme for video queries on the Web. In *Proceedings of the 2007*

IEEE/WIC/ACM International Conferences on Web Intelligence and Intelligent Agent Technology—Workshops, Silicon Valley, CA, November 2–5, 119–122.

Money, A., and Agius, H. 2008. Feasibility of personalized affective video summaries. In *Affect and Emotion in Human–Computer Interaction, Lecture Notes in Computer Science, Vol. 4868*, eds. C. Peter and R. Beale. Berlin, Germany: Springer-Verlag.

O'Reilly, T. 2006. Web 2.0 compact definition: Trying again. *O'Reilly Radar* (December 10), http://radar.oreilly.com/archives/2006/12/web-20-compact-definition-tryi.html.

Papadopoulou, S., Ignat, C., Oster, G., and Norrie, M. 2006. Increasing awareness in collaborative authoring through edit profiling. In *Proceedings of the International Conference on Collaborative Computing: Networking, Applications and Worksharing (CollaborateCom 2006)*, Atlanta, GA, November 17–20.

Pea, R., Lindgren, R., and Rosen, J. 2006. Computer-supported collaborative video analysis. In *Proceedings of the 7th International Conference on Learning Sciences*, Bloomington, IN, June 27–July 1, pp. 516–521.

Sarma, A., Noroozi, Z., and van der Hoek, A. 2003. Palantir: Raising awareness among configuration management workspaces. In *Proceedings of the 25th International Conference on Software Engineering*, Portland, OR, May 3–10, pp. 444–454.

Shen, H., and Sun, C. 2005. Syntax-based reconciliation for asynchronous collaborative writing. In *Proceedings of the International Conference on Collaborative Computing: Networking, Applications and Worksharing (CollaborateCom 2005)*, San Jose, CA, December 19–21.

Sieg, A., Mobasher, B., and Burke, R. 2007. Web search personalization with ontological user profiles. In *Proceedings of the 16th ACM Conference on Information and Knowledge Management*, Lisbon, Portugal, November 6–10, pp. 525–534.

Tang, L., Liu, H., Zhang, J., Agarwal, N., and Salerno, J. J. 2008. Topic taxonomy adaptation for group profiling. *ACM Transactions on Knowledge Discovery from Data* 1(4): 1–28.

Tapiador, A., Fumero, A., Salvachua, J., and Aguirre, S. A. 2006. A Web collaboration architecture. In *Proceedings of the International Conference on Collaborative Computing: Networking, Applications and Worksharing (CollaborateCom 2006)*, Atlanta, GA, November 17–20.

Tjondronegoro, D., and Chen, Y.-P. 2002. Content-based indexing and retrieval using MPEG-7 and X-Query in video data management systems. *World Wide Web* 5(3): 207–227.

Voss, J. 2007. Tagging, Folksonomy & Co.: Renaissance of manual indexing? In *Proceedings of the 10th International Symposium for Information Science*, Cologne, Germany, May 30–June 1, pp. 234–254.

William, K. 2006. Exploiting "the world is flat" syndrome in digital photo collections for contextual metadata. In *Proceedings of the 8th IEEE International Symposium on Multimedia (ISM '06)*, San Diego, CA, December 11–13, pp. 341–347.

Yoo, W. S., Suh, K. S., and Lee, M. B. 2002. Exploring factors enhancing member participation in virtual communities. *Journal of Global Information Management* 10(3): 55–71.

Chapter 2

Research Directions toward User-Centric Multimedia

Bernhard Reiterer, Janine Lachner, Andreas Lorenz, Andreas Zimmermann, and Hermann Hellwagner

2.1 Introduction

Building upon considerable successes in the multimedia area over the last decades, the research community is now facing the goal of having multimedia content (particularly images, audio, and video), devices, and applications converge into systems that end users can utilize conveniently. In this respect, home environments comprise homes as *spaces* of multimedia convergence, and advanced mobile devices of nomadic users constitute *points* of convergence. The European Network of Excellence INTERMEDIA aims at developing a research roadmap for user-centric handling of multimedia content in and beyond home environments with various devices. The project seeks to progress beyond approaches that focus on homes and devices toward a truly user-centric convergence of multimedia. The project vision is to place the user into the center of such multimedia systems, where services (multimedia applications) and the means for interacting with them (devices and interfaces) converge.

Specific aspects of human–computer interaction related to user-centric multimedia applications introduce several challenges for ensuring the usability of such systems. According to the authors' experience, context awareness and the personalization of both multimedia content and user interfaces may be the most critical issues. Additionally, despite a human-centered design process, the final deployment of multimedia applications may require instant adaptation of the functionality due to increasing situational dynamics. Therefore, the INTERMEDIA project envisions a software framework that provides developers with a means for improving the usability of user-centric multimedia software at both construction and deployment times. This software framework empowers developers to easily and flexibly create applications that closely meet their respective requirements and to adopt the human-centered computing paradigm (Jaimes et al. 2007) to diverse application scenarios involving multimedia content.

This chapter focuses primarily on the challenges involved in the creation of a conceptual framework as a basis of the software framework elaborated in a later step. It provides considerations about requirements for the design, development, and functioning of user-centric multimedia software that need to be reflected by such a framework. Section 2.2 outlines important research and technology fields pertaining to the concept of user-centric multimedia. Section 2.3 covers two of the aforementioned key areas: context awareness and user interface personalization, which are closely coupled in much of the current research. Section 2.4 introduces basic aspects of multimedia adaptation and subsequently two adaptation approaches that might serve as reference points for future research. Section 2.5 builds mainly on the two preceding sections and provides constructive considerations toward the realization of a system that satisfies the gathered requirements. Finally, we draw our conclusion in Section 2.6.

2.2 Vision of User-Centric Multimedia

The concept of user-centric multimedia provides freedom to a modern nomadic person to consume multimedia content without the requirement to carry a range of mobile devices by providing personalized access to media regardless of device type. It will extend personal media spaces for a nomadic life by removing spatial constraints in our daily activities.

Our general vision of user-centric multimedia is that a user should have access to multimedia applications and services

- Offered by the surrounding environment
- And/or providing personal/personalized content
- In an easy-to-use and intuitive way
- Regardless of the device type and physical position
- Seamlessly across various networks
- Through a personalized interface
- According to her or his commands, gestures, and behavior
- As sensed by the environment

Key to this vision is the idea that users can interact using personalized interfaces and consume their personalized content regardless of their location, the particular set of physical devices used for interaction (on the body or in the environment), and other environmental influences, rather than forcing users to organize their lives around the computational technologies required for multimedia access.

The term *user-centered system design* was used by Norman as early as 1983. In the meantime, Norman's observations on work in related areas made him emphasize that role-related terms like *user, driver, patient,* and so on, should be used with care in order to avoid hiding the fact that one is talking about other persons (Norman 2008), and that the "human-centered design" should be advanced toward "activity-centered design" (Norman 2005). Thus putting weight on the fact that systems (and things) should not simply offer a collection of features to be used for a huge set of possibly small tasks but do their best to help in specific activities.

In order to operationalize the term *user-centric multimedia*, we roughly define a system's degree of compliance to the user-centric multimedia paradigm as the usefulness of the system at aiding users in optimizing the utility of multimedia factors in their activities.

One thing we can learn from Norman's considerations is that we should avoid proposing another multipurpose framework that is so generic, powerful, and complicated that we cannot enumerate a reasonable set of activities that it improves: situations in which it really helps without errors are rather special cases. In accordance with this statement, we now provide a scope of activities that should be supported by a user-centric multimedia system, emphasizing that similar activities and ways to assist in them might be found in future work.

The most relevant activity we wish to support is the consumption of multimedia content. But it comes in diverse specializations with different requirements and potentials for optimization, and it involves different subactivities. It can be seen in many cases as a person's main activity (although the person might in fact be quite passive due to the currently dominant noninteractive types of media), but multimedia consumption as a side occupation must also be taken into account. Having, for example, music or the television running while doing something else is very common, and in such cases, the main occupation has a great influence on the way the media consumption can be optimized: we may want the lights dimmed if we are watching a movie, but if we are cooking while watching a movie, we would not want dim lights because we would risk chopping off a finger instead of a piece of potato. In addition, the reduced attention for the visual content might allow for a lower video quality, while a higher audio volume or a different audio output device might be required, and any textual information might need to be transformed to audio because otherwise it would be useless because of the distance to the screen. Things get more complicated if we consider a group of persons participating in the same media consumption but maybe with different parallel activities—we want to allow a person on the move to continue to get the best possible media experience utilizing any available renderer device.

If content is consumed for entertainment, a user interface is usually supposed to disappear so as not to waste resources for itself that are needed for the content presentation (e.g., parts of the screen or processor time). An important related activity that requires interface personalization is the management of media content (e.g., the selection of content to be played or the exchange of content with a visiting or remotely connected friend's repository, as far as allowed by rights). Straightforward views of the file system's directory structure are not helping the activity much for huge content repositories. Browsing and searching repositories based on diverse content properties (e.g., singers, actors, influencing artists, genres, keywords, depicted places, moods conveyed by music, objective quality measures, or subjective ratings) should be available. Due to the diversity of properties that persons might wish to utilize, a generally accepted best practice for an interface can hardly be designed. Instead, convenient methods for supporting a user's preferred ways of accessing repositories should be offered, also taking into account that the trade-off between interface complexity and functionality differs between users and that a good compromise should be offered as a default.

Another relevant multimedia activity is communication, and most of the following considerations can also be applied to it.

Figure 2.1 illustrates the approach of user centricity where the user is situated in the center of a multimedia environment. The three most important aspects of user centricity for multimedia systems—personalized interfaces, context awareness, and content adaptation—are illustrated around the user. In a user-centric environment, the user should be able to select her or his favorite devices for interaction, although in many cases the devices to be used are determined automatically. Similarly, users may want a system to know what content they would enjoy in a certain situation, and in other cases they may want an interface tailored to their own preferences and characteristics for selecting and managing content. Content adaptation is the technology that optimizes the experience that users get from consuming the selected content on the devices of choice.

To realize a vision like this, significant advances in a number of research and technology fields must be made. For example, content annotation and an efficient and interoperable content description mechanism guarantees that the user gets her or his content of interest. Content discovery methods and the process of selecting content have to take into account the user's preferences and a variety of usage environment factors. Other areas that must be considered are digital rights management and privacy and security issues (i.e., authentication and authorization). Regarding the delivery of multimedia data over dynamic networks, it is important to address robust transmission, quality of service, the mobility of users, as well as energy-efficient delivery. Furthermore, the design of devices, software, and interfaces must be considered for the consumption of the content. However, these areas are important for a vast number of scenarios regarding multimedia delivery, not only for a typical user-centric approach where they have a supporting but less vital role.

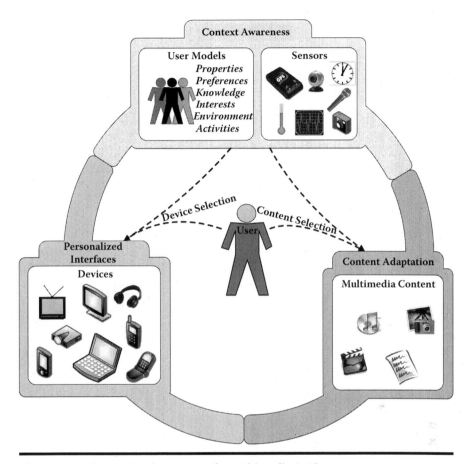

Figure 2.1   The user in the center of a multimedia environment.

In this chapter, we concentrate on three areas that are especially significant for user-centric scenarios: personalized interfaces, context awareness, and content adaptation.

2.3 Personalization and Context Management

As a major aspect of user-centric multimedia systems, users should be able to communicate with the system using a natural, personalized interface to issue commands and express preferences. Personalization allows users to interact with a system in a way that is adapted to their needs, knowledge, interests, or other characteristics. Jameson (2003) defines systems automatically performing adaptation to the individual user in a nontrivial way as *user-adaptive systems.*

2.3.1 Adaptation Targets

The major aims of personalized adaptive systems are improvements in effectiveness and efficiency of user interaction together with higher user satisfaction. An adaptive system provides a set of features that can be adapted. These are called *adaptation targets*. Algorithms that control the adaptation need to know how to deal with adaptation targets, and thus developers must take them into account explicitly. The modifications of such adaptation targets as parts of an adaptive system may be immediately visible or noticeable to the user, or the adaptation effects may be hidden from the user and reveal their impact at a later point in time. Context-aware and user-aware applications comprise five targets of adaptation that can be tailored to the context and the user (Zimmermann 2008):

> *Human–computer interaction* covers the modality of entering commands or data and receiving information and services. In a ubiquitous computing system, traditional modalities for data input (e.g., a keyboard) are expanded by other information acquisition methods such as sensors. The same holds for traditional information presentation displays (e.g., a screen), which can be extended by every possible actuator that may have influence on the environment, such as motors or LEDs.
>
> The *information presentation* regards the front end of the adaptive system and comprises methods required for the output of relevant information. In addition, the information presentation addresses how information is received by the user, since the information should be presented in a way that facilitates its processing and perception. In particular, the issue of choosing the appropriate media and content is of concern and requires appropriate coordination with the modality chosen for human–computer interaction.
>
> *Functionality* refers to the capabilities of the application that are needed to perform tasks at the back end and thus the means to solve a single task or a set of tasks. Functionality may or may not be easy to use, and the amount provided can be reduced or increased during an adaptation process.
>
> *Information selection* and *service selection* cover the content, density, and depth of the presented information. For example, the information selection process can be adapted with respect to the knowledge and expertise of the user. In addition, this adaptation target affects the functionality and complexity of the services required by the user.
>
> The *knowledge base* considers the collection, organization, and retrieval of knowledge about the user, the context, and the application itself. The adaptation of the knowledge base of an adaptive system covers operations such as systematic selection of data about the user that is considered relevant or the deletion of entries from the usage history.

2.3.2 *Properties of Users and Context*

In user-oriented systems, the adaptation of the system behavior to its current user is the main focus of interest. It is common to base the adaptation process on a model of the user containing demographic data and other personal characteristics of the user or shared attributes of group members, possibly enhanced by a goal (task) model. Additionally, in order to provide adaptive services in mobile and ubiquitous computing, a context model has to be added.

The application scenario described in Section 2.2 demonstrates examples of changing conditions that might trigger an adaptation. According to Zimmermann (2008), such characteristics can be categorized into interindividual, intraindividual, and environmental differences. The following subsections provide in-depth descriptions of these differences.

2.3.2.1 *Interindividual Differences and Intraindividual Differences*

Among the users of computer applications, several differences exist in multiple dimensions. Such differences can be categorized into interindividual and intraindividual differences. Interindividual differences address the characteristics of a user that result in varieties among different users. Intraindividual differences particularly refer to changes in such characteristics, and so both categories must be considered in conjunction.

Physiological characteristics like disabilities are of major concern for application designers. Additionally, there is a broad spectrum of psychological personality characteristics such as emotions, self-confidence, motivation, beliefs, and idols, which are difficult to assess automatically. The same holds true for the user's level of factual, general, and domain-specific knowledge (e.g., beginner or expert), which is a valuable source for adaptive operations.

Intraindividual differences consider the evolution of a single user over time as well as variable requirements for a certain task at different times. User requirements may change over a period of time, since the activities and goals of the user evolve. Thus, the system has to be continuously adapted to conform to the increasing experience and changing interests of the user. For example, a user might be overstrained when first using a system but miss some advanced features as soon as her or his expertise increases. In the same manner, the need for highly flexible and adaptable systems is driven by changing requirements for the tasks that are to be accomplished with the system.

The following list describes several user-related characteristics that are primarily relevant for multimedia applications:

Preferences: The possibility of defining personal preferences is one of the most popular sources of adaptation and can be reused in different applications. Common preference settings provided by applications include the language, color schemes, layouts for menus and content directories, and security prop-erties. For more complex systems, we can imagine that a variety of prefer-ences regarding the devices to be used or the modality of presentation and interaction, should be considered.

Interests: Being aware of the user's interests and disinterests constitutes an important prerequisite for the content adaptation. The user's interests can be employed to filter or select the multimedia content that is presented to the user. One example of content selection, is that the user can define her or his individual interests by creating personal playlists. Alternatively, genre and categories of selected contents can be used to recommend content the user might be interested in.

Knowledge and expertise: The user's level of factual, general, and domain-specific knowledge is a valuable source for adaptive operations. Possible indicators of knowledge and expertise include the level of detail of information the user requests as well as the frequency of usage. Knowledge determines both the content and the interface: as the user gains experience, the more she or he is able to use more complex user interfaces with advanced features and to con-sume more detailed information.

2.3.2.2 Environmental Differences

Environmental differences result from the mobility of computing devices, appli-cations, and people, which leads to highly dynamic computing environments and requires taking into account context factors (e.g., location information, cur-rently available network bandwidth, capabilities of the current media renderer, and natural environment characteristics). Thus, the user and her or his context can be continuously monitored to guarantee personalized media consumption with the best possible media quality.

The context-aware functionality of a user-centric multimedia application must be conclusive in order to make the adaptation decisions of the application accessible to the user and to allow an override of the behavior. For the user of a converged multimedia application, the lack of conclusiveness bears the risk of getting into sit-uations in which the context-aware behavior implemented by the developer is inap-propriate or undesired. If the user becomes subordinate to automatic mechanisms, she or he will abandon the useful context-aware functionality of the multimedia application (Dey et al. 2001; Henricksen and Indulska 2005).

Derived from Zimmermann and colleagues (2007), the following context attri-butes are considered important in a user-centric multimedia application:

Location: In mobile and ubiquitous computing environments, physical objects, devices, and humans are spatially arranged and often moving. The location describes location models that classify the physical or virtual residence of an entity as well as other related spatial information like speed and orientation.

Furthermore, a location may be described either in an absolute manner or relative to something else. Models for physical locations can be discriminated into quantitative (geometric) location models and qualitative (symbolic) location models (Stahl and Heckmann 2004). In addition to physical locations, virtual locations cover technical types of locations such as the position within the network identified by an IP address or a unified resource locator of a Web page.

Time: The time subsumes temporal information such as the current time, the time zone, time intervals, and any virtual time. In user-centric multimedia systems, a clear model of time and time intervals is essential because most statements are related over the temporal dimension. In combination with the ability to capture and express recurring events (e.g., always on Sundays), time intervals constitute a significant feature for modeling user characteristics. Furthermore, the time also covers the evaluation of the interaction of users with the system, which creates a continuous user profile. Such a history forms the basis for accessing past information, analyzing the interaction history, inferring the usage habits of users, and predicting future behavior.

Environment: User-centric multimedia systems rely on the adaptation of media to characteristics of available devices in the environment. There is an increasing variety of available devices with specific properties, capabilities, software specifications, operating systems, and available media players. The content selection, presentation, and interaction settings have to be adapted depending on the screen or display size, the bandwidth and reliability of the accessible network connection, and further properties. From a technical perspective, services in the environment can be used by multimedia applications. Such services might include Web services, client-server applications, or any functionality provided by a networked appliance (such as a projector). In addition, the presence of people currently residing in the environment might be relevant. For example, if access control or service personalization requires the users' identities or profiles, or if common or concurrent activities are to be optimized for a group of users. Furthermore, sensors installed in the environment provide the multimedia application with information regarding the temperature, brightness, or sound levels.

2.3.3 Approaches to User Modeling

The knowledge about the user that is necessary for adaptation is held in a container usually referred to as the *user model*. With the evolution of systems from desktop applications to mobile and ubiquitous systems, several approaches for user modeling have been developed. Considering different architectures of multimedia services, we will briefly describe the key approaches and their potential for multimedia services in the following subsections.

2.3.3.1 Monolithic User Modeling

In the classic approach for personalized system development, the application contains specific user-modeling components inside the personalization engine. This engine is closely connected with the application logic for sharing the same host. The derived knowledge from local sensors is usually written to an internal database, mapping user attributes to their values.

First, monolithic user modeling and integrated personalization engines work for all multimedia systems that do not share user attributes with others, including applications running on desktop PCs as well as for isolated mobile applications. As an important advantage, the close relation to the internal application logic reduces the complexity of system design, user-modeling overhead, and network traffic, resulting in potential increased performance (memory, time). Nowadays, the installation of a database for persistent storage of user data does not confront desktop PCs with performance problems. In contrast to personal computers, the need for a local knowledge base is often incompatible with the limited resources of mobile devices.

> Example: An audio player manages playlists for its users on the local hard disk. Another player on a mobile device also manages playlists for one of these users.

For sharing user attributes (e.g., if the user wants to work with the same setup on different devices or with several multimedia services), applications need to explicitly synchronize with the other applications. One drawback of this approach is that the synchronization might annoy users and introduce extra effort. Additionally, this approach may cause considerable network traffic, and potentially complex methods are needed to avoid inconsistencies.

2.3.3.2 User-Modeling Servers

Several generic user-modeling servers support adaptation by providing user-modeling services to application systems (Fink 2004; Kobsa 2007). Because users might form groups to share content with others or to interact with each other in a shared session, we consider both user groups and single users.

In order to enable different applications on different hosts to have access to the same knowledge and to adapt consistently, the knowledge base about the user is separated from the internal application logic. User-modeling servers (Fink and Kobsa 2000) work as an application-external knowledge base. The inferred knowledge about the user is delivered to the server that hosts the information for different applications. Furthermore, this approach enables small devices, even with limited memory and computing power, to access meaningful user models over a network.

User-modeling servers are required if users want access to several installations of a multimedia service in a consistent manner or if the same service is accessed from different devices. Of particular interest are use cases in which desktop and mobile applications have shared access to a multimedia service. The mobile applications then has a location-independent access point to the knowledge base. As a consequence, the step toward ambient multimedia systems is well supported by user-modeling servers providing access from different devices and applications to one and the same knowledge base.

> Example: A server hosts models of users of an audio player application. Any application having access to the server can request delivery of the model for any user.

When different applications have application-specific models on several servers, consistent management of the user models is required.

2.3.3.3 Modularization of User Models

For sharing user models between applications, the modularization of user-related knowledge is proposed for example, by Chepegin et al. (2004). Their architecture focuses on the role of external user models. To give access to a centralized user-modeling service, the common user-model exchange language UserML (Heckmann and Krüger 2003) is used, this supports the communication between different user-adaptive systems that base their decisions on the state of the same central user model.

The modularization enables interchanging only parts of an overall model: application A and application B are enabled to put together their knowledge, and any application is enabled to download it from the server. If modules overlap, specific conflict resolving will be necessary. This approach is applicable for use cases in which different multimedia systems on heterogeneous devices access one and the same personal attributes, like personal playlists or favorite actors. In turn, the modularization supports downloading of user-model fragments that actually were brought in by another party, enabling an integrated set of attributes of a group of users, like a group playlist or an actor's fan club. For any ambient multimedia service, the ability to exchange separate modules between (parts of) applications is an important advantage. Based on a central user-modeling server, the approach is appropriate if the server is accessible at any time when an adaptation is to be performed.

> Example: A server hosts models of users of several audio player applications. Any application having access to the server can request delivery of a complete model or just a playlist for any user or group of users.

2.3.3.4 Ubiquitous User Modeling

For the mobile user, a personal device will continuously connect to local networks and therefore will have access to all information available in this network. A centralized solution fails because of its inability to cope with a high degree of change, which requires that the solution be both self-configurable and robust to interruption. This implies that monolithic user modeling is replaced by distributed user-model fragments (Vassileva 2001). The knowledge about the user (i.e., the current state of the user model), is merged from all the information that can be requested from components reachable in the current context.

Embedding computation into the environment and everyday objects would enable people to move around and interact with information and computing more naturally and casually than they currently do. One of the goals of ubiquitous computing is to enable devices to sense changes in their environment and to automatically adapt and act on the basis of these changes according to user needs and preferences. There are approaches that apply user-modeling techniques to meet the specific requirements of ubiquitous computing (e.g., Kay et al. 2003). In such approaches, the term *ubiquitous user modeling* refers to user modeling for ubiquitous computing. In Heckmann (2007), special attention is given to the requirement of sharing user models, stating that ubiquitous user modeling describes ongoing modeling and exploitation of user behavior with a variety of systems that share their user models. Just as the structure of a ubiquitous service is subject to change depending on the environmental settings and personal attributes, the structure of the user model itself is also subject to adaptation. From this point of view, Lorenz and Zimmermann (2006) define a ubiquitous user model as a base of the knowledge currently available about a user of a ubiquitous service whose structure is subject to change in unpredictable manners and without explicit notification. Specifically, mobile multimedia services coping with unknown environments in changing locations and multimedia services embedded into the environment that are coping with different accessing users, will profit from ubiquitous user models to keep the content and structure of the knowledge base up to date.

> Example: The model of a user of an audio player application is distributed on several user devices and environmental devices. When the user moves to another location, songs that were available only at the former location are removed from the playlist.

2.3.4 Approaches to Context Management

In order to develop user-centric applications, the considered attributes must be gathered and managed in a conclusive way (Zimmermann et al. 2005). Different approaches for context management have been identified (Winograd 2001). Context widgets are building blocks that aim to hide the complexity of gathering and managing context information from the application by encapsulating complex sensor functionality. The one-dimensional context information is communicated over the network by messages and callbacks. In service-based approaches, on the other hand, clients have to discover and establish a connection to each service that provides relevant context information. This architecture lacks global context management and is thus more flexible; however, each component has to manage an increased amount of functionality (e.g., network connections). Another approach is the blackboard model, which is implemented as a shared message board where sensor components provide the context information for the applications. This architecture consists of a centralized server that is responsible for routing the messages from the sensors to the processing components.

2.4 Content Adaptation

Ubiquitous use of media content requires the adaptation of content to the current context. For example, a user on the move wants to watch a streamed movie whose frame size exceeds the display size of her or his mobile device and whose bit rate is larger than the available network bandwidth. In a different scenario, a user wants to see a summary of a news broadcast that skips the society topics, or a blind user wants to receive the best available audio quality instead of the video stream. Media adaptation is currently a very active research topic.

Adaptation may involve various kinds of manipulations resulting in the fulfillment of the user's needs. The spectrum of such manipulations has been subdivided in various ways, and so different flavors have been given to the concept of adaptation itself.

2.4.1 Concepts for Adaptation

Chang and Vetro (2005) provide an overview of adaptation as a taxonomy and a conceptual framework for multimedia adaptation systems as a reference for future work in the field. With respect to the *entity* that is subject to adaptation, they first introduce the notion of the *adaptation space*, which is made up of the adaptation steps that can be applied to the entity, resulting in different representations of the entity. Such different representations can be mapped to the *resource space*, which quantifies resources required for using the representation, and to the *utility space*, which yields the usefulness of the representation for different purposes. The goal of adaptation should be to perform a path taken from the adaptation space so that the resulting entity representation's mapping to the utility space yields the maximal value for a given measure in comparison to all other representations that would be reachable in the adaptation space, which lie within a previously specified subspace that corresponds to the available resources for a given situation.

The ideal design process of an adaptation system takes into account the set of entities that can be processed on the one hand and the properties of the three spaces on the other hand. Entities as the units for which adaptation operations are defined can also be located at more detailed levels of granularity: "pixel, object, frame, shot, scene, syntactic components, as well as semantic components" (Chang and Vetro 2005).

In Chang and Vetro (2005), a classification of adaptation operations into the following categories is suggested:

Format transcoding produces a representation of an entity in a different format from the original one. Transcoding receives its importance from the fact that applications and terminals often lack the ability to decode some of the many formats that are widespread nowadays.

Selection/reduction removes components from the original entity, usually in order to save resources. The components affected by reduction can be at different levels (e.g., shots or frames out of a video, pixels out of frames, or bit planes out of pixels). Reductions that reduce characteristics such as the bit rate, frame rate, or frame resolution of content are also thought of as a type of transcoding.

Replacement operations replace media elements with different ones. A typical application provides a summary of a video instead of the whole video for browsing purposes. The authors note that the replacement content need not be derived from the original content. For example, a similar but smaller photograph of a certain building might already be available, making actual processing of the original content unnecessary. As a further example, inserting text that replaces the audio track for the hearing impaired might be retrieved from a Web source if it is not available in the original content.

Synthesis allows content to be synthesized from existing content with a result that provides an improved experience. Synthesized content is often used as replacement content (e.g., speech might be synthesized for a news ticker if the user leaves home and wants to continue receiving its content without a visual device).

In addition to these categories, any operation for manipulating multimedia content makes sense in certain adaptation scenarios.

In Pereira and Burnett (2003), the impact of adaptation on the experience that a user gets by consuming content is emphasized. While many adaptations of certain content are possible, the entertaining value or the transport of knowledge can be reduced so far below an acceptable rate that it may be worth considering canceling the content's delivery under the given circumstances.

MPEG-21 Digital Item Adaptation (DIA) (ISO/IEC 2004) defines standardized structures for describing factors relevant for adaptation, collectively known as Usage Environment Descriptions (UEDs). UEDs deal with characteristics from the areas covered in Section 2.3, such as terminal capabilities, location and movement, network conditions, and users' preferences and perception impairments. Based on such descriptions, the application of a variety of adaptation operations can be steered as outlined in the following subsections, where we briefly introduce two adaptation approaches that can serve as starting points for advancing toward user-centric multimedia systems.

2.4.2 Utility-Based Multimedia Adaptation

The approach of utility-based multimedia adaptation (Prangl and Hellwagner 2007; Prangl et al. 2007) aims to maximize a user's multimedia experience. For every user, a comprehensive utility model is constructed. It is derived not only from usual adaptation constraints such as terminal capabilities and network conditions but also includes the factors such as intuitive rules, the user's judgments, perceptual impairments, demographic features, and favorite content types. An example of a utility-related hypothesis validated in the course of this research is that for different genres, various quality features have different priorities. Adaptation decision making is based on values that were statistically obtained from experiments with a number of test users. For finding the optimum adaptation decision, different algorithms were implemented and compared. A heuristic hill-climbing method performed best.

In terms of the conceptual framework from Chang and Vetro (2005), this approach considers a limited adaptation space (i.e., the transcoding class of operations), but for this scope it provides extensive research on the trade-off between resource usage in a constrained resource space and maximizing the score in the utility space for a given user, taking into account many aspects of her or his individual properties and context.

2.4.3 Knowledge-Based Media Adaptation

Adaptation is increasingly shifting toward user centricity. In the long-term, the growing set of user characteristics and preferences to be supported require open and intelligent solutions.

The knowledge-based multimedia adaptation (koMMa) framework (Jannach and Leopold 2007; Leopold et al. 2004) can be used to set up intelligent adaptation servers. The idea underlying the framework resulted from the observation that there are a growing number of possible constraints in content adaptation and personalization. Besides well-known transcoding problems such as changing coding formats or spatial and temporal resolutions, the user's constraints and preferences may require more complex processes (e.g., various kinds of splitting and merging content in order to select the relevant parts for the user). The conclusion drawn here is that the monolithic approaches to adaptation cannot cope with the full spectrum of possible requests, especially as the world of multimedia continues to evolve. Thus, the koMMa framework is designed to dynamically integrate simple, well-defined adaptation operations into an adaptation server. A multimedia content adaptation request is transformed into an artificial intelligence planning problem (cf. Russell and Norvig 2003), composing complex adaptation tasks from simple operations. Solutions to such a problem include the arrangement of the available operations that can then be executed by the server. The output of this execution is a version of the multimedia content that suits the user's needs.

Operations can be added to a running adaptation server without any programming effort. Instead, declarative descriptions of the operations are required for the planning process. The initial state for the planning problem is automatically derived from MPEG-7 (Manjunath et al. 2002) descriptions of the source content. Similarly, goals to be fulfilled by the plan are constructed from MPEG-21 DIA UEDs.

Considering the taxonomy from Chang and Vetro (2005), we could say that this approach imposes no real limitations on the adaptation space but in turn lacks the ability to explore the resource space in order to find a solution that gives the highest utility. The planner approach only cares about satisfying the given resource constraints, although actions are usually described in a way that avoids wasting resources (e.g., scaling the frame size to the actual display size instead of any smaller dimension), which in many cases might yield the best utility.

2.5 Implications

Reviewing the results of the previous sections, we get a clearer picture of the roadmap toward the vision of user-centric multimedia.

2.5.1 User Modeling and Context Management

Regarding context, there are much data that can be collected and managed, and while these basic tasks are not trivial and may require considerable infrastructure to be done properly, it is still unclear for many observable characteristics how they should be used, especially in user-centric multimedia systems.

For most scenarios of such systems, typically in the home environment, the deployment of rigorous infrastructures for user modeling and context management may be difficult (unless they are already present for other purposes). Thus, a multimedia system dealing with context should be able to work with incomplete context data in a wide range of configurations, interpreting the context sources that are available on a best-effort basis and explicitly taking into account its own imperfections. Context management, the gathering of knowledge, and subsequent reasoning might not always be in full accordance with a user's actual intentions and environment. Thus, the system shall incorporate techniques that allow the user to take back decisions of the system, update its beliefs, and use alternatives for regathering knowledge if previous results have proven wrong.

Also, if many types of context information are available, maintaining a comprehensive collection of the context data independent of its effective usage might be a waste of resources; thus a system using context might be more efficient if it sticks to a kind of pull-based policy. This means that the knowledge required for a decision is requested only as it is needed. Besides reducing state maintenance efforts in the context management system, such an approach also naturally limits the amount of knowledge that is consulted for making decisions, thus also making reasoning more efficient.

2.5.2 Advanced Interfaces for Converging Devices

We are used to issuing quite detailed commands to our electronic devices. However, this is because the devices require it, not because we would prefer it that way. It is still true that switching on a television or a transistor radio often does not require the parameter of what content to show or play at start, but it is because the device's manufacturer created a standard behavior that simply stays set to the last channel received at the time of switching off or always switching to the first channel in the register at power-up. We doubt that modern multimedia systems should be designed with such rigid standard behavior, but to a great extent they are. Most of today's media player software programs start with the last used playlist when they are invoked, but if they had the chance to take into account context information, they could do better. Of course, cases in which the user is annoyed by the system's choices are to be avoided as much as possible.

Most current multimedia environments are collections of monolithic components, each with individual interfaces (both to the user and to their vicinal components, if any), resulting in unnecessarily limited scopes of applications. With multimedia content consumed in an environment where many network devices serve various purposes, some of which can act as sensors for context and others as actuators with different possible relations to multimedia consumption, it seems natural to extend the control of multimedia-related tasks to arbitrary networked devices for enhancing the overall result. An improved experience similar to what the amBX systems (amBX 2008) achieve can also be imagined by using nonspecialized devices that are already available in the environment (e.g., colored lights, vibrating hardware, and air conditioning systems).

A convergence of components that opens the door to new joint efforts satisfying more of people's needs does not necessarily require those components to be built as parts of one huge and complex system. Instead, standards and interfaces provide a key to joining diverse components for reaching common goals. Examples of technologies that ease the dynamic integration of components into larger functionalities are UPnP (universal plug and play) (The UPnP Forum 2008), DLNA (Digital Living Network Alliance 2008), Web Services (Lafon 2008) (also their semantic descriptions), and DPWS (Microsoft Corporation 2006). Some of them are especially well suited for multimedia devices and digital homes. MPEG-7 and other standards ease the interchange of content metadata. For adaptation tools, MPEG-21 DIA provides the means for describing not only many relevant characteristics of users and their environments but also the properties of adaptation operations, including utility measures computed from parameter values. All of these standards can aid in dynamically integrating the components of a useful user-centric multimedia system.

2.5.3 *Extending Multimedia Adaptation Decision Taking*

For adaptation, the decision-taking component is the point at which user models and context information are required. Given those, the scope of an adaptation decision-taking engine can be extended to cover all multimedia-related aspects of a user-centric system that have been discussed in this chapter: optimizing users' media experiences in dynamic conditions while reducing the manual effort involved in such and related activities, especially by personalizing interfaces for supporting tasks and by anticipating what decisions of the system fit the users' preferences best.

As mentioned by Pereira and Burnett (2003), a multimedia system built as an extension of an adaptation engine can consider the user's context for judging what content is currently appropriate, taking into account, for example, the user's body physics values. MPEG-7 user preferences, especially when using conditional preferences (e.g., for different locations, daytimes, weekdays, time of year, and holiday seasons), are a valuable source for context-dependent content selection. But if those are not available for the given context, or if there is a reason to mistrust them in the current context (e.g., a calendar indicates a holiday during the week, which allows for the conclusion that the user might prefer "Sunday music"), the system might "want" to consult other information sources (e.g., user profile pages in a Web-accessible social networking system) or a usage history, or the system might simply ask the user, ideally via a speech interface.

We are aiming to build a system that integrates various networked devices, many of which can be multimedia devices, and others that might be sensors or other digital home components. All of these devices offer operations that can be remotely invoked. The system itself also has the capability to perform basic actions, such as initiating some interaction with the user. Given a task to be fulfilled, the system plans what actions it should execute, and for this planning, the actions are described by their parameters, preconditions, and effects. Since not all knowledge is assured to be given initially, the planning process might give all of the required details first. Instead, some actions will involve preconditions that require certain knowledge of the reasoner itself, and other actions might provide just that knowledge.

The envisioned approach builds on the idea that there are multiple ways of gathering certain knowledge, and thus, such knowledge-achieving actions will be abstract descriptions that are to be instantiated later. So, the planner will produce plans that are complete but not fully concrete (i.e., they may contain abstract actions). Given such a plan, a different reasoning component complements the planner by judging how an abstract action is to be resolved. In this aspect, the approach discussed here resembles hierarchical planning (cf. Russel and Norvig 2003), although it must be noted that the separation between pure planning and different kinds of reasoning is essential. That is because planners are generally not designed to do numerical optimization comparisons of the utility of alternatives and similar tasks, thus the overall reasoning presented here cannot be considered to be one hierarchical planning algorithm. Parts of the reasoning process are intended to be not fully specified beforehand.

Section 2.4 indicates that it is not trivial to sufficiently consider the adaptation space, resource space, and utility space in adaptation decisions. Nevertheless, it is feasible to find adequate solutions for problems that are sufficiently limited by borders within those spaces. We therefore see multiple components for finding adaptation decisions as parts of the extended decision-taking engine. Reasoning on a higher level might show that one task in a given problem can be solved by transcoding, so the utility space and resource space can be explored for the small adaptation space, which is restricted to transcoding. In a previous step, a planner—with less regard to the relations between utility space and resource space—can be applied for checking if the given problem can be solved at all. After successfully finding a plan, optimization techniques can determine the values of the variable parameters in the plan.

A major aim of our future work will thus be the development of a system that dynamically integrates components monitoring and adapting the environment; interacting with users; and providing, adapting, and consuming media content, controlling them altogether in order to enact their joint functionality in the most appropriate way.

2.6 Conclusion

In this chapter, personalized user interfaces, context awareness, and multimedia content adaptation were discussed as the most important areas to achieve user-centric multimedia. One of the objectives of the NoE INTERMEDIA is to develop solutions and provide a software framework for the problems addressed earlier in order to make progress toward the vision of user-centric multimedia applications and services.

The earlier sections of this chapter indicate important requirements for the envisioned user-centric multimedia framework. In addition to its basic functionality of comfortable sharing and distribution of content to any suitable device, the adaptation of a multitude of factors must be incorporated. A basic set of such factors considered in many adaptation scenarios are terminal and network capabilities. However, the INTERMEDIA project is focusing on user-centric multimedia convergence and thus attempts to cover in particular the properties, context, and activities of the user. Context management and user modeling are crucial, although it is important to keep in mind that they can hardly give perfect results in many real-world environments.

Section 2.5 exposed future directions derived from the discussion of the most relevant fields in user-centric multimedia. The lack of user-centric aspects could turn into a huge barrier for the success of multimedia systems to come. We believe that our considerations can help break this barrier.

Acknowledgment

This work is supported by the NoE INTERMEDIA funded by the European Commission (NoE 038419).

Bernhard Reiterer is a research assistant and PhD student in the multimedia communication (MMC) research group at the Institute of Information Technology (ITEC) at Klagenfurt University, Austria, where he received his Diplom-Ingenieur (MSc) in computer science (2007). He is currently focused on intelligent systems for automating multimedia environments and home devices.

Janine Lachner is a university assistant in the MMC research group at the Institute of Information Technology, Klagenfurt University, Austria. Her current research areas are user-centric multimedia systems and multimedia communication in ad-hoc networks, especially in the context of disaster management and mobile emergency response.

Andreas Lorenz completed his masters in computer science at the University of Kaiserslautern, Germany, in 2001. He joined the Information in Context research group of the Fraunhofer Institute for Applied Information Technology in Sankt Augustin, Germany, in the spring of 2002. He is a research associate and PhD candidate in the research field of human–computer interaction in ambient computing environments. His other research interests include user-modeling and user-adaptive systems, mobile and nomadic information systems, and software engineering.

Andreas Zimmermann received his diploma in computer science and electrical engineering from the University of Kaiserslautern, Germany, in 2000. After 1 year of working as a product innovation manager at TRAIAN Internet Products in Bonn, Germany, and as a consultant for T-Systems in Aachen, Germany, he joined the Information in Context research group at the Fraunhofer Institute for Applied Information Technology (FIT) in Sankt Augustin, Germany. In 2007, he received his PhD in the field of context-aware computing. His other research interests include areas such as nomadic systems, end-user control of ubiquitous computing environments, and artificial intelligence. Within the scope of two European projects that he currently manages, he is responsible for the user-centered design process and for the design of software architectures.

Hermann Hellwagner is a full professor of informatics at the Institute of Information Technology at Klagenfurt University, Austria, where he leads the multimedia communications research group. His current research areas are distributed multimedia systems, multimedia communications, quality of service, and adaptation of multimedia contents. Dr. Hellwagner is a member of the ACM, the IEEE, the German Informatics Society (GI), and the Austrian Computer Society (OCG).

References

amBX 2008. amBX. http://www.ambx.com (accessed May 27, 2008).

Chang, S.-F., and A. Vetro. 2005. Video adaptation: Concepts, technologies, and open issues. In *Proceedings of the IEEE*, Volume 93, 148–158.

Chepegin, V., L. Aroyo, P. D. Bra, and D. Heckmann. 2004. User modelling for modular adaptive hypermedia. In *Proceedings of the Workshop on Semantic Web for E-Learning*, 366–371.

Dey, A., D. Salber, and G. Abowd. 2001. A conceptual framework and a toolkit for supporting the rapid prototyping of context-aware applications. *Human–Computer Interaction 16*, 97–166.

Digital Living Network Alliance. 2008. DLNA. http://www.dlna.org (accessed May 27, 2008).

Fink, J. 2004. *User Modeling Servers—Requirements, Design, and Evaluation*. Amsterdam, Netherlands: IOS Press.

Fink, J., and A. Kobsa. 2000. A review and analysis of commercial user modeling servers for personalization on the World Wide Web. *User Modeling and User-Adapted Interaction 10*(2–3), 209–249.

Heckmann, D. 2005. *Ubiquitous User Modeling*. Ph.D. thesis, Saarland University, Saarbrücken, Germany.

Heckmann, D., and A. Krüger. 2003. User modelling markup language (UserML) for ubiquitous computing. In P. Brusilowsky, A. Corbett, and F. de Rosis (Eds.), *Proceedings of the 9th International Conference on User Modelling*, 403–407. Springer-Verlag.

Henricksen, K., and J. Indulska. 2005. Developing context-aware pervasive computing applications: Models and approach. *Pervasive and Mobile Computing 2*, 37–64.

ISO/IEC. 2004. ISO/IEC 21000-7:2004. Information Technology—Multimedia Framework—Part 7: Digital Item Adaptation.

Jaimes, A., D. Gatica-Perez, N. Sebe, and T. S. Huang. 2007. Human-centered computing: Toward a human revolution. *IEEE Computer 40*(5), 30–34.

Jameson, A. 2003. Systems that adapt to their users: An integrative overview. In *Tutorial presented at 9th International Conference on User Modelling*, Johnstown, PA.

Jannach, D., and K. Leopold. 2007. Knowledge-based multimedia adaptation for ubiquitous multimedia consumption. *Journal of Network and Computer Applications 30*(3), 958–982.

Kay, J., B. Kummerfeld, and P. Lauder. 2003. Managing private user models and shared personas. In *Proceedings of the Workshop on User Modelling for Ubiquitous Computing*, 1–11.

Kobsa, A. 2007. Generic user modeling systems. In P. Brusilovsky, A. Kobsa, and W. Nejdl (Eds.), *The Adaptive Web: Methods and Strategies of Web Personalization*. Berlin: Springer-Verlag.

Lafon, Y. 2008. W3C Web Services Activity. http://www.w3.org/2002/ws (accessed May 27, 2008).

Leopold, K., D. Jannach, and H. Hellwagner. 2004. A Knowledge and Component Based Multimedia Adaptation Framework. In *Proceedings of IEEE Sixth International Symposium on Multimedia Software Engineering (ISMSE '04)*, 10–17.

Lorenz, A., and A. Zimmermann. 2006. Adaptation of ubiquitous user-models. In *Workshop on Ubiquitous User Modeling*.

Manjunath, B. S., Philippe Salembier, and Thomas Sikora, eds. 2002. *Introduction to MPEG-7*. New York: Wiley.

Microsoft Corporation. 2006. Devices Profile for Web Services. http://specs.xmlsoap.org/ws/2006/02/devprof/devicesprofile.pdf (accessed May 27, 2008).

Norman, D. A. 1983. Design principles for human–computer interfaces. In *CHI '83: Proceedings of the SIGCHI Conference on Human Factors in Computing Systems,* New York, 1–10. Association for Computer Machinery.

Norman, D. A. 2005. Human-centered design considered harmful. *Interactions 12*(4), 14–19.

Norman, D. A. 2008. A fetish for numbers. *Interactions 15*(2), 14–15.

Pereira, F., and I. Burnett. 2003. Universal multimedia experiences for tomorrow. *IEEE Signal Processing Magazine 20,* 63–73.

Prangl, M., and H. Hellwagner. 2007. A Framework for Personalized Utility-aware IP-based Multimedia Consumption. In *IEEE International Symposium on a World of Wireless, Mobile and Multimedia Networks (WOWMOM).*

Prangl, M., T. Szkaliczki, and H. Hellwagner. 2007. A framework for utility-based multimedia adaptation. *Transactions on Circuits and Systems for Video Technology 17*(6), 719–728.

Russell, S., and P. Norvig. 2003. *Artificial Intelligence: A Modern Approach* (2nd ed.). Englewood Cliffs, NJ: Prentice-Hall.

Stahl, C., and D. Heckmann. 2004 Using semantic Web technology for ubiquitous location and situation modeling. *Journal of Geographic Information Sciences CPGIS 10,* 157–165.

The UPnP Forum. 2008. Universal Plug and Play (UPnP) Forum. http://www.upnp.org (accessed May 27, 2008).

Vassileva, J. 2001. Distributed user modelling for universal information access. In Winograd, T. Architectures for context. *Human–Computer Interaction, Special Issue on Context-Aware Computing 16*(2–4), 401–419.

Zimmermann, A. 2008. *Context-Management and Personalisation: A Tool Suite for Context- and User-Aware Computing.* Ph.D. thesis, University of Aachen, Germany.

Zimmermann, A., A. Lorenz, and R. Oppermann. 2007. An operational definition of context. In *Proceedings of the 6th International and Interdisciplinary Conference on Modeling and Using Context (CONTEXT '07),* 558–571.

Zimmermann, A., M. Specht, and A. Lorenz 2005. Personalization and context management. *User Modeling and User-Adapted Interaction 15*(3–4), 275–302.

Chapter 3

User-Centered Adaptation of User Interfaces for Heterogeneous Environments

Jan Meskens, Mieke Haesen,
Kris Luyten, and Karin Coninx

3.1 Introduction

User-centered adaptation of user interfaces (UIs) has become increasingly important over the last years for two main reasons: the diversity of end-user devices and
the diversity in end-user profiles. The former has been the motivation for the development of many of the automatic UI adaptation techniques found in the literature.
Examples of such approaches that focus on adaptation of the UI presentation are
supple [19], artistic resizing [16], and comets (context-moldable widgets) [14]. The
diversity in end-user profiles has been limited to adapting the user interface according to the preferences of the end users. Traditionally, UI adaptation mechanisms
based on user preferences focused on two aspects: tailoring the style of the presentation according to the user's liking, and presenting only parts of the user interface
that are important for the user's role. Few of these approaches, however, consider
accessibility preferences as part of the general user preferences. Supple is an example

of an approach that considers the physical disabilities of the user [20]. Luyten, Thys, and Coninx [33] used an MPEG-21-based user profile to adapt the user interface according to that specific user profile.

The aforementioned approaches have one thing in common: they try to adapt the user interface automatically at runtime. UI adaptations are no longer controlled by designer choices but are steered by end-user profiles and end-user devices. Adaptation after design can lead to user interfaces that are no longer consistent with the model that the designer had in mind while creating the initial interface. It can even lead to user interfaces that behave differently than they were intended to behave. In the worst case, the behavior is wrong, and the user interface is misleading rather than helpful in accomplishing a task.

In this chapter, we combine a process framework for multidisciplinary user-centered software engineering processes (MuiCSer) with tools and techniques that steer UI adaptability (or plasticity) at runtime on many devices. MuiCSer ensures that different stakeholders, such as designers and end users, are involved in creating the user interface in order to take both the overall and the generic requirements into account. The combination of the designer and end-user input determines the UI adaptations that should be supported at runtime. We explicitly choose to support both the design and runtime stages to create adaptable user interfaces because we strongly believe that UI adaptability can be optimized only by combining the result of the design efforts with the end-user context.

The goal we strive for in this work is the creation of a generic process that supports the creation of user interfaces that can adapt according to the context of use, while both the designer and the end user can steer and constrain this adaptation. A context of use is defined here as the combination of an end user who interacts with the user interface and the computing device that is used by the end user to access the user interface. Figure 3.1 illustrates the relations among the topics discussed in this chapter to obtain our goal.

1. MuiCSer, which enables investigating end users and evaluating design decisions by means of several artifacts, such as UI prototypes
2. A unified model structure that contains important information collected during a MuiCSer process, especially information about the presentation of the user interface (including the design decisions), the end users of the future application, and the devices that these users possess
3. An overview of existing tools such as Gummy [34] that can be used for structuring the unified model during a MuiCSer process, with special attention to the way these tools support transitions between the different stages of MuiCSer
4. A runtime adaptation process that reasons about the information contained in the model and adapts the user interface according to the current context of use so that the adaptation process does not break the adaptation constraints made during a MuiCSer process (we label this behavior as *design-constrained plasticity of the user interface*)

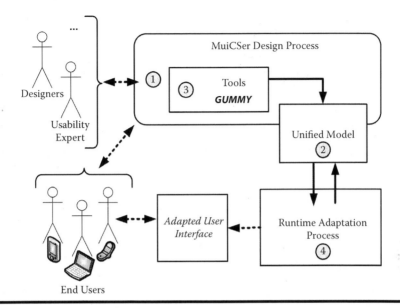

Figure 3.1 **User-centered adaptation of user interfaces for heterogeneous environments.**

Gummy [34], a multidevice UI design tool, plays an important role in the approach presented here. It helps designers and domain experts to rapidly create mid- and high-fidelity prototypes for multiple devices, and at the same time, it allows designers to specify the adaptation constraints of a UI design in order to ensure design-constrained plasticity. Example constraints are the minimum and maximum sizes of a button and the different fonts that a textlabel may have. In Gummy, these adaptation constraints can be specified with relation to the size of the user interface (e.g., a certain widget's minimum size can be specified for all display sizes between 200 × 300 and 600 × 800).

3.2 MuiCSer Process Framework

MuiCSer, illustrated in Figure 3.2 [21], is a generic process subdivided into steps that are commonly used for UI design processes. Contrary to most other approaches, MuiCSer supports multidisciplinary teams using a mix of manual design and development efforts and automatic transformations.

User-centered design (UCD) approaches recommend focusing on the end user during the entire design and development cycle in order to optimize the user experience provided by the delivered software [3,24,27,39]. MuiCSer is based on the same user-centered principles but combines both human–computer interaction (HCI) and traditional software engineering techniques. At the first stage of

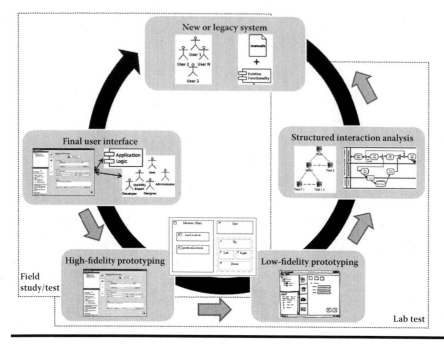

Figure 3.2 MuiCSer, our framework for multidisciplinary user-centered software engineering processes. The dark arrow indicates the overall design and development direction. The light arrows indicate feedback from evaluation, verification, and validation efforts.

MuiCSer, interaction designers carry out a user and task analysis to obtain user requirements. When developing adaptable user interfaces, these observations are also useful in discovering the preferences of end users and determining the information to include in the user and device profiles. If MuiCSer is employed to redesign an existing system, studying manuals and a legacy system can also provide an understanding of functional requirements.

Because the results of this first stage can be very diverse and are mostly specified in a narrative style, there is a need to structure these functional and nonfunctional requirements before designers and developers can create prototypes. The structured interaction analysis allows the creation of various models based on the results of the first stage. Models created during this stage usually contain user tasks and their interrelationships, the link between the user interface and the application logic, and presentation models.

The use of well-structured models instead of narrative information guarantees a better understanding of the future application by the multidisciplinary team and prevents some parts of the prototype from being overlooked. Furthermore, tool support can be provided to create and maintain models or even to reason about the information contained in the models, which improves the traceability and visibility of artifacts created using MuiCSer processes. Tools that can be used during the structured interaction analysis and other stages of MuiCSer are introduced later in this chapter.

After modeling information about the future application and its end users, the results of the first stages of MuiCSer processes contribute to the prototypes. The design of low-fidelity prototypes in the early design stages allows inexpensive changes after evaluation and verification by end users and the multidisciplinary team. These low-fidelity prototypes gradually evolve into high-fidelity prototypes containing more functionality. Usually, high-fidelity prototypes provide sufficient interactivity to evaluate the design in a usability lab or in the natural environment of the end user. The more functionality is available in the high-fidelity prototype, the closer this prototype comes to the final user interface. Later in this chapter, we present how Gummy [34] can be used to create high-fidelity prototypes for heterogeneous environments.

MuiCSer supports iterative design and development, meaning that artifacts can be managed using a central repository. This improves the visibility and traceability during the development and after the deployment of a user interface. This transparency and availability of information in various formats make MuiCSer a powerful approach for supporting multidisciplinary teams.

3.3 Models

The MuiCSer process framework takes advantage of the vast body of experiences with model-based UI development (MBUID) techniques. MBUID has been successfully applied to create context-sensitive user interfaces [10,12] (i.e., user interfaces that adapt automatically according to the context of use). The most important drawback of MBUID techniques is their use of abstract models and automatic transformations to translate these models into concrete user interfaces without further input of the end user or designer. It has been difficult to make tool support for a user interface that adapts according to its context of use while adhering to the design decisions made during its creation.

The second stage of MuiCSer, the structured interaction analysis, results in several models. Among those, our approach uses three models to orchestrate the runtime adaptation of the user interface: the presentation model, the user model, and the device model. More models can be involved in UI generation to allow for more specific tailoring of the user interface, but for our goals, these three models suffice. Each of the models describes a specific aspect of an interactive system that must be considered in the runtime adaptation process. The *presentation model* describes the UI structure, style, and content. This model is created by the UI designers and developers and is used to generate the final user interface that is shown to the user. The *user model* describes the end user and is concerned with a specific user group

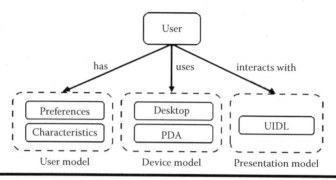

Figure 3.3 Structure of the information model.

(e.g., color-blind people) or even an individual user. Whereas the former contains less detail and is thus more generic, the latter contains a combination of details specific for a single user. The model can be created at design time but is often completed at runtime when the system can detect the user capabilities and preferences. Finally, the *device model* describes one or more devices that are used by the end user. The capabilities of these devices play an important role in deciding how to adapt the user interface so that the user can access it with his or her own devices.

To ease processing, we combine different models into one unified model that encompasses all the information required to generate a suitable user interface. The combined information model, an overview of which is shown in Figure 3.3, is specified by using the Web Ontology Language (OWL) [42]. Because OWL relies on the Resource Description Framework (RDF) [42] notation, a language that can describe graph structures, it can describe the individual entities contained in the models and the inter- and intrarelations among these entities. Once this unified language relates the different models, queries over the combined information from these models that could be useful for UI adaptation are relatively easy to accomplish.

3.3.1 Presentation Model

The development of multidevice personalized user interfaces requires the underlying presentation model to be sufficiently flexible to describe user interfaces for several possible situations. XML-based User Interface Description Languages (UIDLs) have proven to be suitable for multiplatform personalized UI design and creation [30]. All the available UIDLs have their own advantages and disadvantages, which mainly follow from the purpose for which the UIDL was built. Two types of UIDLs are described here: form-based UIDLs and high-level UIDLs. A form-based UIDL describes user interfaces close to the final user interface and thus makes UI rendering easy. High-level UIDLs (HLUIDLs) are highly portable and describe user interfaces independently of a toolkit or platform, thus providing more flexibility (or plasticity) and requiring a more complex transformation to obtain the final user interface. Several types of XML-based UIDLs are discussed in the remainder of this section.

3.3.1.1 Form-Based UIDLs

Most form-based UIDLs typically support a predefined one-to-one mapping between XML tags and UI components. For example, when such a UIDL defines a `<button>` tag, this button will always be represented by the same predefined button in the final user interface: the designer does not have the flexibility to customize how the UIDL tags are mapped onto the concrete UI elements.

The XML User Interface Language (XUL) [25], developed by the Mozilla project, is an XML-based language for describing window layout. An XUL UI description can be rendered with an XUL-renderer or within the Mozilla browser. Furthermore, XUL can be combined with other browser-compatible languages such as Cascading Style Sheets (CSS), RDF, and JavaScript. Microsoft's eXtensible Application Markup Language (XAML) is an XML-based language that can serialize objects and properties defined in the Microsoft .NET Framework. The XAML syntax focuses on defining the user interface for the Windows Presentation Foundation (WPF) and is therefore separate from the application code behind it. XForms [17] is an XML description format that represents the next generation of Forms for the Web. The three main parts of an XForms document are the data model, the instance data, and the user interface. These three components permit separating the structure of the model from its presentation, thus stimulating reuse: one model can be reused in different user interfaces. UI descriptions described in XForms are more flexible than XUL or XAML because in most XForms implementations, designers can choose how to render the input elements used in their UI description.

3.3.1.2 High-Level UIDLs

Form-based UIDLs are not flexible enough for our approach because they cannot define user interfaces in a platform-, toolkit-, and metaphor-independent way. This flexibility can be achieved by means of HLUIDLs, which describe user interfaces on a higher level of abstraction. Two well-known HLUIDLs are the User Interface eXtensible Markup Language (UsiXML) and the User Interface Markup Language (UIML). The former follows an MBUID approach, while the latter is a canonical metalanguage that makes it easy to create a new UIDL containing a custom set of abstractions.

UsiXML [18,28] describes a user interface on the four layers of abstraction that were introduced by the Cameleon Reference Framework [7]. By means of a set of predefined transformation rules (e.g., abstractions or refinements), a UI description can be transformed between these levels. For example, a user interface written for a certain platform and interaction modality can be *abstracted* to a toolkit-independent or modality-independent level. This abstract description can then be *refined* into a final user interface for a new interaction modality and/or platform. Although there is a lot of flexibility introduced in UsiXML, it permits using only a predefined set of abstractions and cannot be extended without altering the language definition.

For our approach, we use UIML [1]. We chose this particular UIDL for three reasons. First, a UIML document has a clear separation of the structure, content, style, and behavior, which allows both multidevice and personalized user interface. Second, the presentation part in the vocabulary section of UIML dynamically maps the generic UIML terms to concrete UI elements. Domain-specific vocabularies contain custom abstractions and can be extended easily without altering the structure of the user interface, making UIML highly platform independent. Finally, UIML has a great practical advantage because of the good and freely available tool support, like renderers such as the UIML.net renderer [31] and the Harmonia rendering engine [22], and several design tools, such as Tide [2] and Gummy [34]. Besides designing user interfaces, Gummy can also be used to specify adaptation constraints in a UI design. Although we do not consider UIML the only usable UIDL, its clear separation of concern makes it the most suitable UIDL for our needs.

3.3.2 User Model

There exist several user-modeling standards that describe user information as well-structured user profiles. One of these is the General User-Model Ontology (GUMO) [23], an ontology for the uniform interpretation of distributed user models in intelligent, semantic, Web-enriched environments. This ontology is described in OWL [42], which enables applications to process information included in documents. In order to make the exchange and interpretation of user models among different systems much simpler, GUMO aims to be a commonly accepted top-level ontology. The main conceptual idea of GUMO is the use of situational statements, dividing the user-model dimensions into three parts: auxiliary, predicate, and range. Using this ontology, a lot of personal information, such as preferences, abilities, and contact information, can be modeled. However, because of its intention to be an upper-level ontology, some detailed information that is valuable for the adaptation process (e.g., color deficiency) is missing.

MPEG-21 [6] is a well-known framework that standardizes the delivery and consumption of multimedia. It contains several parts of technology that can be used independently, such as Intellectual Property Management and Protection, Digital Item Adaptation, and Reference Software. For the modeling of detailed user information, we can rely on part 7 of this framework, Digital Item Adaptation (DIA) [41]. DIA focuses on universal multimedia access through different terminals, networks, and users. As proposed by Luyten, Thys, and Coninx [33], the Usage Environment Description Tools within DIA can be used as input for the adaptation of the user interface. The combination of GUMO and MPEG-21 results in an easily extendable and detailed user model suitable for the adaptation of user interfaces.

3.3.3 Device Model

A computing device is characterized by three important features: the device type (e.g., smartphone, tablet PC), the operating system installed on the device (e.g., Windows mobile), and the available toolkits (e.g., .NET Compact Framework, Java Swing). Consequently, a model that describes a computing device available for, or preferred by, the end user must at least take these three elements into account.

The User Agent Profile (UAProf) [38] specification can be used for describing and transmitting capability and preference information (CPI) about a device. UAProf is an extension of WAP 2.0 (Wireless Application Protocol 2.0) that enables the end-to-end flow of CPI among a WAP client, intermediate network points, and the origin server. The biggest limitations of UAProf, however, come from its purpose to model only mobile devices, and thus this language is not expressive enough for our approach.

We also use part 7 of the MPEG-21 standard, DIA [41], to model user information. In addition to the personalization of media, DIA can be used to describe the adaptation of the content according to the characteristics and capabilities of the devices used to access the content. DIA allows us to describe the terminal capabilities regarding software and hardware. This standard is only usable with a wide variety of end-user devices and overcomes the limitations of UAProf.

For now, we can model the device, the operating system, and the available toolkit(s) using DIA. However, it is important to know not only the toolkits that are available but also how these toolkits can be used to render our UI description on the target device. In order to describe this information, we can rely on the UIML vocabulary description. This vocabulary describes how to map the abstractions used in the presentation model to the elements of the toolkit. Thus, a computing platform will be described using a combination of DIA and a UIML vocabulary.

3.4 Designing for Transformation

The results of each stage in a MuiCSer process are one or more artifacts. Each artifact constructed at a certain stage is the result of a transformation from previously created artifacts. Transformation from one artifact to another can take place in several ways. We introduced a classification of five transformation or mapping mechanisms in a previous work [11]:

- *Artifact derivation*: Constructing a new artifact using the information of an existing artifact
- *Partial artifact derivation*: Partially deriving an artifact from an existing artifact
- *Artifact linking*: Connecting different artifacts to each other, capturing how they are related

■ *Artifact modification*: Applying changes made by the human designer to an artifact
■ *Artifact update*: Updating an artifact from another artifact to which a human designer or an algorithm has made changes or added properties

The use of appropriate tools is helpful in creating artifacts and transforming a particular artifact into another one. The right tools significantly decrease the complexity of making an adaptable multidevice user interface, because the users of these tools are unaware of the different transformation paths one can take among artifacts. By selecting suitable tools according to the project and the multidisciplinary team, collaboration within the team can be stimulated, and the resulting prototypes will be based on all the know-how available in the team. In this section, we will discuss some of the tools that can be used in a MuiCSer process and their popularity in a multidisciplinary team.

As part of our discussion, we will introduce Gummy, a graphical design tool that can assume different roles in the design of an adaptive user interface. Both designers and domain experts can use Gummy to create user interfaces, which can then be easily plugged into our runtime adaptation process. In this process, end users can directly test these interfaces and provide their input.

3.4.1 Tools

MuiCSer supports UI design and development by multidisciplinary teams. For creating, transforming, and managing several artifacts, appropriate tool support is needed. Table 3.1 associates roles in a multidisciplinary team with tools available for user-centered software engineering. The roles listed in the first column are based on ISO 13407 [27]; the tools in the first row are based on literature that describes UCD processes and tools. We associated the tools with roles according to our own experiences while carrying out case studies in a multidisciplinary team and based on literature that describes tools. The tools in the left column are accessible for a wide range of roles in the multidisciplinary team.

The other tools are used mostly by software developers and designers. We define *transformation tools* as tools that are accessible for two or more roles in a multidisciplinary team and provide support for at least one of the aforementioned transformation or mapping mechanisms.

The mapping of these tools on MuiCSer is presented in Figure 3.4. Some of these tools cover many stages of MuiCSer and are explicitly developed to design multidevice user interfaces. Teresa [37], for instance, supports several artifacts (e.g., task models and abstract user interfaces), which are spread over three stages and can be transformed semiautomatically. Although these transformations provide a high consistency between artifacts and the user interfaces for the different devices, the tool supports little creativity of designers. Damask [29], on the other hand, concentrates on the early-stage prototyping by designers using layers to specify which

Table 3.1 Tools That Support MuiCSer and Their Accessibility in a Multidisciplinary Team

	End-user	Purchaser, manager of user	Application domain specialist	Systems analyst, systems engineer, programmer	Marketer, salesperson	UI designer, visual designer	Human factors and ergonomics expert, HCI specialist	Technical author, trainer, and support personnel
Word Processor [3]		√	√	√	√	√	√	√
Presentation [3]		√	√	√	√	√	√	√
Spreadheet [3]		√	√	√	√	√	√	√
Drawing [3]		√	√	√	√	√	√	√
Paper [3]	√	√	√	√	√	√	√	√
PDF viewer [3]		√	√	√	√	√	√	√
Paint Program [3]						√		√
Simple Programming [3]				√				
HTML (site) editor [3]				√		√		
Animation tool [3]						√		
Advance programming [3]				√				
CTTE [37]				√		√		
TaskSketch [8]				√		√		
Vista [5]				√		√		
CanonSketch [8]				√		√		
Teresa [38]				√		√		
SketchiXML [13]	√					√		
Damask [29]				√		√		
GrafiXML [35]				√		√		
Gummy [34]		√	√	√		√		
IntuiKit [9]				√		√		

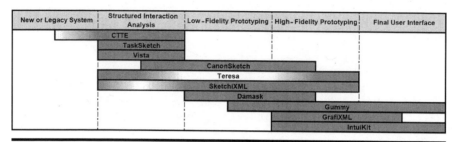

New or Legacy System	Structured Interaction Analysis	Low–Fidelity Prototyping	High–Fidelity Prototyping	Final User Interface
	CTTE			
	TaskSketch			
	Vista			
	CanonSketch			
	Teresa			
	SketchiXML			
	Damask			
			Gummy	
			GrafiXML	
			IntuiKit	

Figure 3.4 A timeline presenting the stages of MuiCSer and how artifact transformation tools can be mapped on it. The gray parts in a bar show on what stages of MuiCSer the tool focuses.

parts of the user interface are common across all devices. This tool allows for a large amount of creativity but does not support the design of high-fidelity prototypes. A wider range of fidelities (from no-fidelity to high-fidelity prototypes) to create prototypes is supported by SketchiXML [13]. Although profiles for multiple platforms are available in SketchiXML, the tool does not support the management of a particular prototype for multiple devices at the same time.

In order to take full advantage of the different viewpoints in the team, several tools can be combined to support the different roles of a multidisciplinary team when employing MuiCSer. For the development of an adaptable system that is often difficult to conceive for nontechnical users, we use Gummy, a tool that is discussed in more detail in the next section.

3.4.2 Gummy

To facilitate the creation of mid- to high-fidelity prototypes for heterogeneous environments, we rely on the Gummy [34] design tool (see Figure 3.5). Gummy is a flexible GUI builder that enables both designers and domain experts to create user interfaces using direct manipulation. The user interfaces created with Gummy are serialized in UIML and can thus be deployed on multiple computing devices. Next to the design of user interfaces, Gummy also allows us to specify adaptation constraints that should be ensured during the runtime adaptation process.

Figure 3.6 illustrates how a designer can use Gummy to generate platform-independent user interfaces. First, he or she provides Gummy with a device model that represents the target device that the user interface is being designed for. According to this model, Gummy automatically loads a workspace that is fully equipped to design interfaces for the selected device. Such a workspace offers a designer a palette that contains all the widgets available on the target device and that he or she can use to construct a user interface. To speed up the creation of user interfaces, a designer does not need to start from scratch: Gummy automatically generates an initial design as a starting point. This initial design is based on a

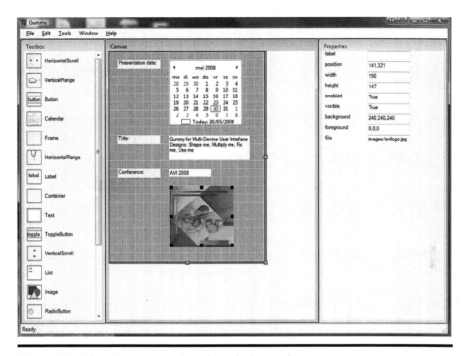

Figure 3.5   The Gummy user interface design tool.

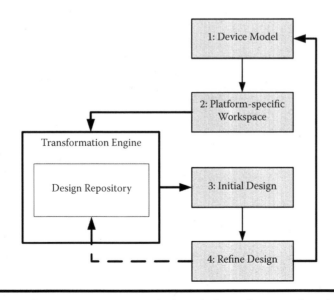

Figure 3.6   Using Gummy to create platform-independent user interfaces.

design repository containing user interfaces that were previously designed for the same task as the new user interface. Finally, a designer can refine this design until he or she reaches the desired result. This design is then added to the design repository as a basis for future designs for other devices. A designer can restart the cycle by providing a new design.

Gummy is not oriented toward designers only. With a slightly modified approach, domain experts can also take part in the design process [32]. Domain experts provide Gummy with a domain model that contains a set of abstractions with which they are familiar. For example, a media player domain model may contain abstractions such as play, stop, song, and playlist. Each of these abstractions is linked to a concrete UI part (e.g., a playlist is linked to a listbox containing all of the songs). Using this domain model, Gummy loads a domain-specific workspace containing a palette with iconographic notations of the domain abstractions. To design a user interface, domain experts drag these abstractions to the design canvas. Once they are placed on the canvas, the concrete representation of the abstraction is shown and can be manipulated. In this way, domain experts can create platform-independent user interfaces.

To constrain the way a user interface adapts, designers can define the values that the properties of each widget can have according to the available screenspace. For example, designers can specify the minimum and maximum sizes a widget can have on a small screenspace (e.g., the screen of a mobile device) and give other constraints for larger screen sizes (e.g., a desktop computer or smartboard). Other examples include the different background colors that a button can take and the number of fonts a text label may have. The constraints specified through Gummy are also serialized in the presentation model and can thus be consulted in the runtime adaptation process, which is the subject of the next section.

3.5 Runtime UI Adaptation

While MuiCSer processes are used to improve the user experience, and the Gummy tool supports the prototyping stages of MuiCSer, the runtime UI adaptation process is built to increase the accessibility of information presented in the user interface. Figure 3.1 shows how the runtime environment fits in the user-centered adaptation process. As described previously, this UI adaptation process takes into account the presentation, user, and device models. In addition, the possible adaptations that can occur are constrained by what the designer specified through Gummy in a MuiCSer design process, which ensures that adaptations do not lead to user interfaces that are unusable by the end user or undesired by the designer or provider.

3.5.1 Adaptation Process

During the adaptation process, information from the device, the user, and the presentation models are used to generate an adapted presentation model respecting the constraints specified by the designer. This presentation model will finally result in an appropriate user interface for the user and the device. An overview of the adaptation process is shown in Figure 3.7.

In the first stage of the runtime adaptation, the user model and device model constructed during the structured interaction analysis are being analyzed by the *Filter Set Generator*. Based on the information found within these models, a set of filters is selected from a repository of available filters. A filter defines an adaptation for specific types of elements contained in the presentation model and changes the values of these elements according to the information collected in the other models. Following are examples of the most important available filters:

- *Color filter*: This allows for the modification of the foreground and background color of the parts in the user interface, such as changing them to colors that are preferred by the user.
- *Content filter*: Parts can have different kinds of content: text, pictures, and so on. The attributes responsible for the content of these parts can be modified using this filter.
- *Visible filter*: Just like the enabled property, UI parts should sometimes be invisible for the user.

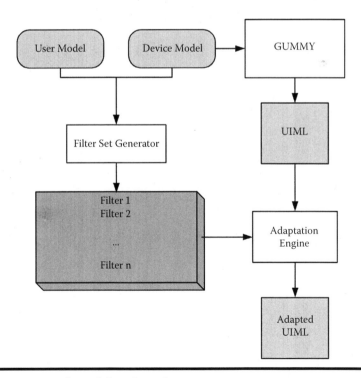

Figure 3.7   Overview of the adaptation process.

- *Font filter*: When the content of the parts is text, the font of the text can be modified. Increasing the size, brightening the color, making the text bold, and so on, can personalize the user interface or make it more accessible.
- *Position filter*: If necessary, this filter could change the position of the parts in the user interface.
- *Size filter*: Changing the size of the parts in the user interface may be necessary when the user interface is migrated to another device with a larger or smaller screen size.

The software architecture provides support for new filters to be plugged in or existing filters to be extended with new behavior. Currently, the filters contain simple rules that are applied on the presentation model and are changed according to the plug-ins or the extensions as required. We plan to extend this approach in the future toward a system that can choose among several algorithms to steer adaptation. The first steps toward a more generic approach have already been explored [15,34]. In the system presented in this chapter, filters are currently generated from a list of rules defining the desired transformations according to some specified information from the models.

After the filters have been generated, the *adaptation engine* receives the set of filters as input, together with the presentation model provided by Gummy. The filters are run on the UIML document, and the property values are changed according to the behavior contained in the filters. However, the adaptation engine always adheres to the design decisions made during the previous phase. For example, the position filter cannot break the placement constraints provided by the designer; it can change the position of a user interface part as long as it satisfies the constraints.

3.5.2 Examples

We demonstrate the applicability of our system by means of some concrete examples. In the first scenario, a remote control application has been created with our approach. Figure 3.8 shows a set of user interfaces for this service that are the result of applying several sets of filters to the original user interface, shown in the upper left. The original user interface serves for users without any specific preferences using a device with a screen size that is sufficiently large. When a device with a smaller screen size is used, the menu controls can be omitted, and only the play controls are presented to the user. The icons can be replaced by large text to ensure that the application is accessible for users who cannot see the details of such icons. Finally, the same user interface is shown, but it is personalized with a different color scheme. Several degrees of visual impairment, such as color-blindness, can be supported in this way.

For the second scenario, a picture viewer service is developed. It shows that filters for the adaptation of the user interface or for the content within a user interface can be easily modified and added. In this scenario, a user with a green–red

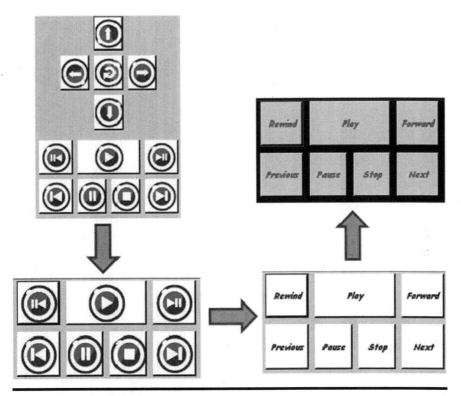

Figure 3.8 UI adaptation using filters.

color deficiency will access the application. When he or she uses the application, the pictures shown in the user interface will be adapted, allowing him or her to see the pictures in full detail, which is not possible showing the original pictures. Figure 3.9 shows the result of applying an adaptation filter, using the algorithm described in [26]. First, the original picture of a cap with red and green colors is shown. When a person with a red–green color deficiency looks at this image, the details of the star in the center of the cap are lost. When the colors of the picture are adapted by our color filter, the details of the star are preserved for this user.

3.6 Discussion

In this chapter, we presented an approach to design user interfaces that can be accessed by users regardless of their preferences, deficiencies, or the device they use. We relied on a process framework for multidisciplinary, user-centered software engineering processes in which different roles can contribute to both the UI design process and a runtime UI adaptation process. The process framework

Figure 3.9 Adaptation for green–red color deficiency.

ensures that both the designer and end-user input are taken into account and thus that the adaptations performed by the runtime process do not lead to user interfaces that are unusable by the end user or undesired by the designer.

During the incremental design process, different roles (e.g., end users and designers) provide their input to construct an overall structured model that contains information about the end users, the end-user devices, and the UI presentation. To ease the construction of this model, transformation tools are used to transform intermediate increments and artifacts toward the final model. The UI presentation and adaptation constraints are modeled through Gummy, a graphical design tool that enables quick design of multidevice mid- and high-fidelity prototypes. At run-time, the runtime adaptation process relies on the constructed model to steer and constrain how a user interface should adapt depending on the context of use.

The approach presented in this chapter is evaluated continuously throughout the MuiCSer process framework. This continuous evaluation leads to more realistic artifacts during the different stages of the design process that should eventually result in better UI adaptations. Because of the underlying tool support, the result-ing UI adaptations can be perceived immediately. In turn, these UI adaptations are evaluated, too. The result of this evaluation provides better insights in the way that end users deal with the adapted user interfaces. This information can be invaluable for the construction of better models during future process iterations.

Currently, only a limited amount of information regarding the device and user is being used in the adaptation process. Therefore, a next step would be to extend the adaptation process to make even more personalized user interfaces. An interest-ing path in this area would be to examine the influence of the social relations of a user regarding the user interface.

Furthermore, a couple of disadvantages of UIML can be addressed. The infor-mation about users and devices influences not only the presentation but also the navigation and the tasks within the user interface. Therefore, the presentation model must be extended with more abstract interface objects, as mentioned in [40]. Our goal is to examine this possibility and to adopt it in the current system.

The current implementation of Gummy permits the specification of adapta-tion constraints only for certain screen ranges. In future versions of the tool, we want to incorporate other criteria, such as the input technology of the target devices, which would allow specifying different adaptation constraints accord-ing to the input technology used. For example, we might incorporate criteria to enlarge the buttons of a user interface when a touch screen is used instead of a pointing device.

Acknowledgments

Part of the research at the Expertise Centre for Digital Media (EDM) is funded by EFRO (European Fund for Regional Development) and the Flemish govern-ment. The VIN (Virtual Individual Networks) and QoE (Quality of Experience) projects are directly funded by the Interdisciplinary Institute for Broadband Technology (IBBT). The MuiCSer process framework and the Gummy tool are based on our experiences in the IWT project AMASS++ (IWT 060051). We also would like to thank Chris Raeymaekers for his contributions to the early versions of this chapter.

Jan Meskens is a PhD researcher at the Expertise Centre for Digital Media (EDM), a research institute of Hasselt University, Belgium. He obtained his MSc in computer science from Hasselt University in 2007 and joined EDM in September that year. Dr. Meskens has been working with User Interface Markup Language (UIML) since 2006, when he wrote his BSc thesis about UIML template parameterization. For his MSc thesis, he created the gummy multiplatform design tool on top of UIML. His research interests revolve mainly around model-driven user interface design, demonstrational user interface design, and user-centered design processes.

Mieke Haesen is a PhD student at Hasselt University, Belgium. She holds an MSc in computer science (2004) from Hasselt University. Since 2004 she has worked as a researcher at the Expertise Centre for Digital Media, a research institute of Hasselt University, where she is actively involved in projects that focus on user-centered design. In 2007, she started her PhD, which concerns user-centered software engineering techniques that support cooperation within multidisciplinary teams. In addition to user-centered design and development processes her research interests include model-based user interface development and multimedia content retrieval. She is a member of ACM Sigchi and the Belgian Professional Association for Human–Computer Interaction.

Kris Luyten is an assistant professor at Hasselt University, Belgium, where he is a member of the Expertise Centre for Digital Media, a research institute. His research interests are model-based user interface development, human–computer interface (HCI) engineering for ambient intelligence, user-centered design of complex systems, and context-aware user interfaces. He is a member of ACM Sigchi and the OASIS UIML Technical Committee. He was the coorganizer of several successful workshops dedicated to user interface description languages and model-based user interface development.

Karin Coninx is a full-time professor at Hasselt University, Belgium, and head of the Department of Mathematics, Physics, and Computer Science. She holds a PhD in computer science and leads the Human–Computer Interaction (HCI) group of the research institute, Expertise Centre for Digital Media. Her research interests include interaction in multimodal/virtual environments, user-centred development approaches, model-based user interface development, and software architectures for ubiquitous systems including distributed and migratable user interfaces. She is the coauthor of more than 180 international publications and was a coorganizer of several workshops.

References

1. Marc Abrams, Constantinos Phanouriou, Alan L. Batongbacal, Stephen M. Williams, and Jonathan E. Shuster. UIML: An appliance-independent XML user interface language. *Computer Networks*, 31(11–16):1695–1708, 1999.

2. Mir Farooq Ali, Manuel A. Pérez-Quiñones, Marc Abrams, and Eric Shell. Building multi-platform user interfaces with UIML. In *Proceedings of CADUI 2002*, pp. 255–266, 2002.
3. Jonathan Arnowitz, Michael Arent, and Nevin Berger. *Effective Prototyping for Software Makers (The Morgan Kaufmann Series in Interactive Technologies)*. San Francisco: Morgan Kaufmann, 2006.
4. Brian P. Bailey and Joseph A. Konstan. Are informal tools better? Comparing DEMAIS, pencil and paper, and authorware for early multimedia design. In *CHI '03: Proceedings of the SIGCHI Conference on Human Factors in Computing Systems*, New York: ACM, pp. 313–320, 2003.
5. Judy Brown, T. C. Nicholas Graham, and Timothy Wright. The Vista environment for the coevolutionary design of user interfaces. In *CHI '98: Proceedings of the SIGCHI Conference on Human Factors in Computing Systems*, New York: ACM/Addison-Wesley, pp. 376–383, 1998.
6. Ian Burnett, Rik Van de Walle, Keith Hill, Jan Bormans, and Fernando Pereira. MPEG-21: Goals and achievements. *IEEE-MULTIMEDIA* 10(4):60–70, Oct.–Dec. 2003.
7. G. Calvary, J. Coutaz, D. Thevenin, Q. Limbourg, L. Bouillon, and J. Vanderdonckt. A unifying reference framework for multi-target user interfaces. *Interacting with Computers* 15(3):289–308, 2003.
8. Pedro Campos and Nuno Jardim Nunes. Practitioner tools and workstyles for user-interface design. *IEEE Software* 24(1):73–80, 2007.
9. Stéphane Chatty, Stéphane Sire, Jean-Luc Vinot, Patrick Lecoanet, Alexandre Lemort, and Christophe Mertz. Revisiting visual interface programming: Creating GUI tools for designers and programmers. In *UIST '04: Proceedings of the 17th Annual ACM Symposium on User Interface Software and Technology*, New York: ACM, pp. 267–276, 2004.
10. Tim Clerckx, Kris Luyten, and Karin Coninx. Dynamo-aid: A design process and a runtime architecture for dynamic model-based user interface development. In R. Bastide, Philippe Palanque, and Jörg Roth, Eds., *Engineering for Human–Computer Interaction and Interactive Systems/DSV-IS*, Berlin: Springer, pp. 77–95, 2004.
11. Tim Clerckx, Kris Luyten, and Karin Coninx. The mapping problem back and forth: Customizing dynamic models while preserving consistency. In *TAMODIA '04: Proceedings of the 3rd Annual Conference on Task Models and Diagrams*, pp. 33–42, 2004.
12. Karin Coninx, Kris Luyten, Jan Van den Bergh, Chris Vandervelpen, and Bert Creemers. Dygimes: Dynamically generating interfaces for mobile computing devices and embedded systems. *Lecture Notes in Computer Science*, 2795:256–270, 2003.
13. Adrien Coyette, Suzanne Kieffer, and Jean Vanderdonckt. Multi-fidelity prototyping of user interfaces. In *Human–Computer Interaction—INTERACT 2007, 11th IFIP TC 13 International Conference*, pp. 150–164, 2007.
14. Alexandre Demeure, Gaëlle Coutaz, Joëlle Calvary, and Jean Vanderdonckt. The Comets Inspector: Towards runtime plasticity control based on a semantic network. In *TAMODIA '06*, pp. 324–338, 2006.
15. Alexandre Demeure, Jan Meskens, Kris Luyten, and Karin Coninx. Design by example of plastic user interfaces. In *CADUI '08: Computer Aided Design of User Interfaces 2008*, 2008. (to appear)
16. Pierre Dragicevic, Stéphane Chatty, David Thevenin, and Jean-Luc Vinot. Artistic resizing: A technique for rich scale-sensitive vector graphics. In *Symposium on User Interface Software and Technology*, pp. 201–210, 2005.

17. Micah Dubinko, Leigh L. Klotz, Roland Merrick, and T. V. Raman. Xforms 1.0. W3C, http://www.w3.org/TR/2003/RECxforms-20031014/, 2003.

18. Murielle Florins, Francisco Montero Simarro, Jean Vanderdonckt, and Benjamin Michotte. Splitting rules for graceful degradation of user interfaces. In *AVI '06: Proceedings of the Working Conference on Advanced Visual Interfaces*, New York: ACM, pp. 59–66, 2006.

19. Krzysztof Gajos and Daniel S. Weld. Supple: Automatically generating user interfaces. In *IUI '04: Proceedings of the 9th International Conference on Intelligent User Interface*, New York: ACM, pp. 93–100, 2004.

20. Krzysztof Z. Gajos, Jing Jing Long, and Daniel S. Weld. Automatically generating custom user interfaces for users with physical disabilities. In *Assets '06: Proceedings of the 8th International ACM SIGACCESS Conference on Computers and Accessibility*, New York: ACM, pp. 243–244, 2006.

21. Mieke Haesen, Karin Coninx, Jan Van den Bergh, and Kris Luyten. MuiCSer: A process framework for multi-disciplinary user-centered software engineering processes. To appear in *Proceedings of HCSE2008, Conference on Human-Centred Software Engineering*, Pisa, Italy, September 2008.

22. Harmonia. *UIML Tools*. http://www.uiml.org/tools/.

23. Dominik Heckmann, Tim Schwartz, Boris Brandherm, Michael Schmitz, and Margeritta von Wilamowitz-Moellendorff. GUMO—The general user model ontology. In *Proceedings of the 10th International Conference on User Modeling*, Berlin: Springer, pp. 428–432, 2005.

24. K. Holtzblatt, Jessamy Burns Wendell, and Shelley Wood. *Rapid Contextual Design. A How-To Guide to Key Techniques for User-Centered Design*. San Francisco: Morgan Kaufmann, 2005.

25. David Hyatt, Ben Goodger, Ian Hickson, and Chris Waterson. *XML User Interface Language (XUL) Specification 1.0*. http://www.mozilla.org/projects/xul/, 2001.

26. Gennaro Iaccarino, Delfina Malandrino, Marco Del Percio, and Vittorio Scarano. Efficient edge-services for colorblind users. In *WWW '06: Proceedings of the 15th International Conference on World Wide Web*, New York: ACM, pp. 919–920, 2006.

27. International Standards Organization. *ISO 13407. Human Centred Design Process for Interactive Systems*. Geneva, Switzerland, 1999.

28. Quentin Limbourg and Jean Vanderdonckt. *Engineering Advanced Web Applications*, Paramus, NJ: Rinton Press, December 2004.

29. James Lin and James A. Landay. Employing patterns and layers for early-stage design and prototyping of cross-device user interfaces. In *CHI '08: Proceedings of the SIGCHI Conference on Human factors in Computing Systems*, pp. 1313–1322, April 2008.

30. Kris Luyten, Marc Abrams, Quentin Limbourg, and Jean Vanderdonckt. Developing user interfaces with XML: Advances on user interface description languages. In *Satellite Workshop of Advanced Visual Interfaces (AVI)*. Expertise Centre for Digital Media, 2004.

31. Kris Luyten and Karin Coninx. Uiml.net: An Open UIML renderer for the .NET Framework. In *Computer-Aided Design of User Interfaces IV*, volume 4. Dordrecht: Kluwer Academic, 2004.

32. Kris Luyten, Jan Meskens, Jo Vermeulen, and Karin Coninx. Meta-GUI-builders: Generating domain-specific interface builders for multi-device user interface creation. In *CHI '08: CHI '08 Extended Abstracts on Human Factors in Computing Systems*, New York: ACM, pp. 3189–3194, 2008.

33. Kris Luyten, Kristof Thys, and Karin Coninx. Profile-aware multi-device interfaces: An MPEG-21-based approach for accessible user interfaces. In *Proceedings of Accessible Design in the Digital World*, Dundee, Great Britain, Aug. 23–25, 2005.

34. Jan Meskens, Jo Vermeulen, Kris Luyten, and Karin Coninx. Gummy for multi-platform user interface designs: Shape me, multiply me, fix me, use me. In *AVI '08: Proceedings of the Working Conference on Advanced Visual Interfaces*, New York: ACM, 2008.

35. Benjamin Michotte and Jean Vanderdonckt. A multi-target user interface builder based on UsiXML. In *Proceedings of ICAS 2008*, Los Alamitos, CA: IEEE Computer Society Press, 2008.

36. Giulio Mori, Fabio Paternò, and Carmen Santoro. CTTE: Support for developing and analyzing task models for interactive system design. *IEEE Transactions on Software Engineering* 28(8):797–813, 2002.

37. Giulio Mori, Fabio Paternò, and Carmen Santoro. Design and development of multi-device user interfaces through multiple logical descriptions. *IEEE Transactions on Software Engineering* 30(8):507–520, Aug. 2004.

38. Open Mobile Alliance. *Wireless Application Protocol: User Agent Profile Specification.* http://www.openmobilealliance.org/tech/affiliates/wap/wap-248-uaprof-20011020-a.pdf, 2001.

39. D. Redmond-Pyle and A. Moore. *Graphical User Interface Design and Evaluation.* London: Prentice Hall, 1995.

40. Jo Vermeulen, Yves Vandriessche, Tim Clerckx, Kris Luyten, and Karin Coninx. Service-interaction descriptions: Augmenting semantic Web Services with high-level user interface models. In *Proceedings of the Engineering Interactive Systems 2007* (Salamanca), March 2007.

41. Anthony Vetro. MPEG-21 digital item adaptation: Enabling universal multimedia access. *IEEE Multimedia* 11(1):84-87, Jan.–Mar. 2004.

42. World Wide Web Consortium (W3C). *W3C Technical Reports and Publications.* http://www.w3.org/TR/.

Chapter 4

Video Adaptation Based on Content Characteristics and Hardware Capabilities

Özgür Deniz Önür and Aydin A. Alatan

4.1 Introduction

The processing capabilities of mobile terminals like personal digital assistants (PDAs) and cellular phones have increased at an unprecedented rate during the previous decade. Accompanied by the much anticipated spread of broadband wireless access, advancements in processing capabilities have led to a wealth of new possibilities for new consumer services. Among the most exciting killer applications of this era is the pervasive access to rich multimedia content on mobile terminals.

The problem of delivering multimedia content through heterogeneous networks to terminals with diverse processing capabilities in a form that suits the end user's unique preferences remains a challenge. It is apparent that a particular representation of content would be satisfactory for a very limited number of situations; consequently, it is mandatory to be able to adapt the multimedia content depending on the requirements of the consumption scenario. The factors that must be considered while determining the best representation of the content include, but are not limited to, network characteristics (maximum bandwidth, bit error rate [BER]), terminal characteristics (central processing unit [CPU] capacity, available video codecs, color capability, display resolution), natural environment (ambient noise, illumination conditions), and user preferences.

This problem has received considerable attention in the image- and video-processing community, and many methodologies and algorithms exist that deal with the adaptation of multimedia content. The process of modifying a given representation of a video into another representation in order to change the amount of resources required for transmitting, decoding, and displaying video is called *video adaptation* [1].

Video adaptation can be classified in many different ways depending on the application scenario used. Some appropriate classifications include the following [2]:

- Semantic-level video adaptation
- Signal-level video adaptation (transcoding)
- Adaptation of scalable streams

Semantic video adaptation can be basically described as the detection of important or relevant fragments of a video clip (like goals in a soccer video or dialog scenes in an interview) and giving higher priority to these segments during the reduction of the resources allocated to the adapted video. Semantic video adaptation of sports videos has been studied extensively in the literature. For instance, in [3], metadata is combined with video analysis to detect important events and players. In [4], nonimportant video segments are replaced with still images, audio only, or text only representations, resulting in significant reduction in the resources required for the consumption (transmission, decoding, and displaying) of a video clip. In [4], an experiment performed with baseball video clips demonstrated that the nonimportant segments occupied more than 50% of the video clip.

In addition to the semantic level, video adaptation can also be performed at the signal level (transcoding). The most straightforward signal-level adaptation of a video stream is performed by fully decoding the source stream to obtain the raw video data and then re-encoding it with the desired video codec and parameters. However, in most cases, it is not computationally efficient to fully decode the video. Many algorithms have been proposed that perform adaptation by partially decoding the stream and, after changing the necessary parameters, reusing compressed domain features that are not affected by the required adaptation (i.e., the motion vectors) instead of totally re-encoding the video. Whether performed by fully re-encoding the bitstream or by reusing compressed domain features, transcoding can be performed at the following levels:

1. *Spatial*: changing the spatial resolution
2. *Temporal*: changing the frame rate
3. *Quality*: changing the quantization parameters, bit plane depth, and so on
4. *Object*: using advanced codecs like MPEG-4, some objects in a video can be retained and others discarded during adaptation

In a typical video distribution scenario, a video server contains high-quality video data that is to be consumed, and the client terminal has to communicate with an intermediate proxy to request a specific video clip. The proxy then relays this request together with the specifications of the client to the server. The server determines the video format that is suitable for the requesting client. The server can then perform the necessary adaptation itself or can inform the proxy of its adaptation decision by sending metadata together with the video stream to be adapted and asking the proxy to perform the actual adaptation.

An alternative approach to providing video content at different levels of quality is the scalable video coding (SVC) approach. In this approach, a single video stream is encoded as a collection of layers that have properties of different quality. Scalable video codecs can provide content scalability on a number of different axes. The most common scalability axes employed in scalable video codecs are the temporal scalability, signal-to-noise ratio (SNR) scalability, and spatial scalability. The scalable extension of h264/MPEG-4 advanced video coding (AVC) is being standardized jointly by the International Telecommunication Union-Telecommunication Standardization Sector (ITU-T) Video Coding Experts Group (VCEG) and the International Organization for Standardization/International Electrotechnical Commission (ISO/IEC) Moving Pictures Expert Group (MPEG). The preliminary coding efficiency results are highly promising [5,6]. Wavelet-based SVC schemes also exist [7]. In [8], an MPEG-21-based real-time SVC streaming system is introduced. The platform allows for adaptation of real-time encoded video streams as well as adapted representation of interactive scenes mixing text, 2D and 3D avatars, audio, and video, including session mobility between terminals with different capabilities. In [9], the distortions introduced by each type of scalability selection (SNR, temporal, and spatial) are investigated. Using objective metrics, a scaling option is selected among several such that the overall distortion is minimized. That is, in order to measure the distortions caused by different scalability selections, an objective function is defined as a linear combination of common visual distortion measures.

The most important factor that determines the success of video adaptation methods is the quality of the adapted video. However, quality metrics that can effectively model the satisfaction of humans for a given content representation are not easy to design.

The subjective user satisfaction pertaining to video content is called the *utility* of the video. Utility can be measured at different levels: the objective level (i.e., peak-signal-to-noise ratio [PSNR]), the subjective levels (i.e., degradation mean opinion scores [DMOS]), or the comprehension level, which measures the viewer's capability in comprehending the semantic information in video content [2]. It has been accepted that the objective measures fail to measure the human satisfaction accurately. The correlation between PSNR and subjective tests has been shown to be about 0.2. It is very difficult to measure the comprehension-level utility because it depends on the users' knowledge, the context domains, and other variables. The most reliable method of measuring user satisfaction on an adapted video is to use subjective quality metrics. However, even this method is not free of problems. It is always difficult to find human subjects to participate in the tests, and the results usually cannot be generalized for different terminals and testing environments.

The first reference to *utility* in the context of video adaptation appears in [10]. In a more theoretical approach, a conceptual framework that models adaptation, as well as resource, utility, and the relationships in between, is also presented in [11]. A content-based utility function predictor is also proposed by [12] in which the system extracts compressed domain features in real time and uses content-based pattern classification and regression to obtain a prediction of the utility function. However, the utility value corresponding to a given adaptation of a video is presented as a function of the video bit rate [12], which contradicts the subjective nature of the utility concept.

A novel method to determine an optimal video adaptation scheme, given the properties of an end terminal on which the video is to be displayed, is proposed in [13]. In this approach, *utility theory* [14] is utilized to model a strictly subjective quantity, *satisfaction*, that a user will get from watching a certain video clip. In [15], the multidimensional adaptation problem is considered. The utility of video clips is determined using subjective video evaluation experiments, and the results are tested using a scalable video codec (MC-3DSBC [16]). However, the processing capabilities of user terminals are not taken into consideration, which limits the usefulness of the results. Most of the evaluated video content is evaluated by five assessors, which is far fewer than the number required to obtain statistically reasonable results.

4.2 Utility-Based Video Adaptation

In this framework, a general video consumption scenario is considered in which a user requests video content from a server to view on a resource-limited mobile device. The proposed system aims to determine the optimal coding parameters that the video should be encoded with in order to maximally satisfy the user. These parameters are determined according to the characteristics of the video content and the hardware capabilities of the viewing device. A utility-based video adaptation system is illustrated in Figure 4.1.

In order to determine the optimal encoding parameters, it is necessary to model the satisfaction of the user associated with viewing a video on a resource-limited device. In the proposed work, the user satisfaction is modeled as a utility function [14]. The utility function is obtained as a weighted sum of the user satisfaction related to two independent aspects of the video: *temporal satisfaction* and *spatial satisfaction*:

$$U_{tot}(h,c) = (1-\lambda)U_{temp}(h,c) + \lambda U_{spat}(h,c) \qquad (4.1)$$

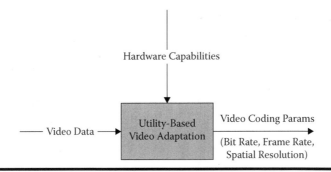

Figure 4.1   A utility-based video adaptation system.

where h denotes the hardware capabilities of the device on which the video will be viewed, and c denotes the content characteristics of the video clip. The constant λ parameter can be set to any value between 0 and 1. The optimal value of this constant is largely dependent on the video content type and individual user preferences.

Following the determination of the optimal video coding parameters, the source video that is maintained at a server can be transcoded to the desired format. Transcoding can be performed either at the server or at an intermediate proxy; however, on-demand transcoding of the requested video stream is usually a resource-intensive operation, and the time that has to elapse before the user can begin to watch the video might reach undesired levels. On the other hand, if an SVC scheme is being utilized, a substream with the required video-encoding parameters can be extracted from the main video stream with low complexity. The recently standardized SVC extension of the H.264/AVC standard, which has quite high coding efficiency, supports many scalability options, such as SNR, temporal, and spatial resolution scalability [6]. Consequently, the SVC extension of H.264/AVC could be an ideal codec to use in adaptive video streaming systems.

4.2.1 Video Content Characteristics

The viewing satisfaction obtained from a video obviously depends on the content itself. While it is possible to tolerate jerky motion on a video clip containing limited movement, such as a scene consisting of an anchorman delivering the news, the principal aspect of satisfaction becomes smooth movements for a sports video containing fast-moving scenes. Similar arguments apply to the spatial aspects of viewing satisfaction.

Thus, the utility models associated with the temporal and spatial satisfaction should be constructed according to the video content characteristics. In this work, video sequences are classified into two classes according to the amount of the motion activity, one class represents *high-motion* activity and the other *low-motion* activity. The ITU's *temporal index* (TI) metric [17] has been utilized as the measure for motion activity in the simulation videos. Similarly, according to their spatial content, all video sequences are also separated into two distinct classes: *low detail* and *high detail*. In this case, ITU's *spatial index* (SI) [17] metric is utilized to measure the amount of spatial detail of the videos. Although SI and TI metrics do not provide a highly precise description of the video content characteristics, their precision is sufficient for the main purpose of this work. Moreover, they can be extracted from the videos in real time, since their complexity is quite low.

4.2.2 Hardware Capabilities

In order to determine the satisfaction a typical user will get from watching a video clip on a particular device, the device's capabilities must be taken into account. The proposed algorithm for user satisfaction modeling must be validated for a wide range of devices before it can be deployed on a real-life video streaming system. In this work, two different classes of devices are studied: high-end PDAs and high-end mobile phones. Such a separation is necessary because these two classes of devices have significant differences in both their hardware and software architectures. For instance, almost all the PDAs in use today have the Windows Mobile® operating system, whereas for mobile phones, there are a variety of operating systems among which Symbian OS is the most common. In addition, most PDAs have specialized hardware for processing graphics, whereas such hardware is very rare for mobile phones. As a result, different hardware metrics are used for quantifying the processing capabilities of these two classes of devices.

Many different hardware performance metrics have been proposed for the quantification of data-processing capabilities of mobile devices [18]. The performance of CPUs measured by using a relatively simple metric, such as the Whetstone [18], which measures the number of floating-point operations per second that the device can perform, can be a sufficient indicator of the video-processing performance of the mobile device. However, especially if the device does have specialized hardware for graphics processing, it can attain much better video-processing performance utilizing graphical processing units (GPUs) and dedicated video memories. In order to measure the performance of such devices, another class of metrics that directly measures the graphics-rendering capabilities of the devices needs to be used because the number of operations that the CPU can perform in unit time is not sufficient to account for the video-processing capabilities of the device.

In this work, for measuring the performance of high-end PDAs, two different metrics are utilized: one is an implementation of the Whetstone metric, and the other is a metric measuring the graphics performance. Both of the metrics employed in this chapter are measured by using MARK 1.03 [19]. In order to obtain a single metric for the overall performance, these two metrics are first normalized and then linearly weighted. For mobile phones, on the other hand, the use of a single metric that measures the performance of the CPU is considered sufficient. Details of the hardware metrics that are used are outlined in Section 4.3.3.

4.3 Subjective Video Evaluation Tests

Through these tests, subjective satisfaction models are obtained for videos with different content characteristics and for hardware with varying capabilities. Separate subjective video evaluation experiments are performed for measuring spatial and temporal satisfactions. Then the temporal and spatial utilities can be combined, as outlined in Equation 4.1, to obtain the total utility function. Bit rate and frame rate that maximize this utility function can be obtained by the help of a suitable optimization algorithm. It is also shown that, by using the result of simulations performed on devices with known hardware capabilities, fairly accurate satisfaction models for other resource-limited devices can be obtained via interpolation. Hence, these results could be generalized for any unknown device to determine the optimal coding parameters for a video clip prior to transmission to the particular device.

4.3.1 Test Methodology

Different methodologies exist for testing the subjective video quality. The most commonly used methodologies are briefly described [20]:

1. *Double-Stimulus Continuous Quality Scale (DSCQS)*: For each sequence, the reference picture and the test picture are shown to the assessor in a random order (i.e., the assessor does not know which one is the reference and which one is the test sequence). The assessor is asked to rate both pictures according to a continuous scale. Usually, the assessor is asked to put a mark on a straight line, where one end of the line denotes the highest quality and the other end the lowest quality.
2. *Double-Stimulus Impairment Scale (DSIS)*: For each test sequence, first a reference picture is shown to the assessor, and the assessor is explicitly told that it is the reference. Then the test picture is shown, and the assessor is asked to grade the impairment in the test picture compared to the reference. Grading is done on a discrete impairment scale with five or seven grading levels.
3. *Single Stimulus (SS)*: The assessors are shown only a single video and are asked to grade the video on a five-point grading scale.
4. *Double-Stimulus Binary Vote (DSBV)*: This is very similar to DSIS, but the assessors are only asked to decide whether or not the test sequence contains a discernible impairment.

Regardless of the testing methodology used, the test sessions should be made up of three phases [20].

4.3.1.1 Training Phase

■ During the training phase, written instructions (so that exactly the same set of instructions can be given to each assessor) should be provided to the assessor that describe the testing methodologies and the grading scales used.

■ The training phase should also include two to three sequences to familiarize the assessor with the timing and the amount of quality variation between test videos that are likely to be encountered during the test. The samples used for the training session should have levels of impairment similar to those in the actual sequences that will be used in the test, but they should not be the same video sequence.

4.3.1.2 Stabilization Phase

■ The first five sequences of each session should be used for stabilization. These sequences should contain some of the best-quality and some of the worst-quality videos so that the entire impairment range is presented to the assessor.

■ The grades given to these five sequences should not be taken into account, and these sequences should later be presented again in the test.

■ The assessors should not know that they are in stabilization.

4.3.1.3 Testing Phase

■ If any reference sequences are used, they should be in ITU-R 601 format (uncompressed 4:2:0 YUV [luminance–chrominance]). The sequences used in the testing phase should be about 10 seconds long.

■ The assessors should be given a limited amount of time to do the grading. Usually, 10 seconds of grading time is ideal.

■ For the test procedure to be compliant with ITU standards, at least 15 assessors should participate in the test. These assessors should not be professionally involved in video quality evaluation.

4.3.1.4 Comparison of DSIS and DSCQS Methods

DSCQS by its nature gives relative results. The assessors do not know beforehand which sequence is a reference and which is a test sequence. Therefore, DSCQS is usually used when the quality of the reference and test sequences are similar. The DSIS is usually used when the reference picture clearly has a higher quality than the test sequence.

4.3.2 Subjective Video Evaluation Experiments

In order to construct a model for the user satisfaction for different video content characteristics, subjective video evaluation tests were performed. The tests were performed in accordance with the subjective video testing principles specified in ITU BT 500-11 *Methodology for the Subjective Assessment of the Quality of TV Pictures* standard [20].

The testing methodology used was a combination of SS and DSIS methods. The assessors were shown reference videos on a desktop computer at the beginning of the test and were asked to rate the impairment in the test videos compared to the reference. The assessors were free to refer back to the reference pictures during these tests; however, they were not obliged to do so.

In order to model the subjective user satisfaction, two different subjective tests were performed, one for modeling the temporal user satisfaction and the other for the spatial user satisfaction. In both tests, the evaluators were asked to rate the impairments in the test video compared to a reference. The reference pictures were coded according to the ITU-R 601 recommendation (with Common Intermediate Format [CIF] resolution and in raw YUV 4:2:0 format) and played on a desktop PC. For both tests, the participants were asked to evaluate the videos by taking into account only the impairments (spatial or temporal) related to the test being performed. For instance, during the motion test, the assessors were asked to evaluate only the motion smoothness of the video clips while disregarding other quality impairments such as blurring and blocking artifacts.

The evaluation tests were performed for two classes of devices separately: PDAs with high data-processing capabilities and mobile phones with rather low data-processing capabilities.

4.3.2.1 High-End PDA Tests

Thirty evaluators, all students at Middle East Technical University (METU), took part in these tests. Four different Windows Mobile PDAs were used for the tests: HP 6340 (hereafter referred to as Device 1), HP 4700 (Device 2), HP 6815 (Device 3), and Siemens Pocket LOOX 600 (Device 4). The hardware performance of these devices, measured by the metrics discussed in Section 4.2.2, are given in Table 4.1.

For the training phase, Coastguard and Flowergarden sequences were used. The tests began after the training; however, the assessors' votes for the first five sequences were disregarded to allow for the stabilization of the assessors' opinions. These five sequences were chosen to include the worst and the best videos to be presented in the test. The videos were later repeated in the test, and their grades were recorded. The total training session lasted no more than 30 minutes, and individual video clips were 10 seconds long. The presentation order of the video clips used in the different testing sessions was always randomly rearranged so that effects like evaluator fatigue were averaged out.

Table 4.1 Hardware Capabilities Benchmark Results

	Whetstone Metric	*Windows Graphics*	*Overall Hardware Metric (h = (w + g)/2)*
Device 1	0.22	0.35	0.29
Device 2	0.85	0.31	0.58
Device 3	0.56	0.56	0.56
Device 4	0.44	0.29	0.36

Table 4.2 SI and TI Values for Well-Known Sequences

Sequence	*SI*	*TI*
Foreman	136.89	39.18
Akiyo	119.45	5.5
Coastguard	135.14	27.77
Mother	76.42	8.35
Bus	155.49	35.4
Hall monitor	128.54	8.09
Flowergarden	152.58	35.57
Mobile	179.94	31.99
Waterfall	64.47	7.27
Soccer	105.28	33.5

For the temporal test, to obtain different models for videos with varying levels of motion activity, two different videos, each representing one of the two video classes (high motion, low motion), were used.

To determine a representative video for each class, the SI and TI values of well-known video sequences were calculated; the results obtained are given in Table 4.2.

The Akiyo sequence, which has the lowest TI value, was used for representing the low-motion activity video class; the Soccer sequence, which has the highest TI value, was used for the high-motion activity class. Similarly, for the spatial test, SI values of the same sequences were measured; the Waterfall sequence was

Figure 4.2 (A) The Akiyo sequence. (B) The Soccer sequence. (C) The Mobile sequence. (D) The Waterfall sequence.

chosen as the representative video for the low-detail class, and the Mobile sequence was chosen as the video for the high-detail class. Figure 4.2 illustrates the Akiyo, Soccer, Mobile, and Waterfall sequences. The presentation order of the video clips was arranged so that the same sequence was never presented on two successive occasions [20]; that is, for instance, during the motion test, an Akiyo sequence was always followed by a Soccer sequence, and vice versa.

The results of the temporal tests (U_{temp}) for Devices 1 and 3 are presented in Figures 4.3 through 4.6. The results shown are the mean opinion scores (MOS) of the subjective ratings of 30 assessors on a 5-grade scale. The videos used in the tests were encoded at Quarter Common Intermediate Format (QCIF) resolution, for four different frame rates (7, 11, 15, 20 fps), and at six different bit rates (50, 100, 150, 256, 512, 1024 kbps).

Figures 4.3 and 4.4 illustrate the test results for the Akiyo sequence for Device 1 and Device 3. It can be observed that the temporal satisfaction of users increases in an exponential manner up to about 11 fps, and for larger frame rates, the utility values saturate. It can also be observed that the utilities do not change significantly, as the bit rate is varied for a given frame rate. These results indicate that the temporal utility is dictated more by the frame rate than by the bit rate of the video clip. It is also worth noting that Figures 4.3 and 4.4 do not show a significant

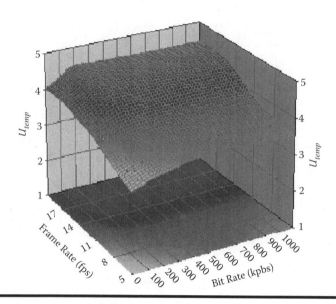

Figure 4.3   Motion test results for Device 1, Akiyo sequence.

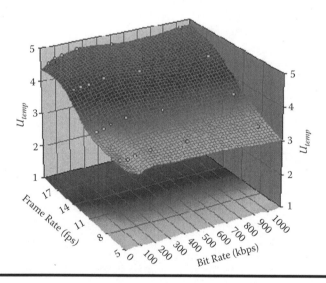

Figure 4.4   Motion test results for Device 3, Akiyo sequence.

performance difference between the two devices. This is expected, because the Akiyo sequence does not contain high-motion activity; the difference in hardware capabilities between the devices does not significantly affect the results. On the other hand, Figures 4.5 and 4.6 illustrate the subjective test results for the Soccer

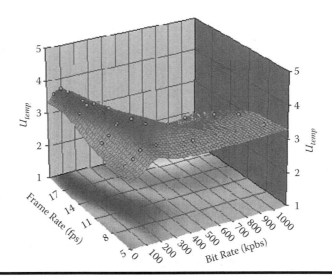

Figure 4.5   Temporal test results for Device 1, Soccer sequence.

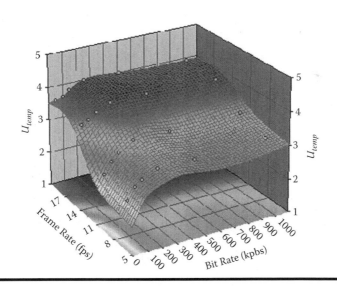

Figure 4.6   Temporal test results for Device 3, Soccer sequence.

sequence. Contrary to the Akiyo sequence results, the results for Devices 1 and 3 are significantly different.

Specifically, when the frame rate is at 20 fps, Device 1 has a severely degraded performance for all bit rates. Device 3 suffers such degradation only when the frame rate is 20 fps and the bit rate is more than 512 kbps. The difference in hardware capabilities of the devices apparently affects the results, especially for high bit rates and frame rates (i.e., coding parameters with the most demanding resource requirements).

The results of the spatial tests are shown in Figures 4.7 and 4.8 for the Mobile and Waterfall sequences, respectively. The videos were encoded for two different spatial resolutions (QCIF 176 × 144, Quarter Video Graphics Array [QVGA] 320 × 240) and six different bit rates (50, 100, 150, 256, 512, 1024 kbps). All tested devices have 320 × 240 resolution on their screens. The spatial tests were performed on only two devices, and their results were averaged together. It was assumed that the processing capabilities of the devices do not affect the results of the spatial test because the spatial satisfaction depends on the resolution and the bit rate at which the video is played, and the introduced impairments are related to the video coding scheme rather than the hardware capabilities of the terminals on which the videos are viewed.

A comparison of Figure 4.7 and Figure 4.8 shows that for the Waterfall sequence, which has a low SI value, the results do not significantly change for QCIF or QVGA resolutions. However, for the Mobile sequence, which has a high SI value, the utility values for the QVGA resolution are significantly better than the values for the QCIF case. This result is also expected because for sequences with a high level of detail, viewing higher resolution content provides significant improvements in the intelligibility of the video.

4.3.2.2 Mobile Phone Tests

Fifteen evaluators, all students at METU, took part in the mobile phone tests. Four different mobile phones were used for the tests: Nokia N81 (hereafter referred to as MP 1), Nokia N 70 (MP 2), Nokia 6670 (MP 3), and Nokia 6300 (MP 4).

For the mobile phones, only the temporal tests were performed. The same procedure outlined in the previous section for high-end PDAs was used for the tests. The same sequences were used for training (Coastguard), and the grades of the first four sequences were disregarded to allow stabilization of the testers' opinions. These videos were later repeated in the test and their grades recorded.

The only significant difference in the test procedure was that the evaluators had to view video clips that they were to grade on two different mobile phones instead of viewing all of the clips in the test on a single device. The evaluators were asked to watch the first two videos on the first mobile phone and the third and fourth videos on the second mobile phone and to proceed in this manner until the end, each time viewing two videos on one of the phones and the next two videos on the other phone. This alternation was done to prevent the evaluators from normalizing their test results for a single device. Previously, it was observed that the evaluators tried to evenly distribute their grades between 1 and 5, which resulted in phones having very low resource-processing capabilities receiving higher grades than the display performance of the device deserved.

To obtain different models for videos with varying levels of motion activity, two different videos, each representing one of the two video classes (high motion, low motion), were used. To determine a representative video for each class, the SI and TI

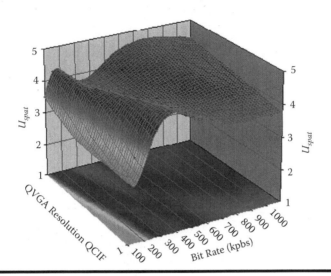

Figure 4.7   Spatial test results, Mobile sequence.

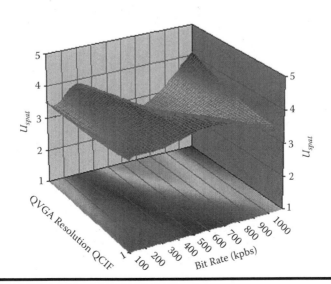

Figure 4.8   Spatial test results, Mobile sequence.

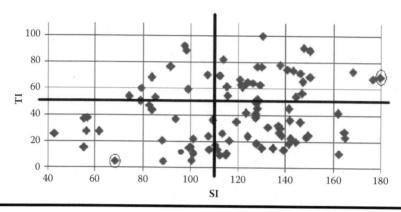

Figure 4.9 SI and TI values.

values of 94 video sequences that were recorded from a variety of Turkish broadcast channels were computed. These SI and TI values were calculated from unencoded .yuv files in 4:2:0 format. Figure 4.9 shows the SI and TI values of the sequences. The circled points are the ones that were used in the temporal tests.

It was observed that the sequences having the highest TI values in the graph do not actually have the highest motion activity. The reason for this is that the TI metric is highly sensitive to shot boundaries because it calculates the motion activity based on pixel value differences in consecutive frames. For video clips that have shot boundaries, the TI value is much higher than the actual motion activity. Based on this observation, all of the video clips with relatively high TI values were reviewed, and the video clip of a basketball game (the circled point to the right of the SI–TI graph) was selected to represent the high-motion class. The video clip having the lowest TI value (an elderly woman talking) was selected to represent the low-motion class.

The results of the temporal tests (U_{temp}) for MP 1, MP 3, and MP 4 are presented in Figures 4.10 through 4.15. The results reflect the MOS of the subjective ratings of 15 assessors on a 5-grade scale. The videos that were used in the tests were encoded at QCIF resolution, for four different frame rates (7, 11, 15, 20 fps), and at seven different bit rates (50, 100, 200, 350, 512,750, 1024 kbps).

Figures 4.10 and 4.11 illustrate that MP 1 successfully displays the video clips for both high-motion and low-motion cases. This result is expected because MP 1 has the highest resource-processing capabilities, as explained in the following section. Examining Figures 4.12 and 4.13, one can see that even though MP 3 displays the low-motion video quite successfully, significant performance degradation occurs for the resource-intensive videos having high bit rates and high frame rates.

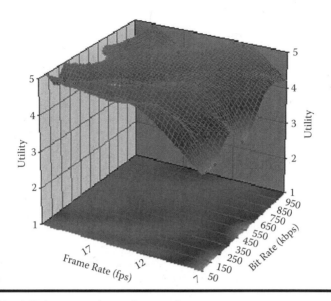

Figure 4.10   MP 1 temporal test, low motion.

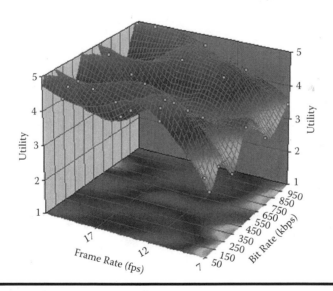

Figure 4.11   MP 1 temporal test, high motion.

MP 4 has the worst performance overall, again this is in accordance with its resource-processing capabilities. Even for the low-motion video, the device has performance degradation, as illustrated in Figures 4.14 and 4.15. For the high-motion case, the results are disastrous: only videos with very low resource requirements (clips with bit rates less than 200k) are played back at acceptable quality levels.

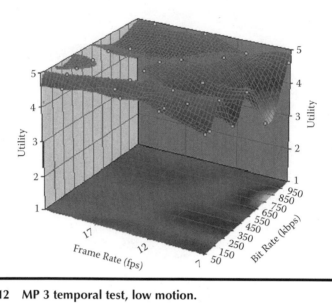

Figure 4.12   MP 3 temporal test, low motion.

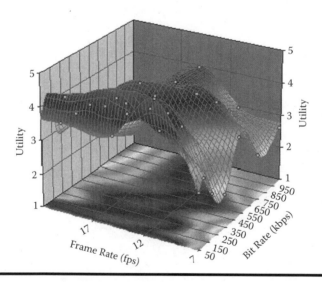

Figure 4.13   MP 3 temporal test, high motion.

4.3.3 Predicting Satisfaction Models for Unknown Devices

It is apparently not practical to perform subjective video evaluation tests for every single device prior to viewing video clips with it. A plausible approach would be to determine utility curves on a limited number of devices for each content class

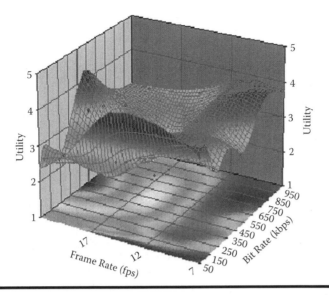

Figure 4.14   MP 4 temporal test, low motion.

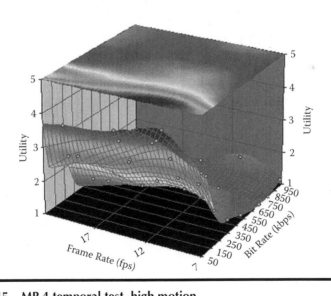

Figure 4.15   MP 4 temporal test, high motion.

(high–low motion activity and high–low spatial detail) and then exploiting these results to predict the spatial and temporal utility curves for the devices with different processing capabilities. For this purpose, a hardware metric representing the overall video-rendering capacity of a mobile device is needed. Different metrics were used for the different classes of devices (high-end PDA and mobile phones) that were studied.

4.3.3.1 Prediction for High-End PDAs

Examining the test results that were presented in the previous sections, the hardware metric was heuristically defined to be the arithmetic average of the Whetstone and graphics metrics that were introduced in Section 4.2.2. The values of Whetstone, graphics, and overall hardware metrics for the devices utilized in the simulations are given in Table 4.2.

In order to be able to calculate the utility curve of a new unknown device, a relation between this newly defined hardware metric and the utility scores of the mobile devices must be established.

To this end, it was assumed that the hardware metric and the utility curves are linearly related as

$$h_n = x_1 \cdot h_1 + x_2 \cdot h_2 + \cdots + x_k \cdot h_k = \sum_i x_i \cdot h_i$$

then

$$U\left(h_n, c\right) = x_1 \cdot U\left(h_1, c\right) + x_2 \cdot U\left(h_2, c\right) + \cdots + x_k \cdot U\left(h_k, c\right) = \sum_i x_i \cdot U\left(h_i, c\right)$$

where h_n is the overall hardware metric for the new device whose utility curve, $U(h_n)$, is to be predicted, and h_1 to h_k are the hardware metrics for the devices whose utility curves would be used to obtain the utility curve of the new device. The content characteristics of parameter c is constant, since the prediction is performed for a particular content class. As an example of using this assumption, the temporal utility curves for Device 3 are predicted by using the curves of Devices 2 and 4, after determining x_1 and x_2 from the available hardware metric values given in Table 4.2. Similar predictions have also been performed for Devices 1, 2, and 4. The estimation of the parameters x_i can be obtained via linear regression for the cases where the number of known devices that are utilized for the prediction of the unknown device is more than two.

Figures 4.16 and 4.17 show the prediction errors between the subjectively determined and predicted utility curves for Device 3. The obtained prediction results are quite promising; for the predictions of the utility curves of Device 3, the prediction error is less than 8% on average.

The performance of the utility-prediction algorithm can be improved, especially for the high bit rates and frame rates, by using a nonlinear relationship between the hardware performance metrics and the utility curves. Obviously, further experiments and devices are required in order to obtain such a nonlinear relation.

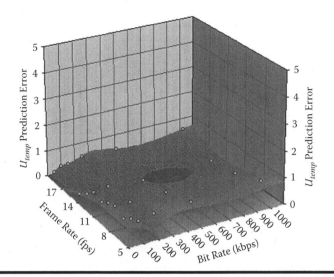

Figure 4.16 Prediction of the utility curves for Device 3, using the utility curves of Devices 2 and 4 for the Akiyo sequence.

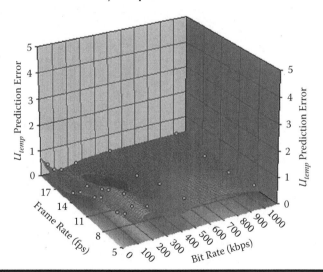

Figure 4.17 Prediction of the utility curves for Device 3, using the utility curves of Devices 2 and 4 for the soccer sequence.

4.3.3.2 Prediction for Mobile Phones

In order to be able to model the resource-processing capabilities of mobile phones, many different performance metrics were investigated. The performance metrics were calculated for 16 different mobile devices, all supporting a Java Micro Edition Environment. The results are shown in Table 4.3.

It was observed that most of the mobile devices on the market run on the ARM (Advanced RISC Machine) family of processors. The clock speed of the processor together with the CPU generation (ARM 9, ARM 11, etc.) gives a strong indicator of the resource-processing capability of the device.

It was observed also that the version and the type of the Java environment significantly affect the results of the performance metrics. This effect becomes more pronounced as the complexity of the performance metric algorithms increases. Thus, simpler metrics gave results that were more correlated with the video-processing capability.

Ad hoc subjective tests were performed to compare the video-processing capability of the devices listed in Table 4.3 with their performance metric results. The "Operations Test" metric, which was developed during the course of the research, had the highest correlation with the subjective video qualities. The Operations Test is a very simple metric that performs basic addition and multiplication operations on w. The fact that this metric has the highest correlation with the video-processing performance suggests that the performance for mobile phones largely depends on the CPU performance, unlike the PDAs, which have specialized hardware for graphics processing.

Following a procedure similar to the one outlined previously for high-end PDAs, utility curves for unknown mobile phones with known hardware metrics were predicted using other mobile phones with known hardware metrics and utility curves. The Operations Test metric was used as the overall metric for mobile phones.

The results for the prediction of the utility curve of MP 2 are shown in Figures 4.18 and 4.19. Figure 4.18 illustrates the prediction of the utility curve for the high-motion video clip using MP 1 and MP 3. The average prediction error for this case is 0.52 (about 10%). Figure 4.19 illustrates the prediction of the utility curve for the low-motion video clip using MP 1 and MP 4. The average prediction error for this case is 0.37 (about 6.5%).

It can be seen that the prediction error for the high-motion video clip is significantly larger than the error for the low-motion video clip. This difference is due to the nonlinear nature of the degradation in the video-rendering performance of mobile phones for video clips having high resource requirements.

4.3.4 Obtaining Optimal User Satisfaction

Figure 4.20 outlines the architecture of a typical adaptive video streaming system. Whenever a new video clip is ingested into the system, the SI and TI values are calculated in real time, and the video is assigned to a particular content class (e.g., high motion and low spatial complexity) in the *content characterization module*. In the content representation module, the video is encoded by using an SCV algorithm, such as the SVC extension of H.264/AVC. Temporal, SNR, and spatial resolution modes scalability are utilized to enable the extraction of video clips having varying levels of quality from the original stream.

Table 4.3 Mobile Phone Performance Metrics

	Nokia 6600	Nokia 6300	Nokia 6630	Nokia 6670	Nokia N81	Nokia N70	Nokia N95	SE P1i	SE W610i	SE K750i
Processor	Arm 9	Arm 9	Arm 9	Arm 9	Arm 11	Arm 9	Arm 11	Arm 9	Arm 9	Arm 9
Clock Speed	104	237	227	123	353	220	326	208	201	110
JVM	JIT	Jazelle	JIT	JIT	JIT	JIT	JIT	JIT	AOT	Jazelle
Fibonacci Test	20641	12652	8828	17532	5135	8828	5743	9472	30347	29231
Operations Test	1828	2040	750	1600	441	735	482	819	900	4602
Operations Float	No float	2778	828	No float	472	828	537	975	1078	7679
Prepare Time	6563	69	2407	6485	692	2406	929	2507	1611	1157
Playback Time	13015	14915	12453	12890	12186	13094	12157	12046	12173	12682
Total Time	19578	14984	14860	19375	12878	15500	13086	14553	13784	13839

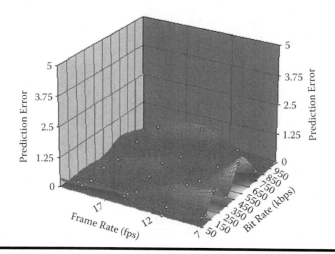

Figure 4.18 **Prediction of the utility curves for MP 2, using the utility curves of MP 1 and MP 3 for a high-motion sequence.**

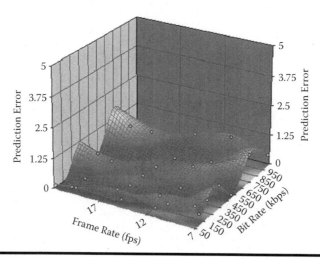

Figure 4.19 **Prediction of the utility curves for MP 2, using the utility curves of MP 1 and MP 4 for a low-motion sequence.**

When a new device requests to view a video clip, the hardware capabilities of the device and the usage environment parameters are recorded and sent to the utility-based adaptation system. For the exchange of this information between the video adaptation system and the end terminal, "MPEG-21 Part-7 Digital Item Adaptation" descriptors can be utilized [21].

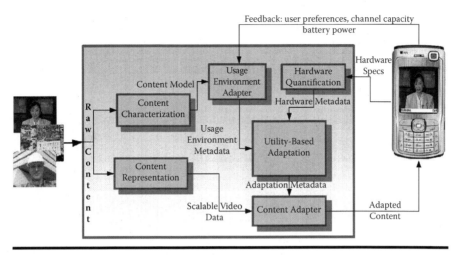

Figure 4.20 Adaptive video streaming architecture.

In the utility-based adaptation module, the spatial and temporal utility curves, which will be used to determine the optimal video coding parameters for the requesting device, are estimated as described in Section 4.3.2. Once the utility curves are obtained, the models for the temporal and spatial satisfaction are combined to obtain the optimal video coding parameters. As presented in Section 4.2, the two models can be combined as a weighted sum given in Equation 4.1, where the weight λ is to be determined by the end user according to his or her preferences. For a given content class, preset λ values can also be utilized for better utility modeling. Obviously, for a video clip having high-motion activity, a λ value close to zero should be used to maximize temporal utility, whereas for a video clip with high spatial detail, λ should be chosen close to unity. In the next step, with λ specified, the optimal video coding parameters are obtained by utilizing a suitable optimization algorithm, such as *simulated annealing* (SA) [22], to find the bit rate, frame rate, and spatial resolution that maximize U_{total}, the overall user satisfaction. Although SA is a computationally demanding algorithm, the execution time is quite small because of the small number of parameters required during optimization.

Once the optimal video coding parameters are obtained, the video coded with the desired parameters can be extracted from the scalable coded stream in the *content adapter module*. The video is then sent to the mobile terminal. A Proof of Concept (PoC) version of the video adaptation system shown in Figure 4.20 has already been implemented and tested.

4.4 Conclusions

The main contribution of this work is the construction of an accurate model of subjective user satisfaction resulting from viewing a video clip on a resource-constrained mobile device. The model is obtained by performing separate subjective tests for formulating the user satisfaction on temporal and spatial aspects of the viewed video clips.

The device capabilities of the terminal on which the final adapted video is viewed is also incorporated into this model. The subjective tests are performed separately for two different classes of devices: high-end PDAs and mobile phones. The device capabilities for both classes are measured using standard metrics. For high-end PDAs, a metric that measures the video-rendering capability is used in combination with another metric that measures the number of floating-point operations per second (FLOPS). For the mobile phones, a single metric measuring the number of arithmetic operations that the device can perform per second was found to be sufficient, since most mobile phones do not employ special hardware for graphics processing.

The approach also accounts for different video content types in terms of temporal and spatial characteristics. Video content characteristics are determined using the ITU's SI and TI metrics. Using these metrics, the incoming video content is separated into four different classes, and unique satisfaction models for each class are constructed. This ensures that the presented approach is content-aware in the sense that a video containing fast-moving scenes is treated differently from a video containing limited motion, or a satisfaction model belonging to a video containing dense texture significantly differs from the model of a video clip containing large, uniform regions.

It is demonstrated that the utility curves obtained through subjective tests for a limited number of devices can be used to generate utility curves for other devices with known hardware capabilities. It is shown that the predictions are performed with less than 10% mean square error.

Finally, an end-to-end architecture for an adaptive video-delivery system that adapts videos according to the video-processing capabilities of the viewing device and the communication channel capacity is proposed.

Özgür Deniz Önür is a doctoral candidate in electrical and electronics engineering at Middle East Technical University, Ankara, Turkey. He received his BS in 2001, and his MSc in 2003, from Middle East Technical University. His research interests include scalable video coding, multimedia adaptation and subjective utility modeling. In 2003, he cofounded Mobilus Ltd., where he currently continues his studies.

Aydin A. Alatan received his BS from Middle East Technical University, Ankara, Turkey in 1990, his MS and DIC from Imperial College of Science, Medicine and Technology, London, U.K. in 1992, and his PhD from Bilkent University, Ankara, Turkey in 1997; all were in electrical engineering. He was a postdoctoral research associate at the Center for Image Processing Research at Rensselaer Polytechnic Institute between 1997 and 1998, and at the New Jersey Center for Multimedia

Research at New Jersey Institute of Technology between 1998 and 2000. In August 2000, he joined the faculty of the Electrical and Electronics Engineering Department at Middle East Technical University. He is a member of IEEE.

References

1. Y. Neuvo and J. Yrjanainen. Wireless meets multimedia: New products and services. *Proceedings of IEEE International Conference on Image Processing*, 2002.
2. S. F. Chang and Anthony Vetro. Video adaptation: Concepts, technologies and open issues. *Proceedings of the IEEE* 93(1): January 2005.
3. B. Li, J. Ericco, H. Pan, and I. Sezan. Bridging the semantic gap in sports video retrieval and summarization. *Journal of Visual Communication and Image Representation* 15, 394–424, 2004.
4. S. F. Chang, D. Zhong, and R. Kumar. Real-time content-based adaptive streaming of sports video. *Proceedings of the IEEE Workshop on Content-Based Access of Image and Video Libraries (CBAIVL '01)*, 139, December 2001.
5. H. Schwarz, D. Marpe, and T. Wiegand. Overview of the scalable h.264/mpeg4-avc extension. *Proceedings of the IEEE International Conference on Image Processing*, 2006.
6. H. Schwarz, D. Marpe, and T. Wiegand. Overview of the scalable video coding extension of H.264/AVC. *IEEE Transactions on Circuits and Systems for Video Technology* 17(9): 1103–1120, September 2007.
7. Min Li and Truong Nguyen. Optimal wavelet filter design in scalable video coding. *Proceedings of the IEEE International Conference on Image Processing*, 2005.
8. M. Wien, R. Cazoulat, A. Graffunder, A. Hutter, and P. Amon. Real-time system for adaptive video streaming based on SVC. *IEEE Transactions on Circuits and Systems for Video Technology* 17(9): 1227–1237, September 2007.
9. E. Akyol, A. M. Tekalp, and R. Civanlar. Content-aware scalability type selection for rate adaptation of scalable video. *EUROASIP Journal on Advances in Signal Processing*, 2007, Article ID 10236.
10. P. Bocheck, Y. Nakajima, and S. F. Chang. Real-time estimation of subjective utility functions for MPEG-4 video objects. *Proceedings of the IEEE Packet Video Workshop (PV'99)*, April 1999.
11. S. F. Chang. Optimal video adaptation and skimming using a utility-based framework. *Tyrrhenian International Workshop on Digital Communications*, Capri Island, Italy, September 2002.
12. Y. Wang, J.-G. Kim, and S. F. Chang. Content-based utility function prediction for real-time MPEG-4 video transcoding. *Proceedings of the IEEE International Conference on Image Processing*, 2003.
13. Ö. D. Önür and A. A. Alatan. Optimal video adaptation for resource-constrained mobile devices based on utility theory. *International Workshop on Image Analysis for Multimedia Interactive Services (WIAMIS)*, 2004.
14. A. L. Golub. *Decision Analysis: An Integrated Approach*. New York: Wiley, 1997.
15. Y. Wang, M. van der Schaar, S. F. Chang, and A. C. Loui. Classification-based multidimensional adaptation prediction for scalable video coding using subjective quality evaluation. *IEEE Transactions on Circuits and Systems for Video Technology* 15(10): 1270–1279, 2005.

16. S. J. Choi and J. W. Woods. Motion-compensated 3D subband coding of video. *IEEE Transactions on Image Processing* 8(2): 155–167, February 1999.
17. Recommendation ITU-R P910. Subjective video quality assessment methods for multimedia applications. 1999.
18. Benchmark Headquarters. http://www.benchmarkhq.ru/english.html?/be_ppc.html, 2008.
19. Wizcode LLC. http://www.wizcode.com/products/view/pocketpc_mark, 2008.
20. Recommendation ITU-R BT.500-11. Methodology for the subjective assessment of the quality of TV pictures. 2002.
21. Information Technology—Multimedia Framework—Part 7: Digital Item Adaptation, ISO/IEC 21 000-7, 2004.
22. S. Kirkpatrick, C. D. Gelatt, and M. P. Vecchi. Optimization by simulated annealing. *Science* 220(4598), 1983.

Chapter 5

Toward Next-Generation In-Flight Entertainment Systems: A Survey of the State of the Art and Possible Extensions

Hao Liu, Ben Salem, and Matthias Rauterberg

5.1 Introduction

Traveling by air, especially long distance, is not a natural activity for humans. The combination of long flight duration, limited space, and an unusual cabin environment in terms of air pressure, humidity, and continuous noise causes physical and psychological discomfort and even stress for a large group of passengers. Excessive stress may cause some passengers to become aggressive and overreactive and may even endanger their health (Sophia 1998; WHO 2005). Airlines commonly install in-flight entertainment systems on long-haul aircrafts to improve passengers' comfort level. Usually, entertainment services are delivered via high-speed communication tools and state-of-the-art entertainment systems, which include audio/video on-demand, games, in-flight e-mail, Internet access, and ever-increasing digital entertainment options.

Comfort is a complex concept consisting of both objective ergonomics requirements and subjective impressions. Dumur, Barnard, and Boy (2004) identify four principles that should guide design of a more comfortable aircraft cabin for passengers: (1) affordance, which concentrates on the efforts the passenger must make to get the service; (2) situational awareness, which ensures that the passenger is aware of events surrounding him or her and of other passengers and the cabin crew in order not to feel lost or confused and to be confident that everything is under control; (3) individualization and customization, which address the individual differences in comfort needs for different passengers; and (4) variability and flexibility, which emphasize the diverse needs of passengers. Regarding in-flight entertainment systems, affordance of the entertainment relates to the efforts that the passenger must make to interact with the system to get personalized entertainment; situational awareness means that the passenger should be aware of what goes on around the in-flight entertainment system in order not to feel lost or confused and to be confident that the system is under his or her control. Because passengers come from highly heterogeneous pools, have different entertainment preferences, and experience different flight situations, individualization and customization of entertainment services can provide passengers better physical and psychological comfort. In addition to these four principles, Liu and Rauterberg (2007) point out the importance of improving the passenger's comfort by reducing his or her negative stress level.

In this chapter, we will describe various ways to extend the capabilities of in-flight entertainment systems to improve the passenger's comfort level. First, we present a comprehensive survey of the state of the art of the currently installed and commercially available in-flight entertainment systems. How these systems are designed and implemented to increase passengers' comfort level is analyzed and their limitations are discussed in Section 5.2. Some possible technologies to enable designing a more comfortable in-flight entertainment system for passengers are presented in Section 5.3. A new framework for next-generation in-flight entertainment systems is presented and research that is being conducted to concretize it are also outlined in Section 5.3.

5.2 Overview of the Current In-Flight Entertainment Systems

After World War II, commercial aviation flights became a daily event in which entertainment was requested by passengers to help the time pass. It was delivered in the form of food and drink services along with an occasional projector movie during lengthy flights. The in-flight entertainment systems were upgraded to CRT (cathode ray tube)-based systems in the late 1970s and early 1980s. Around the same time, CRT-based displays began to appear over the aisles of aircrafts. In the mid-1990s, the first in-seat video systems began to appear (see Figure 5.1), and

Figure 5.1 In-seat LCD-based in-flight entertainment systems. (From "Airbus A380 lands in Sydney," by Luke A., 2007. Retrieved March 27, 2008 from CNET's Web site: http://www.cnet.com.au/laptops/0,239035611,339283273-8s,00.htm.)

liquid crystal display (LCD) technology started to replace CRT technology as the display technology of choice for overhead video. In the late 1990s and early 2000s, the first in-seat audio/video on-demand systems began to appear (Wikipedia n.d.). Today, as technology advances, except for audio/video on-demand services, the entertainment services are also delivered in the form of games, in-flight e-mail, Internet access, and ever-increasing digital entertainment options.

In this section, the current in-flight entertainment systems in the aircrafts of major airlines are investigated. Then the latest commercially available in-flight entertainment systems provided by major players in this field are investigated. Finally, the current in-flight entertainment systems are analyzed to see whether they are designed and implemented in accordance with the five design principles listed in Section 5.1.

5.2.1 Currently Installed In-Flight Entertainment Systems

To allow each airline the freedom to configure its aircrafts according to its budgets and market demands, both airplane producers (Boeing and Airbus) and major in-flight entertainment system providers provide customized in-flight entertainment systems to their customers. Liu (2006) investigated the current installed in-flight entertainment systems in the aircrafts of airlines of Lufthansa, Air France, British Airways, American Airlines, Delta Airlines, and Japan Airlines, which are top airlines in Europe, North America, and Asia from a total scheduled passengers point of view (WATS 2006).

Generally, the in-flight entertainment services provided by these airlines might be divided into two categories. In passive services, the user-system interaction levels are very low; passengers simply enjoy a chosen form of entertainment presented to them in an organized and packaged form. Examples of passive entertainment services are audio and video on-demand, audio and video broadcasting, e-books, and moving-map systems. Active entertainment services allow users to actively interact with the entertainment system and to determine the entertainment service content by interaction with the system. Gaming is one example of this active entertainment. The exact entertainment services provided by an airline depend on factors such as the aircraft type, the business model of the airline, and class seats (first class, business class, and economy class).

All the in-flight entertainment systems installed in the investigated airlines' aircrafts are implemented on the basis of preset concepts of what customers like and require as a homogeneous passenger group with similar tastes and desires. The systems present the same interface and entertainment content to each passenger regardless of individual differences in age, gender, ethnicity, entertainment preferences, and so on. If the user wants specific entertainment services during air travel, he or she must interact with the in-flight entertainment system by means of touch screen, remote controller, or similar device (see Figure 5.2) to browse and select the desired entertainment services. If the user selects a game to play, he or she can use the remote controller to interact with the system to play the game. If the available choices are many, or if the passenger is not familiar with the service category structure, or if the interaction design is poor (e.g., Japan Airlines' remote controller has more than 20 keys), the passenger tends to get disoriented and may be unable to find the most appealing entertainment services. However, if the available choices are limited (e.g., most airlines investigated provide only a few movies during a flight), the chance for the passenger to find desired entertainment services is slim. Under these circumstances, the in-flight entertainment system does not contribute to improving the passenger's comfort level; on the contrary, it may exacerbate the passenger's stress.

Figure 5.2 Interactions between the passenger and the in-flight entertainment system. Left: KLM (n.d.). (From "Economy class," by KLM, n.d. Retrieved March 1, 2008 from KLM's Web site: http://www.klm.com/travel/au_en/travel_tools/book_a_flight/ebt_help/help_classes.htm.) Right: ArtsyKen (n.d.). (From "In-flight entertainment," by ArtsyKen, n.d. Retrieved March 1, 2008 from Artsyken's Web site: http://artsyken.com/2003_12_01_archive.php.)

5.2.2 Commercially Available In-Flight Entertainment Systems

Liu (2006) investigated the latest commercially available in-flight entertainment systems provided by three major producers: Panasonic, Thales, and Rockwell Collins. The Panasonic Matsushita X-series in-flight entertainment system is the first in-flight entertainment system to be based on the research of passenger preferences and consumer trends worldwide. The X-series delivers high-speed communication tools and state-of-the-art entertainment, including audio/video on-demand, in-flight e-mail, Internet access, and ever-increasing digital entertainment options. Passengers are in complete control of selecting from the options provided to them. TopSeries™ is Thales's premier family of in-flight entertainment systems that provides integrated solutions for entertainment, e-mail, Internet access, and in-seat laptop power. The latest system is I-5000 in which all digital video and audio on-demand with greater bandwidth use a Gigabit Ethernet network. TopSeries's efficient design integrates broadband communications, in-seat power, and entertainment capability onto one platform. The system's unique modular design can simultaneously support overhead, in-seat distributed, and on-demand content distribution on a single aircraft. Rockwell Collins provides several TES series in-flight entertainment systems. Among them, eTES has not only all of the benefits of TES, such as audio/video on-demand and interactivity, but also the same high-speed network connectivity that users experience at home and in the office. The system provides dynamically built menu pages, which are generated based on each request, creating a truly individualized passenger experience. For example, all eTES pages can be created in French if that is the language selected by the passenger; banner ads for Paris-based restaurants and tourist attractions can be automatically generated should the flight's destination be Paris. Passengers can select from the options provided to them. Movie titles, language choices; and start, stop, fast-forward, rewind, and pause controls are all at their fingertips. Not only will passengers enjoy content delivery the way they want it, but airlines will also know exactly what passengers are listening to and watching. eTES collects usage statistics to assist airlines in determining an optimal content mix, thereby minimizing content costs and maximizing passenger satisfaction.

5.2.3 Discussions and Conclusions

In this section, seven major airline currently installed in-flight entertainment systems were investigated. Five principles of designing a more comfortable in-flight entertainment system for passengers were taken into consideration—(1) affordance, (2) situational awareness, (3) individualization and customization, (4) variability and flexibility, and (5) negative stress reduction—and, the following conclusions were drawn:

1. All of the airlines investigated present the same interface and entertainment contents to each passenger. By means of a touch screen, in-seat controller, or remote control, the passenger can browse the same menu and select the desired audio/video programs from the provided options. However, finding

the desired program is not easy. First, the passenger must know how to use the interactive tools. Second, if the passenger is not familiar with the airline's specific entertainment service categories and the available options are many, he or she is forced to browse numerous selections before finding the desired audio/video program. On the other hand, if the available entertainment options are limited, the chances of finding the desired service are slim. The current systems have much room to improve in affordance, individualization and customization, and variability and flexibility design aspects.

2. None of the airlines that were investigated explored how entertainment services can be used to reduce passengers' negative physical and psychological stresses systematically, actively, and intelligently. For example, considering the limited space and safety constraints, the airlines usually provide some in-chair physical exercise tips either in paper flyers in front of the passenger's seat or in electronic texts in the entertainment systems (QANTAS Airlines n.d.). However, according to our investigation, most passengers tend to ignore these exercise tips. Therefore, a more engaging solution is necessary.

The latest commercially available in-flight entertainment systems provided by major players Panasonic Matsushita, Rockwell Collins, and Thales were investigated. Their latest products aim to provide customized in-flight entertainment to the airline according to the airline's budgets and market demands. For example, Rockwell Collins eTES aims to provide personalized entertainment services to the passenger by offering dynamically built personalized menu pages, collecting usage statistics to assist airlines in determining an optimal entertainment content mix, and so on. Thales's TopSeries I-5000 in-flight entertainment system's modular and functionality-based design makes it more flexible and extendable. However, as shown in Figure 5.3, these systems did not explore passengers' personal profiles, passengers' biosignals, the flight situation, or other factors, in order to provide

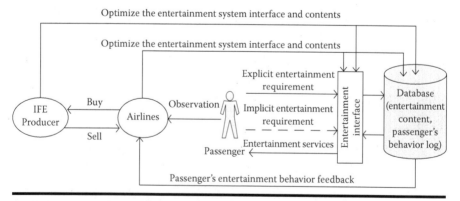

Figure 5.3   The adaptive relation between an in-flight entertainment (IFE) system producer, airline, passenger, and IFE system.

context-aware, personalized entertainment services intelligently. These systems also failed to explore how entertainment services can be used to reduce passengers' negative stresses systematically, actively, and intelligently.

5.3 Extending the Capabilities of In-Flight Entertainment Systems to Increase Passengers' Comfort Actively and Intelligently

In this section, technologies that enable a new in-flight entertainment system to increase passengers' comfort level actively and intelligently are identified. First, the context-adaptive system that enable context-aware in-flight entertainment service provision is explored. Second, user profiling, which can be used to personalize adaptations and decrease unnecessary dialog between the user and the system, is described. Third, the related works of using entertainment to reduce negative stresses are investigated. Fourth, the theory of cybernetic control systems, which use information, models, and control actions to steer toward and maintain their goals while counteracting various disturbances, is introduced. Finally, a new framework for next-generation in-flight entertainment systems that integrates the context-adaptive system, control system, user profiling, and methods of using entertainment to reduce negative stresses is presented, and various research opportunities for concretizing it are identified.

5.3.1 Context-Adaptive Systems

In the 1980s, the focus of user-adaptive systems was a user model defined by personal characteristics and preferences together with a task model defined by task characteristics (Edmonds 1981; Kobsa and Wahlster 1989). Later, in the 1990s, interest developed beyond user-adaptiveness and moved more generally to context-adaptiveness. Context may be defined as "any information that can be used to characterize the situation of an entity; an entity is a person, place, or object that is considered relevant to the interaction between a user and an application, including the user and applications themselves" (Dey and Abowd 1999). In this abstract definition, "any" information that is relevant to characterize the situation of an entity is used to specify context. This definition is correct, meaning that for different domains and different purposes, context has specific definition elements. Early in the history of computers, they were only used for business. As information technology advanced, computers were also used for leisure and at places other than the workplace. It therefore made sense to include other dimensions in the definition of the context of use. Four dimensions often are considered for context: (1) the location of the user in either the information space or the physical space; (2) the identity of the user, implying the user's interests, preferences, and knowledge;

(3) the time of use (working hours, weekend, etc.); and (4) the environment of the current activity (Schilit et al. 1994; Dey and Abowd 1999). These dimensions are currently exploited for embedded, ambient, or disappearing computing (Streitz and Nixon 2005).

The architecture of a context-adaptive system includes at least context sensing, context modeling, context adaptation, and service delivery components (Baldauf 2007). With the support of the architecture, three adaptation steps can be distinguished: (1) the interaction logging function records and categorizes all incoming interaction events according to predefined dimensions of characteristics of the usage process (Rauterberg 1993); (2) the result of this recording and categorization is reported to a central adaptation inference function (Schröder et al. 1990); (3) this adaptation inference function analyzes the incoming interaction event messages, evaluates them according to predefined rules and algorithms, and generates specific adaptation activities to be performed (Bartneck et al. 2006).

There is already a long literature involving the successful context-adaptive applications in several areas. Three areas are of prominent importance: (1) mobile shopping assistants (Kaasinen 2003), (2) mobile tour guides (Petrelli and Not 2005), and (3) mobile learning assistance (Klann et al. 2005). In all these systems, the current location of the user and corresponding domain objects in the environment were continuously identified and mapped to the interests and tasks of the user.

5.3.2 User Profiling

The information about a user that reflects his or her needs, requirements, and desires (NRDs) on the preferred system behaviors, explicitly or implicitly, is called a user profile or a user model (Salem and Rauterberg 2004). It is usually integrated into the system to impart the user knowledge to the system to enable automatic personalized system behavior adaptations and avoid "unnecessary" dialog between the system and the user.

Kay (2001) identified three main ways that a user model can assist in adaptation: (1) It can interpret user actions, such as a mouse action or the user's speech via audio input, to eliminate the ambiguity; a user model can help the system interpret such information. (2) The user model can drive the internal actions of the system. This is the goal of systems that filter information, select the right system functionalities, and so on, on behalf of the user. (3) Machine actions can be controlled by a user model to improve the quality of the interaction. A very simple example might involve the system tailoring its presentation form to the user. More sophisticated cases involve the adaptation of the content as well as the form of the presentation.

An adaptive system, whether user-adaptive or context-adaptive, needs the user profile to represent a user's NRDs on the desired system behaviors to enable adaptations and avoid unnecessary user-explicit inputs. For user-adaptive systems in which the user and task characteristics are considered for adaptations, the formation of the user profile is a subset of the intersection between the real-world user model and the system's available behaviors. For the context-adaptive systems in which the context of use is also considered for system-behavior adaptation, the main content of the user profile is a subset of the intersections among the real-world user model, the available system behaviors, and the context of uses (see Figure 5.4). Context of uses are the actual situations under which the service is delivered to the user. The information items in this subset can reflect the user's NRDs on the preferred system behaviors under the contexts of use explicitly or implicitly. For example, the user profile in Yu and colleagues (2004) is composed of two parts: user's preferences and history of activities (tracks). The user can update the preferences according to specific contexts of use. The history is ordered by a time–space and theme (e.g., a conference). In a similar example, presented in Suh and colleagues (2005), the user profile information is categorized as static or dynamic. Static information is personal information such as name, age, and address books. Dynamic information includes the user's system behavior preferences, which depend on the context of use.

Currently, the user-profile modeling approaches for adaptive systems fall into two categories: (1) in the hierarchical tree modeling approach, the user is modeled by dimensions (e.g., knowledge, interest), and each dimension can be further refined with subdimensions (Goel and Sarkar 2002); (2) in the rule-based language modeling approach, the desired delivery of services relates to the context of use with if-then logic (Oppermann 2005). The advantage of the hierarchical tree approach is that it is well organized and easy to understand; the disadvantage is that it can express only static characteristics. The advantage of the rule-based language approach is that it is based on clear formalism and can be used to express some of the user's dynamic characteristics, such as context-aware user preferences. The disadvantages are that its expressive power is limited, and it is difficult to model the relationships among rules.

Generally, there are three approaches to acquire user profile information: it is entered explicitly by the user, learned implicitly by the system, or both. For some static information about the user, such as demographic information, it is reasonable to let the user provide it. But it may not be ideal to let the user explicitly enter some of the dynamic information, such as user preferences, because such information depends on the context of use and may change over time. Prior researchers have

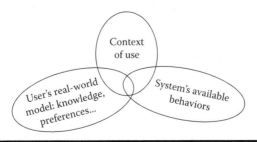

Figure 5.4   User profile for context-adaptive systems.

explored the usefulness of implicit feedback (Kelly and Teevan 2003) to acquire user preferences because the feedback is easy to collect and requires no extra effort from the user. Most researchers have succeeded in this and obtained good results.

5.3.3 Methods of Using Entertainment Services for Stress Reduction

As the first step toward a complete solution, this chapter explores how music and games can be used to reduce the listener's or player's negative psychological and physical stresses.

5.3.3.1 Music

There is much literature involving the use of music for stress reduction. David and Robert (1999) showed that "relaxing" music can be used to decrease stress and increase relaxation in a hospital waiting room. Steelman (1991) looked at a number of studies of music's effect on relaxation where tempo was varied and concluded that tempos of 60 to 80 beats per minute reduce the stress response and induce relaxation, while tempos between 100 and 120 beats per minute stimulate the sympathetic nervous system. Stratton and Zalanowski (1984) conclude that there is a significant correlation between degree of relaxation and preference for music. User preferences, familiarity with, or past experiences with the music have an overriding effect on positive behavior change than do other types of music. Based on these studies, a preassumption can be made that user-preferred music that is familiar and that has tempos of 60 to 80 beats per minute can have a better stress reduction effect than other music. Not only can the music be used directly for stress reduction, it can also be used to improve the user's positive performance. Lai (2005) presented an experiment on the effects of music on sleep disorders. He found that soft, slow music could be used as a therapy to promote sleep quality. The tempo of the music being listened to appears to be an important parameter here. Lesiuk (2005) measured the effect of music listening on state positive affect, work quality, and time-on-task of computer information systems developers. Results indicated that state positive affect and quality of work were lowest with no music, while time-on-task was longest when music was removed. Narrative responses revealed the value of music listening for positive mood change and enhanced perception on design while working.

5.3.3.2 Games

Muscle contraction is very important in reducing physical discomfort. Muscle activity helps to keep blood flowing through the veins, particularly in the deep veins. Depending on the genre and the playing devices of the games, the user must move in certain patterns, resulting in exercise-like muscle activity (Nintendo n.d.). The user may thereby improve his or her physical comfort level through game play.

5.3.4 Cybernetics Control Systems

Cybernetics is the science that studies the abstract principles of organization in complex systems. It is concerned not so much with system components as with how the system functions. Cybernetics focuses on how systems use information, models, and control actions to steer toward and maintain their goals while counteracting various disturbances. Being inherently transdisciplinary, cybernetic reasoning can be applied to understand, model, and design systems of any kind: physical, technological, biological, ecological, psychological, social, or any combination of these (Heylighen and Joslyn 2001).

A simple control system scheme (see Figure 5.5) is a feedback cycle with two inputs: the goal, which stands for the preferred values of the system's essential variables; and the disturbances, which stand for all the processes in the environment that the system does not have under control but that can affect these variables. The system starts by observing or sensing the variables that it wishes to control because they affect its preferred state. This step of perception creates an internal representation of the outside situation. The information in this representation must then be processed in order to determine (1) in what way it may affect the goal and (2) what is the best reaction to safeguard that goal. Based on this interpretation, the system then decides on an appropriate action. This action affects some part of

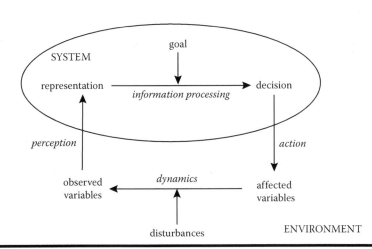

Figure 5.5 Basic components of a control system. (From Cybernetics and second-order cybernetics by F. Heylighen and C. Joslyn, 2001. In R. Meyers, Ed., *Encyclopedia of Physical Science and Technology*, vol. 4. Orlando, FL: Academic Press, pp. 155–170. With permission.)

the environment, which in turn affects other parts of the environment through the normal causal processes or dynamics of that environment. These dynamics are influenced by the set of unknown variables, which we call the disturbances. This dynamic interaction affects, among others, the variables that the system keeps under observation. The change in these variables is again perceived by the system, which again triggers interpretation, decision, and action, thus closing the control loop (Heylighen and Joslyn 2001).

5.3.5 A New Framework for Next-Generation In-Flight Entertainment Systems

In this section, we present a new framework for next-generation in-flight entertainment systems. It integrates the concepts of context-adaptive systems, user profiling, methods of the use of entertainment services for stress reduction, and cybernetics control systems to provide entertainment services that improve the passenger's comfort level during air travel. In Figure 5.6, the system starts by observing the passenger's physical and psychological states (modeled on the passenger's biofeedback signal) that it wishes to control. This step of perception creates an internal representation of the passenger's physical and psychological situation. The information in this representation must be processed in order to determine (1) whether the passenger is comfortable and (2) what are the best entertainment services to improve the passenger's comfort level. Based on this interpretation, and referring to the user profile, the system then decides on an appropriate entertainment service provision. The passenger is an adaptive system: his or her perception creates an internal representation of the entertainment service. This perception affects the passenger's physical and psychological states. During this process, the passenger's physical or psychological states may also be influenced by a set of variables such as unfavorable air pressure, humidity, and continuous noise in the aircraft cabin. The change in the passenger's physical and psychological states is again perceived by the system, again triggering the adaptation process and thus closing the control loop. The entertainment preference of the passenger depends on the context of use, which include, for example, the passenger's physical and psychological states and the activity he or she is pursuing. In Figure 5.6, if the system recommends entertainment services that the passenger does not like, he or she may reject the recommended services and select the desired entertainment or just shut down the system. By mining the context-of-use data, entertainment services selected by the passenger, and the passenger's explicit and implicit feedback on the system's recommendations, the system can automatically learn and adapt to the passenger's preferences. Thus, the more that the passenger uses the in-flight entertainment system, the more intelligent and personalized the system's recommendations become.

The following is a brief discussion of the framework for next-generation in-flight entertainment systems with the comfort design principles described in Section 5.1.

1. *Affordance*: This framework makes it possible for the passenger to get personalized entertainment services with less effort. For example, the more time that a passenger spends on board an airline's plane, the better the user profile and biosignal model based on his or her past behaviors can be built. Thus, more personalized services can be provided intelligently by the system.
2. *Situational awareness*: In the framework, if the passenger does not like the recommended entertainment services, he or she can decline the recommendation and personally select his or her preferred entertainment services. In this way, the framework ensures the passenger that the entertainment is under his or her control.
3. *Individualization and customization*: The user profiling technology used in the framework enables the personalized entertainment service provision. The user preference learning component ensures that the user's entertainment preference is tracked, learned, and updated.
4. *Variability and flexibility*: The framework enables the passenger to choose preferred entertainment services from among many options to fulfill different and diverse entertainment needs.
5. *Negative stress reduction*: As described in this section, the framework can provide the passenger with personalized stress-reduction entertainment services, actively and intelligently, if he or she is under stress.

To implement the framework into a real-world in-flight entertainment system, a lot of research must be done including:

1. Passengers' psychological and physical state modeling with signal outputs from biosensors that monitor, for instance, blood pressure and heart rate.
2. Passengers' personalized psychological and physical comfort points definition under different contexts of use based on psychological and physical state models.

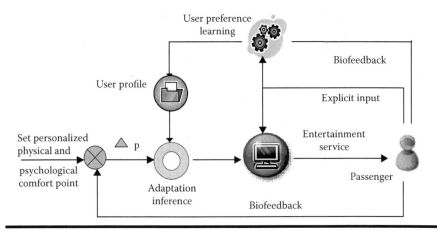

Figure 5.6   A new framework for next-generation in-flight entertainment systems.

3. A user profile model that reflects passengers' NRDs on preferred in-flight entertainment system behaviors, explicitly or implicitly.
4. A user preference learning algorithm that can learn the passenger's entertainment preference with as few explicit inputs as possible.
5. User-desired entertainment service recommendation algorithms that not only consider the possible change of available entertainment content but also avoid the "tunnel effect" of the recommendation.

5.4 Conclusions

In-flight entertainment systems play an important role in improving passengers' comfort level during air travel. Today, the current in-flight entertainment systems have made significant progress in providing user-preferred entertainment services with user-friendly interfaces, interaction mode design, ever-increasing entertainment options, and so on. However, despite all of these advances, the current generation of in-flight entertainment systems surveyed in this chapter still has much room for improvement so that systems intelligently provide personalized entertainment for recreation as well as personalized stress-reduction entertainment for stress-free air travel. In this chapter, we first introduced five principles to design a more comfortable in-flight entertainment system. Then, the currently installed and commercially available in-flight entertainment systems were investigated, and we checked how they are designed and implemented relating to these principles. The state-of-the-art enabling technologies that can be used to design a better in-flight entertainment system to improve the passenger's comfort level were explored. Finally, we presented a new framework based on the integration of investigated technologies for next-generation in-flight entertainment systems. We also identified research that is yet to be done to transform the framework into a real-world in-flight entertainment system. We hope that the framework presented in this chapter will advance the discussion in the aviation community about next-generation in-flight entertainment systems.

Acknowledgment

This project is sponsored by the European Commission DG H.3 Research, Aeronautics Unit under the 6th Framework Programme, contract number AST5-CT-2006-030958.

Hao Liu is a third year PhD candidate in the Department of Industrial Design at the Eindhoven University of Technology, the Netherlands. His PhD topic is a new music adaptive framework design for stress-free air travel which is sponsored by the European project SEAT under the 6th Framework Programme. Liu has a bachelor's degree in electrical engineering and a master's degree in computer science.

His research interests include context-aware computing, ambient intelligence and interactive media.

Ben Salem received a master's degree in architecture in 1993. He then pursued post-graduate education in electronics and received a doctorate in 2003. During his career, he has been involved in various projects dealing with hardware platforms (robots, interaction devices, and sensors) and the development of novel applications (virtual theatre, smart environments, and adaptive and personalized systems).

His current interests include kansei media and entertainment, game design, robotics, user experience and modeling the brain. He is author and co-author of numerous publications and has been involved with both academic research projects and industrial projects. He has worked in England, the Netherlands and Japan. He is currently an assistant professor with the Department of Industrial Design, at Eindhoven University of Technology, the Netherlands.

Matthias Rauterberg received a BS in psychology in 1978 at the University of Marburg, Germany; he also received a BA in philosophy in 1981 and a BS in computer science in 1983 from the University of Hamburg, Germany. He has an MS in psychology (1981) and an MS in computer science (1986), also from the University of Hamburg, Germany, and a PhD in computer science and mathematics (1995) at the University of Zurich, Switzerland.

He was a senior lecturer for usability engineering in computer science and industrial engineering at the Swiss Federal Institute of Technology (ETH) in Zurich, Switzerland, where he was later head of the Man-Machine Interaction (MMI) research group. Since 1998 he has been a full time professor of human communication technology, first at IPO Center for User System Interaction Research, and later at the Department of Industrial Design at the Eindhoven University of Technology, the Netherlands. From 1999 until 2001 he was director of IPO. He is now the head of the designed intelligence research group at the Department of Industrial Design at the Eindhoven University of Technology.

He was the Swiss representative in the IFIP TC13 on human–computer interaction (HCI) from 1994-2002, and the chairman of the IFIP WG13.1 on HCI and Education from 1998-2004. He is now the Dutch representative in the IFIP TC14 on entertainment computing and the founding vice-chair of this TC14. He has also been the chair of the IFIP WG14.3 on entertainment theory since 2004. He was appointed as visiting professor at Kwansei Gakuin University, Japan from 2004-2007. He received the German GI-HCI Award for the best PhD in 1997 and the Swiss Technology Award for the BUILD-IT system in 1998. Since 2004 he has been a nominated member of the Cream of Science Award in the Netherlands —the 200 top-level Dutch researchers—and amongst the 10 top-level Eindhoven University of Technology scientists. He has over 250 publications in international journals, conference proceedings, and books. He acts as editor and member of the editorial board of several leading international journals.

References

Baldauf, M. (2007). A survey on context-aware systems. *International Journal of Ad Hoc and Ubiquitous Computing* 2(4): 263–277.

Bartneck, C., Masuoka, A., Takahashi, T., and Fukaya, T. (2006). The learning experience with electronic museum guides. *Psychology of Aesthetics, Creativity, and the Arts*, 0(1): 18–25.

David, A. T., and Robert, R. (1999). Customer stress-relaxation: The impact of music in a hospital waiting room. *International Journal of Service Industry Management* 10(1): 68–81.

Dey, A. K., and Abowd, G. D. (1999). Towards a better understanding of context and context-awareness. College of Computing, Georgia Institute of Technology. Technical Report.

Dumur, E., Barnard, Y., and Boy, G. (2004). Designing for comfort. In D. de Waard, K. A. Brookhuis, and C. M. Weikert (Eds.), *Human Factors in Design*. Maastricht, Netherlands: Shaker Publishing, pp. 111–127.

Edmonds, E. A. (1981). Adaptive man–computer interfaces. In M. C. Coombs and J. L. Alty (Eds.), *Computing Skills and the User Interface*. London: Academic Press, pp. 4–10.

Goel, M., and Sarkar, S. (2002). Web site personalization using user profile information. In P. De Bra, P. Brusilovsky, and R. Conejo (Eds.), *Adaptive Hypermedia and Adaptive Web-Based Systems. Proceedings of the Second International Conference (AH 2002)*, pp. 510–513. *Lecture Notes in Computer Science*, Vol. 2347. Berlin: Springer-Verlag.

Heylighen, F., and Joslyn C. (2001). Cybernetics and second-order cybernetics. In R. Meyers (Ed.), *Encyclopedia of Physical Science and Technology, Vol. 4*. Orlando, FL: Academic Press, pp. 155–170.

Kaasinen, E. (2003). User needs for location-aware mobile services. *Personal and Ubiquitous Computing* 7, 70–79.

Kay, Judy. (2001). User modeling for adaptation. In C. Stephanidis (Ed.), *User Interfaces for All: Concepts, Methods, and Tools*. Mahwah, NJ: Erlbaum, pp. 271–294.

Kelly, D., and Teevan, J. (2003). Implicit feedback for inferring user preference: A bibliography. *SIGIR Forum* 37(2), retrieved March 1, 2007, from http://www.acm.org/sigs/sigir/forum/2003F/teevan.pdf.

Klann, M., Humberg, D. et al. (2005). iManual: Mobile endgeräte als kontextsensitive integrierte bedien und hilfesysteme. *Wirtschaftsinformatik* 47(1), 36–44.

Kobsa, A., and Wahlster, W. (1989). *User Models in Dialog Systems*. Berlin: Springer.

Lai, H., and Good, M. (2005). Music improves sleep quality in older adults. *Journal of Advanced Nursing* 49(3): 234–244.

Lesiuk, T. (2005). The effect of music listening on work performance. *Journal of Psychology of Music* 33(2): 173–191.

Liu, H. (2006). State of art of in-flight entertainment systems and office work infrastructure. Deliverable 4.1 of European Project Smart Technologies for Stress-Free Air Travel, Technical University of Eindhoven.

Liu, H., and Rauterberg, M. (2007). Context-aware in-flight entertainment system. In M. J. Dainoff (Ed.), *Proceedings of Posters at HCI International: Part X* (LNCS CD-ROM [ISBN 978-3-540-73332-4]), pp. 1249–1254, Berlin: Springer.

Oppermann, R. (2005). From user-adaptive to context-adaptive information systems. *i-com* 3, 4–14.

Panasonic Matsushita. (n.d.). In-flight entertainment systems. Retrieved November 25, 2006, from http://www.mascorp.com/products.html.

Petrelli D., and Not, E. (2005). User-centered design of flexible hypermedia for a mobile guide: Reflections on the hyperaudio experience. *User Modeling and User-Adapted Interaction (UMUAI)* (Special Issue on User Modeling in Ubiquitous Computing), pp. 85–86.

QANTAS Airlines. In-flight workout. Retrieved May 20, 2007, from http://www.qantas.com.au/info/flying/inTheAir/yourHealthInflight#jump3.

Rauterberg, G. W. M. (1993). AMME: An automatic mental model evaluation to analyze user behavior traced in a finite, discrete state space. *Ergonomics* 36(11): 1369–1380.

Rockwell Collins. (n.d.). In-flight entertainment product catalog. Retrieved November 25, 2006, from http://www.rockwellcollins.com/ecat/at/xxProductList.html?smenu=3.

Salem, B. I., and Rauterberg, G. W. M. (2004). Multiple user profile merging (MUPE): Key challenges for environment awareness. In P. Markopoulos, J. H. Eggen, and E. Aarts (Eds.), *Ambient Intelligence: Second European Symposium, EUSAI 2004*, Eindhoven, pp. 196–206, Berlin: Springer.

Schilit, B. N., Adams, N. et al. (1994). Context-aware computing applications. In *Workshop on Mobile Computing Systems and Applications*, Santa Cruz, CA, pp. 85–90.

Schröder, O., Frank, K.-D., Kohnert, K., Möbus, C., and Rauterberg, M. (1990). Instruction-based knowledge for a functional, visual programming language. *Computers in Human Behavior* 6(1): 31–49.

Sophia, K. (1998). Sky rage. *Flight Safety Australia* (July), pp. 36–37.

Steelman, V. M. (1991). Relaxing to the beat: Music therapy in perioperative nursing. *Today's OR Nurse* 13, 18–22.

Stratton, V. N., and Zalanowski, A. H. (1984). The relationship between music, degree of liking, and self-reported relaxation. *Journal of Music Therapy* 21(4): 184–92.

Streitz, N., and Nixon, P. (2005). Disappearing computer. *Communications of the ACM* 48(3): 33–35.

Suh, Y., Kang, D., and Woo, W. (2005). Context-based user profile management for personalized services. *Proceedings of the First International Workshop on Personalized Context Modeling and Management for UbiComp Applications*, Tokyo, Japan, September 11, pp. 64–73.

Thales. (n.d.). In-flight entertainment systems. Retrieved November 25, 2006, from http://www.thalesgroup.com/all/pdf/ife_brochure.pdf.

WATS. (2006). *World Air Transport Statistics Special 50th Edition*. International Air Transport Association.

Wikipedia. (n.d.). In-flight entertainment. Retrieved March 1, 2008, from http://en.wikipedia.org/wiki/In-flight_entertainment.

World Health Organization. (2005). Travel by air: Health considerations. Retrieved March 1, 2008, from http://whqlibdoc.who.int/publications/2005/9241580364_chap2.pdf.

Yu, S., Spaccapietra, S., Cullot, N., and Aufaure, M. (2004). User profiles in location-based services: Make humans more nomadic and personalized. *Proceeding of IASTED International Conference on Databases and Applications*, Innsbruck, Austria, February 17–19, pp. 71–76.

Chapter 6

Toward an Adaptive Video Retrieval System

Frank Hopfgartner and Joemon M. Jose

6.1 Introduction

With the increasing availability of new tools and applications to record, broadcast, and stream videos, there is a need to create new retrieval engines to assist users in searching and finding scenes that they would like to see within different video files. Research to date has a particular emphasis on the system side, resulting in the design of retrieval tools that assist users in performing search sessions. However, because the effectiveness of current video retrieval systems is anything but satisfying for users, more sophisticated research is needed to increase the retrieval performance to a level similar to their textual counterparts.

Unlike text retrieval systems, retrieval of digital video libraries is facing a challenging problem: the semantic gap. This is the difference between the low-level data representation of videos and the higher level concepts that a user associates with video. In 2005, the panel members of the International Workshop on Multimedia Information Retrieval identified this gap as one of the main technical problems in multimedia retrieval (Jaimes et al. 2005), carrying the potential to dominate the research efforts in multimedia retrieval for the next few years. Retrievable information such as textual sources of video clips (i.e., speech transcripts) is often not reliable enough to describe the actual content of a clip. Moreover, the approach of using visual features and automatically detecting high-level concepts, which have been the main focus of study within the international video processing and evaluation campaign TRECVID (Smeaton et al. 2006), turned out to be insufficient to bridge the semantic gap.

One approach to bridge the semantic gap is to improve the interfaces of video retrieval systems, enabling users to specify their information demand. However, as the performance of state-of-the-art systems indicates, interface designs are, so far, not advanced enough to provide such facilities. A promising approach to solve this problem is to incorporate an adaptive retrieval model, which automatically adapts retrieval results based on the user's preferences. An adaptive retrieval model can be useful to significantly reduce the number of steps that the user has to perform before he retrieves satisfying search results. Sebe and Tian (2007) point out that to develop an adaptive model for retrieving multimedia content, sophisticated research in various areas is needed, including research in the acquisition of user preferences and how to filter information by exploiting the user's profile.

Arezki and colleagues (2004) provide an example to explain the challenge of different user preferences: when a computer scientist enters the search query "java" into a search engine, she is most likely interested in finding information about the programming language. Other people, however, might expect results referring to the island of Java in Indonesia or to a type of coffee bean bearing this name. A classical approach to capture these different preferences is profiling. User profiles can be used to create a simplified model of the user that represents his or her interests on general topics. Commercial search engines incorporate such profiles, the most prominent being Google's iGoogle and Yahoo!'s MyYahoo! Query expansion is used to gather users' interests, and search results are reranked to match their interests.

The named services rely on users' explicitly specifying preferences, a common approach in the text retrieval domain. By giving explicit feedback, users are forced to update their need, which can be problematic when their information need is vague (Spink et al. 1998). Furthermore, users tend to provide insufficient feedback on which to base an adaptive retrieval algorithm (Hancock-Beaulieu and Walker 1992).

Deviating from the method of explicitly asking the user to rate the relevance of retrieval results, the use of implicit feedback techniques helps by unobtrusively learning the user's interests. The main advantage being that users are relieved from providing feedback: it is given unintentionally. An example is when a user prints out a Web page, which may indicate an interest in that Web page. The basic assumption is that during a search, users' actions are used to maximize the retrieval of relevant information. Implicit indicators have been used and analyzed in other domains, such as the World Wide Web (Claypool et al. 2001) and text retrieval (Kelly and Teevan 2003; White et al. 2004), but rarely in the multimedia domain. However, traditional issues of implicit feedback can be addressed in video retrieval because digital video libraries facilitate more interactions and are hence amenable to implicit feedback. Hopfgartner and Jose (2007) have shown that implicit feedback can improve retrieval in digital video library retrieval systems.

A challenging problem in user profiling is the users' evolving focus of interest. What a user finds interesting on day A might be completely uninteresting on day B, or even on the same day. The following example illustrates the problem: Joe Bloggs is rarely interested in sports. Thus, during Euro 2008, the European Football Championship, he is fascinated by the euphoria exuded by the tournament and follows all of the reports related to the event. After the cup final, however, his interest abates again. How to capture and represent this dynamic user interest is an unsolved problem.

Moreover, a user can be interested in multiple topics, which might evolve over time. Instead of being interested in only one topic at one time, users can search for various independent topics such as politics or sports, followed by entertainment or business. We can capture this evolution of information need by capturing the implicit factors involved in such a retrieval system.

In this work, we investigate the following research questions: Which implicit feedback that a user provides can be considered as a positive indicator of relevance and can hence be used to adapt his or her retrieval results? How must these features be weighted to increase retrieval performance? It is unclear which features are stronger and which are weaker indicators of relevance. Moreover, we aim to study how the users' evolving interest in multiple aspects of news should be considered when capturing the users' interests. Answering these questions will shed light on implicit relevance feedback, a necessary step toward an adaptive retrieval model.

This chapter is organized as follows: A brief introduction of related work is given in Section 6.2. In Section 6.3, we discuss research questions that must be solved in order to develop an adaptive retrieval model. To tackle the research questions, we introduce NewsBoy in Section 6.4; NewsBoy is a personalized multimedia application designed to capture the user's evolving interest in multiple aspects of news stories. NewsBoy is a Web-based video retrieval system that enables us to spread the system to a large population, such as to all students on a university campus. In order to offer an attractive news video retrieval system to the general public, the system is based on an up-to-date news video corpus. NewsBoy automatically processes the daily BBC One news bulletin, divides the broadcast into story segments, and recommends news stories by unobtrusively profiling the user according to his interactions with the system. The news aspects are identified by clustering the content of the profile.

6.2 Background

In the following discussion, we introduce the multifaceted research domains, which are important in the scope of this work. In Section 6.2.1, we provide an overview of the field of interactive video retrieval. We explain the idea of personalized retrieval by incorporating user profiles in Section 6.2.2 and introduce the users' evolving interest in different aspects of news in Section 6.2.3. Finally, the idea of feature ranking is introduced in Section 6.2.4.

In the scope of this research, we aim to rely on both user studies and a simulated user evaluation. Performing user studies is a popular methodology to evaluate interactive retrieval systems. The approach of simulating users to fine tune retrieval systems has been studied before (e.g., Hopfgartner and Jose 2007; Vallet et al. 2008; White et al. 2007), the results being promising to follow the methodology. The evaluation framework is presented in Section 6.2.5.

6.2.1 Interactive Video Retrieval Systems

One of the biggest tracks within TRECVID is the interactive search task. In this track, users have to interact with a video retrieval interface in order to retrieve predefined topics. Research on interactive video retrieval has been an important stepping stone for the development of large-scale video retrieval systems such as YouTube and Google Video. Snoek and colleagues (2007) identified an architecture framework for most state-of-the-art video retrieval engines such as those presented in Snoek and colleagues (2005), Campbell and colleagues (2006), and Rautiainen and colleagues (2005). This framework can be divided into an indexing engine and a retrieval engine, the first component involves the indexing of the video data. This process starts with a shot segmentation stage, which will split a single video into a sequence of *shots*. A shot is a sequence of the video that is visually related, with boundaries between shots typically being marked by a scene cut or fade. Each shot will vary in size, most being very short (typically a few seconds). For each shot, example frames—key frames—are extracted to represent the shot. The shot is used as the element of retrieval: each shot is separately indexed by the system, and the results of searches are presented as a list of shots.

In the news domain, a specific unit of retrieval is the news *story* (Boreczky and Rowe 1996). Examples can be stories about a political event, followed by a story about yesterday's football match or the weather forecast. Therefore, it is necessary to identify and merge those shots that semantically form one story. However, the structure of news broadcasts directly depends on the programming director's taste, so finding a general applicable approach of automatically segmenting a broadcast video into its news stories is a challenging task (Chang et al. 2005). With respect to the current systems, indexing shots and stories can be incorporated at visual, textual, and semantic levels. Huang (2003) argues that speech contains most of the semantic information that can be extracted from audio features, and according to Chang et al. (2005), text from speech data has been shown to be important for key term/named entity extraction, story boundary detection, concept annotation, and topic change detection. In literature, the most common text sources are teletext (also called closed-caption), speech recognition transcripts, and optical character recognition output. Hopfgartner (2007) compares different state-of-the-art video retrieval systems, concluding that the text sources for systems differ significantly from each other. Heesch and colleagues (2004) include closed-caption transcripts, automatic speech recognition (ASR) output, and optical character recognition output in their index, whereas Foley and colleagues (2005) index speech recognition output only.

The indexing and related retrieval methods make up the "back end." The second component, the "front end," is the interface between the computer and the human user. Graphical user interfaces give the user the opportunity to compose queries, with the retrieval engine handling these queries, combining returned results, and visualizing them. A detailed survey of different interface approaches is provided by Hopfgartner (2007). In the remainder of this section, we focus on systems that incorporate the idea of providing users with a news video retrieval system that is based on daily news videos.

Pickering and colleagues (2003) record the daily BBC news and capture the broadcasted subtitles. The news broadcast is segmented into shots, and key frames are extracted to represent the shot. Shots are merged to form news stories based on the subtitles. Therefore, they extract key entities (nouns, verbs, etc.) from the subtitles and calculate a term weighting based on their appearance in the teletext. The interface of their system is Web based* and provides browsing and retrieval facilities. Their work has concentrated on summarizing news videos; adapting retrieval results to the user's need has not been considered in their system.

Morrison and Jose (2004) introduced the Web-based news video retrieval system VideoSqueak. They record the BBC One evening news and use the captured subtitles to identify story units. The subtitles of the broadcast are the retrieval source. They evaluate different presentation strategies for multimedia retrieval. However, they have not studied the user behavior in news retrieval systems.

6.2.2 Personalization

Web 2.0 facilities enable everyone to easily create their own content and to publish it online. Users can upload videos on platforms such as YouTube, share pictures on Flickr, or publish anything in a weblog. Two direct consequences of this development can be identified. First, it leads to a growing quantity of content presented in a multimedia format. Second, information sources are completely unstructured, and finding interesting content can be an overwhelming task. Hence, there is a need to understand the user's interest and to customize information accordingly.

A common approach to capture and represent these interests is user profiling. Using user profiles to create personalized online newspapers has been studied for a long time.

Chen and Sycara (1998) join Internet users during their information seeking task and explicitly ask them to judge the relevance of the pages they visit. Exploiting the created user profile of interest, they generate a personalized newspaper containing daily news. However, providing explicit relevance feedback is a demanding task, and users tend not to provide much feedback (Hancock-Beaulieu and Walker 1992).

---

* A demo can be found online at http://www.doc.ic.ac.uk/~mjp3/anses.

Bharat and colleagues (1998) create a personalized online newspaper by unobtrusively observing the user's Web-browsing behavior. Although their system is a promising approach to release the user from providing feedback, their main research focus is on developing user interface aspects, ignoring the sophisticated retrieval issues.

Smeaton and colleagues (2002) introduced Físchlár-News, a news video recommendation system that captures the daily evening news from the national broadcaster's main television channel. The Web-based interface of their system provides a facility to retrieve news stories and recommend stories to the user based on his or her interests. According to Lee and colleagues (2006), the recommendation of Físchlár-News is based on personal and collaborative explicit relevance feedback. The use of implicit relevance feedback as input has not been incorporated. Profiling and capturing the users is an important step toward adapting systems to the user's evolving information interest.

6.2.3 Evolving User Interest

In a retrieval context, profiles can be used to contextualize the user's search queries within his or her interests and to rerank retrieval results. This approach is based on the assumption that the user's information interest is static, which is, however, not appropriate in a retrieval context.

Campbell (1995) argues that the user's information need can change within different retrieval sessions and sometimes even within the same session. He states that the user's search direction is directly influenced by the documents retrieved. The following example explains this observation:

> Example: Imagine a user who is interested in red cars and uses an image retrieval system to find pictures showing such cars. His first search query returns several images, including pictures of red Ferraris. Looking at these pictures, he wants to find more Ferraris and adapts the search query accordingly. The new result list now consists of pictures showing red and green Ferraris. Fascinated by the rare color for this type of car, he again reformulates the search query to find more green Ferraris. Within one session, the user's information need evolved from red cars to green Ferraris.

Based on this observation, Campbell and van Rijsbergen (1996) introduced the ostensive model that incorporates this change of interest by considering when a user provides relevant feedback. In the ostensive model, providing feedback on a document is seen as ostensive evidence that this document is relevant for the user's current interest. The combination of this feedback over several search iterations provides ostensive evidence about the user's changing interests. The model considers the user's changing focus of interest by granting the most recent feedback a higher impact over the combined evidence. Various forms of this model have been developed and applied in image retrieval (Urban et al. 2003) and Web search scenarios (Joho et al. 2007).

6.2.4 Relevance Ranking

Most information retrieval systems such as Google and Yahoo! attempt to rank documents in an increasing order of relevance. A major challenge in the field is how to judge whether a document is relevant to a given query. One approach is to rank the results based on query-dependent features, such as the term frequency of a document and the distribution of each term in the entire collection. Hence, for each query, the results are ranked according to a dynamic relevance score. However, better retrieval performance can be achieved by transforming a document's query-independent features into a static relevance score and including this in the overall relevance score. Thinking of a textual corpus such as the World Wide Web, query-independent features can be the number of hyperlinks that point to a document or the length or creation time of a document. Here, the major challenge is combining scores and defining good functions that transform the documents into applicable weighting schemes. Craswell and colleagues (2005) explain that a retrieval model that incorporates these query-independent features must answer basic questions. The first question is whether the feature is needed to adjust the weighting of a document. It might not be necessary to incorporate the weighting of a specific feature if the initial weighting is already appropriate. The second question is how different features shall alter the weighting of a document. And finally, the model should predict that the created weighting best represents the document.

According to Craswell and colleagues (2005), various approaches have been studied to combine different features, rank-based and language modeling priors being the most promising. Fagin and colleagues (2003) and Cai and colleagues (2005) combined features by creating document ranking lists for each feature and merging these lists based on their score. The advantage of this approach is that the diversified weighting used in the different feature ranking lists does not matter, as the combined list takes only the score within each list into account.

Kraaij and colleagues (2002) calculated prior probabilities for various features such as page length and URL type to increase the precision of a text retrieval system. Even though they concluded that using priors to combine independent features can improve the retrieval performance, they argue that choosing a wrong prior can decrease the performance. It is therefore important to identify when a prior is useful.

6.2.5 Evaluation Framework

A common approach to study users' behavior of interacting with a computer system is to perform a user study, to monitor users' interactions, and to analyze the resulting log files. Such an analysis will help to identify good implicit indicators of relevance, as it can help to answer basic questions: What did the user do to find the information he or she wanted? Can the user behavior be used to improve retrieval results?

To get an adequate impression of users' behavior when interacting with a video retrieval system, we need a large number of different users interacting with the system, which is necessary to draw general conclusions from the study (i.e., by analyzing user log files). Additionally, nonexpert users should be interacting with the system, as they will interact in a more intuitive way than expert users. However, it is not practical to conduct such a study in all situations, mainly due to the cost associated with them. Besides, it is hardly possible to benchmark different parameter combinations of features for effectiveness using user-centered evaluations.

An alternative way of evaluating such user feedback is by the use of simulated interactions. In this approach, a set of possible steps are assumed when a user is performing a given task with the evaluated system. Finin (1989) introduced one of the first user simulation modeling approaches. This general user-modeling system (GUMS) allows software developers to test their systems by feeding them simple stereotyped user behavior. White and colleagues (2007) proposed a simulation-based approach to evaluate the performance of implicit indicators in textual retrieval. They simulated user actions as viewing relevant documents, which were expected to improve the retrieval effectiveness. In the simulation-based evaluation methodology, actions that a real user may take are assumed and used to influence further retrieval results. Hopfgartner and colleagues (2007) introduced a simulation framework to evaluate adaptive multimedia retrieval systems. In order to develop a retrieval method, they employed a simulated evaluation methodology that simulated users giving implicit relevance feedback. Hopfgartner and Jose (2007) extended this simulation framework and simulated users interacting with state-of-the-art video retrieval systems. They argue that a simulation can be seen as a pre-implementation method that will give further opportunity to develop appropriate systems and subsequent user-centered evaluations. Vallet and colleagues (2008) used the concept of simulated actions to try and mimic the interaction of past users by simulating user actions based on the past history and behavior of the users with an interactive video retrieval system. Their study has proven to facilitate the analysis of the diverse types of implicit actions that a video retrieval system can provide.

Analyzing these research efforts leads to the conclusion that, even though simulation-based studies should be confirmed by user studies, they can be a cheap and repeatable methodology to fine tune video retrieval systems. Hence, user simulation is a promising approach to further study adaptive video retrieval, at least as a preliminary step.

6.3 Research Framework

The scope of this research is to develop an adaptive video retrieval model that automatically adapts retrieval results to the user's information needs. In the previous section, we introduced various aspects that are relevant within this scope, including an introduction to interactive video retrieval, personalization approaches, users' evolving interests, ranking approaches, and different evaluation methodologies. In this section, we focus on research questions that must be tackled in order to develop an adaptive video retrieval system. We are particularly interested in the following problems:

1. Which implicit feedback a user provides while interacting with an interface can be considered as a positive indicator of relevance?
2. Which interface features are stronger indicators of relevance, or put another way, how shall these features be weighted in order to increase retrieval performance?
3. How should the user's evolving interest in multiple aspects of news be incorporated when retrieval results are reranked in accordance to the user's interest?

Once the user's intentions and information needs are clear, systems can be built that take advantage of such knowledge and optimize the retrieval output for each user by implementing an adaptive video retrieval model.

In order to study the first research question, we will provide users with different video retrieval interface approaches for different interaction environments, such as desktop PCs and iTV boxes. Hence, the users are required to interact differently with the interfaces. The difference has a strong influence on users' behavior, making the importance of implicit indicators of relevance application-dependent. Comparing user interactions with different applications should help to identify common positive indicators. The research will be conducted around two different applications where we can monitor user feedback: desktop computers and television. The specific characteristics of these environments are introduced below.

- *Desktop Computers*: The most familiar environment for the user to conduct video retrieval is probably on a standard desktop computer. Most adaptive video retrieval systems have been designed to run under such an environment. The interface can be displayed on the screen, and users can easily interact with the system by using the keyboard or mouse. We can assume that users will take advantage of this interaction and hence give a high quantity of implicit feedback. From today's point of view, this environment offers the highest possibility for implicit relevance feedback. An example interface is introduced in Section 6.4.2.
- *iTV*: A widely accepted medium for multimedia consumption is television. Watching television, however, is a passive procedure. Viewers can select a program using a remote control, but changing the content is not possible. Recently, interactive TV is becoming increasingly popular. Using a remote control, viewers can interact directly when watching television (e.g., they can participate in quiz shows). In news video retrieval, this limited interaction is a challenge. It will be more complex to enter query terms (e.g., by using the

channel selection buttons as is common for remote controls). Hence, users will possibly avoid entering keywords. On the other hand, the selection keys and a display on the remote control provide a method to give explicit relevance feedback. For example, the viewer sees a video segment on television, then uses the remote control to judge the relevance of this segment.

A well-studied research methodology in the information retrieval community to evaluate different parameters or environments is to perform user studies. Analyzing users' interactions with different interface approaches will help us to understand how users interact with this application and will lead to further knowledge of which interface features are general indicators of relevance. Furthermore, we will use the simulation methodology introduced in Section 6.2.5 by exploiting the user log files, as applied by Hopfgartner and colleagues (2008), and analyzing the effect of different feature weighting schemes on retrieval performance. This analysis should help to distinguish stronger and weaker indicators of relevance and hence will answer our second research question.

Moreover, we aim to study the users' evolving interests and different ranking approaches in order to answer the third research question. In the next section, we introduce NewsBoy, the system we aim to use to further investigate our research questions. Our first choice is to rely on the previously introduced ostensive model. NewsBoy introduces an example interface designed for use on desktop computers and incorporates a simple approach to capturing the users' evolving interests based on the ostensive model.

6.4 NewsBoy Architecture

In order to study our research questions, we need many users interacting with a video retrieval system. Hence, we developed NewsBoy, a Web-based news video retrieval system based on Asynchronous JavaScript and XML (AJAX) technology for personalized news retrieval. This will enable us to spread the system to a large population (e.g., all students on a university campus). AJAX takes away the burden of installing additional software on each client (assuming that JavaScript is activated and a Flash Player is running on the client side). Due to the popularity of Web 2.0 technology, users get used to interacting with complex applications using their browser only. This familiarity might motivate them to use the system on a regular basis to retrieve broadcasting news.

Figure 6.1 illustrates the conceptual design of the system. As the graphic shows, NewsBoy can be divided into five main components, four running on a Web server and one, the user interface, on the client side. The first component is the data collection. The process of recording, analyzing, and indexing a daily news broadcast to create a data collection is introduced in Section 6.4.1. The retrieval back end, the second component of NewsBoy, administers the data collection. We

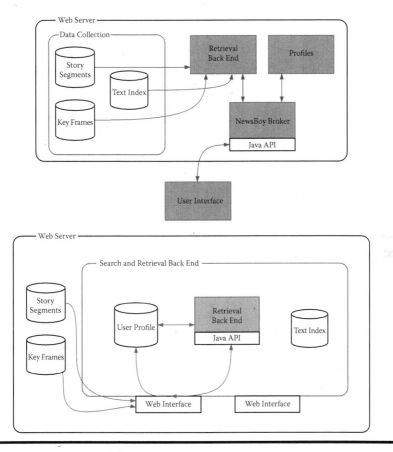

Figure 6.1 NewsBoy architecture.

use MG4J,* an open source full-text search engine. As discussed in Section 6.3, we aim to provide users with different interface approaches for different interaction environments, such as desktop PCs or iTV boxes. One interface approach designed for use on desktop PCs, the third component of the NewsBoy architecture, is introduced in Section 6.4.2. In Section 6.4.3, we introduce the concept of capturing the users' interests in user profiles by interpreting their interactions with these interfaces. It is the fourth component of the NewsBoy system and aims to answer the third research question by incorporating the ostensive model.

6.4.1 Data Collection

In recent years, the retrieval of news video data has been the main focus of research in the field of interactive video retrieval. A main reason for the concentration on

---

* http://mg4j.dsi.unimi.it/.

this domain is the international TRECVID (Smeaton et al. 2006) workshop, which provided a large corpus of news videos in the last few years. However, the latest data collection consisting of news video was recorded in late 2005. While these videos can be used to measure the system-centered research approaches, it is not recommended to base long-term user studies on this old data set. Most likely, potential users will get bored with the outdated data, which eventually results in a lack of motivation to search for interesting topics within the corpus and hence biases the study. One method to avoid this effect is to provide users with up-to-date news videos.

In this section, we describe the process of recording a daily news bulletin and will introduce our approach of segmenting the broadcast into news stories, the unit of retrieval in our system. We focus on the regional version of the BBC One O'Clock news. The program covers international, national (United Kingdom), and regional (Scotland) topics, which are usually presented by a single newsreader. The BBC enriches its television broadcast with Ceefax, a closed-caption (teletext) signal that provides televisual subtitles. The bulletin has a running time of 30 minutes and is broadcasted every day from Monday to Friday on BBC One, the nation's main broadcasting station. Both analog and digital broadcasts can be received by aerial antennas. In addition, the BBC streams the latest program on its Web site.

Figure 6.2 illustrates the architecture for recording, analyzing, and indexing the news program broadcasted by BBC Scotland. The process is divided into a shot boundary-detection and key-frame-extraction task, followed by the creation of a text transcript. Both shot boundaries and text transcript are used to identify story units.

The video/audio stream is downloaded from the BBC Web site, where it is provided in Windows Media Format (WMF) as an online stream. Adopting the techniques introduced by O'Toole and colleagues (1999) and Browne and colleagues (2000), we used a color histogram-based method to detect shot boundaries in our video files. Furthermore, we detected example key frames by calculating the average color histogram for each shot and extracted the frames within the shot that were closest to the average. In an additional step, we combined the key frames belonging to the same shot to form an animated presentation of the shot.

Further, we captured the teletext by decoding the aerial transmission signal of the BBC. The BBC's Ceefax system was developed to provide televisual subtitles for the deaf. They are manually created, so that the semantic quality of the text is reliable. However, the text is not synchronized with the actual speech. According to Huang (2003), the mean delay between speech and teletext is between 1 and 1.5 seconds. Furthermore, the transcript does not always represent the whole spoken text but more likely a shortened version of the sentences. While these two drawbacks are acceptable when the text is considered as an additional service to accompany the news program, it can be problematic when used as the source of a content analysis. Therefore, we created a second text transcript by performing an ASR using the Sphinx III* system.

---

* http://cmusphinx.sourceforge.net/

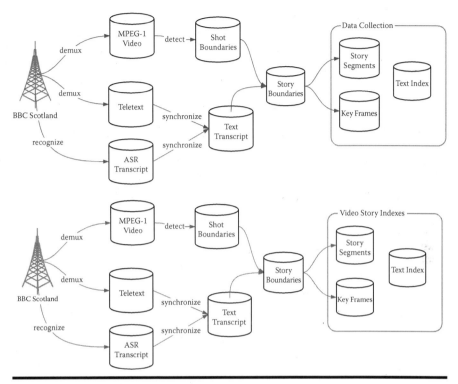

Figure 6.2   System architecture of the capturing and indexing process.

Sphinx III is a speaker-independent speech recognition system which, according to Huang (2003), is the best-performing tool for news video data sets. For recognition, we used the open source acoustic models, language models, and dictionaries provided under the Open Source license. As these are U.S. English models, the recognition of the BBC news broadcast, mainly spoken in British English, is rather weak. This means that the teletext transcript contains more correct words, while the transcript provides correct time codes for positively identified terms. It is therefore necessary to improve the text transcript. Following Huang (2003), we merged both closed-caption and ASR transcripts by aligning closed-caption terms with time codes and synchronizing these terms with the time codes of the ASR transcript. Within a sliding window of plus/minus 2.5 seconds around the time code of a term appearing in the teletext list, we calculated the Levenshtein distance for each word. If the distance stays below a predefined threshold, we merged the ASR transcript's time code with the word found in the teletext list. Terms are considered to be actual spoken terms when they appear in both streams within the defined time window. However, in several cases, no matching term is available within the time window. In this case, we assumed that the quality of the speech recognition output is too poor and hence used the teletext term and its output only.

Figure 6.3 Speaker segments.

As most stories on the BBC One O'Clock news are introduced by the anchorman or a speaker in the background, we divided the audio stream into speaker segments using the free available tool mClust.* We then analyzed the text transcript of these speaker segments to identify whether the segments could be merged to a story segment candidate. In the first step, we merged "interview" segments that were segments spoken by the same speaker and interrupted by a short speaker segment.

Figure 6.3 illustrates an example. Three different speakers are identified: S_1, S_2, and S_3. The speaker segment S_2 is surrounded by two segments of speaker S_1. Assuming that speaker S_1 is a journalist who interviews speaker S_2 and afterward continues with the story, we merged the three mentioned segments into one story segment candidate. In the next step, we scanned the segments for *signal terms* such as "Welcome to . . . ," "Thank you . . . ," or "Let's speak to . . . ," which indicate the end or beginning of a story. Further, we used the Spearman rank-order correlation to compute the degree of similarity between neighbored segments. The correlation returns values were between −1 and 1, where 0 shows that there is no correlation between the segments and 1 shows that they are a perfect match. White and colleagues (2003) showed the use of a similarity threshold of 0.2 in a text retrieval scenario, which we found useful in this case. Moreover, we matched the detected story unit candidates with the detected shot boundaries, assuming that a news story always begins with a new shot. To further enrich the segmented stories, we used the General Architecture for Text Engineering (GATE)† to identify persons, locations, and relative time mentioned in the transcript.

6.4.2 Desktop PC Interface

In this section, we present an example interface as it can be used in a desktop PC environment. It provides various possibilities to supply implicit relevance feedback. Users interacting with it can

- Expand the retrieved results by clicking on it.
- Play the video of a retrieved story by clicking on "play video."

---

* http://www-lium.univ-lemans.fr/tools.
† http://gate.ac.uk/.

■ Play the video for a certain amount of time.
■ Browse through the key frames.
■ Highlight additional information by moving the mouse over the key frames.

Figure 6.4 shows a screenshot of the interface; its features are described in the following section. The interface can be divided into three main panels: search panel (A), result panel (B), and clustered search queries (C). In the search panel (A), users can formulate and carry out their searches by entering a search query and clicking the button to start the search. BM25 (Robertson et al. 1994) is used to rank the retrieved documents according to their relevance to a given search query.

Once a user logs in, NewsBoy displays the latest news stories in the result panel (B). This panel lists a maximum of 15 retrieval results; further results can be displayed by clicking the annotated page number (1). The results can be sorted by their relevance to the query or chronologically by their broadcasting date (2). Results are presented by one key frame and a shortened part of the text transcript. A user can get additional information about the result by clicking on either the text or the key frame. Doing so expands the result and presents additional information, including the full-text transcript, broadcasting date, time, channel, and a list of extracted named entities such as persons, locations, and relative times (3). In the example screenshot, the second search result has been expanded. The shots forming the

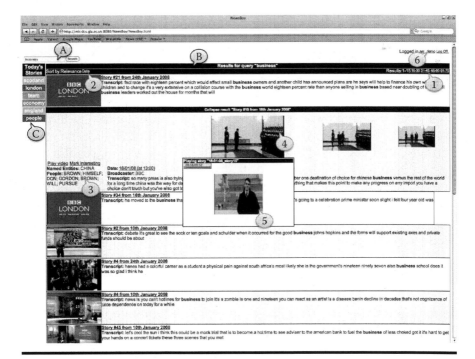

Figure 6.4   Example of a desktop PC environment interface.

news story are represented by animated key frames of each shot. Users can browse through these animations by clicking on the key frame. This action centers the selected key frame and surrounds it by its neighbored key frames. The key frames are displayed in a fish-eye view (4), meaning that the size of the key frame grows larger the closer it is to the focused key frame. In the expanded display, a user can also select to play a video or to mark it as interesting. Clicking on "play video" starts playing the story video in a new panel (5).

NewsBoy recommends daily news videos based on the user's multiaspect preferences. These preferences are captured by unobtrusively observing the user's interactions with the NewsBoy interface. By clustering the content of the profile, NewsBoy identifies different topics of interest and recommends these topics to the user. The interface presents these topics as labeled clusters on the left side of the interface (C). Each cluster represents a group of terms; hence, when a user clicks on the term, a new search is triggered, using the selected terms as a new query. Results are displayed in the result panel.

On the top of the interface, the users can edit their profile by clicking on their username (6). This action will pop up a new frame where the top weighted terms of each cluster are listed, and the user can edit the terms or the aligned weighting. Furthermore, the user can manually add new weighted terms.

6.4.3 Profile

User profiling is the process of learning the user's interest over an extended period of time. Several approaches have been studied to capture a user's interest in a profile, the most prominent being the weighted keyword vector approach. In this section, we introduce the approach and the problems that occur in capturing this interest in a profile.

In the weighted term approach, interests are represented as a vector of weighted terms where each dimension of the vector space represents a term aligned with a weighting. Hence, in order to capture the user's interest, terms aligned with the story item with which a user interacted should be extracted and weighted with the feedback based on the user's interaction. The weighting of the terms are updated when the system submits a new set of weighted terms to the profile, starting a new iteration, j. Hence, the interaction I of a user i at iteration j is represented as a vector of weights

$$\overrightarrow{I_{ji}} = \left\{ W_{ij1} \ldots W_{ijv} \right\}$$

where v indexes the word in the whole vocabulary V. The weighting W_{ij} depends on the implicit relevance feedback provided by a user i in the iteration j while interacting with an interface. Identifying an optimal weighting for each interface feature W_{ij} is one of the research questions we aim to study. Once the weighting has been determined, representative terms from relevant documents are extracted and assigned with an indicative weight to each term, which represents its weight in the term space. In a simple model that we proposed, we extracted non-stopwords v from the stories that a user interacted with in the iteration j and assigned these terms with the relevance weighting W_{ijv}. Furthermore, the profile $\vec{P_i}$ of user i can be presented as a vector containing the profile weight PW of each term v of the vocabulary:

$$\vec{P_i} = \{ PW_{i1} \dots PW_{iv} \}$$

6.4.3.1 Capturing Evolving Interest

The simplest approach to create a weighting for each term in the profile is to combine the weighting of the terms over all of the iterations. This approach is based on the assumption that the user's information interest is static, which is, however, not appropriate in a retrieval context. The users' information needs can change within different retrieval sessions, and we aim to study how this change of interest can be incorporated.

Campbell and van Rijsbergen (1996) proposed in their ostensive model that the time factor must be taken into account (i.e., by modifying the weighting of terms based on the iteration in which they were added to the user profile). They argued that more recent feedback is a stronger indicator of the user's interest than is older feedback. In our profile, the profile weight for each user i is the combination of the weighted terms v over different iterations j:

$$PW_{iv} = \sum_j aj W_{ijv}$$

We included the ostensive factor, denoted a_j, to introduce different weighting schemes based on the ostensive model. We have experimented with four different functions to calculate the weighting, depending on the nature of aging:

- Constant weighting
- Exponential weighting
- Linear weighting
- Inverse exponential weighting

Results of a user-centered evaluation of these weighting functions are discussed in Hopfgartner et al. (2008b). Figure 6.5 plots the normalized functions for up to 10 iterations. It can be seen that all of the functions, apart from the constant weighting, reduce the ostensive weighting of earlier iterations. The weighting depends on the constant $C > 1$. The functions are introduced in the remainder of this section.

6.4.3.1.1 Constant Weighting

The constant weighting function does not influence the ostensive weighting. As Equation 6.1 illustrates, all terms are combined equally, ignoring the iteration

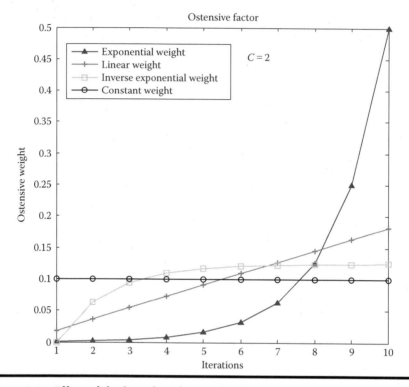

Figure 6.5 Effect of the introduced ostensive factors over 1 to 10 iterations.

when a term was added or updated. The constant weighting can be seen as a baseline methodology that does not include any ostensive factor.

$$a_j = \frac{1}{j_{max}} \tag{6.1}$$

6.4.3.1.2 Exponential Weighting

The exponential weighting as defined in Equation 6.2 gives a higher ostensive weighting to terms that have been added or updated in older iterations. It is the most extreme function because the ostensive weighting of earlier iterations decreases distinctly.

$$a_j = \frac{C^j}{\sum_{k=1}^{j_{max}} C^k} \tag{6.2}$$

6.4.3.1.3 Linear Weighting

Equation 6.3 defines the linear weighting function. The ostensive weighting of earlier iterations decreases linearly. This function linearly reduces the ostensive weighting of earlier iterations.

$$a_j = \frac{C_j}{\sum_{k=1}^{j_{max}} C^k} \tag{6.3}$$

6.4.3.1.4 Inverse Exponential Weighting

The inverse exponential weighting defined by Equation 6.4 is the most contained function. Compared to the other functions, the ostensive weighting of early iterations decreases more slowly.

$$a_j = \frac{1 - C^{-j+1}}{\sum_{k=1}^{j_{max}} 1 - C^{-k+1}} \tag{6.4}$$

6.4.3.2 *Capturing Multiple Interests*

All components introduced in the previous sections communicate through the NewsBoy Broker, the fifth component of the system illustrated in Figure 6.4. The task of the broker is to personalize the system by identifying the user's multiple interests in different aspects. Our methodology of identifying these aspects, the third research question, is introduced in the following.

We base our approach on the assumption that news topics consist of a number of particular terms that appear in all stories about this topic. News stories about soccer, for example, might consist of unique terms such as *goal, offside, match*, or *referee*. We capture implicit feedback when a user interacts with these stories. The terms of these stories are extracted and, along with the implicit weighting, stored in the profile. Hence, as the particular terms are added with the same weighting, they are close neighbors in the profile's vector space.

In this work, we limited the number of different aspects to a maximum of six. Therefore, we sorted the terms in the user's profile according to his or her profile weighting and identified the terms that had the five biggest distances to the neighbored terms. We used these identified weighted terms to cluster the remaining profile terms accordingly. Each cluster represents one aspect of the user's interest.

The top weighted terms of each cluster were used as a label to visualize the aspect on the left-hand side of the NewsBoy interface (marked C in Figure 6.4). Clicking on this label triggers a retrieval with the top six weighted terms of this aspect being used as a search query.

6.5 Discussion

When comparing video and text retrieval systems, one notices a large difference in retrieval performance. State-of-the-art systems are not yet advanced enough to understand the user's interest and to identify relevant video scenes. The semantic gap has been identified as the main reason for this problem. While humans can easily understand the content of images or videos, computers cannot. Different approaches are currently being studied to bridge this gap, the most prominent being the automatic detection of high-level concepts in a video. However, this approach has been neither efficient nor effective enough. A second approach is to improve the query formulation schemes so that a user can accurately specify queries. However, as the performance of state-of-the-art systems indicates, interface designs are not advanced enough to provide users with facilities to enter their information needs. Hence, we argue that there is a need for more sophisticated interfaces to search for videos.

In this work, we proposed to adapt retrieval based on the user's interaction with video retrieval interfaces. In the text retrieval domain, the approach of interpreting the user's actions as implicit indicators of relevance turned out to be an effective method to increase retrieval performance. In the video retrieval domain, however, little is known about which implicit feedback can be used as implicit indicators of relevance. We focused on three questions: The first problem was which implicit feedback that a user provides can be considered as a positive indicator of relevance and can hence be used to adapt retrieval results. The second problem was how these features have to be weighted in order to increase retrieval performance. It is unclear which features are stronger and which are weaker indicators of relevance. Moreover, we argued that the users' evolving interest in multiple news aspects must be considered when capturing the users' interests.

We discussed different evaluation approaches to tackle this research problem, including performing a user study in order to analyze the user's interactions with a video retrieval system and simulating users by exploiting log files of the users' interactions with the system. As a basis of our research, we introduced NewsBoy, a Web-based news video retrieval system. NewsBoy captures and processes the daily BBC One O'Clock news bulletin and provides an interface to access this data. The introduced system can be seen as a medium which can be used to answer the introduced research questions.

Acknowledgment

This research was supported by the European Commission under the contract FP6-027026-K-SPACE.

Frank Hopfgartner is a doctoral candidate in information retrieval at the University of Glasgow, Scotland. He holds a Diplom-Informatik (2006) from the University of Koblenz-Landau, Germany. His research interests include interactive video retrieval with a main focus on relevance feedback and adaptive search systems. He is a member of the British Computer Society.

Joemon M. Jose is a reader at the Department of Computing Science, University of Glasgow, Scotland, and leader of the multimedia information retrieval group. He is interested in all aspects of information retrieval including theory, experimentation, evaluation, and applications in the textual and multimedia domain. His current research focuses around the following three themes: adaptive and personalized search systems; multimodal interaction for information retrieval; and multimedia mining and search. He is a member of the BCS, IET, ACM, and the IEEE Computer Society.

References

Arezki, R., P. Poncelet, G. Dray, and D. W. Pearson. (2004). Web information retrieval based on user profiles. In *Proceedings of Adaptive Hypermedia and Adaptive Web-Based Systems*, pp. 275–278. Berlin: Springer.

Bharat, K., T. Kamba, and M. Albers. (1998). Personalized, interactive news on the Web. *Multimedia Systems* 6(5): 349–358.

Boreczky, J. S., and L. A. Rowe. (1996). Comparison of video shot boundary detection techniques. In *Storage and Retrieval for Image and Video Databases (SPIE)*, pp. 170–179.

Browne, P., A. F. Smeaton, N. Murphy, N. O'Connor, S. Marlow, and C. Berrut. (2000). Evaluating and combining digital video shot boundary detection algorithms. In *IMVIP 2000: Proceedings of the Irish Machine Vision and Image Processing Conference*. Belfast, Northern Ireland.

Cai, D., X. He, J.-R. Wen, and W.-Y. Ma. (2004). Block-level link analysis. In *SIGIR '04: Proceedings of the 27th Annual International Conference on Research and Development in Information Retrieval*, pp. 440–447. New York: ACM Press.

Campbell, I. (1995). Supporting information needs by ostensive definition in an adaptive information space. In *MIRO '95: Workshops in Computing*. Berlin: Springer.

Campbell, I., and C. J. van Rijsbergen. (1996). The ostensive model of developing information needs. In *Proceedings of CoLIS-96, 2nd International Conference on Conceptions of Library Science*, pp. 251–268.

Campbell, M., A. Haubold, S. Ebadollahi, M. R. Naphade, A. Natsev, J. Seidl, J. R. Smith, J. Tešić, and L. Xie. (2006). IBM research TRECVID-2006 video retrieval system. In *TRECVID 2006: Text Retrieval Conference, TRECVID Workshop*, Gaithersburg, MD, November 2006.

Chang, S.-F., R. Manmatha, and T.-S. Chua. (2005). Combining text and audio-visual features in video indexing. In *ICASSP '05: Proceedings of Acoustics, Speech, and Signal Processing Conference*, pp. 1005–1008.

Chen, L. and K. Sycara. (1998). WebMate: A personal agent for browsing and searching. In K. P. Sycara and M. Wooldridge (Eds.), *Proceedings of the 2nd International Conference on Autonomous Agents (Agents '98)*, pp. 132–139. New York: ACM Press.

Claypool, M., P. Le, M. Wased, and D. Brown. (2001). Implicit interest indicators. In *Intelligent User Interfaces*, pp. 33–40.

Craswell, N., S. Robertson, H. Zaragoza, and M. Taylor. (2005). Relevance weighting for query independent evidence. In *SIGIR '05: Proceedings of the 28th Annual International*

ACM SIGIR conference on Research and Development in Information Retrieval, pp. 416– 423. New York: ACM Press.

Fagin, R., R. Kumar, K. S. McCurley, J. Novak, D. Sivakumar, J. A. Tomlin, and D. P. Williamson. (2003). Searching the workplace Web. In *WWW '03: Proceedings of the 12th International Conference on World Wide Web*, pp. 366–375. New York: ACM Press.

Finin, T. W. (1989). GUMS: A general user modeling shell. In A. Kobsa and W. Wahlster (Eds.), *User Models in Dialog Systems.* Berlin: Springer, pp. 411–430.

Foley, E., C. Gurrin, G. Jones, C. Gurrin, G. Jones, H. Lee, S. McGivney, N. E. O'Connor, S. Sav, A. F. Smeaton, and P. Wilkins. (2005). TRECVid 2005 experiments at Dublin City University. In *TRECVid 2005: Text Retrieval Conference, TRECVID Workshop*, Gaithersburg, MD.

Hancock-Beaulieu, M., and S. Walker. (1992). An evaluation of automatic query expansion in an online library catalogue. *Journal of Documentation* 48(4), 406–421.

Heesch, D., P. Howarth, J. Magalhães, A. May, M. Pickering, A. Yavlinski, and S. Rüger. (2004). Video retrieval using search and browsing. In *TREC2004: Text REtrieval Conference*, Gaithersburg, MD.

Hopfgartner, F. (2007). *Understanding Video Retrieval.* Saarbrücken, Germany: VDM Verlag.

Hopfgartner, F., and J. Jose. (2007). Evaluating the implicit feedback models for adaptive video retrieval. In *ACM MIR '07: Proceedings of the 9th ACM SIGMM International Workshop on Multimedia Information Retrieval*, pp. 323–332.

Hopfgartner, F., J. Urban, R. Villa, and J. Jose. (2007). Simulated testing of an adaptive multimedia information retrieval system. In *CBMI '07: Proceedings of the 5th International Workshop on Content-Based Multimedia Indexing*, pp. 328–335.

Hopfgartner, F., D. Hannah, N. Gildea, J. M. Jose. (2008). Capturing multiple interests in news video retrieval by incorporating the ostensive model. In *Proceedings of the Second International Workshop on Personalized Access, Profile Management, and Context Awareness in Databases,* Auckland, New Zealand, pp. 48–55, 08.

Hopfgartner, F., T. Urruty, R. Villa, N. Gildea, and J. M. Jose. (2008a). Exploiting log files in video retrieval. In *JCDL '08: Joint Conference on Digital Libraries.* p. 454, New York: ACM Press.

Huang, C.-W. (2003). Automatic closed-caption alignment based on speech recognition transcripts. *ADVENT Technical Report*, University of Columbia.

Jaimes, A., M. Christel, S. Gilles, S. Ramesh, and W.-Y. Ma. (2005). Multimedia information retrieval: What is it, and why isn't anyone using it? In *MIR '05: Proceedings of the 7th ACM SIGMM International Workshop on Multimedia Information Retrieval*, pp. 3–8. New York: ACM Press.

Joho, H., R. D. Birbeck, J. M. Jose. (2007). An ostensive browsing and searching on the Web. In *Proceedings of the 2nd International Workshop on Context-Based Information Retrieval*, pp. 81–92. Roskilde University Research Report.

Kelly, D., and J. Teevan. (2003). Implicit feedback for inferring user preference: A bibliography. *SIGIR Forum* 32(2).

Kraaij, W., T. Westerveld, and D. Hiemstra. (2002). The importance of prior probabilities for entry page search. In *SIGIR '02: Proceedings of the 25th Annual International ACM SIGIR Conference on Research and Development in Information Retrieval*, pp. 27–34. New York: ACM Press.

Lee, H., A. F. Smeaton, N. E. O'Connor, and B. Smyth. (2006). User evaluation of Físchlár-News: An automatic broadcast news delivery system. *ACM Transactions on Information Systems* 24(2), 145–189.

Morrison, S., and J. Jose. (2004). A comparative study of online news retrieval and presentation strategies. In *ISMSE '04: Proceedings of the IEEE Sixth International Symposium on Multimedia Software Engineering*, pp. 403–409. Washington, DC: IEEE Computer Society.

O'Toole, C., A. Smeaton, N. Murphy, and S. Marlow. (1999). Evaluation of automatic shot boundary detection on a large video test suite. In *Proceedings of Challenges in Image Retrieval*, Newcastle, U.K.

Pickering, M. J., L. Wong, and S. Rüger. (2003). ANSES: Summarisation of news video. *Image and Video Retrieval* 2788, 481–486.

Rautiainen, M., T. Ojala, and T. Seppänen. (2005). Content-based browsing in large news video databases. In *Proceedings of the 5th IASTED International Conference on Visualization, Imaging, and Image Processing*.

Robertson, S. E., S. Walker, S. Jones, M. Hancock- Beaulieu, and M. Gatford. (1994). Okapi at TREC-3. In *Proceedings of the Third Text Retrieval Conference (TREC 1994)*, Gaithersburg, MD.

Sebe, N., and Q. Tian. (2007). Personalized multimedia retrieval: The new trend? In *MIR '07: Proceedings of the International Workshop on Multimedia Information Retrieval*, pp. 299–306. New York: ACM Press.

Smeaton, A. F. (2002). The Físchlár Digital Library: Networked access to a video archive of TV news. In *TERENA Networking Conference 2002*, Limerick, Ireland.

Smeaton, A. F., P. Over, and W. Kraaij. (2006). Evaluation campaigns and TRECVID. In *MIR '06: Proceedings of the 8th ACM International Workshop on Multimedia Information Retrieval*, pp. 321–330. New York: ACM Press.

Snoek, C. G. M., M. Worring, D. C. Koelma, and A. W. M. Smeulders. (2007). A learned lexicon-driven paradigm for interactive video retrieval. *IEEE Transactions on Multimedia* 9(2), 280–292.

Snoek, C. G. M., M. Worring, J. van Gemert, J.-M. Geusebroek, D. Koelma, G. P. Nguyen, O. de Rooij, and F. Seinstra. (2005). MediaMill: Exploring news video archives based on learned semantics. In *Multimedia '05: Proceedings of the 13th Annual ACM International Conference on Multimedia*, pp. 225–226. New York: ACM Press.

Spink, A., H. Greisdorf, and J. Bateman. (1998). From highly relevant to not relevant: Examining different regions of relevance. *Information Processing Management* 34(5), 599–621.

Urban, J., J. M. Jose, and C. J. van Rijsbergen. (2003). An adaptive approach towards content-based image retrieval. In *Proceedings of the 3rd International Workshop on Content-Based Multimedia Indexing*, pp. 119–126.

Vallet, D., F. Hopfgartner, and J. Jose. (2008). Use of implicit graph for recommending relevant videos: A simulated evaluation. In *ECIR '08: Proceedings of the 30th European Conference on Information Retrieval*, pp. 199–210. Berlin: Springer.

White, R., M. Bilenko, and S. Cucerzan. (2007). Studying the use of popular destinations to enhance Web search interaction. In *ACM SIGIR '07: Proceedings of the 30th International ACM SIGIR Conference*, pp. 159–166. New York: ACM Press.

White, R., J. Jose, C. van Rijsbergen, and I. Ruthven. (2004). A simulated study of implicit feedback models. In *ECIR '04: Proceedings of the 26th European Conference on Information Retrieval Research*, pp. 311–326. Berlin: Springer.

White, R. W., J. M. Jose, and I. Ruthven. (2003). An approach for implicitly detecting information needs. In *CIKM '03: Proceedings of the 12th International Conference on Information and Knowledge Management*, pp. 504–507. New York: ACM Press.

Chapter 7

On Using Information Retrieval Techniques for Semantic Media Adaptation

Sébastien Laborie and Antoine Zimmermann

7.1 Introduction

The diversity of information on the World Wide Web increases extensively in terms of media types (texts, images, sounds, and videos), formats (e.g., avi, mpeg, jpeg, gif), and specific characteristics (e.g., quality, size). In this context, Internet access devices have to adapt continually to new technologies, which is true not only for desktop computers with their Web browsers but also for many new-generation mobile devices (e.g., laptops, PDAs, mobile phones, portable multimedia players). However, in spite of this evolution, some devices cannot execute specific medias, particularly emergent formats, because of hardware or software limitations (e.g., screen size, memory, bandwidth) or even user preferences (e.g., language, handicap).

In order to ensure universal access to information, a document complying with the target device constraints must be provided instead of the incompatible document. This chapter focuses on media item adaptation. To avoid ambiguity, we call a *media item* an atomic multimedia object such as a single picture or video.*

Usually, media item adaptation is performed by transforming the content of the media into a compatible one. Unfortunately, this is often time consuming, and adapting nascent technologies requires new implementations.

To overcome these limitations, our approach consists of replacing incompatible media items with compatible ones selected from a set of possible alternatives, using information retrieval techniques. Indeed, retrieving documents is fast, compared to some transformations, such as transcoding or transmoding. Furthermore, we argue that if these alternatives are found on the Web, which constantly evolves according to emergent technologies, our proposal takes advantage of the most recent formats with a single implementation.

Accordingly, we define an adaptation framework composed of several modules that interact with the World Wide Web. As a first step, media items available on the Web are indexed according to their descriptions. Then, the adaptation process consists of retrieving the most similar description of an adapted media item satisfying the target profile. Although this framework has not yet been implemented, we show that existing information retrieval techniques, particularly Web search engines, are already capable of promising—yet limited—results.

The World Wide Web is evolving into the Semantic Web (Berners-Lee et al. 2001), where annotations are even more expressive and may overcome heterogeneity or incompleteness of semantic descriptions. This could ensure a more accurate retrieval process. Our adaptation framework is still valid in this context because many existing Semantic Web technologies can be used to implement its modules.

The remainder of this chapter is articulated as follows. First, we present the related work and divide it into two parts: one concerning media adaptation (Section 7.2.1) and the other concerning existing technologies used to annotate and retrieve Semantic Web documents (Section 7.2.2). We then motivate our approach by providing concrete examples in Section 7.3. Section 7.4 presents the main adaptation architecture, including a description of each module, illustrated by examples. Section 7.5 details how currently developed Semantic Web technologies can be used within our adaptation mechanism. Possible limitations and open problematics are discussed in Section 7.6.

7.2 Related Work

7.2.1 Media Adaptation

A fair amount of research has been conducted on media item transformation and summarization: InfoPyramid (Smith et al. 1999) manages the different variations

---

* Other terms are media element, multimedia object, and media object.

of media items with different modalities and fidelities; NAC, a Negotiation and Adaptation Core (Lemlouma and Layaïda 2001) seeks to transform incompatible media items efficiently using predefined transcoding components; Asadi and Dufour (2004) use MPEG-21 resource adaptation tools; and Soetens and colleagues (2004) use Web services compositions for media transformation.

Unfortunately, these systems change a specific format into another specific format. As a result, an implementation must be conducted for each format. Moreover, the computation costs of media transformation are considerable for large data such as long videos and will overload low-capacity devices.

To avoid excessive response times, some multimedia description languages offer authors the capability of specifying explicit alternatives (e.g., Rousseau et al. 1999; Bulterman et al. 2005). However, doing so is rather cumbersome and must be conducted for each conceivable execution profile. Additionally, it cannot take advantage of a dynamically evolving network like the Web (e.g., if a referenced media item moves, it will not be accessible anymore, and the alternative will not work).

Similar to our approach, the work described in Zhang and Vines (2004) uses the World Wide Web to select the translation of the text from Chinese to English, and vice versa. More precisely, the approach uses Web-based search engines to automatically find probable translations by looking for the most frequent co-occurrences of terms. Nevertheless, it translates only words or small phrases, while one could need a summarized text or a new formulation of the text, which could be captured by a semantic annotation.

7.2.2 Semantic Information Retrieval and Description

This chapter particularly advertises the use of semantic technologies to enhance the retrieval of media alternatives. We herein describe existing techniques for representing, annotating, retrieving, and using semantic descriptions, especially in the context of the Semantic Web.

Several formalisms for semantically describing documents, particularly multimedia documents, are defined in the literature. Although RDF* (Manola and Miller 2004) is the W3C standard for providing semantic descriptions for any kind of resource, early Semantic Web information retrieval tools advertised the use of other formalisms, such as Conceptual Graphs in WebKB (Martin and Eklund 1999); OHTML, an extension of HTML, which embeds semantic annotations in Quest (Bar-Yossef et al. 1999); DAML+OIL (McGuiness et al. 2002), which predates the Web Ontology Language (OWL) (McGuiness and van Harmelen 2004) in OWLIR (Shah et al. 2002); and simple XML (Chinenyanga and Kushmerick 2002; Fuhr and Großjohann 2000; Egnor and Lord 2000).

---

* Resource Description Framework.

However, it is now clear that RDF has been accepted as the de facto standard for resource description in the Semantic Web. There are many ways of providing RDF descriptions for a resource. Most often, RDF metadata are found in separate XML files, but it is also possible to embed an RDF in other existing XML sub-languages such as SMIL* (Bulterman et al. 2005), MPEG-7 (Martínez 2004), or XHTML (McCarron et al. 2007). In particular, RDFa (Adida and Birbeck 2008) is an emerging standard from the W3C that allows implementing RDF descriptions within XHTML pages in a convenient way.

Nonetheless, for better interoperability, it is preferable to agree on a common vocabulary. For instance, a system may assume that all RDF descriptions conform to a common audiovisual ontology (Isaac and Troncy 2004). A more flexible approach would allow for the use of multiple ontologies, as presented in Isaac and Troncy (2005). In Section 7.5, we discuss more precisely the difficulties and possible solutions for dealing with heterogeneity.

Concerning semantic information retrieval, Swoogle (Ding et al. 2005) is one of the earliest Semantic Web search engines. More recent implementations of Semantic Web retrieval services are Watson (d'Aquin et al. 2007), which mainly indexes ontologies; Sindice (Tummarello et al. 2007), which offers links to the places where a resource is described (while not being able to actually query the documents themselves); DBpedia (Auer et al. 2007), which is in fact an "RDFized" version of Wikipedia;[†] and SWSE (Harth et al. 2007), a general-purpose Semantic Web search engine, which also indexes HTML files converted to RDF.

In order to motivate the use of information retrieval in the context of media adaptation, the next section presents several examples that show the appropriateness of our approach.

7.3 Motivating Examples

Consider a movie trailer, encoded in an AVI format, which is found online. This video can potentially be consulted by several Internet access devices, some of which, due to their profiles (i.e., technical characteristics or user preferences), are unable to execute the original media item. For example, in Figure 7.1, on the left-hand side, the desktop computer is able to play the movie trailer; however, on the right-hand side, the mobile phone profile indicates that no videos can be executed, while the PDA profile indicates that neither videos nor images can be played.

In order to execute the original media item on various platforms, this one must be adapted. A simple method to adapt media items could be to browse the Web and select an alternative media item that conforms to the target profile. For example, in Figure 7.1, the mobile phone may execute the movie poster that is related to the

---

* Synchronized Multimedia Integration Language.
† http://en.wikipedia.org.

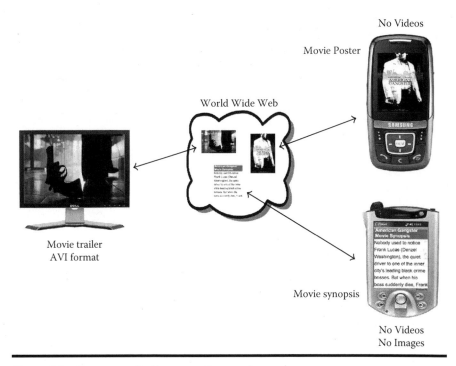

Figure 7.1   Access media items anytime and anywhere.

movie trailer, while the PDA may execute its movie synopsis. For most commercial movies, this information is easily found on the Web in several formats, especially on the movie studio's Web site. Other cases may arise when sharing images or videos of famous persons (e.g., Albert Einstein, Brad Pitt), masterpieces (e.g., Mona Lisa, The Last Supper), monuments (e.g., Eiffel Tower), sports events, and so on.

Using existing search engines, the Web contains many versions of the same information. For instance, we can find many media types, with various formats and characteristics, for the 2004 tsunami in Indonesia, as shown in Table 7.1. Whatever the target media type or characteristics, the response time is almost instantaneous. Obviously, this time does not take into account the selection of an appropriate solution, but a suitable result conveying that the initial information is found quickly.

Even if the media item is executable on the target, the profile may specify other constraints, such as language, content protection, or personal preferences, that necessitate adaptation. Our approach is still usable and effective in this context. Eventually, adaptation is also useful when, though the media item is executable, the end user is not satisfied and wants an alternative (e.g., finding different points of view, camera angles).

In the following section, we describe an architecture that takes advantage of the profusion and diversity of the content of the Web in order to adapt media information.

Table 7.1   Results Provided by Google Search Engines with the Query "Tsunami December 2004"

Media Type	Media Characteristic	Number of Results	Response Time
Videos[a]	All durations	171	0.025s
	>20 minutes	12	0.013s
	4–20 minutes	45	0.02s
	<4 minutes	104	0.027s
Images[b]	All sizes	77,200	0.03s
	Large	2,310	0.11s
	Medium	73,700	0.09s
	Small	2,720	0.1s
Text[c]	Any	1,540,000	0.23s
	English	1,230,000	0.23s
	French	39,700	0.21s
	Indonesian	76,200	0.37s

Source: Laborie & Zimmermann; "A Framework for Media Adaptation Using the Web and the Semantic Web"; *IEEE SMAP* 2007, 33–37. With permission.

[a] http://video.google.com.

[b] http://images.google.com.

[c] http://www.google.com.

7.4 A Framework for Media Adaptation

Our goal is to retrieve from the Web a media item that matches two requirements:

1. It must be executable on the target device (i.e., it must conform to the target profile).
2. It has to convey the same information as the original media item or at least provide a message as close as possible to the original one.

Figure 7.2 gives an overview of the framework. The top part of the figure is a simplified representation of the World Wide Web, where each media item is identified by a URI (m_1, m_2, etc.), including the initial one. Moreover, each description d_i refers to exactly one media item's URI. The descriptions may be Web pages, formal annotations, or automatically generated metadata available on the Web.

On the bottom part, we find the adaptation component that takes a source media URI and a target profile as input and produces as output a replacement media item that conforms to the profile. Its architecture uses four modules: (a), (b), (c) and (d). Each module and the overall component are detailed and exemplified in the following. Figure 7.3 presents a sample of the database's content.

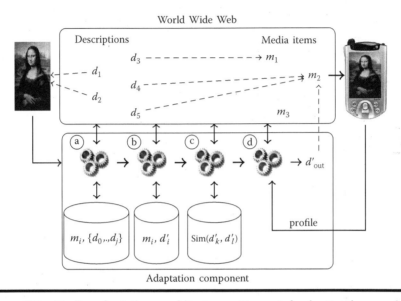

Figure 7.2 **Media adaptation architecture. (From Laborie & Zimmermann; "A Framework for Media Adaptation Using the Web and the Semantic Web"; *IEEE SMAP* 2007, 33–37. With permission.)**

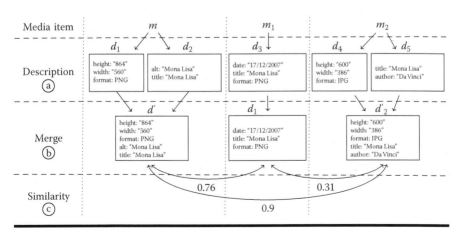

Figure 7.3 **An example of the content of the databases of each module.**

7.4.1 Description Association (a)

This module can be equated to the indexing processes of search engines. It is used to retrieve all the descriptions related to a particular media item. The descriptions are indexed and cached in a database, and constantly updated by automatic Web mining techniques. It may happen that a media item is related to several descriptions. More precisely, the index table associates to each media item's URI the set of descriptions that refers to it on the Web. The stored descriptions can be in any format as long as their structure can be understood by the next module.

> *Example*: An image search engine can index pictures according to their characteristics and textual annotations found on the source code of HTML files containing the picture. In particular, the attribute `alt` is an important feature for this indexing process. Possibly, the attribute `title` and the text surrounding the picture can be used too.
>
> Consider a Web page[*] that displays a photograph of the painting Mona Lisa by Leonardo da Vinci. It contains the following `img` HTML tag:
>
> ```
> <img src="monalisa.png" alt="Mona Lisa" title="Mona Lisa"/>
> ```
>
> This image, named *m* in Figure 7.3, is encoded in PNG format in resolution 560 × 864.[†] This media description corresponds to d_1 in Figure 7.3, while d_2 refers to the `alt` and `title` attributes, which serve as a textual description for the picture. In information retrieval systems, this textual information is internally represented as vector indexing terms with their frequency in the document and in the corpus (known as the tf-idf weighting scheme), according to the vector space model (Manning et al. 2007).

7.4.2 Description Aggregation (b)

This module takes a set of descriptions as input and produces a description that aggregates all of the information found in the input descriptions. This operation is needed because media annotations are usually poor individually, while merging them would enrich the media description. Data integration techniques used for this purpose can be as simple as concatenating textual descriptions or making an index of keywords, or they can be very elaborate database integration methods (Ziegler and Dittrich 2004). The aggregated descriptions are cached and updated as soon as a new description is found by the previous module or when an existing description is updated.

> *Example*: Although this module may not have an equivalent in existing search engines, it is easy to define the merge of two document vectors, particularly if it uses the tf-idf computation. Indeed, inverse document frequency is not affected

---

[*] The Web page is http://www.inrialpes.fr/exmo/people/zimmer/smap2007/monalisa.html.
[†] The picture URI is http://www.inrialpes.fr/exmo/people/zimmer/smap2007/monalisa.png.

by the merging operation because the number of terms in the corpus is preserved. However, term frequency strongly depends on the size of the textual document, so the merge has to take into account the relative size of both merged documents.

In our example, the merge is applied when two descriptions are referring to the very same URL within two different Web pages. Consider the media item m of Figure 7.3 associated with the descriptions d_1 and d_2. It is possible to group the descriptions into one single description, d', which contains all descriptions.

7.4.3 Description Similarity (c)

When media descriptions have been aggregated in such a way that only one unique description corresponds to a given media item, these have to be compared in order to find the most similar ones according to the input document. More precisely, a pairwise comparison using data or metadata similarities is computed for each pair of descriptions, and the results are cached too, and updated when an aggregated description changes. An example of a similarity measure applied on Web pages can be found in Broder and colleagues (1997).

> *Example*: While it does not clearly appear in typical Web search engines, this module is indeed almost always implemented in common information retrieval systems. In fact, with the vector space model described above, textual queries are treated in exactly the same way as textual documents; that is, their internal representation is a vector of terms and tf-idf weight. This way, in order to provide ranked results for the query, this vector is compared to the document vectors using a similarity measure. The most used measure is the cosine measure (Manning et al. 2007). In Web search engines, similarity is computed at query time because queries are freely written by the end users, so they are not known in advance. In our architecture, the query corresponds to the description of a given media item, which is also indexed. Therefore, all similarities can be calculated at indexing time, speeding up significantly the response time.
>
> In Figure 7.3, $Sim(d', d_1') = 0.76$ and $Sim(d', d_2') = 0.9$. Hence, the description d' related to the media item m is closer to the description d_2' corresponding to m_2 than to the description d_1' corresponding to m_1.

7.4.4 Description Selection (d)

This process selects the first description d'_{out} that conforms to the target device environment constraints and personal profile from among an ordered set of alternative media descriptions.

> *Example*: Results can be filtered using advanced Web search engines options or preferences. Google's search options allow selecting only particular images such as "medium images." Filters can also be applied to the format of the image: JPEG, GIF, TIFF, and so on. In most existing information retrieval systems, this is implemented as an ad hoc functionality.

7.4.5 Adaptation Component

The inputs of the overall component are the initial media URI and the target profile. The URI is used to retrieve the corresponding aggregated description d'_i from module (b). Then, it computes the list of aggregated descriptions ordered by similarity with d'_i. Finally, this ordered list and the target profile are sent to the last module, which returns a description that refers to the adapted media item (m_2 in Figure 7.2) that will be sent to the target device.

> *Example*: In order to find an alternative image on the Web, we could use a search engine by typing the content of the `alt` attribute—in our case, this attribute value is "Mona Lisa"—as the query, then select the results that match the constraints of the target device. This manual process is illustrated by Figure 7.4 and Figure 7.5, which are screenshots of the results of Google Image Search according to this query.[*]
>
> As you may notice in Figure 7.4, the first answer conveys the same message as the original one (i.e., both are the same paintings of Mona Lisa). However, for the same description and a different profile (small images), Figure 7.5 provides unsatisfactory results because even if there exists a small Mona Lisa image, the first results are completely different from the initial Mona Lisa image.

Even though the World Wide Web is vast and diverse, current descriptions about content available on the Web are heterogeneous, partial, and imprecise. Moreover, in the description above, we focused on textual descriptions, while more and more annotations are using semantics. Considering these issues, we believe

Figure 7.4 Mona Lisa medium images from Google Images. (From Laborie & Zimmermann; "A Framework for Media Adaptation Using the Web and the Semantic Web"; *IEEE SMAP* 2007, 33–37. With permission.)

---

[*] Note that Google results vary according to several factors, for instance, time, precise domain (.com, .co.uk, .fr, etc.), and user profile for people with a Google account.

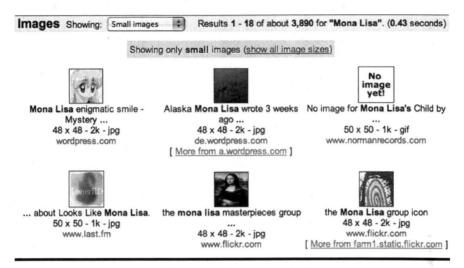

Figure 7.5 **Mona Lisa small images from Google Images. (From Laborie &
Zimmermann; "A Framework for Media Adaptation Using the Web and the
Semantic Web";** *IEEE SMAP* **2007, 33–37. With permission.)**

that using Semantic Web technologies would significantly improve our adaptation
mechanism by

- Adding expressivity (e.g., with RDF triples like `Da_Vinci is_a Painter`)
- Providing deductive capabilities (e.g., `Mona_Lisa was_painted by Da_Vinci` implies that `Mona_Lisa is_a Painting`)
- Solving heterogeneity problems (e.g., with assertions like `La_Gioconda same_as Mona_Lisa`)

The next section updates the description of our architecture by considering
Semantic Web technologies, such as RDF descriptions (Manola and Miller 2004),
ontologies, and ontology matching and merging, and it discusses new problems
posed by these techniques.

7.5 Media Adaptation by Semantic Web Retrieval

When media items are annotated with semantic descriptions, the selection of the
alternative media item can be far more accurate. In this section, we describe how
our framework could be implemented with currently developed Semantic Web
technologies. In particular, we refer to many existing works that would appropriately fit in with the architecture presented in Section 7.4. We use Figure 7.6 to
illustrate a possible scenario on the Semantic Web.

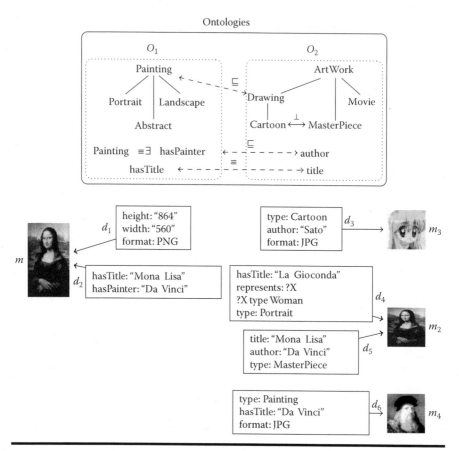

Figure 7.6 Media descriptions using Semantic Web technologies.

7.5.1 Scenario

First, we assume that media descriptions are now represented in RDF (Manola and Miller 2004) and use terminologies specified in OWL ontologies (McGuiness and van Harmelen 2004), as shown in Figure 7.6.* In this example, d_1 and d_2 describe the initial media item, from which we display a sample in Descriptions d_1 and d_2.

Descriptions d_1

```
<rdf:Description rdf:about="&ex;monalisa.png">
 <exif:height>864</exif:height>
 <exif:width>560</exif:width>
```

* The examples of RDF descriptions and OWL ontologies can be found at http://www.inrialpes.fr/exmo/people/zimmer/smap2007/monalisa.html.

```
<dc:format>PNG</dc:format>
</rdf:Description>
```

```
Description d₂
```

```
<rdf:Description rdf:about="&ex;monalisa.png">
 <O1:hasTitle>Mona Lisa</O1:hasTitle>
 <O1:hasPainter>Da Vinci</O1:hasPainter>
</rdf:Description>
```

Descriptions d_3, d_4, d_5, and d_6 refer to potential alternatives. Notice that the properties and concepts are defined in ontologies; hence, it allows inferring knowledge that is not explicitly written in the description. For instance, the axiom *Painting* ≡ ∃*hasPainter* in ontology O_1 means that if something has a painter, then it is a painting. and vice versa. Now, d_2 stipulates that the initial media item was painted by "Da Vinci." Therefore, the image is a painting. Furthermore, *Cartoon* ⊥ *MasterPiece* in O_2 signifies that *Cartoon* and *MasterPiece* are disjointed concepts. Thus, d_5 does not describe a cartoon.

In this scenario, the target device has a technical limitation that forbids it to display PNG files. Moreover, the user also specified a restriction in his personal profile, which imposes that only paintings are presented. In the next sections, we show that we can still use the same adaptation framework with these semantic descriptions, although with a different implementation.

7.5.2 Module (a)

A simple solution for indexing and retrieving Semantic Web documents resides in tokenizing RDF descriptions, after which they can be indexed and retrieved with classical IR techniques. In this case, the underlying semantics of the formalism is not exploited, but a preprocessing can be done in order to infer new knowledge before the tokenization process occurs. This method is algorithmically efficient but does not take enough advantage of the semantics of the descriptions. This process is described in Finin and colleagues (2005), where it is called *swangling*. In such situations, the other modules are the same as described previously.

A more accurate solution is to index real RDF descriptions, which allows for inferring at query time. Recently, several attempts to index Semantic Web documents on the Web were conducted. A Semantic Web search engine, such as Swoogle (Ding et al. 2005) and SWSE (Harth et al. 2007), automatically crawls the Web to index RDF descriptions, which can be retrieved. Among other services, it is possible to search by URI, so that all descriptions of a given resource can be retrieved. This is precisely what our framework needs for module (a).

7.5.3 Module (b)

The task of merging RDF descriptions of a single resource can be as simple as putting together all RDF descriptions by using the *RDF merge** operation, which merely consists of a set-theoretic union of RDF triples. The basic merge operation applied to our example would render the RDF/XML description as below.

RDF Merge of d_1 and d_2

```
<rdf:Description rdf:about="&ex;monalisa.png">
  <exif:height>864</exif:height>
  <exif:width>560</exif:width>
  <dc:format>PNG</dc:format>
  <O1:hasTitle>Mona Lisa</O1:hasTitle>
  <O1:hasPainter>Da Vinci</O1:hasPainter>
</rdf:Description>
```

However, in many cases, this notion of merging is not satisfactory. For instance, descriptions d_4 and d_5 refer to the same media item and yet use a different terminology. Still, we can intuitively assume that *hasTitle* and *title* have the same meaning. Therefore, an equivalence relation could be asserted to solve this heterogeneity problem. In addition, other relations may exist between two ontologies, such as subsumption (e.g., a *Painting* in O_1 is a kind of *Drawing* in O_2) because two ontologies, however different, may describe the same domain of knowledge. In order to reason simultaneously with descriptions from different ontologies, it is necessary to discover and define the semantic relationships that exist between multiple ontologies. This activity is called *ontology matching* (Euzenat and Shvaiko 2007). Matching ontologies results in an ontology alignment (i.e., a set of correspondences between terms). They are represented as dashed arrows in Figure 7.6 and as an RDF/XML-rendered alignment format (Euzenat 2004) in the example below.[†]

Sample Alignment between O_1 and O_2

```
<Alignment>
  <xml>yes</xml>
  <level>0</level>
  <type>**</type>
  <onto1>&O1;</onto1>
  <onto2>&O2;</onto2>
```

---

[*] A definition of an RDF merge can be found at http://www.w3.org/TR/2001/WD-rdf-mt-20010925/#merging.

[†] The example alignment is defined in http://www.inrialpes.fr/exmo/people/zimmer/smap2007/alignment.rdf.

```
<map>
  <Cell>
    <entity1 rdf:resource="&O1;Painting"/>
    <entity2 rdf:resource="&O2;Drawing"/>
    <measure rdf:datatype="&xsd;float">1.0</measure>
    <relation>subClassOf</relation>
  </Cell>
  <Cell>
    <entity1 rdf:resource="&O1;hasPainter"/>
    <entity2 rdf:resource="&O2;author"/>
    <measure rdf:datatype="&xsd;float">1.0</measure>
    <relation>subPropertyOf</relation>
  </Cell>
  <Cell>
    <entity1 rdf:resource="&O1;hasTitle"/>
    <entity2 rdf:resource="&O2;title"/>
    <measure rdf:datatype="&xsd;float">1.0</measure>
    <relation>=</relation>
  </Cell>
</map>
</Alignment>
```

In our case, they are used to adequately merge individual descriptions. A basic yet efficient way to implement module (b) is to unify terms that have been proved equivalent by a distributed reasoner and then apply a simple RDF merge. In the general case, there are several possible ways to merge data, and a proper merging tool still has to be defined.

7.5.4 Module (c)

Computing similarities is also quite difficult when comparing heterogeneous semantic descriptions. Examples of similarity measures for comparing ontology-based metadata can be found in Maedche and Zacharias (2002). Also, semantic similarities are defined for comparing terms of ontologies, for instance with the algorithm OLA (Euzenat and Valtchev 2004). These existing technologies can correctly implement module (c). More precisely, the similarity between two individuals is usually computed by evaluating and combining the similarities of their attributes and properties.

In the example shown in Figure 7.6, the attribute values of *hasTitle* of d_2, d_4, and d_6 can be directly compared and are quite different. This will decrease the similarity. Conversely, d_2, d_4, and d_6 all imply that the pictures are paintings, which should increase the similarity. Indeed, according to ontology O_1, something that has a painter is a painting, and all portraits are paintings. Until now, nothing allows the system to discriminate between m_2 and m_4. However, a correspondence asserts that *hasTitle* is equivalent to *title*, so the two attributes can be compared. Therefore,

d_2 and d_5 will be quite similar because of their titles. As a result, the merging of d_4 and d_5 will have a high overall similarity with the merged description $d_1 \oplus d_2$, whereas the similarity of d_6 with $d_1 \oplus d_2$ will be assessed as lower because the title does not match. Finally, the similarity of d_3 with $d_1 \oplus d_2$ will be quite low because they do not have much in common. Consequently, m_2 will most likely be preferred to the other ones.

7.5.5 Module (d)

Finally, the filter module (d) can select the adapted media item not only according to its technical specification but also according to its semantic description. For instance, if the target has a content protection, only media items that are asserted to be nonviolent would be retained. Likewise, as specified in our scenario in Section 7.5.1, the target profile stipulates that only paintings must be presented and PNG files are forbidden. This kind of profile may be detailed in a Composite Capability/Preference Profiles (CC/PP) description (Klyne et al. 2001), which extends RDF vocabulary for describing user preferences or device characteristics. In turn, CC/PP can be extended to specify the profiles of a certain device, such as UAProf (WAG 2001). This again may require ontology matching techniques if the profile is not encoded with the same vocabulary as the media description.

In Figure 7.6, m_2 is described as a Portrait in d_4, which is a kind of Painting according to ontology O_1, and m_4 is de facto a Painting. Hence, these pictures would be candidate adaptation solutions. Besides, m_3 is a Cartoon and cannot be proved to be a Painting. Therefore, the filter module will discard this media item. Finally, as stated above, module (c) computed a higher similarity for m_2 than for m_4, so the former will be retained as the adaptation solution.

In summation, all of the presented modules can be adapted to the Semantic Web using technologies that are either implemented or on the verge of being so. Nevertheless, the framework we have presented has some limitations and raises several issues that we discuss in the next section.

7.6 Discussion

As we pointed out in Section 7.3, it is useful to find media item alternatives on the Web in some relevant circumstances. Nonetheless, it may happen that no appropriate alternative can be retrieved. For instance, it is disputable that a relevant replacement for personal data (e.g., family photographs), small events, or uncommon objects would be found at all on the Web.

In such a case, a media transformation technique certainly leads to better results. However, more and more personal media items are now stored on publicly available Web sites like Flickr* or Picasa† for pictures and Youtube,‡ Dailymotion,§ or Metacafe¶ for videos; not to mention personal weblogs.

Yet, if an implementation uses a URL to identify pictures, it is most likely that very few descriptions will refer to the same media item, because pictures are usually duplicated when reused in Web pages. For this reason, URIs must be kept different from URLs, and descriptions referring to different URLs can in fact annotate the same URI. Indeed, identical images with different URLs can be spotted by computing their checksum. These images would receive the same URI, which would enrich the merged description.

Another critical issue for which our method would probably not offer the best solution is the problem of multimedia document adaptation. In multimedia, the different media items composing a document are generally connected temporally, spatially, rhetorically, or semantically. For that matter, other adaptation frameworks, such as presented by Laborie and colleagues (2007), are better adapted. By contrast, replacing media items individually would most likely destroy the articulation of the author's discourse. This issue is therefore left to some further investigation.

Furthermore, it is still unclear how the Semantic Web version of our approach would perform concretely, because most of the works mentioned in this chapter are still preliminary when it comes to implementation. Some of them do not even have a prototype, while others, though fully developed, are still lacking large-scale test cases. In any case, it is expected that semantics-based retrieval techniques will operate at least as well as fully syntactic systems.

Ultimately, our last but not least self-criticism is about copyright issues. Indeed, while the author or sender of the original media item is responsible for choosing an adequate media, our fully automatic approach might carelessly select an authored item that should not be transmitted to any target individuals. Again, if copyright annotations are attached to candidate media items (e.g., Creative Commons), the filter module would easily discriminate copyrighted elements.

7.7 Conclusion

In this chapter, we proposed a novel approach for adapting medias using information retrieval techniques. In particular, we devised an architecture that uses the World Wide Web's diversity and profusion to adapt media items. We also used Semantic Web technologies to deal with semantic gaps, heterogeneity, and partial descriptions, thus improving this adaptation framework.

---

* http://www.flickr.com.
† http://picasa.google.com.
‡ http://www.youtube.com.
§ http://www.dailymotion.com.
¶ http://www.metacafe.com.

We showed that existing Web-based technologies can already implement an efficient system in terms of computational time. We also envisioned how current Semantic Web technologies nearly accomplish with accuracy the task that we motivated here.

As a future development, this framework could be implemented as a Web service, while environment constraints (profiles) may be defined using CC/PP (Klyne et al. 2001), ontologies based on OWL, and descriptions written in RDF. Another interesting prospect that we envisage is to broadcast several alternatives that are sufficiently close to an initial description, *even when there is no initial media item*, because this framework is used to discover alternative media items according to the proximity of their description to the original media description. This can be paralleled with the act of automatically generating a document according to a description. Last, this framework could be integrated into a more general multimedia adaptation system mixing semantic media adaptation with structural and compositional adaptations.

Sébastien Laborie acquired his PhD in computer science at Joseph Fourier University, Grenoble, France. His thesis topic, semantic adaptation of multimedia documents, is at the crossroads of multimedia document interpretation, language semantics, and device adaptation. His recent research interests are related to using semantic Web technologies in multimedia content. His research findings have been published widely in edited books and he has presented his work at several international conferences including some hosted by the IEEE and ACM.

Antoine Zimmermann is a doctoral candidate in computer science at Joseph Fourier University, Grenoble, France. The topic of his thesis concerns the semantics of networked knowledge. His research interests include distributed knowledge representation and reasoning, ontology modularity, and Semantic Web technologies. He has published his research findings in the proceedings of prestigious international conferences and actively participated in European projects.

References

Ben Adida and Mark Birbeck. (2008). RDFa primer: embedding structured data in web pages. W3C working draft, World Wide Web Consortium. http://www.w3.org/TR/xhtml-rdfa-primer/.

Mariam Kimiaei Asadi and Jean-Claude Dufourd. (2004). Knowledge-based and semantic adaptation of multimedia content. In *Knowledge-Based Media Analysis for Self-Adaptive and Agile Multimedia Technology*, pp. 285–293.

Sören Auer, Christian Bizer, Georgi Kobilarov, Jens Lehmann, Richard Cyganiak, and Zachary G. Ives. (2007). Dbpedia: A nucleus for a web of open data. In Karl Aberer, Key-Sun Choi, Natasha Fridman Noy et al., editors, *The Semantic Web, 6th International Semantic Web Conference, 2nd Asian Semantic Web Conference, ISWC*

2007 + ASWC 2007, Busan, Korea, November 11–15, 2007, vol. 4825 of Lecture Notes in Computer Science, pp. 722–735. Berlin: Springer.

Ziv Bar-Yossef, Yaron Kanza, Yakov A. Kogan, Werner Nutt, and Yehoshua Sagiv. (1999). Querying semantically tagged documents on the World-Wide Web. In *NGIT '99: Proceedings of the 4th International Workshop on Next Generation Information Technologies and Systems*, pp. 2–19. Berlin: Springer.

Tim Berners-Lee, James Hendler, and Ora Lassila. (2001). The Semantic Web. *Scientific American*, 284(5): 34–43.

Andrei Z. Broder, Steven C. Glassman, Mark S. Manasse, and Geoffrey Zweig. (1997). Syntactic clustering of the Web. *Computer Networks and ISDN Systems*, 29(8–13): 1157–1166.

Dick Bulterman, Guido Grassel, Jack Jansen, Antti Koivisto, Nabil Layaïda, Thierry Michel, Sjoerd Mullender, and Daniel Zucker. (2005). Synchronized Multimedia Integration Language (SMIL 2.1). World Wide Web Consortium. http://www.w3.org/TR/SMIL2/.

Taurai Tapiwa Chinenyanga and Nicholas Kushmerick. (2002). An expressive and efficient language for XML information retrieval. *Journal of the American Society for Information Science and Technology*, 53(6): 438–453.

Mathieu d'Aquin, Claudio Baldassarre, Laurian Gridinoc, Sofia Angeletou, Marta Sabou, and Enrico Motta. (2007). Watson: A gateway for next generation Semantic Web applications. In *Poster Session of the International Semantic Web Conference, ISWC 2007*.

Li Ding, Rong Pan, Tim Finin, Anupam Joshi, Yun Peng, and Pranam Kolari. (2005). Finding and ranking knowledge on the Semantic Web. In *Proceedings of the 4th International Semantic Web Conference*, LNCS 3729, pp. 156–170. Berlin: Springer.

Daniel Egnor and Robert Lord. (2000). Structured information retrieval using XML. http://www.haifa.il.ibm.com/sigir00-xml/final-papers/Egnor/index.html.

Jérôme Euzenat. (2004). An API for ontology alignment. In *Proceedings of the 3rd International Semantic Web Conference*, vol. 3298 of LNCS, pp. 698–712. Berlin: Springer.

Jérôme Euzenat and Pavel Shvaiko. (2007). *Ontology matching*. Heidelberg: Springer.

Jérôme Euzenat and Petko Valtchev. (2004). Similarity-based ontology alignment in OWL-Lite. In Ramon López de Mantaras and Lorenza Saitta, editors, *Proceedings of the 16th European Conference on Artificial Intelligence*, pp. 333–337. Amsterdam: IOS Press.

Tim Finin, James Mayfield, Anupam Joshi, R. Scott Cost, and Clay Fink. (2005). Information retrieval and the Semantic Web. In *HICSS '05: Proceedings of the 38th Annual Hawaii International Conference on System Sciences*, Track 4, p. 113.1. Washington, DC: IEEE Computer Society.

Norbert Fuhr and Kai Großjohann. (2000). XIRQL: An extension of XQL for information retrieval. In Ricardo Baeza-Yates, Norbert Fuhr, Ron Sacks-Davis, and Ross Wilkinson, editors, *Proceedings of the SIGIR 2000 Workshop on XML and Information Retrieval*. New York: ACM Press. http://www.haifa.il.ibm.com/sigir00-xml/index.html.

Andreas Harth, Aidan Hogan, Renaud Delbru, Jürgen Umbrich, Sean O'Riain, and Stefan Decker. (2007). SWSE: Answers before links! http://www.cs.vu.nl/ pmika/swc-2007/SWSE.pdf.

Antoine Isaac and Raphal Troncy. (2004). Designing and using an audio-visual description core ontology. In Aldo Gangemi and Stefano Borgo, editors, *Workshop on Core Ontologies in Ontology Engineering*, vol. 118.

Antoine Isaac and Raphal Troncy. (2005). Using several ontologies for describing audio-visual documents: A case study in the medical domain. In Paola Hobson, Yiannis Kompatsiaris, John Davies, and Ant Miller, editors, *Workshop on Multimedia and the Semantic Web*.

Graham Klyne, Franklin Reynolds, Chris Woodrow, Hidetaka Ohto, Johan Hjelm, Mark H. Butler, and Luu Tran. (2001). Composite Capability/Preference Profiles (CC/PP): Structure and Vocabularies 1.0. World Wide Web Consortium. http://www.w3.org/TR/CCPP-struct-vocab/.

Sébastien Laborie, Jérôme Euzenat, and Nabil Layaïda. (2007). Multimedia document summarization based on a semantic adaptation framework. In *Proceedings of the International Workshop on Semantically Aware Document Processing and Indexing*, pp. 87–94. New York: ACM Press.

Sébastien Laborie and Antoine Zimmermann. (2007). A framework for media adaptation using the Web and the Semantic Web. *IEEE*, 33–37.

Tayeb Lemlouma and Nabil Layaïda. (2001). The negotiation of multimedia content services in heterogeneous environments. In *Proceedings of the 8th International Conference on Multimedia Modeling*, pp. 187–206. Amsterdam: IOS Press.

Alexander Maedche and Valentin Zacharias. (2002). Clustering ontology-based metadata in the semantic web. In *Proceedings of the 6th European Conference on Principles of Data Mining and Knowledge Discovery*, pp. 348–360. London: Springer.

Christopher D. Manning, Prabhakar Raghavan, and Hinrich Shütze. (2007). *An Introduction to Information Retrieval*. New York: Cambridge University Press, pp. 109–133.

Frank Manola and Eric Miller. (2004). RDF Primer. World Wide Web Consortium. http://www.w3.org/RDF/.

Philippe Martin and Peter Eklund. (1999). Embedding knowledge in Web documents. *Computer Networking*, 31(11–16): 1403–1419.

José M. Martínez. (2004). MPEG-7 Overview v.10. ISO/IEC JTC1/SC29/WG11/N6828. http://www.chiariglione.org/mpeg/standard/mpeg-7/mpeg-7.htm.

Shane McCarron, Masayasu Ishikawa, and Murray Altheim. (2007). XHTML 1.1: Module-based XHTML, Second Edition. W3C recommendation, World Wide Web Consortium. http://www.w3.org/TR/xhtml11/.

Deborah L. McGuinness, Richard Fikes, James Hendler, and Lynn Andrea Stein. (2002). DAML + OIL: An ontology language for the Semantic Web. *IEEE Intelligent Systems*, 17(5): 72–80.

Deborah L. McGuinness and Frank van Harmelen. (2004). OWL Web Ontology Language Overview. World Wide Web Consortium. http://www.w3.org/TR/owl-features/.

Franck Rousseau, J. Antonio García-Marcías, José Valdeni de Lima, and Andrzej Duda. (1999). User adaptable multimedia presentations for the World Wide Web. In *Proceedings of the 8th International Conference on World Wide Web*, pp. 1273–1290. Elsevier.

Urvi Shah, Tim Finin, and Anupam Joshi. (2002). Information retrieval on the Semantic Web. In *CIKM '02: Proceedings of the 11th International Conference on Information and Knowledge Management*, pp. 461–468, New York: ACM Press.

John R. Smith, Rakesh Mohan, and Chung-Sheng Li. (1999). Scalable multimedia delivery for pervasive computing. In *Proceedings of the 7th ACM International Conference on Multimedia (Part 1)*, pp. 131–140. New York: ACM Press.

Peter Soetens, Matthias De Geyter, and Stijn Decneut. (2004). Multi-step media adaptation with Semantic Web services. In *Proceedings of the 3rd International Semantic Web Conference*, Hiroshima.

Giovanni Tummarello, Renaud Delbru, and Eyal Oren. (2007). Sindice.com: Weaving the open linked data. In Karl Aberer, Key-Sun Choi, Natasha Fridman Noy et al., editors, *The Semantic Web, 6th International Semantic Web Conference, 2nd Asian Semantic*

Web Conference, ISWC 2007 + ASWC 2007, Busan, Korea, November 11–15, 2007, vol. 4825 of Lecture Notes in Computer Science, pp. 552–565. Berlin: Springer.

Wireless Application Protocol Forum. (2001). WAG UAProf. http://www.openmobilealliance. org/tech/affiliates/wap/wap-248-uaprof-20011020-a.pdf.

Ying Zhang and Phil Vines. (2004). Using the Web for automated translation extraction in cross-language information retrieval. In *Proceedings of the 27th Annual International ACM SIGIR Conference on Research and Development in Information Retrieval*, pp. 162–169. New York: ACM Press.

Patrick Ziegler and Klaus R. Dittrich. (2004). Three decades of data integration: All problems solved? In *IFIP Congress Topical Sessions*, pp. 3–12. Toulouse, France: Kluwer.

Chapter 8

Interactive Video Browsing of H.264 Content Based on Just-in-Time Analysis

Klaus Schöffmann and Laszlo Böszörmenyi

8.1 Introduction

With the rapid dispersion of video technology, not only are the number of videos but also the areas of their usage growing fast. Besides entertainment, a large number of application domains, such as learning, health care support, and disaster management, rely increasingly on audiovisual material. A common characteristic of these emerging applications is that videos are not just watched sequentially. We are often not interested in the entire movie; rather, we need to find certain video segments as fast as possible. An important special case is that we want to be able to identify a video we do *not* need quickly. Tools for efficient and user-friendly navigation both in video archives and inside of single videos are urgently required.

Even modern soft video players operate in a manner as invented for traditional VCR devices in the 1960s, mainly for entertainment. They provide such well-known interaction features as play, pause, stop, and fast-forward/backward. Additionally, they usually offer a timeline that allows more or less (rather less) precise jumping to a particular point in time within a video. In a large user test with 200 persons, researchers [5] found that the preferred method for browsing a video with a VCR-like control set in order to find a specific part is the *speed-switching* technique, followed by simple *straight viewing.* Speed-switching is browsing a video sequentially by using different playback speeds (e.g., fast-forward and play). However, even with techniques like speed-switching, finding a specific segment within a large video file remains a difficult and time-consuming task.

A lot of research has already been done in the area of *video abstraction* (also called *video summarization*) to improve the interactivity of digital video. The purpose of video abstraction is to create a short summary of a long video. While video abstraction is mainly used to facilitate browsing of large video databases, video abstracts can also enable nonlinear navigation within a single video sequence. However, video abstracts do not provide a level of interaction, as required in many applications.

In this chapter, we present the architecture and implementation of a flexible tool that enables efficient, powerful, and interactive navigation in video data.

An important aspect of our tool is that video analysis is performed on compressed data only and thus can be done very fast. Video files are usually stored in a compressed form, and not only video encoding but also video decoding requires high processing power; operating on compressed data is therefore a significant advantage from the efficiency point of view. Although content analysis in the pixel domain (i.e., on decompressed data) will usually produce better results, the preprocessing time and memory required for decoding are often not available.

Beyond its simple interaction mode, which is similar to a common video player, our tool provides features such as (1) skimming roughly through the video, (2) watching an on-demand-created video abstract/skim of a particular sequence or of the entire video, and (3) several presentation modes of different scenes in parallel in time and/or in space. Moreover, the tool allows users to efficiently extract representative parts of the video (e.g., key frames) and to dynamically switch between several presentation modes. Instead of enforcing any "best" presentation mode or limiting the navigation interface to either some genres or content features, we expect the user to know which content feature is the most appropriate one to support his or her browsing task ideally.

8.2 Related Work

Several approaches for video browsing have been presented. Most of them use *shots* as a base unit of navigation.

Arman and colleagues [2] proposed to use the concept of *key-frames* (denoted as *Rframes* in their work), which are representative frames of shots, for browsing the content of a video sequence. In their approach, key-frames are extracted by using content-based analysis of motion, shape, and color. Zhong and colleagues [7] proposed a hierarchical shot clustering method based on color histograms and the K-means algorithm. Moraveji [14] showed that using feature-based *color bars* in the timeline of a standard video player can significantly improve the subjective task of content-based seeking. Similar to that work, Barbieri and colleagues [3] have recommended using a *color-slider* that conveys the dominant background color of a shot. The concept of the *ZoomSlider* was proposed by Hurst and Jarvers [8] to overcome the scalability problem of standard time-sliders. Liu and colleagues [13] used automatic text extraction methods to improve content browsing of news videos. Truong and Venkatesh [18] considered two basic forms of video abstracts: key-frames and video skims. Komlodi and Marchionini [10] revealed in their user study that key-frame approaches such as storyboards are still the preferred methods for seeking, even if additional time is required to interact with the user interface (scroll bars) and for eye movements. Dynamic approaches such as slideshows often display the content with a fixed frame rate and do not allow the user to adjust it. An alternative approach to the linear storyboard display is to present key-frames in a layered/hierarchical manner [17]. At the top level, a single key-frame represents the entire video, whereas the number of key-frames is increased at each level. If additional semantic information is extracted (e.g., an *importance score*), key-frames may be displayed in different sizes, drawing the user's attention to important key-frames in the first place [20,19]. These scores can also be applied to dynamic approaches to adjust the playback speed, skipping unimportant scenes. Similar to our approach, Divakaran and colleagues [6] take advantage of information extracted from the compressed domain of the video. Their approach is based on the hypothesis that the intensity of motion activity is a measure of the summarizability. To skip over less interesting parts (i.e., parts of the video with low-motion activity), the playback rate is adjusted dynamically. In most approaches, the basic units are shots, but often we are interested in all of the shots belonging to the same topic (i.e., semantic units). Divakaran and colleagues propose analyzing the audio channel to detect speaker changes and generate a list of topics afterward. The proposed video content analysis of S. Lee and colleagues [12] is also similar to ours. It detects shot boundaries, selects an appropriate set of key-frames, and generates XML-based metadata describing the video content. Their metadata do not conform to any accepted standard (such as MPEG-7); therefore, the interoperability with other systems is not guaranteed. Besides, only MPEG-1 and MPEG-2 are supported, and their approach is restricted to utilizing key-frames to summarize video content.

As concluded in Truong and Venkatesh [18], the optimal visualization of summarized content remains an open question. The lack of a consistent evaluation framework is a common complaint, leading to proprietary evaluation methods in the different visualization approaches. Starting in 2003, the TRECVID evaluation meetings [16] (which were already part of TREC [1] in 2001 and 2002) focus on content-based retrieval from digital video via open, metrics-based evaluation.

Although there has been a lot of work in that area, existing methods/solutions for video browsing lack interactive navigation in combination with a flexible presentation of the content, as we suggest. Furthermore, many solutions are based on features extracted from the pixel domain, which is a significant performance drawback if used for on-demand (i.e., on-the-fly) scenarios.

8.3 System Architecture

This section describes the system architecture used by our video browsing tool.

8.3.1 Overview

As shown in Figure 8.1, the first step in our video browsing system is the segmentation of a video into basic units, which in our case are shots. The segmentation information (i.e., the frame at which a shot has been detected and the length of that shot) is stored in an MPEG-7 file. The *unit classification* step performs some further content analysis and extracts several low-level features for each frame (for details, see Section 8.5). For all the frames of a shot, the per-frame values of one particular feature are summed up and divided by the number of frames in that shot in order to compute an average feature value for one shot and one feature. This average value is used as an importance score for a shot (related to one particular feature) and added to the MPEG-7 file. For every shot, the frame with the highest feature value is selected to be the representative frame for that shot (respectively for each feature). The frame numbers of selected representative frames are also stored in the MPEG-7 file.

The visualization component uses the MPEG-7 file for three purposes: (1) to split up the entire content into shots, (2) to prioritize shots (i.e., to sort the shots based on their importance score according to a feature selected by the user), and (3) to present

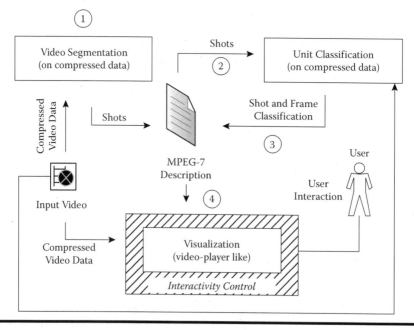

Figure 8.1   Overview of the system architecture.

a representative frame for each shot. The *interactivity control* component is responsible for changing the visualization of the content according to the user input.

8.3.2 Video Segmentation

The first step is a video segmentation process, which is used to find the elementary units (i.e., *shots*) in the entire video sequence (see Figure 8.1). As an output, a list of shot boundaries is returned, specified in an MPEG-7-compliant format. Since this segmentation is done in an on-demand fashion (e.g., when a user opens a video file), it must operate in a very efficient (fast) way. Schöffmann and Böszörmenyi [15] describe an efficient shot-detection algorithm that can be used for fast video segmentation because it operates in the early stages of the compressed domain. It is targeted on H.264/AVC, the most recent state-of-the-art video coding standard used in practice today. The proposed algorithm has been shown to work reliably for different encoders and to produce sufficiently exact results. Furthermore, it is approximately 5 to 10 times faster than just decoding the video file. This fast operation makes it perfectly suited for an on-demand video segmentation as needed by the tool described in this chapter.

8.3.3 Unit Classification

The aim of the unit classification process is to rate the importance of single units (these are shots and representative frames) in the video. Thus, based on the shot boundaries detected by the video segmentation process, it calculates an importance score for each shot and each frame. The result is an importance value for each unit, which is further used by the visualization component to structure the segmented content of a video.

In principle, several well-known low-level features that can be calculated from the pixel data can be used for that classification step (e.g., motion activity, color layout, scalable color, color histograms). However, if the aimed use case of the video browsing tool is operation in an on-demand fashion, where the video being browsed is accessed by the tool for the first time, an intensive content analysis based on pixel data is often impossible due to the following conflicting reasons:

- The predominant part of digital videos is stored in a compressed form (e.g., MPEG-1/2, MPEG-4, H.264).
- Thus, obtaining the pixel data can be expensive in both time and memory.
- The low-level feature extraction itself can be very time consuming (e.g., for motion activity).
- Especially for the purpose of on-demand video browsing, where users may not know exactly what the searched scene looks like, users prefer a highly interactive tool with immediate feedback (and maybe somewhat limited precision) instead of a highly precise but computation-intensive tool that causes long waiting times.

Therefore, instead of using a complex but precise low-level feature extraction from the pixel domain, we use features directly available from the compressed domain. In the case of the H.264/AVC encoding, the set of these features is unusually rich and can therefore assist users who are performing astonishingly "intelligent" search operations. Section 8.5 discusses the feature extraction from the compressed data in more detail.

8.3.4 Visualization and Interactivity

The visualization and interactivity module uses the results of the segmentation and classification processes. It is the most important part of our architecture because it is the interface to the user. There are three (partly conflicting) goals for the user interface: *simplicity*, *flexibility*, and *interactivity*. While our tool should be able to be used in a similar manner to common video player software, it should also provide the possibility of flexible searching and concisely imparting the content. It should enable rich interactivity to the end user. Furthermore, the tool should be applicable to a large set of different video genres (e.g., news, documentaries, sports, trailers). The details are described in Section 8.4.

8.4 Interactive User Interface

Because of the requirements mentioned above, we have decided to provide three basic navigation modes (views). These views have in common that the content is displayed in a page-based, matrix-aligned arrangement, whereas the size of the matrix (columns × rows) can be specified by the user. In the example given in Figure 8.2, the user has chosen a 4 × 4 display, where 16 *video windows* are shown simultaneously. Every window acts as an entry point into the video and shows a preview image (i.e., a key-frame) of its content. The selection of the key-frame is based on the importance score calculated by the unit classification process. Every window contains time information, which shows the relative position of the current frame to the entire video, and a time-slider to move quickly forward or backward in the selected video window. In any view, the user is allowed to start one or several video windows, increase or decrease the playback rate of one particular video window, perform ascending or descending sorting of the video windows, or switch a video window to full-screen mode. When several video windows are in playback mode, we use the mouse pointer to select which window should get the audio/sound focus. In the following, let us consider the individual features in detail. Note that even though these are really low-level features, in interactive usage they can lead to semantically rich results.

8.4.1 Chronological Shot Navigation

In this navigation mode, all detected shots of the entire video are displayed in chronological order, as illustrated in Figure 8.2. If the number of shots exceeds

Figure 8.2 **Chronological view of shots.**

the number of displayed video windows, buttons for page navigation (forward/backward) are displayed.

This navigation mode is useful for quickly browsing through the whole video sequence in a sequential manner. It is especially useful if the searched scene is expected to be either at the beginning or at the end. If, for example, we are looking for the result of a competition, it is obvious that it is somewhere at the end. Applying the chronological view in reverse order gives the result immediately.

8.4.2 Feature-Based Shot Navigation

Feature-based shot navigation is somewhat similar to chronological shot navigation. However, the shots are sorted not in relation to time but in relation to an importance score of the selected feature. The user can switch between several different features and thereby determine which shots are displayed at the beginning of the shot list. In our current prototype, the importance score is calculated by the unit classification process based on the features described in Section 8.5.

Feature-based navigation is useful in situations where the user has some knowledge of what the scene looks like (e.g., the scene is very dark, there is a zoom, there

Figure 8.3   Feature-based view of shots.

is something moving from left to right). In that case, the searched scene will appear at the beginning of the shot list when the proper feature has been selected and the classification process works correctly. This mode is also very convenient when a user is looking for similar shots, because the feature-based sorting will usually group such shots together. If, for example, we apply the *fast motion* feature for ski jumping, then we will get scenes of the moment that the skiers jump off the top—with almost 100% accuracy. If we apply the *motion down* feature for the same, we get the skiers driving down the jump. These examples show how a user with some domain knowledge can semantically gain rich answers from low-level features. An example is shown in Figure 8.3.

8.4.3 Hierarchical Navigation

With hierarchical navigation, the whole video sequence is uniformly separated into as many windows as the user has selected. For instance, in a 2 × 2 view in which four windows are displayed, each window represents exactly one-quarter of the whole content. When users are interested in one particular part, they can go one step deeper into the hierarchy and again perform a uniform distribution of the

Figure 8.4 Hierarchical view.

selected part. This can be continued until the frame granularity is reached and no more partitioning can be made. Of course, it is also possible to move upward in the hierarchy. Figure 8.4 shows an example of the hierarchical navigation mode. Note the gray bars at the bottom of each window, denoting the time area of the content in relation to the entire video sequence.

This navigation mode seems well suited for searching scenes for which the time position can be roughly estimated. Moreover, this mode is perfectly suited for quickly getting knowledge about the content of a video. Together with the possibility of flexibly changing the number of displayed video windows, this mode enables the user to automatically generate a *table of contents* on almost any granularity level.

8.5 Feature Extraction from H.264

A compressed bitstream encoded with the state-of-the-art video coding standard H.264/AVC [9] provides a lot of useful information about the content of the video. This information is tediously computed by an encoder in a time-consuming encoding process. Therefore, it seems to be a good idea to take advantage of this valuable information instead of throwing it away. Even though the result may be less accurate compared to features extracted from pixel data of the decompressed domain, the H.264/AVC coding offers considerably rich opportunities.

8.5.1 Macroblock Type Distribution

H.264/AVC allows the storage of several different types of macroblocks in one single frame. More precisely, a frame may consist of *intracoded, predicted, bipredicted,* and *skipped* macroblocks. Which type of a macroblock an encoder chooses for an area of 16 × 16 pixels depends on the content. An encoder will use similar distributions of macroblock types for similar frames and, thus, shots as well. Therefore, the average distribution of macroblocks is a powerful feature for the content-based clustering of shots. From our experimental results, we have seen that the following features are especially well suited for the purpose of shot clustering (n denotes the starting-frame number of a shot, k the length of a shot, and I_i / S_i the number of intracoded/skipped macroblocks in frame i):

■ Average number of intracoded macroblocks (this can be denoted as the *energy* of a shot). This value will be high if the content of the shot heavily or rapidly changes over time. It will be low if the content is relatively constant over time.

$$\frac{\sum_{i=n}^{n+k} I_i}{k} \quad (8.1)$$

■ Average number of skipped macroblocks (this can be denoted as the *homogeneity* of a shot). This value represents the opposite of the average number of intracoded macroblocks. This value will be high when the content of a shot is relatively constant over time. It will be low if the content changes heavily.

$$\frac{\sum_{i=n}^{n+k} S_i}{k} \quad (8.2)$$

■ Average relation of intracoded to skipped macroblocks (this can be denoted as the *energy-to-homogeneity relation* of a shot, or how big the energy-rich regions are in relation to the homogeneous regions in the shot).

$$\frac{\sum_{i=n}^{n+k} \frac{I_i}{S_i}}{k} \quad (8.3)$$

8.5.2 Macroblock Partitioning Scheme

In H.264/AVC, macroblocks (with a size of 16 × 16 pixels) can be further partitioned into smaller blocks down to the size of 4 × 4 pixels. Which partitioning scheme is used by the encoder mainly depends on the *energy distribution* of the block. As an example, consider Figure 8.5, where three predicted macroblocks of

Figure 8.5   Macroblock partitioning example.

a news video are shown. The encoder has decided to use 4×4 partitions for the area containing the mouth of the moderator and 8×16 partitions for the area containing the cheeks, while the macroblock to the left (containing the homogeneous background) uses a 16×16 partition.

Typically, the partitioning scheme used for frames containing the same content remains the same as well. The shot segmentation algorithm proposed in Schöffmann and Böszörmenyi [15] is also based on this observation. It is apparent that similar scenes within a video sequence use similar partitioning schemes too. Therefore, we believe that the *macroblock partitioning scheme* (MPS) is another well-suited feature for the purpose of shot clustering. We use the following two properties of the MPS:

1. Average number of macroblock partitions in a particular spatial area (denoted by PA_i).

$$\frac{\sum_{i=n}^{n+k} PA_i}{k} \tag{8.4}$$

2. Histogram comparison based on a histogram H_P consisting of 15 bins* according to the macroblock-related partition sizes defined in the H.264/AVC [9] standard (except for partitions of intracoded macroblocks[†]):

$$H_p = \{P^{16\times16},\ P^{16\times8},\ P^{8\times16},\ P^{8\times8},\ P^{8\times4},\ P^{4\times8},\ P^{4\times4},$$
$$B^{16\times16},\ B^{16\times8},\ B^{8\times16},\ B^{8\times8},\ B^{8\times4},\ B^{4\times8},\ B^{4\times4},\ S^{16\times16}\}$$

We compare the partitioning histogram (H_p) for one shot with the H_p of another shot in order to cluster the shots based on their *similarity* (n denotes the starting-frame number of a shot, k the length of a shot, and H_p the partition histogram).

$$\frac{\sum_{i=n}^{n+k} x_i}{k} \quad \forall x \in H_p \tag{8.5}$$

---

[*] In our experimental results, we have not used partition types of bipredicted macroblocks due to the baseline profile limitation of our current implementation.

[†] Schöffmann and Böszörmenyi [15] describe why intracoded macroblocks are not used.

8.5.3 *Intraprediction Mode Histogram*

H.264/AVC uses intraprediction for intracoded macroblocks. The standard defines four prediction modes for 16×16 partitions and nine prediction modes for 4×4 partitions. In general, encoders use similar intraprediction modes for similar content. Thus, we use that relation for the purpose of shot clustering as well. In our current implementation, we compare averaged intraprediction mode histograms to cluster shots based on their *similarity*. Therefore, we use a histogram HI consisting of 13 bins according to the intraprediction modes defined in the H.264/AVC standard [9]:

$$H_I = \{DC^{16\times16},\ Hor^{16\times16},\ Plane^{16\times16},\ Vert^{16\times16},$$
$$DC^{4\times4},\ DDL^{4\times4},\ DDR^{4\times4},\ HD^{4\times4},$$
$$Hor^{4\times4},\ HU^{4\times4},\ Vert^{4\times4},\ VL^{4\times4},\ VR^{4\times4}\}$$

$$\frac{\sum_{i=n}^{n+k} x_i}{k} \qquad \forall x \in H_I \tag{8.6}$$

8.5.4 *Dominant Motion*

The dominant direction and intensity of motion are popular examples of useful features that can support video browsing, as shown in past research [6]. The values of motion vectors allow for the deduction of a lot of information about the content. For the purpose of video browsing, we use the dominant motion direction (see Figure 8.6) and intensity of motion.

For the latter feature, we use the averaged length of motion vectors in the compressed bitstream (L denotes the length of the motion vectors stored for macroblock b in frame i; NB_i denotes the number of macroblocks in frame i).

$$\frac{\sum_{i=n}^{n+k} \sum_{b=0}^{NB_i} L_{ib}}{k} \tag{8.7}$$

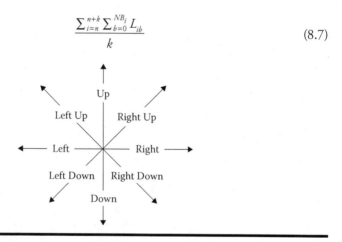

Figure 8.6 Motion direction classification.

8.5.5 Shot Length

The length of a shot is often a significant value for some types/genres of video. One example is the duration of advertisement clips in TV broadcastings or TV shows. Another example is the introduction of news stories in a news show. Several other TV shows contain repeating content that is very similar in duration. In the *Who Wants to Be a Millionaire* show, for example, sorting by the clip-length feature clusters all of the questions together, since the questions in this show are similar in their duration.

8.5.6 Color Information

It is also possible to extract color information from the compressed data. However, currently, we have only evaluated the usage of *brightness*, extracted from DC* coefficients, for the purpose of shot clustering.

8.6 Experimental Results

The concepts discussed in the previous section were evaluated on several test sequences recorded from TV. In order to evaluate the feature-based browsing, video sequences in which similar scenes appear repeatedly have been selected:

- V1: 74 minutes of ski-jumping consisting of 1350 shots (detected by our segmentation algorithm [15] used with $TH_p = TH_I = 0.4$ as thresholds)
- V2: 51 minutes of *Who Wants to Be a Millionaire* (Austrian version) consisting of 661 shots
- V3: 12 minutes of daily news consisting of 200 shots

All three of these sequences were encoded with x264 [11] using Baseline Profile with 2048 KBit/s and a resolution of 368 × 288 pixels. Due to space limitations, only short excerpts of content-based browsing for a few features are presented here. Figure 8.7 shows excerpts of screenshots of our video browsing tool, in which the shots are clustered according to a particular feature extracted from compressed data. The timestamps displayed in the right bottom corner of each shot shows which segments of the entire video sequences have been selected, respectively. Only a few examples are shown in the figure; however, we have implemented all of the features discussed in the previous section and tested them with several video sequences. From our experience, we can conclude that features extracted from the compressed domain provide a great benefit for the purpose of shot clustering in video browsing tools.

---

* The DC coefficient is the DCT (Discrete Cosine Transforms) coefficient for which the frequency is zero in both dimensions.

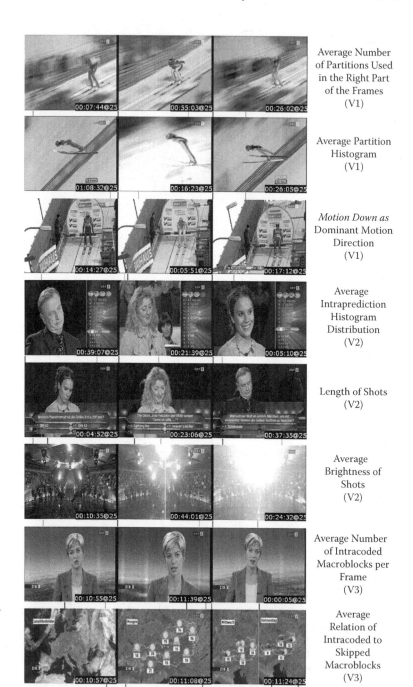

Figure 8.7 Examples of content-based browsing using different features extracted from compressed data.

8.7 User Study

8.7.1 Test Setup and Environment

With 5 female and 15 male multidisciplinary volunteer students, between 20 and 30 years old, we evaluated our video browsing tool in a usability lab equipped with tools like screen recording, mouse-tracking, and eye-tracking. As test content, we used

- A popular TV sitcom, 45 minutes long, 303 shots
- A popular TV show containing interviews and music performances of celebrities, 150 minutes long, 2132 shots
- *Who Wants to Be a Millionaire* (Austrian version), 51 minutes long, 661 shots
- A recording of a downhill skiing competition (women), 50 minutes long, 375 shots

From the set of four videos, we selected several small scenes of 10 to 120 seconds duration. A test person was requested to find a particular scene in a particular video sequence. For some exercises, the requested scene was shown to half of the participants before they started their search; for the other half, we explained the content using natural language. This was done to find out how the behaviors of users differ if they know the scene visually rather than only having heard it explained in words. Similarly, we wanted to evaluate how their behaviors differed if they roughly knew the time position of the searched scene. Thus, for a few exercises, we gave half of the participants some hints as to where the searched scene should be contained. We decided whether participants should use a standard video player (VLC 0.8.6) or our video browsing tool for each corresponding task. This separation was done using a half-by-half manner per question.

In order to avoid familiarization effects, each person received a different permutation of the exercises. Overall, we had 69 exercises that needed to be solved with the standard video player and 59 exercises to be solved with our video browsing tool. At the end of the test, each person was asked to fill out an evaluation form containing a standardized System Usability Score (SUS) [4] questionnaire and some other subjective questions with open answers.

8.7.2 Evaluation

The test revealed a lot of interesting results. First, when users were asked to search for a specific scene within a video as fast as possible, they tried to find some heuristics in order to perform the task efficiently. Mostly, these heuristics were based on some time-related clues. For example, when a scene within a skiing video should be found, where a specific skier starts, users tried to organize their search based on the tricot-number of the skier. In this case, the timeline was used to randomly select some scenes where any starting number could be seen, and the user tried to estimate the position where the searched skier starts. In another video, a popular sitcom, we asked participants to find a scene where an actress calls a taxi at night. In that case, most users, especially those who had some knowledge about the sitcom, reasoned that this scene must happen after a social event late at night. Thus, they searched for both night scenes and scenes of a social event.

With the standard video player, the users mainly interacted with the time-slider, which was incrementally moved forward while playing the video and moved backward (and maybe forward again) if the searched scene was not found. Some of the users switched to fast-forward when they guessed that the searched scene was about to appear but could not be found by using the time-slider. The eye-tracker has shown that using the time-slider is not very efficient because users must move their eyes from the time-slider to the content and back. It is interesting that the users tended to grasp the time-slider with the mouse and move it to a specific position instead of directly clicking onto that position. The reason for this might be that different video players use different interaction behaviors for the time-slider (e.g., some of them provide a fast-forward preview by dragging the slider, and others do not; some only do stepwise increments of the slider position, comparable to scrollbar behavior, when clicking outside the time-slider into the timeline). Still worse, the behavior of the time-slider usually depends on the file format of the video. For instance, if there is no index information available from the file, the time-slider often works in a very coarse mode only.

The tests with our video browsing tool showed that

- 59% of all tasks were solved by using the chronologically ordered shot view.
- 32% of all tasks were solved by using the hierarchical view.
- 9% of all tasks were solved by using the feature-ordered shot view.

The explanation for this behavior is surely that users have a preference for a chronological search strategy, which is essentially how a hierarchical view is organized. One reason for this preference could be that users have learned to search in a chronological way since the early days of analogical videotapes. It is interesting that many participants based their search mainly on static key-frames (i.e., preview pictures) from the displayed windows, even in the hierarchical view. Instead of starting some videos of the current view, many users just scanned all the pictures* of the current page and moved on to the next page if the projected picture of the searched scene was not found.

Instead of starting some videos, the participants increased the number of simultaneously displayed windows† and concentrated on the static pictures. The average number of simultaneously displayed windows per page was 25 (5 × 5),

---

* Several times users scanned the whole page in such a hurried way that they overlooked the searched scene.

† Sometimes to an unmanageable number like 13 × 13!

averaged from all tasks during our tests. Figure 8.8 shows the distribution of the preferred number of parallel windows used by our participants (averaged over all exercises). From our tests, we can conclude that users accept a relatively high number of simultaneous video windows for the purpose of searching; however, they will start a video only when they are pretty sure that the clip or section must contain the searched scene. Users often change the number of simultaneously displayed video windows between different tasks and within one task as well. How many windows are selected seems to depend on

- Type and quality of the video content
- Searched scene
- Personal preferences

As mentioned, the participants decided to use the feature-based view—as the best-suited search method for their current task—only a few times. Although we limited the number of eligible features to only a few reasonable ones for each corresponding video, and the first page sometimes contained the answer to the question, many users never opened the feature-based view. Some users switched to the features-based view but were irritated when the first pages in that view did not contain the answer. It seemed that some of the users were confused because the shots in the feature-based view are not ordered chronologically. The eye-tracker revealed that almost no users checked which feature was selected in the feature-based view. Thus, the preselected feature was often the only feature used. However, those users who tried to solve the task with the feature-based mode were usually the fastest in finishing their task.

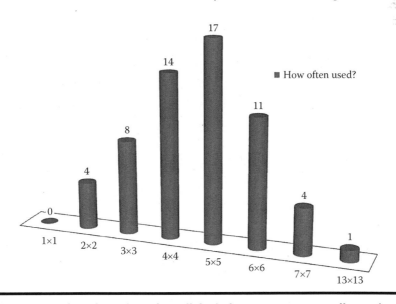

Figure 8.8 Preferred number of parallel windows (average over all exercises).

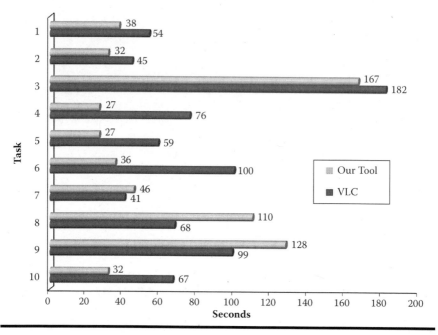

Figure 8.9 Averaged solve times.

We tried to compare the results from the VLC player and our video browsing tool regarding the solve times. However, from this first test, it is difficult to deduce meaningful results regarding solve times because there were too many tasks for the relatively small number of participants. Nevertheless, as we can see from Figure 8.9, the solve time for 70% of the tasks was lower with our video browsing tool than with VLC. In some cases, it is significantly lower (e.g., only 36 seconds instead of 100 seconds for task 6), while in two of the three cases when it is higher, it is only a bit higher (e.g., 46 seconds instead of 41 seconds for task 7). More intensive user tests must be performed in order to make a more comparative evaluation.

8.7.3 Questionnaire and SUS

At the end of the test, each participant was asked to complete a questionnaire with some standardized questions used to compare the SUS [4] and some questions with free text answers. Altogether, users rated the VLC player with a total SUS score of 69 and our video browsing tool with a total SUS score of 75. In Figure 8.10, the average SUS ratings for all of the questions are shown.*

---

* This diagram shows the average of the plain rating per question without the multiplication with 2.5 (as used for the overall SUS value [4]). The score contribution for Questions 1, 3, 5, 7, and 9 is scale position minus 1, and for Questions 2, 4, 6, 8, and 10, it is 5 minus the scale position.

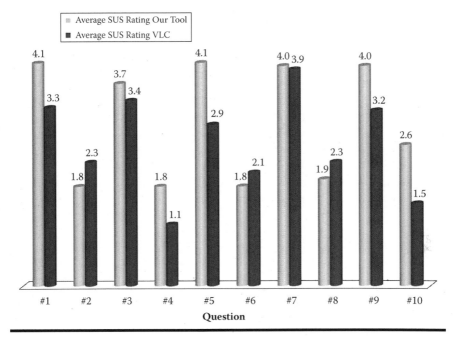

Figure 8.10   Average SUS rating according to the question number.

While many users found that they needed to learn a lot to use our video browsing tool (Question 10) and that they might need the help of a technical person to use the system (Question 4), they also felt confident using the system (Question 9), and thought that they would like to use our tool frequently (Question 7). It is interesting that almost all of the female participants found that using the VLC player was more complex than using our tool (Question 2). In addition, most users found that the video browsing tool was easier to use than the VLC player (Question 3).

8.8 Conclusions

In this chapter, some novel research concepts were presented for efficient and interactive video browsing; these concepts should overcome the current drawbacks of video interaction. We defined an architecture that allows for combining our browser with external tools because it uses the standardized MPEG-7 format for the annotation of videos. Furthermore, we described the visualization concepts used to provide a flexible and interactive user interface that can be used for many purposes. We explained how low-level features directly extracted from the compressed data can be used for the purpose of video browsing. We also presented the results of a first user study, which showed that users can benefit from such a video browsing tool.

We conclude that there is a real demand for video browsing tools that help users to find particular scenes within videos faster and easier than with standard video players.

In general, users are very open to new interfaces that offer later benefits. To the question—*Have you ever been annoyed when searching a scene with a common video player?*—more than 90% of the participants answered yes. All of the participants believed that our tool would help them to find clips within a video faster. We were surprised that the majority of users wished to change the number of simultaneously displayed windows to the quite high number of 25 instances. Neither did we expect that in the case of such a mosaic-formed preview of the video, users mainly concentrated on the preview pictures. This is an important insight that will be the basis for further improving our user interface. Our test also showed that users avoided using the feature-based navigation because of the nonchronological sorting. Moreover, in our current prototype, it is difficult for a user to determine the relevance of one particular feature in the content of the video (e.g., for how many shots and how long? in relation to the usage of which other features?).

We are currently working on an extended version of our prototype that integrates suggested improvements from our first user study. The next step is to continue larger user studies with the improved prototype.

Klaus Schöffmann is a university assistant and doctoral candidate at the Institute of Information Technology at Klagenfurt University, Austria. He received his MSc in 2005. His master's thesis focused on the design and implementation of a video session migration system. After his studies, he continued to work on distributed multimedia systems at the M3 Systems Lab in Klagenfurt before accepting a position at Klagenfurt University in September 2005. He teaches practical courses about distributed multimedia systems, operating systems, and distributed systems. In his current research he is focusing on video browsing and video summarization in the compressed domain of H.264/AVC.

Laszlo Böszörmenyi is a full professor and the head of the Institute of Information Technology at Klagenfurt University, Austria. He is a member of the ACM, IEEE, and OCG; and deputy head of the Austrian delegation to the Moving Picture Experts Group (MPEG, the ISO/IEC JTC1/SC29 WG11). He is a founding member of the European chapter of the Special Interest Group on Multimedia (SIGMM). His research, is currently focusing on distributed multimedia systems, with special emphasis on adaptation, video delivery infrastructures, advanced video coding, and multimedia languages. He has authored several books and regularly publishes in refereed international journals and conference proceedings. He has organized several international conferences and workshops.

References

1. Text Retrieval Conference (TREC) series, National Institute of Standards and Technology (NIST), 1992–2008, http://trec.nist.gov/overview.html, last accessed: 10/10/2008.
2. F. Arman, R. Depommier, A. Hsu, and M.-Y. Chiu. Content-based browsing of video sequences. In *MULTIMEDIA '94: Proceedings of the 2nd ACM International Conference on Multimedia*, pp. 97–103, 1994. New York: ACM Press.
3. M. Barbieri, G. Mekenkamp, M. Ceccarelli, and J. Nes-vadba. The color browser: a content-driven linear video browsing tool. In *Proceedings of the IEEE International Conference on Multimedia and Expo*, pp. 627–630, 2001.
4. J. Brooke. SUS: A "quick and dirty" usability scale. *Usability Evaluation in Industry*, 1996.
5. C. Crockford and H. Agius. An empirical investigation into user navigation of digital video using the VCR-like control set. *International Journal of Human–Computer Studies*, 64(4): 340–355, 2006.
6. A. Divakaran, K. Peker, R. Radhakrishnan, Z. Xiong, and R. Cabasson. Video summarization using MPEG-7 motion activity and audio descriptors. Technical Report TR-2003-34, Mitsubishi Electric Research Laboratories, May 2003.
7. D. Zhong, H. J. Zhang, and S. F. Chang. Clustering methods for video browsing and annotation. In *Proceedings of SPIE Conference on Storage and Retrieval for Media Databases*, 2670: 239–246, 1996.
8. W. Hurst and P. Jarvers. Interactive, dynamic video browsing with the ZoomSlider interface. *In Proceedings of the IEEE International Conference on Multimedia and Expo*, pp. 558–561, 2005.
9. ISO/IEC ITC 1/SC 29/WG 11. ISO/IEC FDIS 14496–10: Information Technology–Coding of audio-visual objects, Part 10: Advanced Video Coding. March 2003.
10. A. Komlodi and G. Marchionini. Key frame preview techniques for video browsing. *Proceedings of the 3rd ACM Conference on Digital Libraries*, pp. 118–125, 1998.
11. Laurent Aimar, Loren Merritt, Eric Petit, Min Chen, Justin Clay, Mans Rullgard, et al. x264: A free H264/AVC encoder, 2008. http://www.videolan.org/developers/x264. html, last accessed: 10/10/2008.
12. S. Lee, W. Ma, and B. Shen. An interactive video delivery and caching system using video summarization. *Computer Communications*, 25: 424–435, March 2002.
13. J. Liu, Y. He, and M. Peng. NewsBR: A content-based news video browsing and retrieval system. *4th International Conference on Computer and Information Technology*, pp. 857–862, 2004.
14. N. Moraveji. Improving video browsing with an eye-tracking evaluation of feature-based color bars. *Proceedings of the 2004 Joint ACM/IEEE Conference on Digital Libraries*, pp. 49–50, 2004.
15. K. Schöffmann and L. Böszörmenyi. Fast segmentation of h.264/avc bitstreams for on-demand video summarization. In S. Satoh, F. Nack, and M. Etoh, editors, *Advances in Multimedia Modeling*, vol. 4903 of Lecture Notes in Computer Science (LNCS), pp. 265–276. Berlin: Springer, 2008.
16. A. F. Smeaton, P. Over, and W. Kraaij. Evaluation campaigns and TRECVID. In *MIR '06: Proceedings of the 8th ACM International Workshop on Multimedia Information Retrieval*, pp. 321–330, 2006. New York: ACM Press.

17. S. Sull, J. Kim, Y. Kim, H. Chang, and S. Lee. Scalable hierarchical video summary and search. *Proceedings of SPIE Conference on Storage and Retrieval for Media Databases*, 4315, 2001.

18. B. T. Truong and S. Venkatesh. Video abstraction: A systematic review and classification. *ACM Transactions on Multimedia Computing, Communications, and Applications*, 3(1): 3, February 2007.

19. S. Uchihashi, J. Foote, A. Girgensohn, and J. Boreczky. Video manga: Generating semantically meaningful video summaries. In *MULTIMEDIA '99: Proceedings of the 7th ACM International Conference on Multimedia (Part 1)*, pp. 383–392, 1999. New York: ACM Press.

20. M. Yeung and B.-L. Yeo. Video visualization for compact representation and fast browsing of pictorial content. *IEEE Transactions on Circuits and Systems for Video Technology*, 7(5):771–785, 1997.

Chapter 9

Personalized Faceted Navigation in Semantically Enriched Information Spaces

Michal Tvarožek and Mária Bieliková

9.1 Introduction

The present Web, along with many Web-based resources, comprises a unique ubiquitous source of information and an environment for collaboration and interaction of many users and businesses. While the amount of available information and the quality and capabilities of information search and processing tools are growing at an incredible rate, so are the size and diversity of the Web's user base and the expectations and requirements of individual users.

Although existing information retrieval (IR) methods are continuously improving, they still fail to address the increasing requirements and expectations of many users with specific needs. For example, most existing search engines such as Google and MSN Live Search employ keyword-based searches, while sharing systems such as Flickr and YouTube might extend this capability with tag-based searches. The infamous "advanced search" interfaces allow users to specify even more complex (keyword-based) queries, optionally with some additional domain-specific attributes (e.g., size, file type for images). Video search sites such as IMDb and MovieLens take complexity to another level by offering (multistep) interfaces with many text fields, drop-down menus, and multichoice listboxes.

However, several studies have repeatedly indicated that typical search queries are short (up to four words, depending on the domain) (Jansen et al. 2003) and that an advanced search is impractical to use for many users (Technical Advisory Service for Images 2008). While existing systems are generally good when searching for very specific items, they do not support browsing and exploratory tasks sufficiently (Yee et al. 2003). Markulla and Sormunen (2000) conducted a field study of journalists and newspaper editors who selected photos for newspaper articles. They reported that "professional users" needed to search on multiple categories yet found an elaborate advanced search interface with about 40 of the input forms being unusable.

The Web is a dynamic open information space, as many "information artifacts"—documents, articles, images, videos, music files, and more—are continuously added, modified, removed, rated, or tagged. Thus, user diversity and the evolution of information and user characteristics over time play a crucial role in effective user-centered IR system design. For example, people who grew up with the Web and the Internet (the "Net Generation") have a natural understanding of this new ubiquitous environment, quite unlike their predecessors (Oblinger and Oblinger 2005). Consequently, they have radically new requirements, expectations, and modes of operation compared to the previous generation of Web users.

Accordingly, current changes include a shift from traditional "lookup tasks" (e.g., fact retrieval) toward more advanced and open-ended learning and investigation tasks (e.g., knowledge acquisition, comparison, aggregation, analysis, planning) collectively described as an *exploratory search* (Marchionini 2006). Furthermore, the trend toward more interaction and active (social) participation encourages the combination and cross-fertilization of approaches from human–computer interaction, information retrieval, the Adaptive Web, and the Semantic Web.

In this chapter, we build upon several existing approaches and describe an enhanced faceted browser, which is built around the view-based search paradigm using faceted navigation (Instone 2004) as a suitable means for exploratory search. We take advantage of Semantic Web technologies (ontologies in particular) (Shadbolt et al. 2006) and adaptation based on an automatically acquired user model to improve usability and reduce information overload via personalization (Brusilovsky 2001; Brusilovsky et al. 2007), ultimately improving overall user experience.

Section 9.2 describes related work in exploratory search and faceted browsing. Section 9.3 outlines our design goals and provides a high-level overview of our approach, while Section 9.4 describes the relevance model used to drive our personalization engine and the corresponding user-modeling at the back end. Next, in Sections 9.5 and 9.6, we describe the details of our personalization approach for facets and restrictions and for search results, respectively. Last, we present our evaluation of the proposed approach in multiple application domains in Section 9.7 and draw conclusions in Section 9.8.

9.2 Related Work

Exploratory search encompasses a broad range of research fields and search and navigation approaches: keyword-based, content-based, and view-based search.

9.2.1 Keyword-Based Search

Keyword-based search is currently used successfully, for example, in all major Web search engines (e.g., Google, Live Search, Yahoo!) thanks to its simplicity and ease of use, while its disadvantages include ambiguity, low expressiveness, and lack of user guidance and interaction. Typical search queries are short (one to three words), though their length varies depending on the domain (Jansen et al. 2003), while advanced search forms are too complex to be practical (Technical Advisory Service for Images 2008). Moreover, "guessing" the right keywords is difficult for many users.

The keyword-based IGroup image search engine presents search results in semantic clusters, thus alleviating some problems with short, general, or ambiguous search queries (Wang et al. 2007). IGroup clusters the original result set into several clusters and provides users with an overview of the result set by means of representative cluster thumbnails and names, which users can choose for further navigation. Thus, IGroup improves usability and makes users' search query formulation easier by providing both query suggestions and browsing by textual category labels.

9.2.2 Content-Based Search

Interactive content-based approaches, such as query-by-example (QBE), have been used in multimedia domains where textual descriptions of instances are sparse, unavailable, or inconsistent with user expectations. The current state of the art in content-based IR and its broader implications are surveyed in Lew and colleagues (2006). Unlike keyword-based search, content-based IR allows users to search interactively: a query is a set of positive (or negative) examples of instances similar to the users' information need.

TagSphere is an approach to visual presentation of search results obtained by QBE information retrieval using collaborative tagging, originally developed for the digital image domain (Aurnhammer et al. 2006). It stresses usability and user interaction in the search process by providing different tools for tag visualization, selection, query construction, and recommendation.

In Ferecatu and Geman (2007), the authors describe mental matching, a QBE-based approach that facilitates exploratory search by bridging the gap between low-level representation of information in databases (i.e., what metadata is available) and high-level semantic descriptions that are meaningful to end users (i.e., how they understand and use them). The approach employs a Bayesian relevance feedback model and allows users to interactively choose the most similar images out of a set of sample images—a "visual query," which the system then matches against other images in the collection.

9.2.3 View-Based Search

Similarly, view-based search interactively guides users by showing them successive views of the respective information space and shows them the available options for further query refinement. In practice, a view-based search is most commonly realized in faceted browsers that are used often, for example, in online shops for product selection. Faceted browsers allow users to formulate queries via navigation by successively selecting metadata terms in a set of available facets and to interactively browse the corresponding search results. Wilson and colleagues (2008) compare three major faceted browsers developed in the course of research projects aimed at discovering new possibilities for view-based searches: Flamenco, mSpace, and RelationBrowser.

mSpace is a domain-specific browser of Resource Description Framework (RDF) data, which provides users with a projection of high-dimensional information spaces into a set of columns (filters) shown in the graphic user interface (GUI), which can be manually added, rearranged, or removed by users (Wilson and Schraefel 2006). The ordering of individual columns in the GUI is important because the contents of the next column are dynamically determined based on the selection in the previous column. If, in the music domain, columns *TimePeriod*, *Composer*, and *MusicPiece* are available, then selecting a time period updates the composer column to display composers only from that period. Similarly, selecting a composer populates the *MusicPiece* column with his or her works.

Flamenco (Yee et al. 2003) stresses interface design and guides users through the information seeking process. Users will first see a high-level overview of the available metadata ("opening"), then refine their query and preview results ("middle game"), and finally explore individual results via horizontal navigation ("endgame"). While in Flamenco the facets are static and predefined, users can manually adapt columns in mSpace to match their needs. Both Flamenco and mSpace support keyword-based searches over the entire information space; however, only mSpace supports keyword-based filtering in individual facets. Moreover, neither Flamenco nor mSpace provide personalization or user adaptation.

The overall user response to these approaches was positive: nearly all users preferred them over a baseline approach/interface. Nevertheless, several of the approaches suffer from scalability and information overload issues. For example, the faceted browser in Yee and colleagues (2003) had an average response time of 3.7 seconds versus 0.3 seconds for the baseline approach. Furthermore, neither of these solutions provides personalized features based on individual users' characteristics. However, even though some of the aforementioned solutions work with RDF data, they do not take advantage of semantic markup for user interface generation and/or personalization in open information spaces.

The BrowseRDF faceted browser (Oren et al. 2006) supports automatic facet generation from arbitrary RDF data and extends the expressiveness of faceted browsing by extending typical faceted queries with RDF semantics (e.g. with existential selection, inverse selection, nonexistential selection). It identifies facets in source data based on several statistical measures—predicate balance, object cardinality, and predicate frequency—yet does not directly address issues of information overload or interface usability and adaptivity.

The faceted browser called /facet (Hildebrand et al. 2006) is intended for heterogeneous information spaces consisting of distributed semantic repositories represented in RDFS. It takes advantage of the *rdfs:subClassOf* and *rdfs:subPropertyOf* properties to process facet restriction hierarchies. Furthermore, /facet supports multitype queries and runtime facet specification, thus greatly increasing flexibility and support for heterogeneous repositories. The multitype capability effectively translates into an additional facet, which is used to specify the target data type. Based on the selection in the type facet, other facets are made available.

Moreover, /facet supports keyword-based searches, which allow users to perform keyword-based search on both data (instances) and metadata (facets and restrictions). Last, /facet supports the grouping of search results based on individual properties and a timeline visualization of dates. However, it does not support personalization or advanced link generation and recommendation techniques. Even though the described approaches present progress in improving search mechanisms, there is still much space left in the sense of combining different approaches together and adapting the resulting approach to individual user needs, ultimately changing the way we search for information in the new Social, Adaptive, Semantic Web.

9.3 Personalized Faceted Navigation Overview

We propose a method for personalized faceted navigation using an enhanced faceted browser, which takes advantage of Semantic Web techniques for ontological knowledge representation and Adaptive Web techniques for personalized facet and search results recommendations. Our primary design goals were

- *Information overload prevention* by recommending relevant content while hiding less relevant content (e.g., facets, restrictions, result attributes)
- *Guidance support* via navigational shortcuts, which streamline navigation in deep/complex faceted hierarchies (e.g., restriction recommendation)
- *Orientation support* by showing additional information/cues, simplifying user decisions about further navigation (e.g., tooltips showing future facet contents)
- *Improved response times* due to selective processing of facets and restrictions, since advanced (semantic) approaches proved to be "time consuming"
- *Universality and flexibility*—suitability to different/changing application domains facilitated by (semi)automatic user interface generations

In order to achieve the aforementioned goals, we took advantage of ontological data representation in Web Ontology Language (OWL):

■ The *domain ontology* describes domain concepts, the relations between them, and their attributes. It contains metadata that describe the structure of the domain model (i.e., classes and properties) as well as actual domain data (i.e., instances). For example, in the scientific publications domain, it describes authors, publications, and venues.

■ The *user ontology* describes the characteristics and preferences of users as well as their broader context: the time, location, and properties of the device and network they use. Since we address generic browsing in large information spaces, we focus on individual user characteristics and omit the issues of acquiring and using a broader user context, which would be required, for example, for mobile applications.

■ The *event ontology* describes the events that occur in the faceted browser and its states during user interaction so that they can be used for the subsequent automated user characteristics acquisition.

The enhanced faceted semantic browser extends the typical request handling of faceted browsers with additional steps that perform specific tasks (see Figure 9.1).

Facet processing is extended with *facet recommendation*—active facet selection, facet and restriction ordering, and annotation—which improve orientation and guidance support, reduce information overload, and alleviate some disadvantages of faceted classification (Figure 9.1, bottom left). If the set of available facets is insufficient (e.g., the refinement options were exhausted), we used dynamic facet generation to add new facets at runtime on a per-user basis, thus allowing the user to further refine the search query.

Search result recommendation extends the processing of search results with support for personalized result ordering, annotation, and view adaptation (Figure 9.1, right). We employed external tools that evaluated the relevance of individual search results, for example, by means of concept comparison with the user model (Andrejko and Bieliková 2008) or via the evaluation of explicit user feedback (Gurský et al. 2006). Subsequently, we reordered the search results or annotated them with additional information. We also generated adaptive views, which showed only selected search result attributes to prevent information overload.

To facilitate automatic user-model acquisition, which was crucial for our personalization approach, we took advantage of the personalized presentation layer described in Tvarožek and colleagues (2007). We logged events that occurred as results of user interaction with the browser and the current state of the browser via a specialized external logging service that preserves the semantics of events (Andrejko et al. 2007) (Figure 9.1, bottom right). The acquired events were processed by the user-modeling back end and in turn retrieved as an updated relevance model, which drove our personalization engine (Figure 9.1, top left).

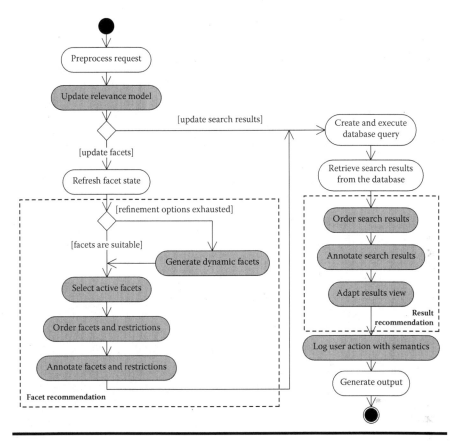

Figure 9.1   Request handling of the enhanced faceted browser, extensions shown in gray.

9.4 Model for Relevance Evaluation

Figure 9.2 shows our user modeling and personalization loop. Our personalization engine logs user actions and their semantics explicitly as opposed to traditional Web server logs, which store them only implicitly in request URLs (Figure 9.2, top). Each logged event uses our event ontology to specify the semantics of the respective user action and also references the domain and user ontologies as required.

Since the detailed description of the event ontology and logging approach is beyond the scope of this chapter, we only give a simplified example. If a user selects New York in a location facet, we log the event *sl:SelectRestriction*, whose attributes are *sl:Facet* and *sl:Restriction* describing the respective URIs of the used facet and restriction: *r:Facet location* and *r:NewYork*.

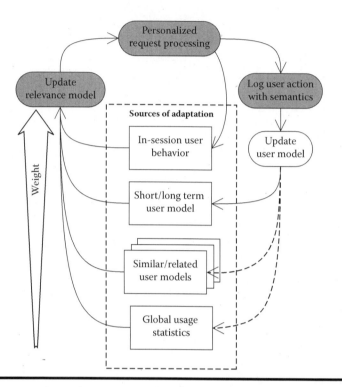

Figure 9.2 Overview of our user-modeling personalization loop (in gray) and the used sources of adaptation (in-session behavior, short- and long-term user preferences, and global usage statistics).

The user-modeling back end provides us with several sources of adaptation, which we employ with different weights depending on how closely related they are to the current user task (Figure 9.2, bottom):

- *In-session user behavior*—user navigation, facet, and restriction selection during the current user session (i.e., user clicks). Frequent use of specific items indicates higher relevance to the current task and/or user interest in the corresponding domain concepts. For example, if *ConferencePaper* is selected as the publication type, showing user interest, additional facets associated with the domain concept *Conference* are likely to be generated in order to allow the user to further refine her query.
- *Short- and long-term user model*—user characteristics acquired during multiple sessions described by their *relevance* to the user and the *confidence* in their estimation in the range ⟨0,1⟩. High relevance in the user model denotes good choices for facet generation and restriction recommendation, while high confidence results in high weights when considering the user's needs.

■ *Similar/related user models*—assumed to belong to users with similar needs and are thus used for relevance evaluation if user-specific data is unavailable or has low confidence. Social user context can be exploited by assigning custom weights to specific relations between users, resulting in social recommendation. Moreover, if usage data about other users are "publicly" available, users might directly browse the trails of their peers (e.g., see what images their friends viewed or what papers their colleagues downloaded).

■ *Global usage statistics*—computed from the overall relevance and usage of individual domain concepts (e.g., facets, restrictions, target objects, whether images, publications, or job offers) from all user models. The overall "popularity" of facets and restrictions increases the likelihood of their recommendation for a specific user, especially if his or her specific preferences are unknown or have low confidence.

Let $L_U(X) = relevance_U(X)$ be the local relevance of concept X from the domain ontology for user U. For example, X might be a facet, a restriction, a search result, or a property. We define $C_U(X)$ as the cross-relevance of X determined as the average local relevance for all users V weighted by their similarity $sim(U,V)$ to user U (Equation 9.1), and $G(X)$ as the global relevance of X defined as its mean local relevance for all users (Equation 9.2).

$$C_U(X) = \frac{\sum\limits_{V \in users} \left(sim(U,V) * L_V(X) \right)}{1 + \sum\limits_{V \in users} sim(U,V)}, U \neq V \tag{9.1}$$

$$G(X) = \frac{\sum\limits_{V \in users} L_V(X)}{|users|} \tag{9.2}$$

To evaluate the user similarity $sim(U,V) \in \langle 0,1 \rangle$, we employ external concept comparison tools (Andrejko and Bieliková 2008). Alternatively, similarity can be evaluated via the sum of square differences in concept relevance between users (Equation 9.3).

$$sim(U,V) = 1 - \frac{\sum\limits_{X \in concepts} \left(L_U(X) - L_V(X) \right)^2}{|concepts|} \tag{9.3}$$

We define $T_U(X)$ as the temporary in-session relevance of concept X determined as the percentage of user clicks on concept X from the total number of clicks on that concept type, such as a facet or a restriction (Equation 9.4).

$$T_U(X) = \frac{Clicks(X)}{1 + TotalClicks} \tag{9.4}$$

Static relevance $S_U(X)$ defines the relevance of concept X based on the user model and the respective confidence in the relevance estimation (Equation 9.5). Dynamic relevance $D_U(X)$ defines the total relevance of concept X based on the user model and the current in-session user behavior (Equation 9.6).

$$S_U(X) = L_U(X) * confidence_U(X) + (C_U(X) + G_U(X)) * (1 - confidence_U(X)) \quad (9.5)$$

$$D_U(X) = S_U(X) + T_U(X) \quad (9.6)$$

As an alternative and/or addition to cross-relevance, we use weighted social relevance $\hat{C}_U(X)$ if social network data for a specific relation $rel(U,V)$ are available (Equation 9.7).

$$\hat{C}_U(X) = \frac{\sum\limits_{rel(U,V) \in relations} (w(rel) * L_V(X))}{|rel(U,V)|} \quad (9.7)$$

9.5 Facet Recommendation

Facet recommendation distinguishes three types of facets adapted at runtime to the specific needs of individual users:

- *Active facets* are fully accessible facets (also known as primary facets), which can be used for faceted query construction and whose content (i.e., restrictions) is visible and entirely processed (e.g., annotated).
- *Inactive facets* are partially accessible facets (also known as secondary facets), which are used in faceted queries if they have active selections. While their content is not directly visible and is thus left unprocessed, they can be activated automatically or per user request.
- *Disabled facets* are partially accessible facets, which are available only after all active/inactive facets are exhausted or on specific user demand. They are not used in queries, and their content is not visible.

9.5.1 Facet and Restriction Personalization

The adaptation process first determines the relevance of individual facets and restrictions in our relevance model (see Section 9.4) and then uses it in these steps:

1. *Active facet selection*: The total number of active facets is reduced to a relatively low number (e.g., two or three facets) because many facets are potentially available in complex information spaces. Active facets are selected based on

relevance and on recency and number of accesses—the most relevant facets or recently/often accessed facets are likely to be active. The rest of the facets are made inactive or left in a disabled state.

2. *Facet and restriction ordering*: All facets are ordered into three groups (active, inactive, disabled) in descending order based on their relevance, with the last used facet always being at the top. Restrictions are ordered alphabetically because alternative orderings based on relevance or the number of matching search results were not well accepted by users as they made it difficult to search for specific items.

3. *Facet and restriction annotation*: Active facet restrictions are annotated with the number of matching instances, the relative number of matching instances by means of font size/type, or directly recommended (e.g., with background color or the "traffic lights" metaphor), effectively providing shortcuts to deeply nested restrictions. Additional tooltips can describe individual facet/restriction meanings (e.g., the *rdfs:comment* annotation in ontologies), annotated child restrictions with relevance, or (personalized) annotations generated by external tools (Návrat et al. 2007).

9.5.2 Dynamic Facet Generation

Normally, facet generation is triggered only when the set of available facets is exhausted, that is, when no or very few active/inactive facets are available.

During facet generation, we examined the attributes of target instances as defined in the domain ontology. For example, for images, we examined attributes of the domain concept *Image* and its associate concepts (via properties), such as *Location* denoting the place where the image was taken.

We searched for eligible candidate properties of individual instance types, which can be used for facet construction based on low-level metadata facet templates used for automated facet construction from the domain ontology (we manually used these templates to create the initial user interface). For example, in the publication domain, a class hierarchy facet for the property *rdf:type* is constructed from the *rdfs:subClassOf* class hierarchy rooted at *pub:Publication*.

Because it is not desirable to generate all possible facets due to their large number, we evaluated the aggregate suitability of individual attributes based on the aforementioned relevance model (see Section 9.4). Last, we determined a suitable presentation method for each new facet and forwarded the resulting set of new facets to the following facet personalization stage. Figure 9.3 illustrates the proposed facet presentation methods:

■ *Simple facets*: Top-level facets based on direct or indirect attributes of target instances—for example, directly for images (the object, keywords, or location) or indirectly (the resolution of the camera used to take the photo).

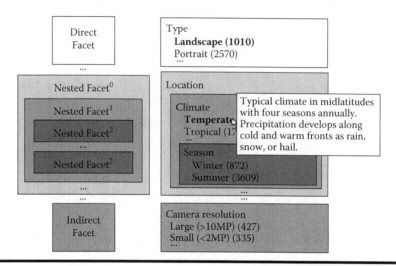

Figure 9.3   Facet presentation methods (left) and adaptation examples (right). Bold text is used for recommendation, tooltips, and instance counts for annotation.

■ *Nested facets:* Facets that in addition to (or instead of) a set of individual restrictions contain a set of *child* facets (e.g., a facet that contains facets for the type of place, popularity, and climate of the location where a photo was taken).

Direct attributes of target instances were presented via simple (direct) facets. If only one indirect attribute of an associated instance type was presented, a simple (indirect) facet was used. If multiple indirect attributes of the same type are presented, a nested facet can be used so that each nesting level corresponds to one level of attribute indirection.

9.6 Search Result Recommendations

Based on the computed relevance and the results of external tools, we performed these recommendation steps:

1. *Search result ordering:* We support simple results ordering—unordered results or ordered based on a single attribute (e.g., date). Additionally, we employed external ordering (relevance evaluation) tools, which evaluate relevance based either on common global preferences or on personalized ratings constructed from explicit user feedback (i.e., rating of instances) (Gurský et al. 2006). Furthermore, we employed external similarity evaluation tools, which enable

users to search for instances similar to a given search result (Návrat et al. 2007).

2. *Search result annotation*: Individual search result attributes are annotated similarly to facets and restrictions. Tooltips show their meanings (*rdfs:comment*) or their properties from the domain ontology. Alternatively, external annotation tools are used to provide custom (personalized) annotations generated from the domain and user ontologies (Návrat et al. 2007). For example, in the movie domain, we can display the suitability of a movie, based on its estimated relevance to the user's preferences, as background color or via emoticons.

3. *View adaptation*: We supported several adaptive views—simple overview, extended overview, thumbnail matrix, and detailed view—which display increasingly more detailed information about individual search results (ontology instances). The attributes of the displayed instances are adaptively chosen and ordered based on their estimated relevance derived from the user model. Moreover, the faceted browser can show instances of different types so that the user can seamlessly switch from browsing/searching for, say, images to videos, then to actors and back to images.

9.7 Evaluation

9.7.1 Architecture and Implementation

For evaluation, we developed *Factic*, a prototype of our enhanced faceted browser (Tvarožek and Bieliková 2007), which implements selected parts of the proposed navigation method based on the faceted browser processing pipeline described in Section 9.3. The overall architecture of our solution was based on the integration and cooperation of several loosely coupled components—software tools—as defined by the personalized presentation layer architecture (Tvarožek et al. 2007). We used Apache Cocoon (cocoon.apache.org) as the underlying portal framework, which is based on the pipelines architectural pattern and thus allowed us to construct different XML-based pipelines to handle our request processing and XML/XSL transformations.

Factic is divided into two relatively independent parts facilitating the presentation of information and adaptation of the GUI, respectively (Figure 9.4, top left). The adaptation part of Factic performs faceted queries and relevance model updates with the successive adaptation of facets and views, while the presentation part transforms its XML output via XSLT into the final XHTML rendered on the client Web browser.

Since Factic relies heavily on user characteristics stored in the user model, it forwards events with semantics occurring during user interaction to the user-modeling back end consisting of components for server-side and client-side user behavior evidence acquisition and user characteristics evaluation (Figure 9.4, center). In our solution, these corresponded to the SemanticLog, Click, and LogAnalyzer tools, respectively (Andrejko et al. 2007). In order to further enhance the functionality offered to end users, Factic also takes advantage of several external information retrieval (CriteriaSearch), relevance evaluation (UpreA/TopK), annotation (Pannda), and concept comparison (ConCom) agents from the application layer of our solution (Figure 9.4, lower center) (Andrejko and Bieliková 2008; Gurský et al. 2006; Návrat et al. 2007).

Last, the aforementioned components all work over common knowledge repositories consisting of the domain ontology, user ontology, and event ontology corresponding to the domain model, user model, and event logs, respectively (Figure 9.4, bottom). We stored the populated domain and user ontologies in the Sesame ontological repository (openrdf.org) for easy access via ontological query languages, and the event logs were stored in a relational database for quick incremental stream processing of incoming events. During the evaluation, we identified

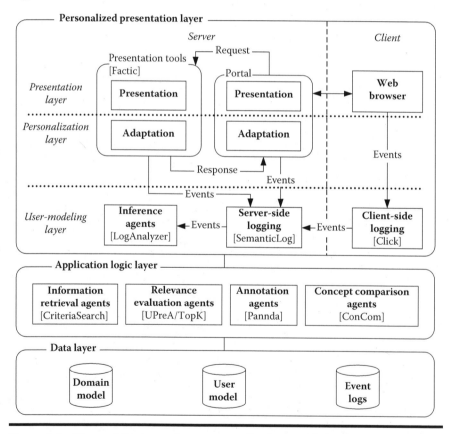

Figure 9.4 The architecture of our personalized presentation layer.

several scalability issues with the ontological repository, which forced us to perform additional optimizations (e.g., caching, query tuning), though satisfactory response times were still difficult to achieve.

9.7.2 Examples and Domains

We applied our approach to three different application domains: online job offers (project NAZOU, nazou.fiit.stuba.sk) (Návrat et al. 2007), scientific publications (project MAPEKUS, mapekus.fiit.stuba.sk), and digital images.

For each domain, we constructed a domain and a user ontology describing the main domain concepts and their properties. The job offer ontology had the most complex schema consisting of some 740 classes with hierarchical classifications up to six levels deep. The publication ontology was of medium complexity with only one hierarchical classification (the ACM classification), while the digital image ontology had a relatively simple flat schema.

We populated the ontologies with instance data of different sizes acquired from publicly available Web resources (e.g., careerbuilder.com, eurojobs.com, profesia.sk, DBLP, Springer, and ACM DL). We worked with several datasets ranging from manually/semiautomatically created "toy-size" datasets having hundreds to thousands of instances, to large automatically acquired datasets in excess of 100,000 instances and several times that many triples.

To demonstrate the flexibility and relative domain independence of our approach, we configured Factic for use in individual application domains (i.e., for their domain and user ontologies). We built upon existing successful faceted browser interface concepts and adaptive hypermedia interfaces. Figure 9.5 shows the sample GUI of our adaptive faceted browser in the digital image domain employing the general faceted browser layout (facets are on the left, query at the top, search results in the center, optional manual search result customization, e.g., sorting, are above search results). Our enhanced faceted browser offers a combined searching and browsing interface and is suited for effective viewing of and navigating in large open information spaces represented by OWL ontologies. It can also be used as an information retrieval tool whereby the search query is visually created via navigation—the selection of restrictions in the set of available facets, which are dynamically adapted to user needs. We also provide users with advanced browsing, searching, and visualization features as described below.

9.7.2.1 Information Overload Prevention

We adaptively reduce the number of accessible items so that users can efficiently focus on the most relevant facets and restrictions without having to scroll several screens down. If users seek images, only facets for the creation date, object, and tags will be displayed, while others concerning image size and acquisition data will be available on demand (Figure 9.5, left).

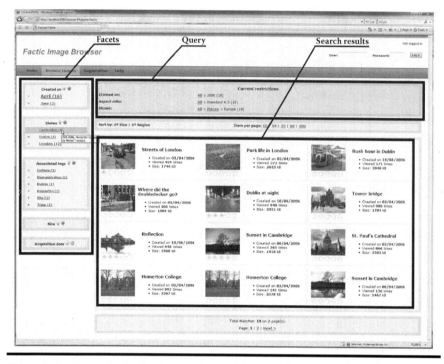

Figure 9.5   Example GUI of our enhanced faceted browser Factic in the digital image domain.

9.7.2.2 Orientation and Guidance Support

We provided visual cues recommending further navigation—the number of instances matching restrictions and textual descriptions of their meanings. Background color indicates restriction recommendations for navigational shortcuts, while "traffic lights" denote their relation to the users' fields of interest (Figure 9.5, left). Individual search results showed additional attributes along with average user ratings (Figure 9.5, center).

9.7.2.3 Query Refinement

If the available set of facets becomes exhausted, additional facets created via dynamic facet generation allow users to refine their queries beyond what would have been possible with statically defined facets.

9.7.2.4 Social Navigation and Collaboration

Collaboration and social networks are considered via global relevance, which describes the overall "popularity" of concepts (i.e., what others think is good), while cross-relevance also considers similarity and/or relations among users. We can also define additional facets based on social network data (e.g., relation types), allowing users to browse their peers' "trails" directly. Hence, users might access facets, which select, for example, only content that is created, viewed, tagged, or rated by their peers.

9.7.3 Experiments and Discussion

We performed several different sets of experiments to validate our approach. Here, we present some of the experimental results in the job offers domain, where our approach proved to be particularly suitable since it is a complex information space with several deep hierarchical classifications (e.g., regions or positions) and intricate concept relations. We experimented with different adaptation, annotation, and recommendation modes. Figure 9.6 illustrates the time and number of user clicks, which represent the total user effort that was necessary to complete a given scenario (i.e., to find a set of relevant job offer instances).

Our evaluation showed that adaptive selection of active facets can significantly reduce the total processing time, which roughly depends on the linear number of displayed facets (assuming an average branching factor). However, the number of clicks increased because the right facets were not always active and thus had to be manually enabled. This resulted in shorter refresh times and consequently shorter total task times.

The recommendation of suitable ontological concepts based on the user model further improved the total task time and also decreased the number of necessary clicks due to the effective creation of navigational shortcuts that allowed users to skip several clicks by directly recommending suitable restrictions within a restriction hierarchy. As before, the number of clicks increased as the number of active facets decreased because more facets had to be manually activated.

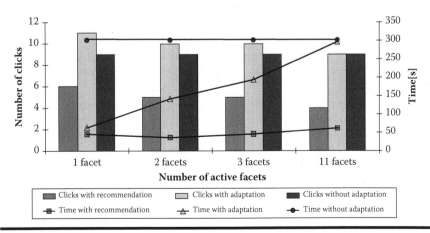

Figure 9.6 Experimental results for different adaptation modes—nonadaptive, with adaptation, with recommendation—for different numbers of simultaneously active facets.

We encountered one significant bottleneck that presently seriously limits the widespread deployment of Semantic Web applications: the immaturity of ontological repositories (we used Sesame) in terms of their query processing speed and query language deficiencies that had to be emulated (missing aggregation and ordering operators in SeRQL-Sesame Rdf Query Language). While SPARQL (SPARQL Protocol and RDF Query Language) addresses some of the problems, the one most crucial aggregate operator, COUNT ( ) (or MINCOUNT ( ) , due to the open world assumption), is still unavailable.

Furthermore, an effective evaluation of Semantic Web approaches is still somewhat difficult because few "good"—rich, complex, and large enough—ontological datasets are available, while the bad scaling of ontological repositories puts a strong bias on every real-world usability study. Our larger datasets yielded only limited results due to their "quality"—their effective use would require extensive preprocessing, which can only be partially achieved by automated means (Dakka et al. 2005).

9.8 Conclusions

We presented a novel method of personalized faceted navigation in semantically enriched information spaces using dynamic facet generation with successive facet recommendation as an enhancement for generic faceted browsers. Our approach is suitable for open information spaces because it is not very susceptible to changes, which are a distinguishing characteristic of open information spaces.

The main advantages of our approach are

- The visual construction of semantic queries via navigation aided by a personalized recommendation of browsing in a faceted browser
- The improved user experience due to decreased information overload and to navigation guidance and orientation support in large information spaces
- The flexible *(semi)automatic interface generation* and *dynamic facet generation* based on semantic metadata from the domain and user ontologies

We already see several promising directions for future research, which are likely to further improve overall user experience. Visual presentation methods for facets and search result overviews and details are likely to improve the understandability of the domain and the available data. Visual navigation in clusters might provide users with the necessary "global" overview of the respective information subspace selected in a faceted browser, while incremental horizontal navigation might be used for details browsing (Tvarožek and Bieliková 2008; Tvarožek et al. 2008). Likewise, the integration of novel social and collaborative approaches as well as the inclusion of mobile application considerations has the potential to improve navigation efficiency and ubiquitous deployment. Last, the design of optimized GUIs from the human–computer interaction perspective with the corresponding usability studies would be of great interest for practical applications.

Acknowledgments

This work was partially supported by the Slovak Research and Development Agency, under contract No. APVT-20-007104, and the Scientific Grant Agency of Slovak Republic, grant No. VG1/3102/06.

Michal Tvarožek is a doctoral candidate in program systems at the Slovak University of Technology, Bratislava, Slovakia, where he also earned a bachelor's degree in informatics (2005) and a master's degree in software engineering (2007). His research interests are in the areas of exploratory information retrieval, adaptive user interfaces, and personalized Web-based systems and user modeling. He has published his research findings in journals and presented his work at several conferences including some supported by ACM, IEEE, and IFIP. He is a member of the Slovak Society for Computer Science.

Mária Bieliková received her master's, summa cum laude, in 1989 and her PhD in 1995, both from the Slovak University of Technology, Bratislava, Slovakia. Since 2005, she has been a full-time professor at the Institute of Informatics and Software Engineering at Slovak University of Technology. Her research interests are in the areas of knowledge software engineering and Web-based adaptive systems, user modeling, and especially the social dimension of personalized Web-based systems in several domains such as educational systems or digital libraries. (A list of selected publications presenting her research results is available at http://www.fiit.stuba.sk/~bielik/—which features more than 100 scientific papers.) She is a member of ACM, a senior member of IEEE and its computer society, and a member of the executive committee of the Slovak Society for Computer Science.

References

Andrejko, A., M. Barla, and M. Bieliková. 2007. Ontology-based user modeling for Web-based information systems. In *Advances in Information Systems Development New Methods and Practice for the Networked Society (vol. 2)*, eds. G. Knapp et al., 457–468. Berlin: Springer.

Andrejko, A., and M. Bieliková. 2008. Investigating similarity of ontology instances and its causes. In *ICANN '08: Proceedings of the International Conference on Artificial Neural Networks*. eds. E. Kurkova et al., LNCS 5164, 1–10. Berlin: Springer.

Aurnhammer, M., P. Hanappe, and L. Steels. 2006. Augmenting navigation for collaborative tagging with emergent semantics. In *ISWC 2006: Proceedings of the 5th International Semantic Web Conference*, eds. I. Cruz et al., LNCS 4273, 58–71. Berlin: Springer.

Brusilovsky, P. 2001. Adaptive hypermedia. *User Modeling and User-Adapted Interaction* 11(1–2): 87–110.

Brusilovsky, P., A. Kobsa, and W. Nejdl, eds. 2007. *The Adaptive Web, Methods and Strategies of Web Personalization*, LNCS 4321. Berlin: Springer.

Dakka, W., P. G. Ipeirotis, and K. R. Wood. 2005. Automatic construction of multifaceted browsing interfaces. In *CIKM '05: Proceedings of the 14th ACM International Conference on Information and Knowledge Management*, 768–775. New York: ACM Press.

Ferecatu, M., and D. Geman. 2007. Interactive search for image categories by mental matching. In *ICCV 2007: Proceedings of the IEEE 11th International Conference on Computer Vision*, 1–8. IEEE.

Gurský, P., T. Horváth, R. Novotný, V. Vaneková, and P. Vojtáš. 2006. Upre: User preference based search system. In *WI '06: Proceedings of the International Conference on Web Intelligence*, 841–844. IEEE.

Hildebrand, M., J. van Ossenbruggen, and L. Hardman. 2006. /facet: A browser for heterogeneous Semantic Web repositories. In *ISWC 2006: Proceedings of the 5th International Semantic Web Conference*, eds. I. Cruz et al., LNCS 4273, 272–285. Berlin: Springer.

Instone, K. 2004. How user interfaces represent and benefit from a faceted classification system. http://instone.org/files/KI-FB-SOASIST.pdf (accessed May 26, 2008).

Jansen, B. J., A. Spink, and J. Pedersen. 2003. An analysis of multimedia searching on AltaVista. In *MIR '03: Proceedings of the 5th ACM SIGMM International Workshop on Multimedia Information Retrieval*, 186–192. New York: ACM Press.

Lew, M. S., N. Sebe, C. Djeraba, and R. Jain. 2006. Content-based multimedia information retrieval: State of the art and challenges. *ACM Transactions on Multimedia Computing, Communications, and Applications* 2(1): 1–19.

Marchionini, G. 2006. Exploratory search: From finding to understanding. *Communications of the ACM* 49(4): 41–46.

Markkula, M., and E. Sormunen. 2000. End-user searching challenges indexing practices in the digital newspaper photo archive. *Information Retrieval* 1(4): 259–285.

Návrat et al., eds. 2007. *Proceedings of the Research Project Workshop: Tools for Acquisition, Organization and Presenting of Information and Knowledge*. Bratislava: STU Press.

Oblinger D., and J. Oblinger, eds. 2005. *Educating the Net generation*. Washington: Educase.

Oren, E., R. Delbru, and S. Decker. 2006. Extending faceted navigation for RDF data. In *ISWC 2006: Proceedings of the 5th International Semantic Web Conference*, eds. I. Cruz et al., LNCS 4273, 559–572. Berlin: Springer.

Shadbolt, N., T. Berners-Lee, and W. Hall. 2006. The Semantic Web revisited. *IEEE Intelligent Systems* 21(3): 96–101.

Technical Advisory Service for Images. 2008. A review of image search engines. http://www.tasi.ac.uk/resources/searchengines.html (accessed May 26, 2008).

Tvarožek, M., M. Barla, and M. Bieliková. 2007. Personalized presentation in Web-based information systems. In *Proceedings of SOFSEM 2007*, eds. J. Van Leeuwen et al., LNCS 4362, 796–807. Berlin: Springer.

Tvarožek, M., M. Bieliková. 2008. Personalized view-based search and visualization as a means for deep/Semantic Web data access. In *WWW'08: Proceedings of the 17th World Wide Web Conference*, 1023–1024. New York: ACM Press.

Tvarožek, M., M. Barla, G. Frivolt, M. Tomša, and M. Bieliková. 2008. Improving semantic search via integrated personalized faceted and visual graph navigation. In *Proceedings of SOFSEM 2008*, eds. V. Geffert et al., LNCS 4910, 778–789. Berlin: Springer.

Tvarožek M., and M. Bieliková. 2007. Personalized faceted navigation in the Semantic Web. In *Proceedings of ICWE 2007*, eds. L. Baresi et al., LNCS 4607, 511–515. Berlin: Springer.

Wang, S., F. Jing, J. He, Q. Du, and L. Zhang. 2007. IGroup: Presenting Web image search results in semantic clusters. In *CHI '07: Proceedings of the SIGCHI Conference on Human Factors in Computing Systems*, 587–596. New York: ACM Press.

Wilson, M. L., and M.C. Schraefel. 2006. mspace: What do numbers and totals mean in a flexible semantic browser? In *The 3rd International Semantic Web User Interaction Workshop at ISWC '06.*

Wilson, M. L., M.C. Schraefel, and R. W. White. 2008. Evaluating advanced search interfaces using established information seeking models. *JASIST: Journal of the American Society for Information Science and Technology*, to appear.

Yee, K. P., K. Swearingen, K. Li, and M. Hearst. 2003. Faceted metadata for image search and browsing. In *CHI '03: Proceedings of the SIGCHI Conference on Human Factors in Computing Systems*, 401–408. New York: ACM Press.

Chapter 10

Personalized Audiovisual Content-Based Podcasting

Elena Sánchez-Nielsen and
Francisco Chávez-Gutiérrez

10.1 Introduction

The amount of multimedia content being produced and consumed on the World Wide Web in video-based podcast environments today is quite large and increasing. Podcast technology represents a shift from mass broadcasting like YouTube or Google Video to personalized media on-demand, where the primary focus is on creating multimedia content for audiences that want to listen/view when they want, where they want, and how they want. Users have traditionally used podcast technology to download their favorite films, interviews, news, product promotions, and educational and cultural content using personalized media with the potential of anytime and anywhere environments.

However, not only is the intrinsic value of multimedia content focused on the advantages of anytime and anywhere environments provided by podcast technology but it also depends on how easily users can search, retrieve, and access it. Thus, effective usage of multimedia content with the purpose of disseminating personalized content using podcast publishing has to deal with the problem of building efficient content annotation and information retrieval tools.

Similar to YouTube, Google Video, and Flickr, users should get interesting multimedia content by only one click. However, when users are interested in a specific topic, the problem arises when they need to download all of the content (the whole file) of the corresponding feed to their portable media and/or desktop computer to retrieve the desired material. This problem gets even worse with the growing size of content files. In order to get the desired information, users have to look for the precise position and/or they have to view all of the content in order to get the answer from the current information. In this context, delivering personalized multimedia content is an important challenge for multimedia environments with podcast publishing.

The use of the MPEG-7 standard (Chang et al., 2001) opens new opportunities to enhance multimedia content annotation and delivery with podcast publishing. On the one hand, information can be categorized by knowledge technologies such as ontologies, and classified at several levels of granularity and abstraction using the different descriptors and description schemes defined in the MPEG-7 framework. On the other hand, the semantic description of multimedia content can be used for personalized requests for material from users. We therefore focus on the opportunities given by the combination of the MPEG-7 standard, metadata annotations, ontologies, and podcast technology for satisfying customized requests. As a result, users can request personalized material, which can be dynamically produced according to users' demand at real time from the podcast information system, and finally, this material can be downloaded and played and replayed via portable media anytime and anywhere.

The remainder of this chapter is organized as follows. Section 10.2 gives an overview of the main topics related to the chapter: (1) the challenges of working with the multimedia content industry, (2) approaches for content delivery distribution, (3) podcast publishing for distributing multimedia content, and (4) the MPEG-7 standard for content annotation. Section 10.3 introduces a scenario that has motivated our work in the context of e-government for legislative multimedia content. Section 10.4 describes our dynamic approach for creating an on-demand system with podcast publishing that is available through parliamentary Web sites in order to provide access to high-quality multimedia content according to individual information needs. Section 10.5 briefly describes the status of the system that is being built and tested for the motivating scenario of legislative information to be available through parliamentary Web sites. Section 10.6 gives concluding remarks and a discussion on future work.

10.2 State of the Art

10.2.1 Facing the Multimedia Content Domain

The management of multimedia content is a task of increasing importance for users who need to archive, organize, and search/retrieve multimedia information in an appropriate fashion. Initially, multimedia companies arranged their multimedia content into file systems, which provided poor naming mechanisms and hierarchical directory structures for organization and searching. This approach has the following drawbacks: (1) the categorization depends on the classification hierarchies used, (2) the logical organization strictly depends on the physical storage system, and (3) identification based on file names alone is often not globally consistent.

The main goal of a good retrieval system is its ability to respond to a user's queries. Customized and easy retrieval of audiovisual data is a main challenge in multimedia management research (Jiménez, 2005), and is currently being addressed by different research groups in diverse applications using semantic technologies. Although semantic technologies are a challenge even for text-based material; for the digital content industry, with huge amounts of nontextual material such as video, the task is even harder. For intelligent processing of multimedia content, it is necessary to incorporate models for concepts and knowledge representation. Tools for efficient storage, classification, retrieval, and editing of multimedia content are essential in order to provide access to high-quality content per individual user preferences or requirements.

There are several approaches to semantically annotating multimedia content (Athanasiadis et al., 2005; Hare, 2006). The aceMedia project (Kompatsiaris et al., 2004) is developing a knowledge infrastructure for multimedia analysis, which incorporates visual description ontology and a multimedia structure ontology. The group has also developed the M-OntoMat Annotizer tool that allows users to manually annotate multimedia items with semantic information. The MIAKT project (Dupplaw et al., 2004) enables the annotation of images with ontologically controlled terms, sometimes derived automatically from content-based image descriptors extracted by image-processing routines from regions of interest indicated by medical experts. Cultural heritage multimedia collections also face important challenges in order to make content accessible to users when data are computed from heterogeneous sources. These problems arise because each institution uses its own metadata formats, and the information is locked away in legacy content management systems. Often, this information is in a structured form, such as articles, reports, and documents.

10.2.2 Content Delivery Distribution

The multimedia content market is growing fast, and it needs solutions for distribution of content collections. This is an important challenge for many industries that are discovering the complexity of managing large multimedia content factories and distribution chains. In this context, content producers, providers, aggregators, and distributors need to adopt innovative approaches in order to cope with large-scale traffic. At the same time, the advent of new mobile and wireless network technologies is facing serious challenges related to business models for multimedia content distribution platforms (Ballon and Van Bossuyt, 2006) where content delivery networks

(CDNs) play a significant role (de Montalvo et al., 2005). Different information delivery methods can be used to disseminate multimedia content through CDNs and the Internet: streaming video, broadcasting, and podcasting.

Streaming video (Wu et al., 2001) is related to the transmission of live video or stored video. There are two models for the transmission of stored video over the Internet: the download mode and the streaming mode. In the download mode, a user downloads the entire video file and then plays back the video file. However, full file transfer in the download mode usually suffers long and unacceptable transfer time. In the streaming mode, the video content need not be downloaded in full: it begins playing while parts of the content are being received and decoded. Because of its real-time nature, video streaming typically has bandwidth, delay, and loss requirements. An example of an architecture of enhanced streaming services in a CND is Prism (Portal Infrastructure for Streaming Media), which allows for distributing, storing, and delivering high-quality streaming media over IP networks (Cranor et al., 2001).

Internet broadcasting (Furht et al., 1998), referred to as webcasting, is related to reprocessed audio or video that is transferred from radio or TV to the Internet. A system with a new video compression technique, IP Simulcast, has been designed for broadcasting multimedia over the Internet (Furht et al., 1999). An approach to introduce metadata based on a TV-anytime standard has been proposed to provide a basic personalized broadcasting service in the education scenario (Ho Kim et al., 2006).

Podcasting (Patterson, 2006) is the distribution of audio or video files, such as radio programs or music videos, over the Internet using either Really Simple Syndication (RSS) or Atom syndication (RSS 2.0) for listening on mobile devices and personal computers.

Subscribing to podcasts allows a user to collect programs from a variety of sources for listening or viewing either online or offline. In contrast, traditional broadcasting provides only one source at a time, and the time is broadcaster-specified. Streaming files from the Internet can remove the specified-time restriction but still offers only one source at a time and requires the user to be connected to the Internet while playing the files. The ability to aggregate programs from multiple sources is a major attraction of podcasts. Unlike podcasts, streaming can also be used to broadcast live events over the Internet at the moment they occur. Although streamed programs, like broadcast radio signals, can be recorded or captured by the receiver, their transient nature distinguishes them from podcast episodes, which arrive readily in an archived form.

10.2.3 Podcast Publishing

Podcasting (Patterson, 2006) is a recent and effective medium by which content providers deliver syndicated Web content (audio/video data) to consumer users. The term is a combination of *iPod*, Apple's portable media device, and *broadcast*.

In addition to being a combination of two words, podcast has two meanings. First, podcasting is the transmission of multimedia files over the Internet. Rather than being received and opened with different plug-ins, podcast files are ready for viewing on a PC or on other devices, such as an iPod. On the PC, users can treat podcast files like any other computer files, viewing them immediately or saving them for viewing at a later date. Second, podcast refers to their content. Frequently, podcasts are files that are sent at regular intervals. For example, many of the morning news programs are available as podcasts on a daily basis to download for listening or viewing at an individual's convenience. Once viewers determine which podcasts they want, they sign up for them and have them delivered automatically whenever their receiving device is connected to the Internet.

Interactions between providers and consumers consist of a two-step process. First, the content providers make audio or video files accessible, which are often referred to as one episode of a podcast, on an available Web server. Then, the content provider acknowledges the existence of these files by referencing them in another file known as the feed. The feed is a machine-readable list of the episodes that may be accessed. This list is usually published in RSS format (RSS 2.0), which provides other information, such as publish dates, titles, and accompanying text descriptions of the series and each of its episodes. The feed is typically limited to a short list of the most recent episodes. Second, a consumer uses a software program called a podcatcher with the purpose of determining the location of the most recent episode and automatically downloads it to a desktop computer and/or portable player. The downloaded episodes can then be played and replayed at any time.

Currently, the use of a subscription feed of automatic delivery of new content is what distinguishes podcast publishing from a simple download or real-time streaming, as outlined in Section 10.2.2. As a result, subscriptions to podcast publishing allow users to collect programs from a variety of sources for listening or viewing offline anytime and anywhere. However, personalized requests by users to create on-demand feeds about specific content have not been included in traditional podcasting systems. In this context, the MPEG-7 standard and ontologies become a key feature for ensuring an appropriate response to users' requests in the distribution of multimedia content.

10.2.4 MPEG-7

MPEG-7 (Chang et al., 2001; Martínez, J. M.), formally named Multimedia Content Description interface, is a standard for the description of multimedia content using machine-consumable metadata descriptors developed by the Moving Pictures Expert Group (MPEG). This standard has been used to model structural and low-level aspects of multimedia documents (Athanasiadis et al., 2005; Vembu et al., 2006) and to describe the semantics of highly structured domains like sports (Tsinaraki et al., 2005).

The MPEG-7 framework consists of Descriptors, Description Scheme (DS), and a Description Definition Language (DDL). Descriptors correspond to representations of features that define the syntax and the semantics of each feature representation. These Descriptors are designed for describing different types of information: (1) low-level audiovisual features, (2) high-level semantic objects, (3) content management, and (4) information about storage media. Description schemes specify the structure and semantics of the relationships among their components. These components may be both Descriptors and Description Schemes. The DDL is used to group several Descriptors and Description Schemes into structured and semantic units. XML Schema language has been used as the DDL (MPEG Systems Group, 2004) for specifying MPEG-7 Descriptors and Description Schemes.

The MPEG-7 standard consists of several parts:

1. MPEG-7 Systems
2. MPEG-7 Description Definition Language
3. MPEG-7 Visual
4. MPEG-7 Audio
5. MPEG-7 Multimedia Description Schemes
6. MPEG-7 Reference Software
7. MPEG-7 Conformance
8. MPEG-7 Extraction and Use of Descriptions

As a result, this standard provides content description tools for content management, organization, navigation, and automated processing. These tools are grouped in different classes according to their functionality:

1. Basic Elements
2. Schema Tools
3. Content Description Tools
4. Content Management Tools
5. Content Organization Tools
6. Navigation and Access Tools
7. User Interaction Tools

With these description tools, different types of descriptions can be created and combined in a single Description Scheme.

Among the MPEG-7 standardized tools for describing different aspects of multimedia content, we focus on the Semantic DS and its components because it represents the main component for describing the semantics of our e-government scenario. In the following sections, this tool is described in more detail.

10.2.5 Semantic Description Tools

The MPEG-7 Semantic DS describes the semantics of multimedia content in terms of events. Events can be viewed as occasions upon which something happens. Objects, people, places, and times can populate such occasions. These entities have properties and states and are interrelated. In MPEG-7, the participants, background, context, and all of the other information that makes up a single narrative are referred to as a narrative world (Benitez, 2002).

A narrative world in MPEG-7 is represented using the Semantic DS, which is described by semantic entities and graphs of their relations. As a result, the data types needed for the semantic description of audiovisual content are defined in a set of Description Schemes rooted in the SemanticBase DS. These Description Schemes are SemanticBase DS, SemanticBag DS and Semantic DS, AgentObject DS, Object DS, Event DS, Concept DS, Semantic State DS, Semantic Place DS, and SemanticTime DS.

10.2.5.1 Abstraction Model

Besides the semantic description of specific instances of multimedia, MPEG-7 semantic description tools allow for the description of abstractions and abstract semantic entities. The AbstractionLevel datatype in the SemanticBase DS describes the level of abstraction that has been performed in the description of a semantic entity. Two different situations are possible: (1) AbstractionLevel is not present in the semantic description; in this case, the description is related to concrete audio-visual material. (2) AbstractionLevel is present in the semantic description; in this case, abstraction is present in the description.

For example, when the attribute dimension of AbstractionLevel is 0, a description of a semantic entity is present, (e.g., the deputy Adan Martin). Higher values of the dimension attribute are used for abstractions of abstractions. For example, Adan Martin is an instance of the deputy class with dimension 1, while deputy is an instance of the person class with dimension 2.

10.2.5.2 Semantic Relations

MPEG-7 defines normative and nonnormative semantic relations. The semantic relation tools include the SemanticRelation CS, which specifies semantic relations among entities that have semantic information. Normative semantic relations describe how several semantic entities are related in a narrative world (e.g., agent, patient, and accompanier). Other normative relations describe how the definitions of several semantic entities relate to each other (e.g., combination, specializes, and exemplifies). Other semantic relations (depicts, symbolized, and context) describe an event taking place at a specific place and time; an object being perceived, referenced, or symbolized in a segment or collection; or a narrative world being the context or interpretation of another narrative world. The complete list of normative relations is illustrated in Benitez (2002).

10.3 Motivating Scenario: Personalized Podcast Publishing for Parliamentary Web Sites

Distributing multimedia legislative content related to plenary sessions (the most important task of parliamentary activity for legislative assemblies) is an important priority for parliaments in order to foster the relationship between citizens and parliament. However, this content has not been generally published to the citizens because (1) plenary sessions generally last more than five hours, which would require citizens to download masses of data and (2) an easy-to-use retrieval system answering the current information need with customized multimedia clips is a challenging goal.

Real-streaming and podcast technology today is being used by parliaments as communication tools to disseminate legislative information. However, the legislative assemblies are at the same time faced with the problem of building citizen-centric services in order to improve customized retrieval of legislative information stored as multimedia content. In particular, the demand is growing for personalized multimedia content that best fits citizens' preferences and/or easy retrieval of audio/video clips of customized interest.

10.3.1 Legislative Assembly Domain

In a European legislative domain, the president of the Legislative Assembly has the power to call and preside over meetings and also to exercise other powers and functions according to the provisions of the law and the Rules of Procedure of the Legislative Assembly. The parliamentary bureau decides on the agenda of meetings. The agendas of meetings are structured according to the different initiatives (subjects) to be processed.

According to the Rules of Procedure of the Legislative Assembly, initiatives introduced either by the government or by the members of the Legislative Assembly will be subjected to a general discussion, where different deputies who belong to different political parties intervene as speakers from the speaker tribune or benches at the debate. The interventions can be performed from different physical places at the plenary sessions. Sometimes a voting procedure related to an initiative is also performed at the agenda of the plenary session.

All the initiatives that can take place at different plenary sessions are defined at a hierarchy of different levels. Among others, the high abstraction of this hierarchy encompasses law projects, government norms, appearances, appeals, nonlaw proposals, questions about popular initiatives, and so on. As a result, these initiatives involve the following actions:

1. Enact, amend, suspend, or repeal laws.
2. Examine and approve funds.
3. Decide on taxation.
4. Approve debts to be undertaken by the government.
5. Debate any issue concerning public interests.
6. Receive and handle complaints from residents.
7. Call persons concerned to testify or give evidence when they exercise powers and functions.

10.3.2 Need for Personalized Podcast Publishing

As an example to introduce the need for personalized podcast publishing in the legislative domain, we will describe a scenario of a particular plenary session that took place during five hours in March 2007 at the legislative assembly of the Canary Islands. The agenda of this plenary session involved different initiatives related to questions from diverse deputies to responsible authorities about modifications of the tourist infrastructures program, inauguration of new hospitals, successions' tax, and new contracts for cleaning services of public administration. Other initiatives concerned the energy and the mining systems, new measurements for the ambient impact on public projects, and information about cultural architecture and art programs. Among the nonproposal laws were a private security contract in public administration and sentences for terrorism. A law proposal from the Commission of Tourism and Transport about the regulation of canary maritime transport finished the plenary session. According to the Rules of Procedure of the Legislative Assembly, the different initiatives introduced either by the government or by the members of the Legislative Assembly were subjected to a general debate, where different deputies who belong to different political parties intervened as speakers from the speaker tribune and/or the benches.

Currently, the content of the different plenary sessions is transcribed to diary sessions, which are published on the Web site. At the same time, some legislative assemblies provide direct emission of a video signal by means of video streaming, or they provide some sections of the most recent plenary session videos, or both. However, citizens, public administration, and businesses in general are not interested in all of the content of every plenary session or in downloading the diary session in text format and searching it for specific topics. With the advent of new technologies, citizens and institutions demand easy and fast retrieval of customized content under the paradigm of anytime and anywhere. For example, tourism businesses focus on legislative modifications of the tourist infrastructures program, while maritime transport businesses focus on regulation of canary maritime transport. Citizens are concerned about the approval of interventions or grants. As a result of diverse interests, some customized requests for podcast information systems could be as follows:

Provide a feed with the interventions about maritime transport regulation.
Provide a feed with all of the help for education.
Provide a feed with all of the grants for persons with diminished physical capacity.
Provide a feed with all of the voting processes with a simple majority vote.
Provide a feed with all of the interventions of the president of the government.

In this context, our challenge is to further support the generation of customized feeds on podcast publishing, by providing a personalized and on-demand podcast system that can be generated in real time and focus on the needs of different citizens, public administration, and businesses.

10.4 Customized Podcast Information System

From a high-level point of view, different processes can be distinguished in the dynamic generation of customized feeds according to user demand in the context of legislative assemblies, for example: (1) descriptions of plenary sessions content, (2) metadata and content generation, (3) fragmentation, and (4) customized feeds delivery. Figure 10.1 illustrates an overview of the system architecture.

10.4.1 Description of Plenary Sessions Content

Description of legislative content is the first process that needs to be carried out in order to develop an efficient multimedia information management system. Ontologies (Fensel, 2001) are a key component for knowledge representation and management because they involve a consensus in the way a particular knowledge domain is described. For this purpose, we use the MPEG-7 standard specifications (Chang et al., 2001) to define an ontology for the description of multimedia content. Using MPEG-7 ontology, the legislative content can be described at different levels of abstraction, and at the same time, this semantic description can be used as a feedback inside our architecture system to make available customized segments' videos. The semantic description of audiovisual content is defined in the Semantic section of the MPEG-7 MDS specification in a set of Description Schemes rooted in the SemanticBase DS, which are shown in Figure 10.2.

In order to describe the different components of the ontology that follow the MPEG-7 specification, we have identified the different elements:

◼ *Events*: Events represent the occasions upon which something happens. According to the Rules of Procedure of the Legislative Assembly, something

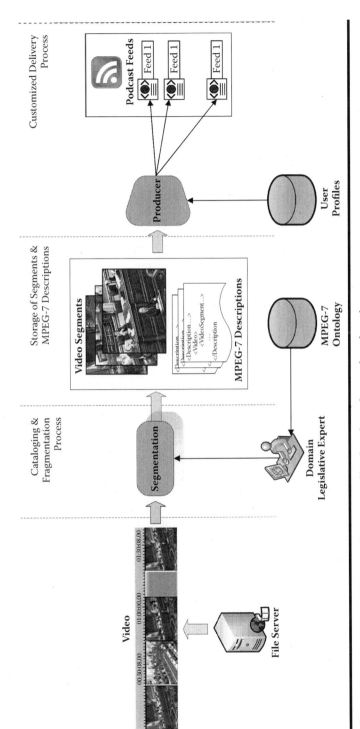

Figure 10.1 System architecture for personalized and on-demand podcasting systems.

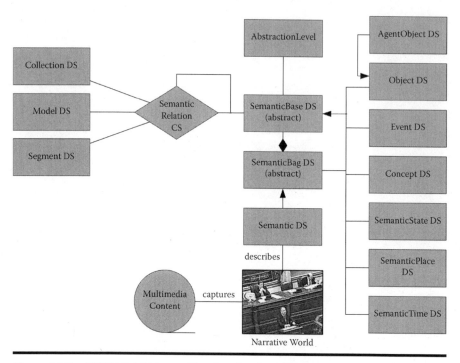

Figure 10.2 MPEG-7 MDS specification for describing semantic descriptions of plenary sessions.

takes place at a plenary session when the different deputies corresponding to the different political parties intervene at the debate of the diverse initiatives to be processed. As a result, we can identify the interventions as the main types of events for a plenary session.

◼ *AgentObjects*: The actors who intervene correspond to the different members of the plenary session. The ontology entities for the representation of person roles are shown in Figure 10.3. In order to define the different levels of abstraction for diverse roles, we used an abstract MPEG-7 Person entity. After the definition of an entity in the domain-specific ontology, it can be instantiated (by means of the AbstractionLevel datatype of the SemanticBase DS) and be associated to specific audiovisual segments (e.g., the audiovisual segments where the deputy "Adan Martin" intervenes).

◼ *ObjectDS*: The agendas of plenary sessions are structured according to the different initiatives that are to be processed. Therefore, every object corresponds to one of the initiatives. Some entities that correspond to the first and second levels of the ontology hierarchy are illustrated in Figure 10.4. The high-level abstraction of the ontology comprises nine different semantic entities. Among the objects are law proposals, law projects, government norms, appearances, communications of government, general debate about the nationality state, appeals, government reports, censure motion, nonlaw proposals, questions about popular initiatives, institutional declarations, different commissions, questions about unconstitutionality, resources about unconstitutionality, and subjects related to different local and regional institutions. Other objects correspond to the description of the initiative to be debated. These descriptions are computed from the Multilingual Eurovoc Thesaurus (Eurovoc), which consists of a database of hierarchical terms with semantic and generic relationships. The European Parliament, the Office for Official Publications of the European Communities, the national and regional parliaments in Europe, and some national government departments and European organizations currently use this thesaurus. Eurovoc includes 21 different fields comprising all the areas of importance for the activities of the European institutions: politics, international relations, European Communities, law, economics, trade, finance, social questions, education and communications, science, business and competition, employment and working conditions, transport, environment, agriculture, forestry and fisheries, agri-foodstuffs, production, technology and research, energy, industry, geography, and international organizations.

■ *Semantic State DS*: One of the most relevant descriptions of a state of the plenary session and the parametric description of its features corresponds to the results of the voting process by the members of the plenary session. A Semantic State describes the corresponding state of the plenary session after a voting process has been performed (e.g., simple majority vote).

■ *Semantic Place DS*: The main event, intervention, and secondary related events can take place at different locations of the plenary session.

■ *Semantic Time DS*: This element is used to describe the semantic time of an initiative being processed (e.g., 21 March 2007, 9:00 A.M.).

10.4.2 Metadata and Content Generation

The metadata of a plenary session are annotated by the catalogers (cataloging experts on the Legislative Assembly's domain) using the domain-specific MPEG-7 ontology described above. A visual annotator interface is provided to catalogers to assist in this process. This interface shows, among other elements, the different events, agents, and objects that can take place at a plenary session. The catalogers select the appropriate terms and relationships from this annotator interface. As a result, every audiovisual segment has an associated single MPEG-7 XML file that describes this specific segment.

Using the MPEG-7 description tools and ontology, this file description includes (1) content management information that describes aspects of creation and production, such as the title, creators, locations, and dates; and (2) content description

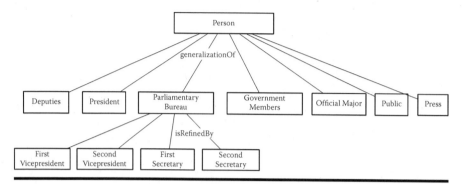

Figure 10.3 The ontology terms for person roles in plenary sessions. (From Elena Sánchez-Nielsen, *Personalized Audiovisual Content-Based Podcasting,* **Taylor & Francis, © IEEE 2007. With permission.)**

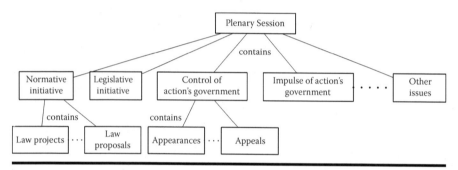

Figure 10.4   First level of hierarchy and some terms of the second level of the ontology terms for the initiatives. (From Elena Sánchez-Nielsen, *Personalized Audiovisual Content-Based Podcasting,* **Taylor & Francis, © IEEE 2007. With permission.)**

that describes the structure, segmentation of the content, and semantics (events, agents, objects, relationships) of the audiovisual content. A partial example shows a temporal decomposition of a plenary session:

```
<TemporalDecomposition>
<VideoSegment id="6LPL0020">
 <TextAnnotation type="title">
      <FreeTextAnnotation>6L/PL-0020.Law Project
      </FreeTextAnnotation>
 </TextAnnotation>
 <TextAnnotation type="description">
      <FreeTextAnnotation>Law project about maritime
          transport in Canary Islands
      </FreeTextAnnotation>
 </TextAnnotation>
...
```

```
<MediaTime>
     <MediaTimePoint>T00:07:58:900F1000
     </MediaTimePoint>
     <MediaDuration>PT00H03M38S00N</MediaDuration>
</MediaTime>

</VideoSegment>
</TemporalDecomposition>
```

Figure 10.5 illustrates a semantic description and its normative relations (such as an object being the patient of an event) to an intervention by a deputy (Adan Martin) from the speaker tribune about a law project (regulation of maritime transport) of legislative initiative type, which corresponds to content related to transport (descriptor computed from the Eurovoc thesaurus). The intervention takes place at 21-03-07 from 9:45 A.M. to 10: 30 A.M.

An extract of a relevant fragment of the MPEG-7 XML file associated with the audiovisual segment illustrated in Figure 10.5 is shown on the next page.

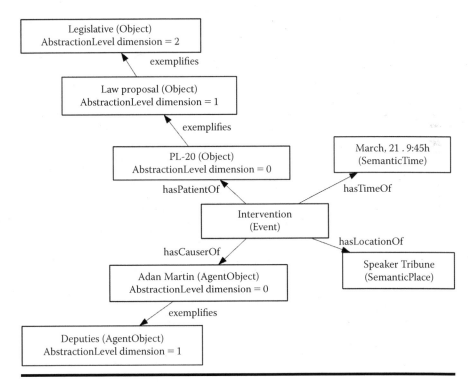

Figure 10.5 **A semantic description of an audiovisual segment related to an event of intervention of a specific deputy. (From Elena Sánchez-Nielsen,** *Personalized Audiovisual Content-Based Podcasting,* **Taylor & Francis, © IEEE 2007. With permission.)**

```
<Description xsi:type="SemanticDescriptionType">
 <Semantics>
        <AbstractionLevel dimension="0"/>
        <Label>
                <Name>Debate of ...6L/PL-0020</Name>
        </Label>
        <!-- ### Description of Event ###  -->
        <SemanticBase xsi:type="EventType" id="INTV1">
                <Label>
                        <Name>Debate ... 6L/PL-0020</Name>
                </Label>
                <Relation type="urn:....:hasPatientOf"
                target="PL-0020"/>
                <Relation type="urn:....:hasCauserOf"
                target="D06055"/>
                <Relation type="urn:....:hasCauserOf"
                target="D06012"/>
                <Relation type="urn:....:hasCauserOf"
                target="D06005"/>
                <Relation type="urn:....:hasCauserOf"
                target="D06048"/>
                <Relation type="urn:....:hasLocationOf"
                target="speakertribune"/>
                <Relation type="urn:....:hasTimeOf"
                target="intv-time"/>
        </SemanticBase>
        <!-- ## Description of Initiative ##  -->
        <SemanticBase xsi:type="ObjectType"
        id="PL-0020">
                <AbstractionLevel dimension="0"/>
                <Label><Name>Law Project</Name></Label>
                <Definition>
                <FreeTextAnnotation>Law Project about
                regulation of Canary maritime
                transport</FreeTextAnnotation>
                </Definition>
                <Relation type="urn:....:isExemplifiedBy"
                target="PL"/>
                <Relation type="urn:....:isExemplifiedBy"
                target="Transport"/>
        </SemanticBase>
        <!-- ## Description of Deputy ##  -->
        <SemanticBase xsi:type="AgentObjectType"
        id="D06055">
                <AbstractionLevel dimension="0"/>
                <Label><Name>
                Adan Martin Menis</Name></Label>
                <Relation type="urn:....:isExemplifiedBy"
                 target="Diputado-obj"/>
```

```
<Agent xsi:type="PersonType">
    <Name>
            <FamilyName>Adan Martin</FamilyName>
    </Name>
</Agent>
</SemanticBase>
```

Figure 10.6 shows the annotator interface that was used to exploit the ontology infrastructure presented in Section 10.4.1 and to annotate the different visual segments of plenary sessions using the main components of the ontology that follow the semantic part of the MPEG-7 MDS specification—that is, agents, events, objects, and semantic state. This annotator tool can also be used to incorporate new elements into the ontology.

10.4.3 Fragmentation

After the cataloging process has been performed, the annotations made by the cataloging experts by means of the visual annotator interface allow for the identification of the start and end of the different segments involved. Each video of each plenary session is divided by an automatic process (fragmentation process in Figure 10.6)

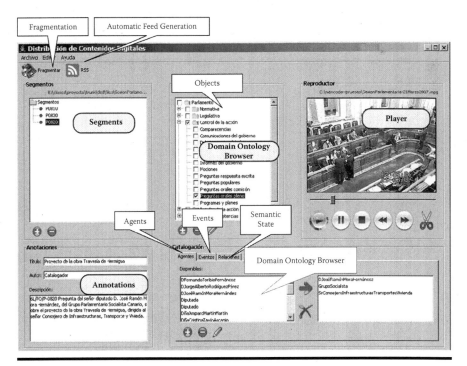

Figure 10.6   An annotator interface for cataloging plenary sessions.

into smaller videos that will have a size that is equivalent to the different segments annotated. This fragmentation process is initially computed according to the 21 different fields of Eurovoc. As a result, when the system is initialized, it provides the 21 available feeds that can be syndicated to the podcast audience.

10.4.4 Customized Feeds Delivery

The basic functionalities required from the podcast audience viewpoint are based on a Web site where users can subscribe to the episodes available from the 21 feeds according to the different fields of Eurovoc and/or can specify their preferences about new personalized episodes with the purpose of generating the new customized feeds in real time.

Via a user-friendly interface, the system provides a structural list of the different preferences that can be initially selected about legislative content. The preferences are based on the main components of the ontology that follow the MPEG-7 MDS specification (described in Section 10.4.1): (1) agents (which corresponds to speakers, e.g., episodes about all of the interventions of the president of the government); (2) objects (related to the different initiatives to be debated and/or associated Eurovoc descriptors, e.g., only episodes about regulation of maritime transport or general episodes about transport); and (3) events (interventions) that relate agents with objects (e.g., all of the episodes in which deputy Adan Martin specifically intervenes about government reports). It should be noted that not only can users select specific instances of the entities of the ontology (agents, objects and events) but they can also combine any instantiations of the specific domain ontology. As a result, users can combine their preferences, selecting the descriptors, initiatives, and/or speakers which they are interested in. For example, when a user specifies "descriptor = tourism, initiative = law project," a new personalized feed in RSS format related to all of the law projects about tourism is automatically generated. After the feed is created, all of the new audiovisual segments that are related to the features that are demanded are made accessible as episodes.

The preferences of every user are translated by the system to a query that is transformed into a new feed in RSS format. Each new request for a customized feed is matched with the existing feeds. If a request is duplicated by a new user, the previously created feed is assigned to the new user. If the request does not match an existing feed, a new feed is generated.

The generation of new episodes for new customized feeds is based on three steps:

1. *Matching*: Because the semantic description of the MPEG-7 XML file associated with every new annotated audiovisual segment contains the different elements (events, agents, objects, and relationships) that correspond to the diverse preferences selected by users, the new episodes can be generated by a means of searching the elements from the semantic description that

matches the queries associated with the feeds created. The elements matched are those that correspond to EventType, AgentObjectType, and ObjectType (see Section 10.4.2).

2. *Fragmentation*: Every new audiovisual segment that matches the query associated with an existing feed is selected from the original video that contains a plenary session by an automatic process in a video file (episode). This episode's size is equivalent to the segment annotated. The start and duration of the episode are computed from the elements MediaTimePoint and MediaTimeDuration of the MPEG-7 file.

3. *Update feed*: After the new episodes have been created, the feed is modified to show the recent episodes. The elements title, summary and duration are computed from the elements title and description associated to the section Content Management Information of the MPEG-7 XML file that describes the audiovisual segment.

10.5 System Status

A first prototype of the customized podcast information system has been implemented with open source software. The main technological benefit inherently characterizing all of the open source solutions is their transparency. Because, by its definition, open source software must always be distributed together with its source code, it is reusable and modifiable by anyone.

The current prototype consists of (1) an annotator interface for cataloging plenary sessions that includes the MPEG-7 legislative ontology described in Section 10.4.1, where new components can be introduced in real time to the specific ontology, and new MPEG-7 ontologies can be imported; (2) a Web site where end users can subscribe to the episodes available from the 21 feeds according to the different fields of Eurovoc and/or a structural list with the purpose of specifying users' preferences about new personalized episodes; and (3) a Java-based application for real-time automatic feed generation based on choices selected by users of the Web site. This application integrates the automatic processes of matching, fragmentation, and update feeds described in Section 10.4.4.

The prototype has been tested from two viewpoints: (1) human cataloging experts who use the annotator interface for cataloging plenary sessions and (2) a group of end users. The practical experience of cataloging experts has been positive in the sense that they have friendly and visual tools for annotating metadata and additional information. Because the annotator interface is user friendly, no specific technical requirements are necessary.

The characteristics of the end users involved in the test of the prototype system are as follows. The average age was 38 years, with a range of 25 to 50. Males represented 75% (6/8) and females 25% (2/8). People with an interest in legislative information represented 50% (4/8). People familiar with podcast technology represented 50% (4/8).

End users concluded that most people learn about what is happening in legislative assemblies from the radio, and the proposed customized system offers a new possibility for users to decide what information they need. People who work at the Legislative Assembly decided to subscribe to the episodes available from the 21 feeds according to the different fields of Eurovoc, while people who work outside of the Legislative Assembly selected personalized episodes. Users were satisfied with the easy-to-use personalized podcast system and the short time needed to select, listen to, and/or view the personalized information. People with no knowledge about podcast technology experienced no technical problems in using this new technology.

10.6 Conclusions and Future Work

In this chapter, we illustrated how the MPEG-7 standard allows the enhancement of the content creation and retrieval for satisfying customized requests dynamically and in real time in podcast environments. MPEG-7 allows us to generate a multimedia ontology, describe multimedia contents, generate dynamic and customized feeds according to the ontology, and update the new episodes of the podcast information system. As a result, a new approach for personalized dissemination of information with podcast publishing was provided. We described our approach using the scenario of the legislative content for parliamentary Web sites. The features widen the potential of e-government in two ways: first, by enabling target audiences to decide on the feeds to be created, and second, by allowing legislative institutions to become more sensitive to the needs and preferences of target audiences, and in particular the citizens because the audiences are clearly identifying and specifying their preferences. Thus, our approach to personalized podcast publishing can also be viewed as a new way of enhancing the participation of citizens and contribute to better legislation. This approach has been tested for the e-government domain, but it can be used in diverse scenarios such as education, religion, audio tours of museums, cultural or historical audio tours of cities, sports, meeting alerts, news dissemination, and more.

Our future work will focus on two research lines. The first will deal with the automatic generation of textual descriptions for video content based on visual features such as facial descriptions in order to generate automatic metadata annotations in the process related to metadata and content generation. The second line of research will focus on improving the way that users specify their preferences in the customized feeds delivery process. Currently, users can select terms from structural lists, where the preferences are selected from the three main components of the ontology that follow the semantic part of the MPEG-7 MDS specification. In this context, we propose to study a concept-based query expansion technique to improve the query formulated by the user in order to translate the information need of the user to expressive formal queries.

Elena Sánchez-Nielsen received a BS in computer science from the University of Las Palmas G.C., Spain, in 1994, and an MS and PhD in computer science and artificial intelligence from the University of La Laguna, Spain, in 1999 and 2003, respectively. Since 1996, she has been involved in various research projects concerning computer vision and perceptual user interface. Since 2000, she has been working as a software architect in various projects related to smart diffusion and retrieval of government contents at the Parliament of the Canary Islands and interoperability problems at the Public Administration. Her research interests include smart multimedia information systems, semantics, video processing, and intelligent systems.

Francisco Chávez-Gutiérrez received a BS in computer science from the University of Las Palmas G.C., Spain, in 1994. He is currently pursuing his PhD in intelligent systems at the Department of Informatics Systems and Computation at the University of La Laguna, Spain. Since 1995, he has been CIO of the Parliament of the Canary Islands, Spain. Since then, he has worked in various projects related to modernization, management, searching, retrieval, and access to digital government content. His research interests include intelligent information systems, Web intelligence, smart distribution, and retrieval of audiovisual contents and metadata descriptions.

References

Athanasiadis, T. H., Tzouvaras, V., Petridis, K. et al. 2005. Using a multimedia ontology infrastructure for semantic annotation of multimedia content. In *Proceedings of the 5th International Workshop on Knowledge Markup and Semantic Annotation (SemAnnot '05)*, Galway, Ireland.

Ballon, P., and Van Bossuyt, M. 2006. Comparing business models for multimedia content distribution platforms. *IEEE Proceedings of the International Conference on Mobile Business (ICMB '06)*.

Benitez, A. B., Rising, D., Jörgerisen, C. et al. 2002. Semantics of multimedia in MPEG-7. In *IEEE International Conference on Image Processing (ICIP 2002)*, Vol. 1, pp. 137–140, New York.

Chang, S. F., Sikora, T., and Puri, A. 2001. Overview of the MPEG-7 standard. *IEEE Transactions on Circuits and Systems for Video Technology*, 11(6): 688–695.

Cranor, C. D., Green, M., Kalmanek, C. et al. 2001. Enhanced streaming services in a content distribution network. *IEEE Internet Computing*, 5(4): 66–75.

de Montalvo, U. W., Ballon, P., and Sokol, J. 2005. Business model scenarios for seamless content distribution and delivery. In *IEEE Proceedings of the International Conference on Mobile Business (ICMB '05)*.

Dupplaw, D., Dasmahapatra, S., Hu, B. et al. 2004. Multimedia distributed knowledge management in MIAKT. In *Proceedings of the 3rd International Semantic Web Conference (ISWC 2004)*, pp. 81–90. Hiroshima, Japan.

Eurovoc. Office for Official Publications of the European Communities. *Eurovoc Thesaurus*. http://europa.eu.int/celex/eurovoc/.

Fensel, D. 2001. *Ontologies: Silver Bullet for Knowledge Management and Electronic Commerce.* Berlin: Springer.

Furht, B., Westwater, R., and Ice, J. 1998. Multimedia broadcasting over the Internet: I. *IEEE Multimedia*, 5(4): 78–82.

Furht, B., Westwater, R., and Ice, J. 1999. Multimedia broadcasting over the Internet. II. Video compression. *IEEE Multimedia*, 6(1): 85–89.

Hare, J. S., Sinclair, P. A. S., Lewis, P. H. et al. 2006. Bridging the semantic gap in multi-media information retrieval. Top-down and bottom-up approaches. In *3rd European Semantic Web Conference*, Budva, Montenegro.

Jiménez, A. 2005. *Multimedia Knowledge: Discovery, Classification, Browsing, and Retrieval.* Ph.D. thesis, Graduate School of Arts and Science, Columbia University.

Kim, Y. H., Lee, H.-K., Choi, J. S. et al. 2006. Study on personalized data broadcasting service using TV-Anytime metadata. In *Proceedings of the IEEE 10th International Symposium on Consumer Electronics. ISCE '06*, pp. 1–6.

Kompatsiaris, I., Avrithis, Y., Hobson, P. et al. 2004. Integrating knowledge, semantics and content for user-centered intelligent media services: The AceMedia project. In *Workshop of Image Analysis for Multimedia Interactive Services (WIAMIS '04)*, Lisboa, Portugal.

Martínez, J. M., ed. ISO/MPEG N6828. MPEG-7 Overview (version 10). http://www.chiariglione.org/mpeg/, last accessed: October 3, 2008.

MPEG Systems Group. 2004. ISO/MPEG N4288, Text of ISO/IEC Final Draft International Standard 15938-2 Information Technology-Multimedia Content Description Interface—Part 2 Description Definition Language.

Patterson, L. J. 2006. The technology underlying podcasts. *IEEE Computer*, 39(10): 103–105.

RSS 2.0 Specification. http://blogs.law.harvard.edu/tech/rss, last accessed: October 3, 2008.

Tsinaraki, C., Polydoros, P., Kazasis, F. et al. 2005. Ontology-based semantic indexing for MPEG-7 and TVAnytime audiovisual content. In *Multimedia Tools and Applications Journal on Video Segmentation for Semantic Annotation and Transcoding*, 26 (special issue): 299–325.

Vembu, S., Kiesel, M., Sintek, M. et al. 2006. Towards bridging the semantic gap in multi-timedia annotation and retrieval. In *Proceedings of the 1st International Workshop on Semantic Web Annotations for Multimedia (SWAMM)*, Edinburgh Scotland.

Wu, D., Hou, Y. T., and Zhu, W. 2001. Streaming video over the Internet: Approaches and directions. *IEEE Transactions on Circuits and Systems for Video Technology*, 11(3).

Chapter 11

Use of Similarity Detection Techniques for Adaptive News Content Delivery and User Profiling

---

Bilal Zaka, Christian Safran, and Frank Kappe

11.1 Introduction

The increased diffusion of communication technologies and their applications has made our lives very information intensive. Exploring, organizing, and preserving this information space are complex tasks that vary with the type of information and its medium of delivery. A huge volume of information is available to individuals in the form of daily news, the sources of which range from conventional print media such as newspapers, radio, and television to more recently developed ways of getting personal and general news via Web portals, e-mail, content syndication, digital media streams, podcasts, and other means. With this variety of sources at hand, it is becoming difficult and time consuming to get the desired information based on the reader's interest and preferences. The user must spend a reasonable amount of time and effort to filter the desired information from all of these sources, especially since different sources are preferable for different types of content. User profiles and preferences that form the basis of adaptive information systems are generally system specific. Profiling techniques used in common information retrieval systems give little or no consideration to user ownership, portability, and reuse of user interest profiles. This is frustrating for users when they have to duplicate filtration efforts at various sources. One research study demonstrates significant negative relationships between information overload and stress, decision making, and job fulfillment [1]. Such an abundance of information affects the natural cognitive capabilities of individuals. According to Basex,* a research firm that predicted information overload as the biggest problem of the year 2008. Information overload has serious effects on the productivity of individuals and can cause the loss of billions of dollars for large organizations. These factors make adaptive reception of information critical in order to fight information overload.

With varying environmental and physical conditions, it is not always desirable or possible to efficiently interact with a number of information systems individually. In this situation, it is preferable to access one central system that provides aggregated access to various sources. In order to provide an effective and suitable way of accessing the system, the interaction must be adapted in modality and media to contextual requirements. Providing multimodal interaction [2] is necessary since the application of the personal computer-based paradigms is not always possible in the conditions described above. In many situations, a telephone or PDA are more readily available than a PC or laptop computer.

Another hurdle in successfully and conveniently navigating through the diverse information base is the constraints posed by interface modality. The increased use of wireless data networks and emerging hand-held devices offer a number of new ways to access information systems. Many information systems already provide specialized layouts and communication interfaces for unconventional devices. However, in most cases, such interfaces are more of a hindrance than a convenience. The design of these unconventional device interfaces compared to conventional desktop devices is still relatively unexplored. The development of revolutionary technologies such as smart phones, digital media players, digital interactive TV, and E-Ink devices marks the evolution from the current desktop computing era to ubiquitous computing. This results in a change in concepts for device interaction and urges researchers to increase the work on new, multimodal systems [3]. Such systems in turn will extend the information paradigm of the computer-based information systems and Internet to these more common platforms. In conventional user interfaces, interaction with a system for precise information retrieval is a lot closer to machine perception of user requirements; input via keyboards/GUIs is interpreted with a higher level of certainty than in multimodal systems where the system's interpretations are probabilistic [4]. Even then, in the case of conventional interfaces, many users have a limited

---

* http://www.basex.com.

knowledge of all of the available information retrieval and filtering techniques (e.g., limitations of vocabulary, awareness of advance search operators). Precision in information retrieval gets more challenging with unconventional modes of interaction. Thus, it is very important to base information filtering and retrieval means on users' spontaneous interaction context and a defined history of interest. Furthermore, it is beneficial to add semantic meanings in multimodal interactions in order to reduce uncertainty and increase the efficiency of communication.

One approach for such a system, with a focus on the individualized delivery of news items and multiple user interface modes, is presented in this chapter. The suggested framework uses conceptual similarity detection techniques for personalized news delivery. It offers a user-controlled, standardized, and portable user interest profiling system. The ongoing user profiling, based on implicit and explicit feedback as well as group preferences, is used to create personal information filters. With a standardized profiling system, it is possible to use personal interest data in a number of existing and upcoming information retrieval applications. The Personalized Interactive Newscast (PINC) system offers a context-aware news item relevance system. It uses term extraction and synonym-set services to link content items and user filters. This approach, based on conceptual semantics, lexical relation, and service-oriented architecture, allows for increased efficiency of the information filtering system. The proposed system also offers an enhanced recommender system. Conventional recommender systems use content-based matching, collaborative filtering, or knowledge-based techniques. A survey and experiments on recommender systems show that more successful systems are those that use a combination of these techniques [5]. Our system takes advantage of the semantic knowledge base and collaborative filtering for its hybrid recommendation capability. The system can also prepare filtered news items as a seamless information source that supports cross-media publication. Multichannel distribution ensures the availability of news content in different media with varying physical and environmental conditions.

11.2 Related Work

The proposed framework addresses news harvesting, metadata extraction, context determination, and filtration for the creation of a personalized newscast. It also deals with cross-media publishing and multimodal interaction for its access. All of the mentioned areas have attracted interest lately, and considerable research has been published on these topics.

Focusing on personalization and filtering functions first, several systems addressing these topics deserve mentioning. Such systems include SELECT [6], one of the early efforts to reduce information overload. It introduces the information environment tailoring to meet individual needs with the help of information filters. These filters provide recommendations derived from an individual's past choices and behavior of other users with similar interests. SELECT emphasizes social and collaborative filters and the importance of a strong rating and feedback mechanism to support filtering of mentioned types. This project also explores the use of implicit as well as explicit feedback techniques to enhance the rating database.

A more recent, ontology-driven user profiling approach is the Quickstep and Foxtrot system [7], which has introduced hybrid content-based and collaborative recommendation techniques with the effectiveness of presenting user profiles in ontological terms. Another project, News [8], also utilizes semantic technologies to extend personalized delivery capabilities of online news content. This system provides an RDF-based news ontology for news item categorization. It also provides annotation components to automatically produce metadata for news items. Social networking sites, blog aggregators that use folksonomies (user tagging of information that they generate or consume) and taxonomies, are becoming popular. Most of us have seen the effectiveness of user collaborative recommender systems while browsing the Amazon portal,* where a recommender system presents items under the labels such as *Customers who bought this item also bought, Customers interested in this title may also be interested in,* and *What do customers ultimately buy after viewing items like this?* In general, we see a tremendous increase in availability of syndicated content and in turn aggregation tools for personalized view. A survey conducted to compare existing news aggregation services in terms of their features and usability reveals that the most desirable features by users are the advanced search functionalities, user-friendly interfaces, quality of sources, browsing, and personalization functionalities [9].

A number of experiments and studies highlight improvements in personalized information access through effective user modeling [10–12]. These approaches include profiling based on user-provided explicit data or implicitly gathered information through an analysis of interests and activities. Research suggests that the automatic capture of user preferences is necessary especially in the case of heterogeneous content and the changing interests of the user. Systems offering personalized content are an appealing alternative to a "one-size-fits-all" approach. This personalization approach is perhaps the major factor in the success of the online e-commerce company Amazon.com. This portal is well known for its personalized service, which starts offering custom store views after just a few mouse clicks and covers a detailed user view and purchase history.

The second focus of the proposed news delivery system is on multimodal interfaces. Although multimodal interfaces are designed with a focus on flexibility and extending usability, few of them can adapt to different user preferences, tasks, or contexts [13]. The same applies to content adaptation in a multimodal approach.

The main problem of the existing solutions is the coverage of only a part of the requirements of the modern user of news systems. Personalization and filtering approaches lack the possibility of being ubiquitously accessible. In a personalization approach, knowledge about the individual user is used and the content is adapted

---

* Amazon: http://www.amazon.com.

according to the user's needs. The collection of this knowledge is an ongoing process that depends on how well user actions are interpreted from various modalities. The effective interpretation of these actions and the conversion into a knowledge base that forms the user models continue to be challenging tasks in multimodal systems. Moreover, many of these approaches do not take into account the particular context of the news domain. This problem can be effectively addressed by using semantic relationships between the input from interaction devices and the collection of entities in a system.

An effective system must be able to aggregate semantically equivalent news content from different sources and present these collectively, arranged and filtered by user and group preferences. Multimodal and cross-media publishing systems can be used to access news content, but generally they lack the support for association by semantic or collaborative equivalence, as described above. The key to adaptive content reception and recommender systems continues to be automated discovery of personal interest, preferences, and environmental and social characteristics. Adaptive systems tend to gather as much information as they can and store it for personalized interaction with the user. Normally, a typical user is not aware of what and how much personal information is stored in an adaptive system, which raises a lot of privacy concerns [14]. One way of addressing the issue of privacy is to provide the user with more control over how the information is stored and processed in a standardized way.

11.3 Design of PINC

PINC aims to enhance the end user's access to news in a way that the previously presented approaches cannot. It provides a solid solution for news harvesting, personalization, and presentation.

11.3.1 News Acquisition and Preprocessing

The aggregated news content of a newscast includes news articles acquired from various syndication services and Web mining. The news content is collected, processed, and indexed on the server side. The intervals for this acquisition process are set by a system user. Information fetching agents responsible for the collection of the news content are easily modifiable and extensible. The plug-in-based crawling agents traverse through the selected sources periodically for the collection of updated information. Fetched news content is relayed to the information preprocessing unit, where the extraction of metadata and categorization is done. This component stores the news entities in the main information repository and builds the information resource knowledge base by extracting meta-information from the fetched content. This extracted meta-information normally includes source, publishing date/time, type of media, author, keywords, and description.

Fetched content and meta-information are normalized to a generalized language form before the creation of an index. This process of normalization is conducted by using natural language processing techniques including part-of-speech (POS) tagging, term extraction, and finding the most common form of each word/term. POS tagging is used to determine the correct syntactical sense of words (verb, noun, adjective, etc.). This syntactical sense is later used to determine the respective group of synonyms. The synonym groups are selected using WordNet* lexical data. The most common word in a selected synonym set, based on its frequency reference in language ontology (tag_count parameter of WordNet), is picked as the normalized representation of a particular word/term. Information normalized in this way, when compared for similarity, provides a greater depth of concept matching. Figure 11.1 depicts the process of normalization and similarity detection for text segments A and B.

Further metadescriptors are generated by applying term extraction on fetched content. A term designates a certain meaning or concept to any information. Different linguistic and statistical techniques for term extraction are in use. They determine the importance of words by consistency, frequency, structural location, and linguistic morphology. Available news category information and generated metadescriptors of fetched news entities are compared for similarity with the system's news category taxonomy. This allows the system to automatically categorize the news entities in a given taxonomy even when little or no classification information is available. In addition, the described approach provides an automated way of using data mining techniques to convert a basic news taxonomy into a rich news ontology. The use of various news sources captures the view of many domain experts, thereby making our news ontology more effective [15]. It works as a rule-based categorization agent, linking news entities and metadata to individual elements of the seed news taxonomy. Similarity detection is used to determine the news item category. Angular measure based on a vector space model determines the relevancy between the news item's meta-information and the news category keywords. This enables the system to go through an iterative process of evaluation, enrichment, and refinement of the news category descriptors. The system maintains the inverted file

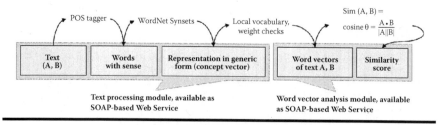

Figure 11.1   Normalization of text to find conceptual similarities.

---

* WordNet: http://wordnet.princeton.edu/.

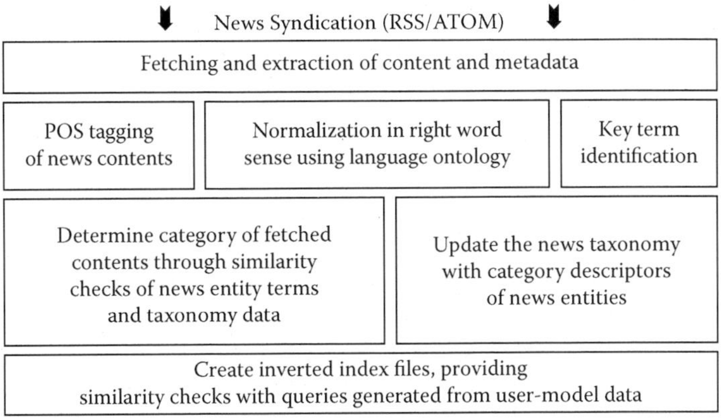

Figure 11.2   Information preprocessing.

index of the normalized contents. Such storage outperforms conventional database systems in terms of faster search and lesser storage requirements. A combination of Boolean and vector space-based similarity models is used to determine the relevance between filter queries (based on user models) and indexed news data. Figure 11.2 gives an overview of information preprocessing and indexing.

11.3.2 Personalization

PINC uses the idea of wrapping heterogeneous data sources into a uniform knowledge representation with semantic annotation. This offers an integrated and personalized view of data [16]. News content can be categorized and characterized using the additional semantic information. The process of annotation is done by using term extraction techniques and enrichment of terms (concept-defining words) with lexical variations. The process of adding greater depth of associated terms to news entities and creating concept vectors is exemplified in Section 11.4. A well-defined user-model structure is the key to the creation of personal views of news entities. A user model is initiated by integrating explicitly stated user preferences in a profile. These preferences may include demographic data, user knowledge skills, capabilities, interests, and the selection of predefined categories. References and links among user models are used to share knowledge about mutual interests in order to form groups and enhance the recommendations by collaborative filtering techniques.

The user-model filters and group/social links are automatically updated based on usage data; this includes explicit tagging, user ratings, and implicit behavior such as selective actions, use frequencies, hardware environment, and location data. Figure 11.3 shows the visual representation of a user model and the process of personalization. A personalized view is created by finding a conceptual equivalence between filters that are available in the user model and normalized news entities processed in information preprocessing.

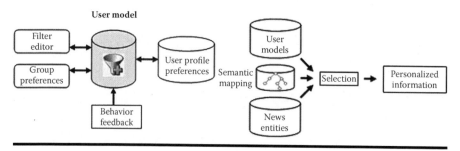

Figure 11.3   User model and personalization.

A growing concern in the context of personalization is privacy. In order to meet the requirement of users for control of their personal data, we decided to integrate Attention Profiling Markup Language (APML).* APML is an XML-based markup language for the description of the user's interests, designed to be shareable and to be controlled by the user. It is intended to improve the ability of an information system to provide information fitting the user's needs, reducing information overload. APML is dedicated to four fundamental rights of the user. First, the profile is the property of the user: his attention is owned and controlled by him. Second, the user has the right to move her attention wherever she wants whenever she wants. Third, the user's attention has worth. He can pay attention to whomever he wishes and receive value. Finally, the user has a right to transparency, being able to see exactly how the attention is being used and, based upon this information, decide who to trust. An APML file contains implicit attention, which is derived automatically from the behavior of the user, as well as explicit attention which is added by the user. For both categories, concepts and sources can be specified, the latter being information sources like a URL or an RSS feed. Each of these elements is assigned a value between 1 and −1, where high positive values indicate a lot of attention and negative values indicate an explicit dislike.

APML is already used in a number of services, most prominently Digg[†] and Bloglines.[‡] Because APML is designed to provide benefits for both advertisers and users, it can be assumed that further services are likely to follow. PINC provides a tool to generate initial profiles from users' browsing habits. To that end, the browser history is scanned, and the visited pages are retrieved and analyzed. Subsequently, terms are extracted. These terms are assigned with attention values between 0 and 1, based on the term frequency. Negative values are ignored in this context. The resulting APML file is provided to the user for editing and can finally be uploaded and incorporated into the personalization process of PINC, presenting an initial interest model.

---

[*] http://www.apml.org.
[†] http://www.digg.com.
[‡] http://www.bloglines.com.

11.3.3 Aggregation

The system acts as a universal news aggregator. It fetches the news content, parses it for metadata enrichment, and stores it in a local repository. In the final aggregation to a newscast, the filtered and arranged news items are retrieved from the repository. The corresponding articles are dynamically fetched from the sources and, appropriate to the content type, either embedded or linked in a NewsML* news envelope. NewsML is a standard by the International Press Telecommunication Council[†] to present news content in text, images, audio, or video using XML. The use of XML at various levels allows ease of data interchange and multimodal publishing.

NewsML is envisioned as a way of standardizing news aggregation for multimedia, multidiscipline, and multimodal delivery. It provides an XML envelope to manage and represent news through its life cycle. This life cycle starts with a definition of a news story along with the comprehensive representation of metadata such as the domain, media, origin, and history. The standard organization also facilitates ease of transformation for enhanced/multimodal user consumption (via XSLT or by any other means). NewsML is currently used by leading newspaper organizations and publishers.[‡]

The information aggregation component of PINC represents an imperative concept of Web 2.0 applications called *mashup*. The term mashup was initially introduced by the modern music community to describe the end result of mixing vocals and music from different songs. In technology, mashup refers to applications that combine content from different sources and present them to users in a seamless manner. Mashups are rapidly spreading their roots, and popular types include map mashups, available through Google MAP API, Microsoft Virtual Earth API, and Yahoo Maps API; shopping mashups like Geizhals[§] and Pricegrabber[¶]; and photo mashups like Flickr. News sources such as Reuters, Associated Press, BBC, CNN, AFP, and APA have used RSS feeds to distribute content for quite some time, and various news mashup applications exist that use all of these feeds to present users with a combined or selective view of content. PINC's aggregation component forms a personalized and context-independent information dataset using content and collaborative filters. This filtration is based on the semantic relations among user models and the meta-information (see Figure 11.3). News items are aggregated into a standardized NewsML structure, which provides a wealth of data interchange for multimodal publishing.

11.3.4 User Interfaces

Current personalized news information systems mainly focus on the presentation of the content via the personal computing paradigm. Technology trends show that in

---

* http://www.newsml.org.
† http://www.iptc.org.
‡ http://www.newsml.org/pages/whouse_main.php.
§ http://www.geizhals.at/.
¶ http://www.pricegrabber.com/.

the coming years, ubiquitous computing will replace the current personal computing era and change the way that users interact with technology. Conventional input/output devices will play a very small role, making way for perceptual user interfaces (PUI) [17] and maximizing the use of natural human communication with digital devices and systems. PUIs demand the capability of automatically extracting the user's needs by translating human interaction with the system. In general, the user input is perceived through the sophisticated analysis of body gestures, voice, and navigation patterns.

In order to follow this direction and provide access to a personal newscast in almost all situations, the PINC framework allows the end user to choose the most appropriate mode for the delivery of personalized news. A dynamic user model containing attention data provides the perception of the user's information needs in multiple modes of interaction. The aggregated data in NewsML form is converted to a specific publishing format using an appropriate XSL transformation. The proposed initial interfaces include World Wide Web access, a speech interface, E-Ink technology, and customizable video.

11.3.4.1 World Wide Web Access

The PINC publishing module provides news and information content for desktop or mobile device browsing via XHTML transformation. The transformation fitting the client specification is achieved through a combination of user-agent sensing and a transparent content negotiation mechanism [18]. An HTTP delivery module contains formatting scripts capable of sensing the user-agent environment variable for browser, OS types, and general display capabilities. A plain user-agent–based adaptive method relies on an up-to-date knowledge base of all of the available browsers and their capabilities; it fails to function in case of nonavailability of data about new clients. This problem is minimized by adding Multimedia Internet Message Extensions (MIME)-based content negotiations between client and server (where supported). The "Accept" header information sent by the client is used to determine the appropriate content format for delivery. The properties of content negotiations sent in the Accept header from the client are media type (with quality parameter), language, encoding, and character set. The added client information helps customize the HTML news presentation for different browsers.

11.3.4.2 Speech Interface

The PINC framework includes a VoiceXML 2.1* browser, supported by compatible text-to-speech (TTS) and automated speech recognition (ASR) engines. VoiceXML (VXML) is a way of defining voice dialogs that take input from the user in the form of dual-tone multifrequency (DTMF) signals or speech phrases and responds with

---

* http://www.w3.org/TR/voicexml21/.

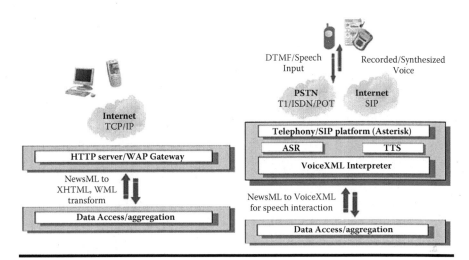

Figure 11.4   HTTP and speech access.

a prerecorded voice or synthesized voice via TTS. This standard is considered the most accepted solution for voice applications on the Web. Figure 11.4 shows the user interaction via HTTP and voice interface.

VXML is an extension of XML designed specifically to provide aural interfaces for Web applications. NewsML is converted to VXML using appropriate XSLT transformations and presented to the end user for voice browsing. The filtered and sorted news items are pushed to the user in the form of interactive voice dialogs. The VXML feed is reorganized based on user browsing interest coming from simple voice commands and keystrokes (DTMF). Figure 11.5 shows a sample VXML newscast snippet.

VoiceXML-based news feed is served to a number of user agents, which include either a standard telephone/mobile phone or Session Initiation Protocol (SIP)-based soft phones. The telephony and SIP interface to the VoiceXML browser is implemented by means of Asterisk[*] IP PBX.

11.3.4.3 E-Ink

One mode of publishing supported by PINC is an output optimized for E-Ink.[†] The technology of this electrophoretic imaging film is based on a new method of converting an electrical signal into a viewable image. Unlike liquid crystal displays (LCDs), an E-Ink display contains electrically charged pigment particles that reflect and absorb light. These particles interact with light in the same way as ink with paper. It results in a bright, high-contrast reflective image that is clearly legible

---

[*] http://www.asterisk.org/.
[†] http://www.eink.com/.

```
<?xml version="1.0" encoding="iso-8859-1" ?>
- <vxml version="2.1">
    <property name="timeout" value="1s" />
    <property name="voicename" value="cepstral callie" />
  + <form id="form1">
  - <form id="form2">
    - <field name="act">
      - <grammar mode="voice" xml:lang="en-US" version="1.0" root="command">
        - <rule id="command" scope="public">
          + <one-of>
          </rule>
        </grammar>
        <prompt bargein="true" bargeintype="hotword" timeout="1s">Can Microsoft make
          Silverlight shine?.The would-be Flash killer works on Windows and Mac OS
          and is headed to Linux, but Web developers want to see it on lots and lots of
          machines before they'll commit.</prompt>
        <option dtmf="1" value="more">more</option>
        <option dtmf="6" value="next">next</option>
        <option dtmf="4" value="back">back</option>
        <option dtmf="5" value="store">store</option>
        <option dtmf="7" value="similar">similar</option>
      - <catch event="noinput nomatch">
          <goto next="#form3" />
        </catch>
      - <filled>
        - <if cond="(act == 'next' || act ==6)">
            <goto next="#form3" />
            <elseif cond="(act == 'back' || act ==4)" />
            <goto next="#form1" />
            <else />
            <submit method="post" namelist="act" next="vxml_interact.php?
              action=showarticle&aid=547" />
          </if>
        </filled>
      </field>
    </form>
```

Figure 11.5   VXML news snippet.

from almost any viewing angle. Films come in a very thin, flexible paper format as well. When the electric field is removed, the particles remain in position, leaving behind a stable image that is readable for days, weeks, even months.

The publishing, media, and content industries have shown a lot of interest in E-Ink displays. The E-Ink device interface in PINC envisions the delivery of personal newspapers on book-like devices such as the Amazon Kindle e-book reader. Figure 11.6 depicts an E-Ink and video-client interface with the system.

11.3.4.4 Video

PINC provides on-demand customized video news via a video media server. In general, IP-TV service is considered to be a simple television broadcast over the Internet; however, there is more to it than simple streaming. IP-TV is a more

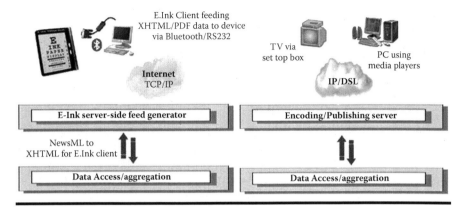

Figure 11.6   E-Ink and video access.

controlled platform capable of user interaction and the delivery of personalized and targeted content. Recent IP-TV platforms integrate multiple ways to trace user choices, preferences, and selections over time. This in turn helps build user attention data for a more personalized video feed. The IP-TV interface takes a selection of video content from the news repository, encodes it into formats suitable for unicast or multicast streaming, and relays it to the client. PINC IP-TV services can be accessed on TV via set-top boxes or media player clients running on various desktop and mobile devices.

11.4 System Architecture

The framework is composed of distributed Web components. The modules responsible for building information needs and performing filtration use an application syndication in the form of Web Services. Such distributed computing gives access to linguistic resources and extensible analysis methods that are necessary for semantic filtering. The personalization module makes use of content filtering with the application of conceptual similarity detection techniques. Collaborative filtering helps to correlate news items for users with similar interests. This approach is effective when the news items, such as movies or voices, have very little metadata to build content-based relevance.

The news acquisition and processing component is based on individual Internet crawling agents. They are responsible for the harvesting of general news entities and personal news from numerous syndication sources. The processing unit extracts metadata from news content and does lexical normalization for conceptual relevancy. The text normalization process provides the semantic mapping between user interest and news items. This process helps generate and store concept term vectors of news data and filter queries based on the user interest model.

The processing of news content in Figure 11.7 shows different stages of concept vector generation. If a filter query containing "risky weather" is used, the system will normalize it in a similar manner (i.e., convert it into "bad weather") and show a higher match with news entity X1, although a query and news entity do not contain exact terms. After the processing of news entities, the information is stored in the system's data repository. The information repository consists of inverted index file structures and a relational database. The inverted list-based index holds the normalized content of news entities. The database maintains user models and news category taxonomy and links tables of news entities in the index with a news taxonomy. News classification and user models are defined in XML. APML-compliant user models are made up of explicit and implicit concept keys. These concept keys

Example of concept vector generation in PINC

News entity X₁:

Runway safety in tough atmospheric conditions is poor, federal report says:
Providing pilots with more accurate information about icy or snowy runways is vital to reducing accidents, said a congressional report Wednesday that blamed safety problems at U.S. airports on sluggish government action.

Response from POS tagger service:

Array ([0] => Runway() [1] => safety(NN) [2] => in(IN) [3] => tough(JJ) [4] => atmospheric(JJ) [5] => conditions(NNS) [6] => is(VBZ) [7] => poor(JJ) [8] => federal(JJ) [9] => report(NN) [10] => says Providing() [11] => pilots(NNS) [12] => with(IN) [13] => more(JJR) [14] => accurate(JJ) [15] => information(NN) [16] => about(IN) [17] => icy(JJ) [18] => or(CC) [19] => snowy(JJ) [20] => runways(NNS) [21] => is(VBZ) [22] => vital(JJ) [23] => to(TO) [24] => reducing(VBG) [25] => accidents(NNS) [26] => said(VBD) [27] => a(DT) [28] => congressional(JJ) [29] => report(NN) [30] => Wednesday(NNP) [31] => that(IN) [32] => blamed(VBD) [33] => safety(NN) [34] => problems(NNS) [35] => at(IN) [36] => U.S(NNP) [37] => airports(NNS) [38] => on(IN) [39] => sluggish(JJ) [40] => government(NN) [41] => action(NN))

Response from term extraction service:

Array ([0] => risky atmospheric conditions [1] => runway safety [2] => congressional report [3] => safety problems [4] => government action [5] => runways [6] => accidents [7] => airports [8] => federal report)

Response from normalization service:

•tough atmospheric conditions -> bad (bad, badness, tough, risky) weather (weather, weather_condition, atmospheric_condition)
•runway safety -> runway (runway, track) guard (guard, safety)
•congressional report -> congress (congress, United States Congress, U.S. Congress, US Congress) account (account, study, written report, news report, story, paper, write up)
•safety problems -> guard (guard, safety) problem (problem, trouble)
•government action -> government (government, authorities, regime, politics, governing, governance, government_activity) action (action, activity)
•runways -> runway (runway, track)
•accidents -> accident (accident, stroke, fortuity, chance event)
•airports -> airport (airport, airdrome, aerodrome)
•Federal report -> federal (federal) account (account, study, written report, news report, story, paper, write up)

Concept vector of news entity X₁:

(bad[1] weather[1] runway[2] guard[2] congress[1] account[2] problem[1] government[1] action[1] accident[1] federal[1])

Figure 11.7 **The process of normalization and concept vector generation.**

are basically terms or keywords used to form information filters. Users can define explicit filters that include the selection of feed sources, predefined category selections, and specification of terms of interest. Implicit filters are made up from user browsing or reading history. News category taxonomy evolves over time; and it is enriched by the flow of fetched news items and metadata.

The personalization component makes use of content and collaborative filters to generate user-adaptive news content in a standard NewsML format. User interest concept vectors are generated from the user model, and if collaborative filtering is enabled, interest vectors from matching user profiles are added to personal news selection filters. These news selection filters are then compared for similarity with the concept vectors of the news entities. Matching news items above a user-specified threshold value are passed on for user presentation.

Modules responsible for information processing and personalization make use of external resources for natural language processing. Access to these linguistic resources (WordNet database, POS tagging rules, term extraction) and similarity checking algorithms are provided via SOAP-based service calls. Such Internet-scale computing (also called cloud computing) provides the system with the capability to efficiently handle complex computational tasks. This is achieved by distributing different components of the system over commodity hardware-based servers across the Internet. At the presentation and data access layers, content is transformed into an appropriate format for delivery through a particular user interface. Interaction modules use browsing and tagging feedback to update the user profile. The interaction component is responsible for caching an active newscast until a user-set timeout or a manual reload occurs. Individual news items or overviews are extracted from the newscast and handed on to the publishing component. Moreover, it relays requests for reload to the information aggregation component and updates the user profile and model by explicit and implicit feedback as well as the information about the news items already read. Finally, it holds the position in an active newscast. Information flow through various components of the system is presented in Figure 11.8.

The publishing component of the system is responsible for the transformation and delivery of the aggregated content to the a specific user interface. The NewsML structure is transformed according to the contextual requirements of the interaction modality and restraints of the interface device. It also embeds feedback mechanisms to (1) give implicit (behavior-based) feedback and (2) give explicit relevance feedback to update the user model. It also provides control mechanisms to navigate through a newscast. Actions by the user are relayed to the interaction component.

The system management component (not shown in the main information flow diagram) is available through a Web-based portal. It offers facilities to system users for editing the base news classification, managing the news repository, managing harvesting agents, and editing user and group models. Moreover, it offers the possibility for all general users to view and edit personal preferences and content filters.

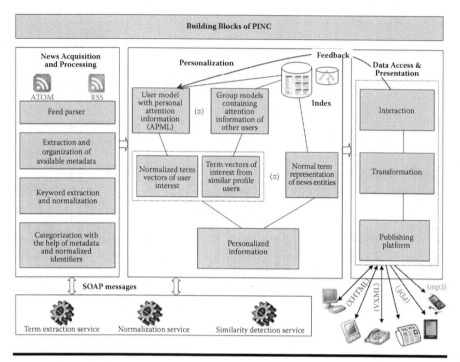

Figure 11.8 PINC architecture.

11.5 Prototype

Based on the proposed architecture, a partial implementation of an interactive newscast with two modes of user interaction has been developed.* The system consists of an information retrieval system to fetch news and information content from affiliated news sites. The news fetching and processing agent is based on a Nutch[†] crawler. The modified parse-RSS and parse-HTML plug-ins are used as fetching agents. These agents traverse through specified feed sources to gather content descriptions and metadata. Fetched content is normalized using specially designed Web Services[‡] integrated with the Nutch crawler. We tested our prototype with external term extraction services from Yahoo! and Topicalizer. It is also possible to use simpler and faster local services that use the removal of stop words and statistical measures to determine keywords. The normalization service uses a WordNet lexical database ported into a local repository.

Lucene, an open source Java-based API for indexing and searching, is used to create a normalized index of fetched news entities. The prototype is developed by

---

* PINC: http://fiicmpc140.tu-graz.ac.at/.
† http://lucene.apache.org/nutch/.
‡ http://fiicmpc140.tu-graz.ac.at/webservices/.

keeping in view the requirements of handling heterogeneous and large collections and news entities. The open source and plug-in-based architectures of Lucene and Nutch allow for ease of modification and handling of multiple content types. The process of detecting similarity is performed in a dynamic manner on an incremental index. The search processing is far more efficient than any conventional database or file-based system. The similarity detection service is based on the vector space model. It creates weighted vectors of content being compared for similarity and user attention filters. These vectors are mapped against the combined local vocabulary of the compared content. The angular measure (dot product) of these vectors is used as a score to determine similarity.

The system has a Web-based management console for user registration, scheduling for content retrieval agents, and profile and interest parameter insertions. The management console furthermore has the capability to add or modify the information retrieval agents, news categories, and interest groups. Based on the user profile, the selected news and information are aggregated as an XML source, which in turn is fed to XSL transformation routines for generating appropriate content for the user's view. The system uses an Apache Web server with mod_negotiation and a PHP (Hypertext Preprocessor) content negotiation library for client-specific automated formatting of XHTML content.

Currently, the system provides access to users with standard desktop browsing support through an application Web server and dialog-based interactive speech browsing through a VXML 2.1-compliant browser. Limited port phone/SIP connectivity is also available for voice access tests. We tested our system with Loquendo's Voxnauta and Voxeo's Prophecy VXML publishing platforms, the latter being freely available with port restriction. Both platforms are capable of VoIP access via SIP clients. Telephony support is added via the Integrated Services Digital Network (ISDN) channel on Asterisk, linking to the voice browser via SIP. A common ISDN-API interface module in Asterisk is used for communication through a basic rate interfaces (BRI) card linking two phone channels to PINC's VXML server.

For vocal presentation, the textual content and dialogs are generated at runtime via the integrated TTS. The archived audio files are converted and transcoded to the proper format, which is suitable for relaying on telephone and Internet channels. The user activities and system access are logged and stored in a behavior database.

11.6 Summary and Future Work

We presented a framework that provides the ability to select adaptive news content from heterogeneous sources and that allows access at any time, from any place. The first goal is achieved by using similarity detection on enhanced metadata to aggregate semantically equivalent news. Collaborative filtering is applied to integrate further news items based on the selection of users with similar interests. The use of adaptive information agents and recommender systems to help users handle the increasing amount of information has increased considerably during last few years. These adaptive systems use content-based, knowledge-based, social, or hybrid filtering mechanisms. A survey [19] about state of the art and possible extensions in recommender systems suggests that despite all of the advances in filtering mechanisms (content/knowledge/social), there is still room for improvement. Possible improvements include less intrusive and improved user modeling, more meaningful and contextual annotation of items, and support for multicriteria ratings. Our research effort tries to fill this gap by the application of conceptual hybrid filtering and a standardized user-modeling approach. This work describes a user-modeling approach that uses both explicit knowledge-based and implicit behavior-based interest data. It stores this information in a reusable format, owned and controlled by individuals, not the system.

The second goal of PINC requirements is met by applying cross-media publishing technologies and integrating multimodal interaction with the system. Thus, a wide range of interfaces can be used to access PINC. An analysis of U.S.-based Internet newspapers found that 86% of these news companies had cross-media publishing support. These publishing modes include print, online, television, and radio [20]. Addition of cross-media publication and multimodal interactions helps overcome inherent weaknesses of any single delivery media. It increases the system audience with alternative access possibilities to meet impulsive user needs. There are efforts to complement news delivery with the addition of one or more media channels [21]. These systems show a need for complementary information infrastructure to filter, link, and present information that satisfies delivery context. In all aspects, PINC is designed for modifiability and extensibility in order to support most of the commonly used information delivery channels. It provides a standardized platform that adds this complementary information infrastructure.

Future work includes user feedback or rating analysis to find the effectiveness of semantic mapping between information needs and news items. We are also exploring the use of a user-modeling component as a user interest profiler. Such a system can be used to automatically create a rich user interest knowledge base. Standardized user attention models provide possibilities of reuse in a number of supporting information retrieval environments.

A complete deployment of the system aims to revolutionize the way a person deals with daily information sources. PINC will provide the convenience of selecting a single most appropriate way of interaction with a vast, personalized body of news, depending on the physical and environmental conditions.

Acknowledgments

Financial support for this research by Styria Media AG, in conjunction with the Endowment Professorship for Innovative Media Technology at Graz University of Technology, is gratefully acknowledged.

Bilal Zaka holds an MSc in electronics from Quaid-i-Azam University, Islamabad, Pakistan. He is systems manager at COMSATS Institute of Information Technology, Pakistan. He received an HEC scholarship to be an overseas researcher in Austria. At present, he is a research fellow and doctoral candidate at the Institute for Information Systems and Computer Media at Graz University of Technology, Austria. His research interests include collaborative Web applications, knowledge management, and multimodal applications for the Internet and computer networks. He has published his research findings in journals and presented his work at several conferences.

Christian Safran is a scientific assistant at the Institute for Information Systems and Computer Media at Graz University of Technology, Austria. He received his diploma in telematics in 2006 and is working on a PhD thesis on collaborative tools for online learning communities. He is a lecturer for Introduction to Structured Programming and Software Development Practical Exercises courses. His research interests include social software, online communities of practice, and the influence of social media on learning.

Frank Kappe completed his study of technical mathematics at Graz University of Technology, Austria in 1988. As part of his PhD dissertation, completed in 1991, he developed the design and a prototype of an Internet-based hypermedia system, "Hyper-G", and then headed its further development until 1996. As a Web pioneer, he developed the first Austrian Web server in 1991, at a time when there were only 12 Web servers in the world, and as an inventor of a content management system, he has published some 60 scientific articles and given numerous talks on hypermedia systems. He commercialized his ideas and cofounded a company, Hyperwave, in 1997. After 10 years as CTO of this company, he is now a professor for innovative media technologies at Graz University of Technology. With his background in academia and industry, he not only looks at technological aspects but also at business models and their impact on society. His current research focus is on virtual worlds and potential applications in academic and commercial environments.

References

1. Klausegger, C., Sinkovics, R. R., and Zou, H. J. Information overload: A cross-national investigation of influence factors and effects. *Marketing Intelligence & Planning*, 2007, 25(7): 691–718.
2. Oviatt, S., Cohen, P. R., Wu, L. et al. Designing the user interface for multimodal speech and gesture applications: State-of-the-art systems and research directions. *Human–Computer Interaction*, 2000, 15(4): 263–322.
3. Larson, J. A., Raman, T. V., and Raggett, D. W3C Multimodal Interaction Framework, W3C Note, May 6, 2003, http://www.w3.org/TR/2003/NOTE-mmi-framework-20030506/.

4. Oviatt, S., and Cohen, P. Multimodal interfaces that process what comes naturally. *Communications of the ACM*, 2000, 43(3): 45–53.

5. Burke, R. Hybrid recommender systems: Survey and experiments. *User Modeling and User-Adapted Interaction*, 2002, 12(4): 331–370.

6. Alton-Schiedl, R., Ekhall, J., van Gelovan, O. et al. SELECT: Social and collaborative filtering of Web documents and news. In *Proceedings of the 5th ERCIM Workshop on User Interfaces for All: User-Tailored Information Environments*, Dagstuhl, Germany, Nov. 28–Dec. 1, 1999, pp. 23–37.

7. Middleton, S. E., Shadbolt, N. R., and De Roure, D. C. Ontological user profiling in recommender systems. *ACM Transactions on Information Systems (TOIS)*, 2004, 22(1): 54–88.

8. Sánchez-Fernández, L., Fernández-García, N., Bernardi, A. et al. An experience with Semantic Web technologies in the news domain. *Workshop on Semantic Web Case Studies and Best Practices for eBusiness*, Ireland, Nov. 2005.

9. Chowdhury, S., and Landoni, M. News aggregator services: User expectations and experience. *Online Information Review*, 2006, 30(2): 100–115.

10. Billsus, D., and Pazzani, M. J. Adaptive news access. *The Adaptive Web*, 2007, 4321: 550–570.

11. Teevan, J., Dumais, S. T., and Horvitz, E. Personalizing search via automated analysis of interests and activities. In *Proceedings of the 28th Annual International ACM SIGIR Conference on Research and Development in Information Retrieval*, Salvador, Brazil, August 15–19, 2005. New York: ACM Press.

12. Kan, L. K., Peng, X., and King, I. A user profile-based approach for personal information access: Shaping your information portfolio. In *Proceedings of the 15th International Conference on World Wide Web*, Edinburgh, Scotland, May 23–26, 2006. New York: ACM Press.

13. Xiao, B., Lunsford, R., Coulston, R., Wesson, M., and Oviatt, S. Modeling multimodal integration patterns and performance in seniors: Toward adaptive processing of individual differences. In *Proceedings of the 5th International Conference on Multimodal Interfaces*, 2003, pp. 265–272. New York: ACM Press.

14. Riedl, J. Guest editor's introduction: Personalization and privacy. *IEEE Internet Computing*, 2001, 5(6): 29–31.

15. Parekh, V., Gwo, J., and Finin, T. W. Mining domain-specific texts and glossaries to evaluate and enrich domain ontologies. *International Conference on Information and Knowledge Engineering*, Las Vegas, NE, June 2004, pp. 533–540.

16. Abel, F., Baumgartner, R., Brooks, A. et al. The personal publication reader. *Semantic Web Challenge, 4th International Semantic Web Conference*, Galway, Ireland, Nov. 2005.

17. Turk, M., and Robertson, G. Perceptual user interfaces. *Communications of the ACM*, 2000, 43(3): 32–34.

18. IETF Draft. RFC 2295, Transparent Content Negotiation in HTTP. March 2008. http://tools.ietf.org/html/rfc2295.

19. Adomavicius, G., and Tuzhilin, A. Toward the next generation of recommender systems: A survey of the state-of-the-art and possible extensions. *IEEE Transactions on Knowledge and Data Engineering*, 2005, 17(6): 734–749.

20. duPlessis, R., and Li, X. Cross-media ownership and its effect on technological convergence of online news content: A content analysis of 100 Internet newspapers.

Paper presented at the annual meeting of the International Communication Association, New Orleans, LA, May 2004, http://www.allacademic.com/meta/p113386_index.html.

21. Ma, Q., Nadamoto, A., and Tanaka, K. Complementary information retrieval for cross-media news content. In *Proceedings of the 2nd ACM International Workshop on Multimedia Databases*, Washington, DC, 2004, pp. 45–54. New York: ACM Press.

Chapter 12

Toward an Adaptive and Personalized Web Interaction Using Human Factors

Panagiotis Germanakos, Nikos Tsianos,
Zacharias Lekkas, Constantinos Mourlas,
Mario Belk, and George Samaras

12.1 Introduction

We are witnessing an extensive and gradual increase in the use of the World Wide Web space, which is a desirable means of communication because of its speed, simplicity, and efficiency. Given the exponential growth of new information sources on the Internet,* the importance of information retrieval and its presentation is critical. Most Web developers create Web pages without taking into account the most important entity of the Internet: the user. The plethora of information and services and the complicated nature of most Web structures intensify the orientation difficulties, as users often lose sight of their original goal, look for stimulating rather than informative material, or even use the navigational features unwisely.

---

* See Internet Domain Survey Host Count: http://www.isc.org.

As the eServices sector rapidly evolves, the need for Web structures that satisfy the heterogeneous needs of its users becomes more evident (Germanakos et al., 2005).

To alleviate such navigational difficulties, researchers have to expend increasing amounts of effort to identify the peculiarities of each user group and design methodologies and systems that can deliver adapted and personalized Web content. The general concept behind all of this is called personalization. Personalization is a broad term, but we can say that all of the solutions offering personalization features meet an abstract common goal: to provide users with what they want or need without expecting them to ask for it explicitly (Mulvenna, Anand, & Buchner, 2000).

Current Web personalization systems use different techniques and paradigms and specific characteristics of the user to create a profile that is used as the primary filtering element for adapting and personalizing Web content with regard to various application fields. Such systems, mostly commercial, include, among others, Broadvision's One-to-One, Microsoft's Firefly Passport (developed by the MIT Media Lab), Macromedia's LikeMinds Preference Server, and Apple's WebObjects. Other, more research-oriented systems include ARCHIMIDES (Bogonicolos et al., 1999), WBI (Barret, Maglio, & Kellem, 1997; Maglio & Barret, 2000), BASAR (Thomas & Fischer, 1997), and mPERSONA (Panayiotou & Samaras, 2004). Significant implementations have also been developed to provide adapted educational content to students using various adaptive hypermedia techniques. Such systems include INSPIRE (Papanikolaou et al., 2003), ELM-ART (Weber & Specht, 1997), AHA! (Brusilovsky, Eklund, & Schwarz, 1998), Interbook (De Bra & Calvi, 1998), and others.

The user profile (Germanakos et al., 2007a, 2008a) is considered to be the most vital component of Web personalization and adaptation systems. In this chapter, we will discuss the importance of user profiles, and will present a comprehensive user profile that incorporates intrinsic user characteristics, such as user perceptual preferences (visual, cognitive, and emotional processing parameters), on top of the "traditional" ones. We introduce an innovative adaptation and personalization architecture, AdaptiveWeb, emphasizing the significance and peculiarities of the various user profile aspects it employs, considered necessary for the provision of an optimized personalization Web-based result.

More specifically, Section 12.2 provides a brief theoretical background, comparing adaptive hypermedia and Web personalization categories and technologies; it presents the user profile fundamentals and investigates a comprehensive user profile that consists of cognitive processing factors; and it depicts a high-level correlation diagram showing the relation between the comprehensive user profile and the information space. Section 12.3 describes the AdaptiveWeb system architecture and gives a brief description of each Web component. Section 12.4 presents the user profile extraction process, as well as the adaptation process, in two application areas of eLearning and eCommerce, describing actual code instances and pseudo-code (with the use of metadata) as well as the semantics used for achieving content adaptation. Sections 12.5, 12.6, and 12.7 present a mature evaluation of the system in both environments. Finally, Section 12.8 concludes this chapter and presents a number of ideas for opportunities for future work.

12.2 Theoretical Background

12.2.1 Constructive Comparison of Adaptive Hypermedia and Web Personalization

In considering adaptation and personalization categories and technologies, we refer to adaptive hypermedia and Web personalization, respectively, because they both make use of a user profile to achieve their goals, and together they offer the most optimized adapted content result to the user. In light of this statement, it is essential to highlight their similarities and differences and to identify their convergence point, which is their objective to develop techniques to adapt what is presented to the user based on the specific user needs identified in the extracted user profiles (Germanakos et al., 2008a; Tsianos et al., 2008a).

Generally, adaptive hypermedia is the manipulation of the link or content structure of an application to achieve adaptation, and it makes use of an explicit user model (Brusilovsky, 2001; Eklund & Sinclair, 2000). Adaptive hypermedia is a relatively old and well-established area of research (Brusilovsky & Peylo, 2003). Educational hypermedia and online information systems are the most popular, accounting for about two-thirds of the research efforts in adaptive hypermedia. Adaptation effects vary from one system to another. These effects are grouped into three major adaptation technologies: adaptive content selection (Brusilovsky & Nejdl, 2004), adaptive presentation (or content-level adaptation), and adaptive navigation support (or link-level adaptation) (Brusilovsky, 2001; Eklund & Sinclair, 2000).

In contrast, Web personalization is the whole process of collecting, classifying, and analyzing Web data and determining, on the basis of these data, the actions that should be performed so that the user is presented with personalized information. Personalization levels have been classified into link personalization, content personalization, context personalization, and authorized personalization (Lankhorst et al., 2002; Rossi, Schwade, & Guimaraes, 2001). The technologies employed in order to implement the processing phases mentioned above, as well as the Web personalization categories, are distinguished into content-based filtering, rule-based filtering, collaborative filtering, Web usage mining, demographic-based filtering, agent technologies, and cluster models (Mobasher et al., 2002; Pazzani, 2005).

As its name implies, Web personalization refers to Web applications exclusively; and it is a relatively new area of research. One could argue that the areas of application of these two research areas are different: adaptive hypermedia is popular for its use in educational hypermedia and online information systems (Brusilovsky, 2001), whereas Web personalization is popular for its use in eBusiness services delivery.

It could be inferred, therefore, that Web personalization has a more extended scope than adaptive hypermedia.

The most evident technical similarities are that they both make use of a user model to achieve their goals, and they have in common two of the adaptation/personalization techniques: the adaptive-navigation support and the adaptive presentation. Finally, it is noteworthy to mention that they both make use of techniques from machine learning, information retrieval and filtering, databases, knowledge representation, data mining, text mining, statistics, and human–computer interaction (Mobasher, Anand, & Kobsa, 2007).

12.2.2 User Profile Fundamentals

The user profile is the core element of most adaptation and personalization systems. According to Merriam-Webster's dictionary, the term *profile* means "a representation of something in outline."* A user profile can be thought of as a set of data representing the significant features of the user.

One of the key technical issues in developing personalization applications is the problem of how to construct accurate and comprehensive profiles of individual users and how these can be used to identify a user and describe the user behavior, especially if the user is moving (Panayiotou & Samaras, 2004). The objective of the user profile is the creation of an information base that contains the preferences, characteristics, and activities of the user. A user profile can be built from a set of keywords that describe the user's interest areas compared against information items.

The user profile can either be *static*, when it contains information that rarely or never changes (e.g., demographic information), or *dynamic*, when the data change frequently. Such information is obtained either *explicitly*, using online registration forms and questionnaires resulting in static user profiles, or *implicitly*, by recording the navigational behavior and/or the preferences of each user (Germanakos et al., 2007a).

12.2.3 Comprehensive User Profile Used in the AdaptiveWeb System

Based on the abovementioned considerations, we introduce a comprehensive user profile, which serves as the main raw Web content filtering module and is used in the AdaptiveWeb system developed for personalizing and adapting the users' environment to their individual perceptual characteristics and needs. This module could accept requests from an entry point module and, after the necessary processing and further communication with a Semantic Web-based content module, provide the requested adapted and personalized results, as we will describe below. The comprehensive user profile has two main components: the user's traditional characteristics and the user's perceptual preference characteristics.

---

* See http://mw1.merriam-Webster.com/dictionary/profile.

12.2.3.1 Traditional User Profile

The traditional user profile contains all of the information related to the user that is necessary for the Web personalization process. It is composed of two elements: (1) the *user characteristics*, which are the "traditional" characteristics such as knowledge, goals, background, experience, preferences, activities, demographic information (age, gender), and socioeconomic information (income, class, job sector); and (2) the *device/channel characteristics*, consisting of information about the device or channel the user is using, such as bandwidth, displays, text writing, connectivity, size, power processing, interface and data entry, memory and storage capacity, latency (high or low), and battery lifetime. Device/channel characteristics are particularly important for creating integrated user profiles of mobile users because these characteristics summarize the unique technical aspects of varied mobile devices. Both user and device/channel characteristics complete the user profile from the user's point of view.

12.2.3.2 User Perceptual Preference Characteristics

User perceptual preference characteristics comprise the new component or dimension of the user profile. The component contains all of the visual attention, cognitive, and emotional processing parameters that complete the user preferences and fulfill the user profile. User perceptual preference characteristics can be described as a continuous mental processing that starts with the perception of an object in the user's attentional visual field and proceeds through a number of cognitive, learning, and emotional processes in direct response to the initial stimulus, as depicted in Figure 12.1.

These characteristics, discussed primarily in Germanakos and colleagues (2007a), formulate a three-dimensional approach to the problem of building a user model that determines the visual attention, cognitive, and emotional processing taking place throughout the whole process of accepting an object of perception (stimulus) until the comprehensive response to it (Germanakos et al., 2005).

The first dimension investigates users' *cognitive style*, the second their *visual and cognitive processing efficiency*, while the third captures their *emotional processing* during the interaction process with the information space.

- *Cognitive styles* represent an individual's typical or habitual mode of problem solving, thinking, perceiving, or remembering and "are considered to be trait-like, relatively stable characteristics of individuals, whereas learning strategies are more state-driven . . ." (McKay, Fischler, & Dunn, 2003). Among the numerous proposed cognitive style typologies (Cassidy, 2004; Kolb & Kolb, 2005; MyersBriggs et al., 1998), Riding's Cognitive Style Analysis (Riding, 2001) is most often used because it applies in a greater number of information distribution circumstances, since it deals with cognitive rather than learning styles. Furthermore, its implications can be mapped on the information

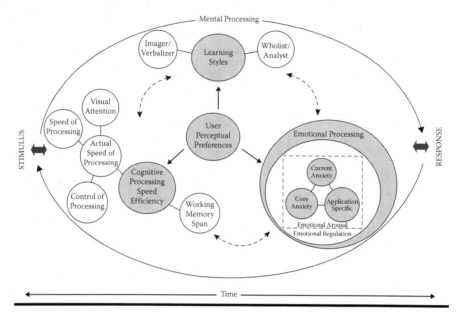

Figure 12.1 User perceptual preference characteristics: Three-dimensional approach.

space more precisely because it consists of two distinct scales that respond to different aspects of the Web. The imager–verbalizer axis affects the way information is presented, and the wholist–analyst dimension is relevant to the structure of the information and the navigational path of the user. Moreover, it is a very inclusive theory derived from a number of preexisting theories that were recapitulated into these two axes.

■ The *cognitive processing* parameters (Demetriou & Kazi, 2001) included in the model are

– Control of processing (the processes that identify and register goal-relevant information and block out dominant or appealing but actually irrelevant information)

– Speed of processing (the maximum speed at which a given mental act may be efficiently executed)

– Working memory span (the processes that enable a person to hold information in an active state while integrating it with other information until the current problem is solved) (Baddeley, 1992)

– Visual attention (based on the empirically validated assumption that when a person is performing a cognitive task, while watching a display, the location of his or her gaze corresponds to the symbol currently being processed in working memory and, moreover, that the eye naturally focuses on areas that are most likely to be informative)

■ *Emotional processing* is a pluralistic construct composed of two mechanisms:
  – Emotional arousal, which is the capacity of a human being to sense and experience specific emotional situations
  – Emotion regulation, which is the way that an individual perceives and controls his or her emotions

Heavy focus is placed on anxiety as the main indicator of emotional arousal because it is correlated with academic performance (Cassady & Johnson, 2002) as well as with performance in computer-mediated learning procedures (Smith & Caputi, 2007).

The construct of emotional regulation includes the concepts of emotional control (self-awareness, emotional management, self-motivation) (Goleman, 1995), self-efficacy (Bandura, 1994), emotional experience, and emotional expression (Halberstadt, 2005). By combining the levels of anxiety with the moderating role of emotion regulation, it is possible to examine how affectional responses hamper or promote learning procedures (Lekkas et al., 2007).

12.2.4 Relating the Comprehensive Profile with the Information Space: A High-Level Correlation Diagram

To illustrate the implications of the three dimensions and their relation with the information space, Figure 12.2 presents a high-level correlation of these implications with selected tags of the information space (a code used in Web languages to define a format change or hypertext link). These tags (images, text, information quantity, links–learner control, navigation support, additional navigation support, and aesthetics) have gone through an extensive optimization representing groups of data affected after the mapping with the implications. The main reason we selected these tags is that they represent the primary subsidiaries of a Web-based content. With the necessary processing and/or alteration, we could provide the same content in different ways (according to a specific user's profile) but without degrading the message conveyed.

The particular mapping is based on specific rules created for the combination of these tags and the variation of their value in order to better filter the raw content and deliver the most personalized Web-based result to the user. As shown in Figure 12.2, each dimension has primary (solid line) and secondary (dashed line) implications on the information space, dynamically altering the weight of the tags.

Regarding learning style, the number of images (few or many) to be displayed, for example, has a primary implication on imagers, while text (more concise or abstract) has a secondary implication. An analyst may primarily affect the links–learner control and navigation support tags, which are secondarily affected by high and medium emotional processing. Emotional processing in turn might secondarily affect the number of images or kind of text to be displayed. The actual

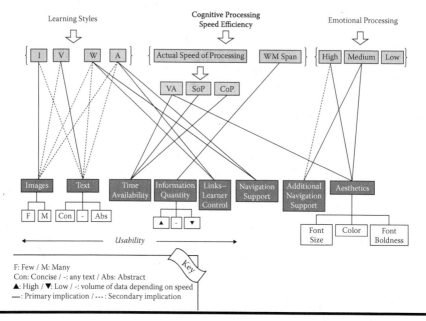

Figure 12.2   Data–implications correlation diagram.

speed of processing parameters (visual attention, speed of processing, and control of processing) and working memory span primarily affect information quantity. Emotional processing primarily affects additional navigation support and aesthetics (as visual attention), while secondary affects information quantity.

Using the data–implications correlation diagram, a user might be identified, for example, with a verbalizer (V)–wholist (W) learning style, an actual cognitive processing speed efficiency of 1000 msec, a fair working memory span (weighting 5/7) with regard to cognitive processing speed efficiency, and high emotional processing. The tags affected in this particular instance are the images (few images displayed), text (any text could be delivered), information quantity (less information because the user's cognitive speed is moderate), links–learner control (less learner control because the user is wholist), additional navigation support (significant because the user has high emotional processing), and high aesthetics (to give more structured and well-defined information with more colors, larger fonts, bold text, and so on, again because of the user's high emotional processing). Note that in the case of internal correlation conflicts, primary implications take over secondary ones.

Additionally, since emotional processing is the most dynamic parameter compared to the others, any changes occurring at any given time can directly affect the yielded value of the adaptation and personalization rules and hence the format of the content delivered.

12.3 AdaptiveWeb System's Architecture

The current system, AdaptiveWeb[*] (see Figure 12.3) (Germanakos et al., 2007b, 2007c), is a Web application that can be ported to both desktop computers and mobile devices. It is composed of five interrelated components,[†] each representing a stand-alone Web-based system:

Component 1, User Profiling Construction: This is the initial step that the user makes for the AdaptiveWeb system's personalization process. It is a vital part of the system. At this point, the user creates his or her comprehensive profile, which will be mapped at a later stage with the personalized content.

Component 2, System Management and Administration: This is the system's back end and is used by the administrators or other authorized users to manage and analyze the personalized user profiles. All of the AdaptiveWeb personalized members' results from the tests taken and questionnaires completed during the User Profiling Construction are processed and shown.

Component 3, Semantic Content Creation: The third component, the system's Semantic Content Editor, is still under study. Using this component, the provider can create his or her own content by defining objects that will be embodied in a given content. The content structure has to be well formatted, and the objects have to be well defined (based on given semantic tags) by the editor in order to give the best results to the end user. The technology used for creating the personalized content is a more expressive semantic Web language, such as Web Ontology Language (OWL) or Resource Description Framework (RDF), used for describing data and to focus on the relation between them.

Component 4, Adaptation and Personalization Process (Mapping Rules): In this section, all of the system's components interact with each other in order to create and give personalized and adapted content to the end user. The author of a page uploads the content on the system's database; the content is mapped according to the system's mapping rules. The mapping rules are functions that run on the AdaptiveWeb server and comprise the main body of the adaptation and personalization procedures of the provider's content according to the user's comprehensive profile. For experimental purposes, we have authored an eLearning environment with a predefined content for adaptation and personalization.

Component 5, AdaptiveWeb Interface: The AdaptiveWeb user interface, called AdaptiveInteliWeb (AIWeb), is a Web application used for displaying the raw or personalized and adapted content on the user's device. The main concept of this component is to provide a framework in which all of the personalized

---

[*] See http://www3.cs.ucy.ac.cy/adaptiveWeb.
[†] The technology used to build each Web system's component is ASP .Net: http://asp.net.

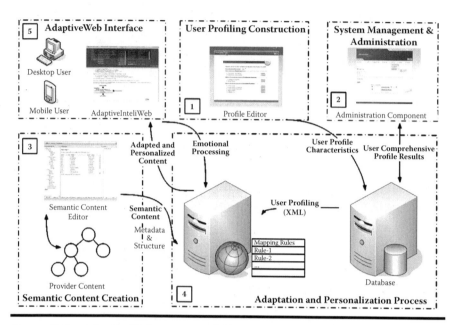

Figure 12.3 AdaptiveWeb system architecture.

Web sites can be navigated. Using this interface, the user navigates through the provider's content. Based on his or her profile, further support is provided to the user via a slide-in panel at the top of the screen, containing all navigation support and learner control attributes that are adjusted accordingly.

12.4 Adaptation Process

12.4.1 User Profile Construction Process

To get personalized and adapted content, a user must create his or her own comprehensive profile. The User Profiling Construction component is responsible for the creation of this content (see Figure 12.4).

At this point, the user must provide traditional and device/channel characteristics and further complete a number of real-time tests (using psychometric tools for measuring attention and cognitive processing efficiency), which are preloaded and executed on the client, in order to get the actual response times of his or her answers as well as to answer predefined questionnaires for generating a cumulative profile. The psychometric instruments we use include the following:

■ Riding's Cognitive Style Analysis (2001) for the learning/cognitive styles dimension

- A series of real-time measurements for the cognitive parameters (speed of processing, control of processing, working memory, and visual attention), similar to tests developed on the E-prime platform[*]
- The Emotional Control 27-item questionnaire that we developed (Cronbach's alpha, 0.76); the Test Anxiety Inventory (Spielberger & Vagg, 1995) to measure application-specific anxiety (educational process, in our case); and the State-Trait Anxiety Inventory (Spielberger, 1983) to measure general (core) anxiety

While users navigate through our application, they can use a sliding anxiety bar, which is part of the interface, to self-report feelings of inconvenience and high levels of anxiety that burden their cognitive effort. This self-report measure will be correlated with general (core) and application-specific levels of anxiety in order to clarify the extent of their correlation and to further optimize the psychometric process.

Our main concern is to ensure openness and interoperability within and among system components. In case an external component wants to access the user's profile, either for adaptation or for historic or statistical calculations, the system must be able to support the extraction of the user's profile. In order to achieve this, the user's profile must be easily extendible and easy to handle. Using XML for implementing the user's profile seems to be the best way to achieve this. XML[†] enables the extendibility we need and enhances interoperability and integration among systems components.

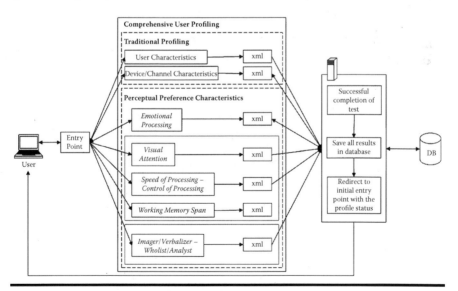

Figure 12.4   User Profiling Construction data flow diagram.

---

[*] See http://www.pstnet.com/products/e-prime/.
[†] See http://www.w3.org/XML/.

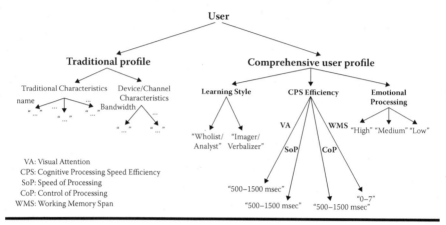

Figure 12.5   The tree structure of the comprehensive user profile XML document.

We have designed a Web Service (a software system designed to support interoperable machine-to-machine interaction over a network) for retrieving the user's comprehensive profile. Depending on the needs of a third-party system that interacts with our system through this middleware, calculations are made and exported in XML. For a better insight, the tree structure of the comprehensive user profile is depicted in Figure 12.5.

12.4.2 Content Authoring and Mapping Process

In order to evaluate the system's performance as well as the impact of our model's dimensions into the information space, we designed two experimental settings in the application fields of eLearning and eCommerce, by authoring predefined content for adaptation and personalization.

The eLearning environment includes a course named Introduction to Algorithms, a first-year eLearning course that aims to provide students with analytic thinking and top-down methodology techniques for further development of constructive solutions to given problems. The eCommerce (Web) environment uses the design and information content of an existing commercial Web site of Sony Style.* This Web site provides product specifications of the Sony Company. We developed an exact replica of the Sony Vaio Notebooks section in http://www.sonystyle.com.

The general methodology and theory behind the content adaptation procedure are the same in both environments, but with slight differences based on the peculiarities and constraints underlined by each environment itself, as we explain in the following sections.

---

* See http://www.sonystyle.com (date extracted: September 19, 2007).

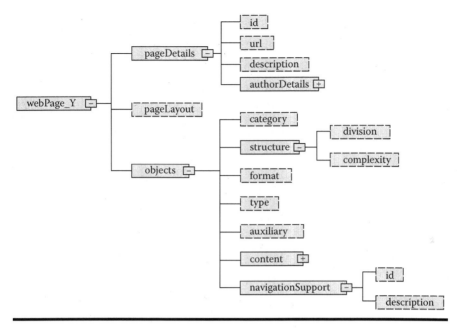

Figure 12.6   Content and structure description schema (eLearning).

To provide insight into the adaptation process and how data flows, we will discuss how the personalized content (the Introduction to Algorithms predefined eLearning environment) interacts with the comprehensive user profile, using specific mapping rules. In Figure 12.6, the content and structure description schema is shown; Figure 12.7 shows the whole adaptation process.

When users want to interact with the adapted and personalized content, they have to give their credentials for retrieving their profile. In this particular example (see Figure 12.7), the user has an imager/wholist learning style, an average knowledge of the subject (computer knowledge) based on the traditional characteristics, an actual cognitive processing speed efficiency of 1200 msec, a fair working memory span (weighting 5/7), and high emotional processing. Using these preferences, the data–implications correlation diagram is evaluated.

Every Web page is detached into stand-alone objects, each one having special characteristics. In our example, the user visits the WebPage_Y Web page. First, the main XML document of this Web page is retrieved; it contains all of the information needed to build the Web page: (1) the page details, such as the URL of the page, an abstract description, and author's details; (2) the page layout, which is a predefined HTML document (supplied by the provider) that specifies divisions/frames in the page for positioning each object; and (3) all objects (text, image, audio, video, etc.) that comprise the content of the Web page (see Figure 12.6).

We now have all of the information that we need for adapting the content: the data–implications correlation diagram based on the user's comprehensive profile and the content description of the particular Web page. The next step is to map the implications with the Web page's content for assembling the final version of the provider's content.

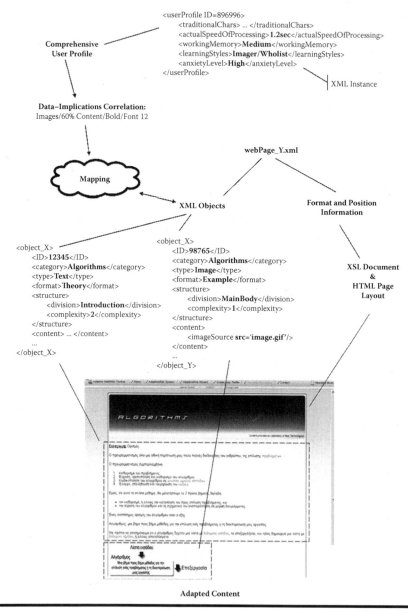

Figure 12.7   The adaptation process.

The interpretation of the user's data–implications correlation diagram results in the following conclusions: (1) the user is an imager, so the provision of visual information is predominant; (2) the user receives 60% of the content which is of average complexity, because this user has a medium cognitive processing speed efficiency, average knowledge of the subject (computer knowledge), and a high level of anxiety; (3) the content will be presented in a 12-point boldfaced font according to the notion of enhancing clear-cut aesthetics for anxious users.

Figure 12.8 shows the mapping process, using our example, explained in pseudocode. Unlike HTML documents, XML documents do not provide formatting or display information. For this purpose, XSL (eXtensible Stylesheet Language) is used, and the author places objects in specified subdivisions of the Web page (HTML layout document).

The content is adapted according to the user's preferences and then loaded onto the user's device. While navigating, the user can change his or her anxiety level by using a dynamic slide bar on the system's toolbar. When the user changes the anxiety level, the server is alerted and a new data–implications correlation diagram is generated with a new adaptation process to take place.

In the eCommerce environment, the mapping process between the Web content and the user's profile is the same as shown for eLearning but does not consider the user's emotional characteristics (e.g., anxiety) because this factor does not usually

---

Algorithm: Mapping Process Phase

Input: User's data–implications correlation diagram (`contentAmount`, `fontSize`, `fontWeight`, `learningStyles`), WebObjects, XSL document, HTML layout

Output: Generate an adapted and personalized Web page

Execute these steps (top-down):

1. For each structure division (`Introduction`, `MainBody`, `Conclusion`), filter out the implication's `contentAmount` of the `WebObjects` in ascending order based on their complexity (`<complexity>`).

2. Further filter each remaining object based on its `<type>` tag:

```
if (learningStyle1 = Imager)
      Add image objects;
elseif (learningStyle1 = Verbalizer)
      Add text objects;
if (object has NavigationSupport Tag){
      var wordDefinitionObject = retrieveWordDefinitions(objectID)
      var navigationSupportType;
      if (learningStyle2 = Analyst)
          getNavigationSupportType(objectID);
          Show description in popup up window;
      elseif (learningStyle2 = Wholist OR learningStyle2 = Intermediate)
          getNavigationSupportType(objectID);
          Show description in tooltip on mouseover;
}
```

3. Format each object based on the `fontSize` and `fontWeight` and the XSL (eXtensive stylesheet).

4. Position each object in the right structure division based on the HTML layout document.

Figure 12.8 Mapping process example (pseudocode).

apply in generic Web environments (i.e., we cannot use the time availability as a constraint to control users' emotional reactions because the navigation time over such Web structures is subject to user discretion).

The main differences between the eLearning and eCommerce environments are the diagrammatical representations of the content (primarily driven by users' typologies) and the provision of extra navigation support tools, devised to be more applicable while interacting with an eCommerce environment. The content and structure description schema in this environment is therefore extended with additional semantic tags, as depicted in Figure 12.9.

Section 12.4.3 explains in more detail the AdaptiveWeb environment, AdaptiveInteliWeb, where all personalized content is shown along with the extra navigation support and learner control that differ according to each user's profile and application area.

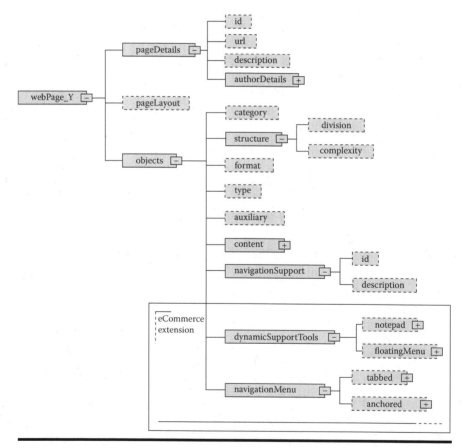

Figure 12.9 Content and structure description schema (extension for eCommerce).

12.4.3 Viewing the Adapted Content: The AdaptiveInteliWeb Environment

The last component of the architecture is the AdaptiveWeb user interface, AdaptiveInteliWeb (see Figure 12.10), which is a Web application used for displaying the raw and/or personalized and adapted content on the user's device—a home desktop, a laptop, or a mobile device.

The main concept of this component is to provide a framework in which all personalized Web sites can be navigated. Using this interface, users interact with the provider's content and, based on their profile, further support is provided via a slide-in panel at the top of the screen containing all navigation support and learner control attributes that are adjusted accordingly. Initially, the interface shows the

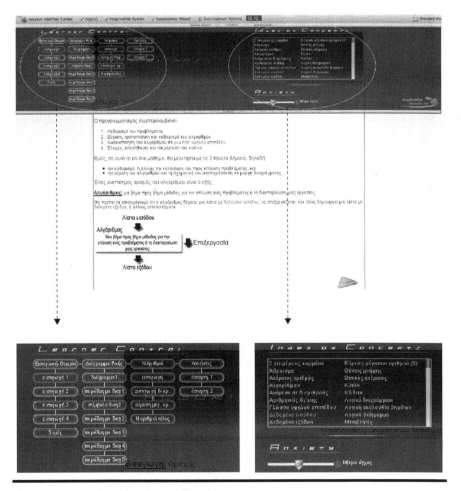

Figure 12.10   The AdaptiveInteliWeb component.

raw, not personalized, content of the provider. When users want to personalize and adapt the content according to their comprehensive profile, they must first enter a username and password. The corresponding profile is loaded onto the server and, in proportion with the individual user's cumulative characteristics, the content of the provider is mapped with the mapping rules, as described earlier.

Sections 12.4.3.1 and 12.4.3.2 review the framework, adjusted to both environments (eLearning and eCommerce), showing the main differences regarding the content adaptation and presentation, as well as the additional navigation support tools used in the eCommerce paradigm.

12.4.3.1 eLearning Environment

Figure 12.11 shows two users, each with a different profile, and the raw content adapted accordingly (with different personalization auxiliary tools provided in each case). The matching process in this case is the same as stated previously; all navigation support and learner control information is kept in the content description XML document as well as in the XSL document and the HTML layout document for the objects' formatting and positioning.

As seen in this figure, the same content has been adapted and a different learner control and different navigation support are provided. Based on theory (Sadler-Smith & Riding, 1999), the analyst–imager has a more analytic diagram with an extra description; the navigation support provided (analytic description of definitions) is in popup windows, so this user can manage the entire lesson, along with its definitions, independently. In the learner control support (the slide-in help panel from the top of the page) is a linkable sitemap of the whole eLearning lesson, plus the entire lesson's definitions in alphabetic order and an anxiety bar for changing the user's current anxiety level. In contrast, the wholist–verbalizer has more text than images and diagrams; the navigation support and learner control support are more restricted and are provided specifically for guidance. The analytic description of a definition is shown in a tooltip only when the user moves the mouse over it, and the learner control shows only the current chapter's pages and allows the user to navigate only to the next and the previous pages. As mentioned before, the wholist user needs more guidance than the analyst user, who prefers to build the lesson as he or she wishes.

12.4.3.2 eCommerce Environment

In the eCommerce environment, the interface is altered as shown in Figure 12.12. The figure depicts an exact replica of the Sony Web site without any personalization, while Figures 12.12b and 12.12c show the same Web site after the personalization and adaptation processes have been initiated, with the content to be adapted according to the user's comprehensive profile.

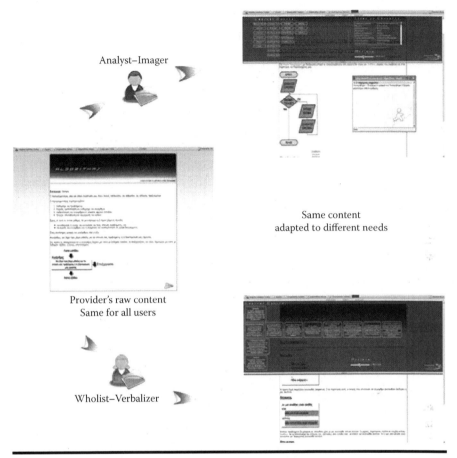

Analyst–Imager

Same content
adapted to different needs

Provider's raw content
Same for all users

Wholist–Verbalizer

Figure 12.11 **Content adaptation according to a user's comprehensive profile (eLearning).**

As we can see, the original environment has been altered according to rules that define the typologies of the users in terms of content reconstruction and supportive tools. For example, a user might be identified as an analyst–imager with low working memory, and therefore the Web environment during the interaction time would be the same as shown in Figure 12.12b. The information will be presented in a diagrammatic form (imager) and enriched with menu tabs (analyst) for easier accessibility with the myNotepad tool (temporary memory buffer) for storing section summaries (low working memory). If the user is identified as a wholist–verbalizer, the content will be automatically reconstructed as in Figure 12.12c, where a floating menu with anchors (wholist) has been added to guide the user to specific parts of the content during interaction. In this case, no diagrammatical presentation is used because the user is a verbalizer.

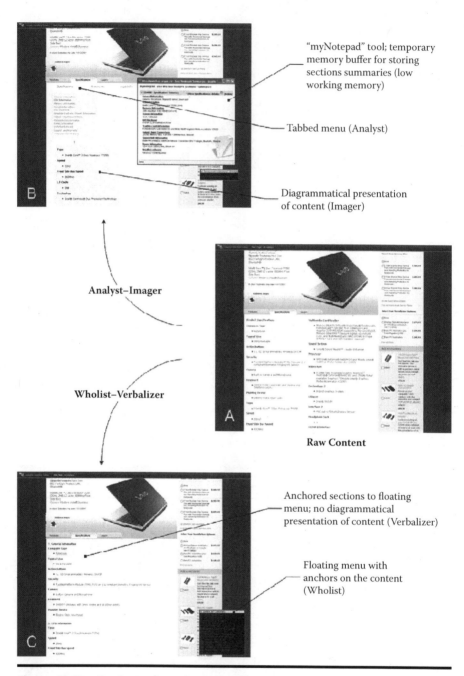

"myNotepad" tool; temporary memory buffer for storing sections summaries (low working memory)

Tabbed menu (Analyst)

Diagrammatical presentation of content (Imager)

Analyst–Imager

Wholist–Verbalizer

Raw Content

Anchored sections to floating menu; no diagrammatical presentation of content (Verbalizer)

Floating menu with anchors on the content (Wholist)

Figure 12.12 Content adaptation according to a user's comprehensive profile (eCommerce).

12.5 Evaluating System Performance

The AdaptiveWeb system is currently in its final stage. All of the components except the Semantic Content Creation have been developed and are running smoothly.

To measure system performance, functional behavior, and efficiency, we ran two different simulations with 100 threads (users) each: (1) users retrieving raw content without any personalization and adaptation taking place and (2) users interacting with adapted and personalized content. In the second scenario, there was a significant increase compared to the raw content scenario, in the number of functions and modules run, such as user profile retrieval, dynamic content adaptation, dynamic learner control tools, and navigational support. Based on the simulations that were made (see Table 12.1), we assume the following: (1) Deviation for raw content is 72 ms, and for personalized content, 110 ms. This difference is expected because the system uses more functional components, such as profile loading and dynamic content, in the case of personalized content. Consequently, this scenario consumes more network resources, causing the deviation of our average to be greater than that of the raw content test. The deviation is not considered to be significantly greater, and this metric result thus proves that the system is stable and efficient. (2) The throughput for the raw content scenario was 14493.17 Kb/min, while the personalized content was 17951.52 Kb/min. Based on the latter results, the system is again considered efficient mainly because the difference in the throughput between the two scenarios is minimal. Taking into consideration that major component functionality is used in the case of personalized content, this small difference suggests the efficiency of the system. (3) The same arguments are true in the case of the average response times. The average response time for the raw content scenario was 138 ms, while the personalized content was 183 ms, signifying a discernible difference among them. However, the system still appears responsive to the user, proving its efficiency.

Table 12.1 Summary Data of Each Simulation Scenario

	Raw Content Scenario	Personalized Content Scenario
Average Response Time	138 ms	183 ms
Deviation	72 ms	110 ms
Throughput	14493.17 Kb/min	17951.52 Kb/min
Median	141 ms	172 ms
Threads (Users)	100 users	100 users

12.6 Evaluation of the eLearning Paradigm

Because of an increased interest in distance education via the Internet, we decided to implement the first phase of our experiments in an eLearning environment, with the corresponding characteristics and constraints imposed by its nature. In this case, we were able to control factors such as previous knowledge of and experience with distributed information as well as the given interaction time of the users with the system, since learning in the context of a specific course is a far more controlled condition than Web browsing. More specifically, we sought to investigate our main research hypotheses:

1. Are the cognitive and emotional parameters of our model significantly important in the context of an educational hypermedia application?
2. Does matching the presentation and structure of the information to users' perceptual preferences increase academic performance?

12.6.1 Sampling and Procedure

The experiment consisted of two distinct phases: phase I was conducted at the University of Cyprus, and phase II was conducted at the University of Athens. The aim of the first experiment was to clarify whether matching (or mismatching) instructional style to users' cognitive style improves performance. The second experiment focused on the importance of matching instructional style to the remaining parameters of our model (working memory, cognitive processing efficiency, and emotional processing).

All of the participants were students from either the University of Cyprus or the University of Athens; phase I was conducted with a sample of 138 students; phase II, with 82 students. 35% of the participants were male, 65% were female, and their ages varied from 17 to 22 years, with a mean age of 19. The environment in which the procedure took place was an eLearning course on algorithms. The course subject was chosen because students of the departments where the experiment took place had absolutely no experience in computer science and traditionally performed poorly. By controlling the factor of experience in this way, we divided our sample into two groups: almost half of the participants were provided with information matched to their perceptual preferences, while the other half were taught in a mismatched way. The match–mismatch factor was their cognitive style (imager–verbalizer, wholist–analyst) at phase I of the experiment, while phase II estimated the effect of matching the actual cognitive speed of processing (time availability based on their type: fast, medium, or slow) and working memory span (complete or broken content provision depending on whether they had high, medium, or low capacity). We expected that the users in the matched condition, in both phase I and phase II, would perform better than those in the mismatched condition.

Table 12.2 Implications for Matched and Mismatched Conditions

	Cognitive Style	*Working Memory*	*Cognitive Processing Speed Efficiency*	*Emotional Processing*
Matched Condition	Presentation and structure of information match user's preference	Users with low working memory are provided with segmented information	Users have at their disposal the amount of time that fits their ability	Users with moderate and high levels of anxiety receive aesthetic enhancement of the content and navigational help
Mismatched Condition	Presentation and structure of information do not match user's preference	Users with low working memory are provided with the whole information	Users' available amount of time does not coincide with their ability	Users with moderate and high levels of anxiety receive no additional help or aesthetics

In order to evaluate the effect of matched and mismatched conditions, participants took an online assessment test on the subject they were taught (algorithms). This examination was taken as soon as the eLearning procedure ended in order to control for long-term memory decay effects. The dependent variable used to assess the effect of adaptation to users' preferences was the participants' score on the online exam.

Note that matching and mismatching instructional styles is a process with different implications for each dimension of our model (see Table 12.2).

12.6.2 Results

As expected, in both experiments, the matched condition group outperformed the mismatched group (Germanakos et al., 2008a, 2008b; Tsianos et al., 2007, 2008b). Figure 12.13 displays the aggregated differences in performance (the dependent variable of examination score) in matched and mismatched conditions.

Table 12.3 shows the differences of means (one-way analysis of variance [ANOVA]) and their statistical significance for the parameters of cognitive style, cognitive efficiency speed, and emotional processing.

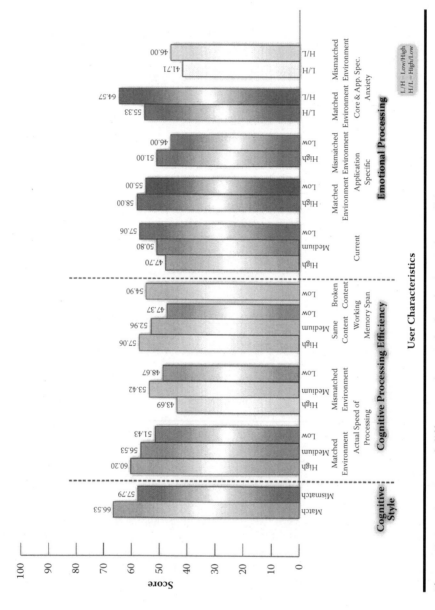

Figure 12.13 Aggregated differences in matched and mismatch conditions.

Table 12.3   Differences of Means in the Matched and Mismatched Conditions

	Match Score	Match n	Mismatch Score	Mismatch n	F	Sig.
Cognitive Style	66.53%	53	57.79%	61	6.330	0.013
Cognitive Efficiency Speed	57.00%	41	48.93%	41	5.345	0.023
Emotional Processing	57.91%	23	48.45%	29	4.357	0.042

In the case of emotional processing, results showed that if an individual reports high levels of anxiety on either the core anxiety or the specific anxiety questionnaire, the matched condition benefits his or her performance (Lekkas et al., 2008). Although we refer to the construct of emotional regulation and the self-report tool, which have both shown statistically significant correlation (negative and positive, respectively) to anxiety, such an analysis is beyond the scope of this chapter.

The relatively small sample that falls into each category and its distribution hamper the statistical analysis of the working memory (WM) parameter. In any case, the difference between those with high WM and those with low WM, when both categories receive nonsegmented (whole) content, approaches statistical significance: 57.06% for those with high WM, 47.37% for those with low WM, Welch statistic = 3.988, $p = 0.054$. This result demonstrates that WM has some effect on an eLearning environment. Moreover, if those with low WM received segmented information, then the difference of means decreases and becomes nonsignificant (57.06% for high WM, 54.90% for those with low WM, Welch statistic = 0.165, $p = 0.687$).

12.7   Evaluation of the eCommerce Paradigm

The second phase of our research was to apply our evaluated information processing model in a setting other than educational (more generic). For the purposes of such an empirical validation, we created an adaptive version of a commercial site in order to investigate users' possible responses to a personalization process.

12.7.1   Sampling and Procedure

In the case of the eCommerce environment, a within-participants experiment was conducted, seeking to explore if the personalized condition serves users better in finding information faster and more accurately. A pilot study that involved a between-participants design demonstrated inconsistent effects, suggesting that a within-participants approach would yield more robust results.

All of the 89 participants were students from the University of Cyprus or the University of Athens, and their ages varied from 18 to 21 years, with a mean age of 19. They accessed the Web environments using personal computers located at the laboratories of both universities, and they were divided into groups of approximately 12 participants. Each session lasted about 40 minutes; 20 minutes for the user-profiling process, while the remaining time was devoted to navigating in both environments, which were presented sequentially (as soon as they were done with the first environment, the second one was presented).

The content was about a series of laptop computers: general description, technical specifications, and additional information was available for each model. We ensured that the original (raw) version of the environment was designed without any consideration of cognitive style preferences, and that the amount of information was so high and randomly allocated that it could increase the possibility of cognitive overload. The personalized condition addressed these issues by introducing as personalization factors both cognitive style and working memory span. The profiling procedure was the same as described previously and involved the same materials.

In each condition, users were asked to fulfill three tasks; they had to find the necessary information to answer three sequential multiple-choice questions that were given to them as they navigated the Web environment. All six questions (three per condition) were about determining which laptop excelled with respect to the prerequisites that were set by each question. There was only one correct answer possible for each question; the users were not required to have hardware-related knowledge or understanding.

As soon as the users finished answering all of the questions in both conditions, they were presented with a comparative satisfaction questionnaire; they were asked to choose which environment was better (on a 1 to 5 scale, 1 being a strong preference for environment A and 5 for environment B) regarding usability and user-friendliness factors.

The dependent variables that were considered as indicators of the differences between the two environments were

1. Task accuracy (number of correct answers)
2. Task completion time
3. User satisfaction

At this point, a few clarifications about the methodology are necessary:

- The users had no knowledge about which one was the personalized condition, nor were they encouraged to use any additional features.
- To avoid training effects, half of the users received the raw condition first (considered as environment A), while the other half started the procedure with the personalized condition (again considered as environment A).

- To avoid the effect of differences in difficulty of each set of the three questions, they were alternated in both environments. Due to a design error, the division was not in half, but 53 participants received the first combination and 36 received the alternate. However, no effect was observed; all of the questions were equal in difficulty.
- The within-participants design allowed for the control of the differences and confiding variables among users.

12.7.2 Implications for an e-Commerce Setting

There are some considerable differences in the way our theoretical model was (partially) implemented in the eCommerce environment as compared to the eLearning setting. For reasons of increased usability, there was no "learner control" panel. Although it was proven a useful tool for learners, we considered that it would be somehow burdening for the case of browsing laptops on the Web.

More importantly, the users with low working memory did not receive segmented content, because that would be impossible considering the absolutely non-sequential pattern of Web browsing. For that reason, we introduced a "myNotepad" tool that allowed users to make entries of goal-related information; this tool was meant to serve as an additional buffer for participants with a low memory span, alleviating disorientation and cognitive load caused by the high amount of information included in the original environment. Users were able to add the link and a general description of the section that they were visiting in this notepad, which allowed them to code large amounts of information. This approach must be further evaluated with working- memory-specific experiments, since there is much depth in the role of working memory and corresponding strategies.

Concerning cognitive style, Table 12.4 shows the implications for each preference. Intermediates received a balance between each opposite preference condition, as with the case of the eLearning experiment described earlier.

12.7.3 Results

The most robust and interesting finding was that the users in the personalized condition were more accurate in providing the correct answer for each task. The same user in the raw condition had a mean of 1 for the correct answer, while in the personalized condition, the mean rose to 1.9. Because the distribution was not normal and the paired-samples t test assumptions were not met, a Wilcoxon signed ranks test was performed, showing that this difference is statistically significant at the zero level of confidence ($Z = -4.755$, $p = 0.000$). This is probably a very encouraging finding, implying that personalization on the basis of these factors (cognitive style and working memory) benefits users within an eCommerce environment as long as there are some cognitive functions (such as information finding) involved, of course.

Table 12.4   Implications for Cognitive Style Preferences in the eCommerce Environment

Imager	Verbalizer	Analyst	Wholist
Presentation of information is visually enhanced in order to resemble a diagrammatical form of representation	The use of text is predominant, unaccompanied by any visual enhancements	The structure of the environment is chunked to clear-cut links to match an analytical way of thinking	The structure of the environment is less segmented and follows a more holistic pattern; users are shown where they are and where they have visited; and a more sequential approach is encouraged

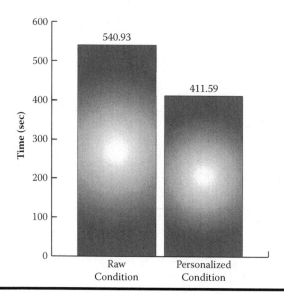

Figure 12.14   The difference in task completion time between the two conditions.

Equally interesting is that users in the personalized condition were significantly faster at task completion. The mean aggregated time of answering all three of the questions was 541 seconds in the raw condition, and 412 in the personalized. A paired-samples t test was performed ($t_{(88)} = 4.668, p = 0.000$) demonstrating significance at the zero level of confidence. Again, this second dependent variable (time) shows that the personalized environment is more efficient (see Figure 12.14).

As it concerns the satisfaction questionnaire, 31 users leaned toward the personalized environment, 38 had no preference, and 20 preferred the raw. This descriptive statistic is merely indicative of whether participants would consciously observe any positive or negative effects of the personalized condition. A considerable percentage leaned toward that condition (or at least users did not seem annoyed by such a restructuring), but overall it cannot be supported that they were fully aware of their increase in performance, as shown by the abovementioned findings.

In sum, the specific experiment shows that users performed better within the personalized environment, and these findings are statistically very robust. It could be argued, of course, that there is no way to be fully aware if information processing is more efficient at a deeper level or if users simply found the personalized condition more to their liking and therefore devoted more conscious cognitive effort. Nevertheless, such an increase in performance, which is consistent with the findings of the eLearning experiments, provides support for the further development and application of our theoretical model beyond the educational level.

12.8 Conclusions and Future Work

The basic objective of this chapter was to introduce a combination of concepts from different research areas, all of which focus on the user. We approached the theoretical considerations and technological parameters that can provide the most comprehensive user profile, under a common filtering element (user perceptual preference characteristics), supporting the provision of the most appropriate and optimized user-centered Web-based result. This chapter made extensive reference to the comprehensive user profile construction and presented an overview of the AdaptiveWeb architecture, indicating the data flow between its various stand-alone components.

Our system and model have been evaluated both in terms of the system's response-time performance and resources consumption as well as with regard to users' learning performance and satisfaction in two different application areas: eLearning and eCommerce.

We conducted a number of experiments to load-test functional behavior and measure the performance of our system. Two different content scenarios of controlled simulation environments were created, measuring average response times, throughput, deviation, and median, run by 100 threads (users).

The empirical study on the field of eLearning indicates an increase in users' learning performance, and we identified a correlation of cognitive processing speed and visual attention processing efficiency of users, as well as intrinsic parameters of emotionality, with the parameters of online content. Moreover, the evaluation results of the eCommerce environments are consistent with our previous findings and perhaps are a little more impressive, considering that such an approach in a noneducational setting is rather novel. It was clearly demonstrated that users' information finding was more accurate and efficient when their cognitive style preference and working memory span are taken into account. The implementation of the rest of our theoretical model and the development of corresponding personalization rules are the next steps of our experimental approach in generic Web settings, aiming to ground, if possible, a set of generic personalization guidelines on the basis of human factors—though it is fully understood how challenging such an endeavor is.

Our system and model have been proven effective and efficient not only regarding the information flow within and between the various stand-alone system components but also in respect to the actual output data gathered. These evaluative results are encouraging for the future of our work because we found that in many cases there is a high positive correlation of matched conditions with performance as well as among the dimensions of the various factors of our model. This fact reveals that the whole approach turned out to be initially successful with a significant impact of human factors in the personalization and adaptation procedure of Web-based environments.

The next step of our work, besides improving the methodology of our experiments in a commercial services Web environment, is the integration of the remaining parameters of our proposed model as personalization factors in the Web. With regard to emotional processing, we are setting up a research framework that will involve the use of sensors and real-time monitoring of emotional arousal (galvanic skin response and heart rate). We also plan to investigate constraints and challenges arising from the implementation of such issues on mobile devices and channels. We will extend our study on the structure of the metadata coming from the providers' side, aiming to construct a Web-based personalization architecture that will serve as an automatic filter adapting the received content based on the comprehensive user profile. The final system will provide a complete adaptation and personalization Web-based solution that satisfies individual users' needs and preferences.

Panagiotis Germanakos is a research scientist at the Laboratory of New Technologies, a faculty member of the Communication and Media Studies Department at the National and Kapodistrian University of Athens, and a faculty member of the Department of Computer Science at the University of Cyprus. He obtained his PhD from the University of Athens in 2008, and his MSc in international marketing management from the Leeds University Business School in 1999. His BSc was in computer science, and he also holds an HND Diploma of Technician Engineer in the field of computer studies. His research interests are in Web adaptation and personalization environments and systems based on user profiling and filters encompassing, among others, visual, mental, and affective processes, implemented on desktop and mobile/wireless platforms. His work has been published in several publications, including coedited books, chapters, articles in journals, and conference contributions. Furthermore, he actively participates in numerous national and EU-funded projects that mainly focus on the analysis, design, and development of open interoperable integrated wireless/mobile and personalized technological infrastructures and systems in the ICT research areas of e-government, e-health, and e-learning; and has extensive experience in the provision of consultancy of large-scale IT solutions and implementations in the business sector.

Nikos Tsianos is a research assistant and doctoral candidate at the New Technologies Laboratory of the Faculty of Communication and Media Studies at the University of Athens, Greece. He holds an MSc in political communications from the University of Athens. His main research area is the incorporation of theories from the psychology of individual differences into adaptive educational hypermedia, the development of corresponding systems, and the empirical evaluation of such systems in the context of an experimental psychology methodology. He has published several articles in conference publications and journals regarding this field of research. He also won the Best Student Paper Award at the Adaptive Hypermedia 2008 conference. He is currently editing a book about cognitive and emotional human factors in Web-learning.

Zacharias Lekkas is a research assistant and doctoral candidate at the New Technologies Laboratory of the Faculty of Communication and Media Studies, University of Athens, Greece. He holds an MSc in occupational psychology from the University of Nottingham. He is interested in the role of emotion in Web-based educational systems and has conducted empirical research on the effect of human factors such as anxiety, emotional moderation, emotional intelligence, self-efficacy, and so forth. Additionally, his research interests include the field of decision making support in adaptive hypermedia and the design of personalized training systems. His work has been published in conference publications, journals, and he has edited books. He also won the Best Student Paper Award at the Adaptive Hypermedia 2008 conference.

Constantinos Mourlas has been an assistant professor in the Department of Communication and Media Studies at the National and Kapodistrian University of Athens, Greece since 2002. He obtained his PhD from the Department of Informatics, University of Athens in 1995, and graduated from the University of Crete in 1988, with a diploma in computer science. In 1998, he was an ERCIM fellow for post-doctoral studies through research in STFC, United Kingdom. He was employed as a lecturer in the Department of Computer Science at the Univeristy of Cyprus from 1999 until 2002. His previous research work has focused on distributed multimedia systems with adaptive behavior, quality of service issues, streaming media, and the Internet. His current main research interest is in the design and the development of intelligent environments that provide adaptive and personalized context to the users according to their preferences, cognitive characteristics, and emotional state. His work has been published in several publications including edited books, chapters, articles in journals, and conference contributions. Dr. Mourlas has taught various undergraduate as well as postgraduate courses in the Department of Computer Science at the University of Cyprus and the Department of Communication and Media Studies at the University of Athens. Furthermore, he has coordinated and actively participated in numerous national and EU-funded projects.

Mario Belk is currently a postgraduate student and research scientist of the faculty of computer science at the University of Cyprus. He obtained his BSc in computer science from the same department. His research interests are in Web adaptation and personalization environments and systems, as well as database systems, ontologies, Internet technologies, and the Semantic Web. He actively participates in numerous national and EU-funded research projects. His bachelor thesis contributed to the publication of several research articles in journals, book chapters, and major international conferences. He worked as a teaching assistant to his professor and the university's vice-rector in the Department of Computer Science. He participated in several business projects as a senior software developer collaborating with Microsoft, IBM, and Marfin Laiki Bank Ltd. After graduation, he plans to pursue a PhD and a career as an academic research scientist.

George Samaras is a professor in the Department of Computer Science at the University of Cyprus. He received a PhD in computer science from Rensselaer Polytechnic Institute, Troy, New York, in 1989. He was previously at IBM Research, Triangle Park, North Carolina, and taught at the University of North Carolina at Chapel Hill, as adjunct faculty from 1990 to 1993. He served as the lead architect of IBM's distributed commit architecture from 1990 to 1994, and coauthored the final publication of the architecture (IBM Book, SC31-8134-00, September 1994). His work on utilizing mobile agents for Web database access received the Best Student Paper Award at the 1999 IEEE International Conference on Data Engineering. His work on e-learning received the Best Student Paper Award of the 2008 International Conference on Adaptive Hypermedia and Adaptive Web-Based Systems. He has a number of patents relating to transaction processing technology and his work has been published in numerous book chapters, technical conference and journal publications. He has served as a proposal evaluator at a national and international levels and has been regularly invited by the European Commission to serve as an external project evaluator and auditor for the ESPRIT and IST Programs (FP5, FP6, FP7). His research interests include e-learning and e-services, Web information retrieval, mobile/wireless computing, context-based services, personalization systems, and database systems. He has also served on IBM's internal international standards committees for issues related to distributed transaction processing (OSI/TP, XOPEN, OMG). He participates in a number of EU IST projects on e-learning and mobile and wireless computing as a scientific coordinator for the Cyprus participation.

References

Baddeley, A. (1992). Working memory. *Science*, 255: 556–59.
Bandura, A. (1994). Self-efficacy. In V. S. Ramachaudran (Ed.), *Encyclopedia of human behavior*, Vol. 4, pp. 71–81. New York: Academic Press.

Barret, R., Maglio, P., & Kellem, D. (1997). How to personalize the Web. In *Proceedings of the Conference on Human Factors in Computing Systems (CHI '97)*, pp. 75–82. New York: ACM Press.

Bogonicolos, N., Fragoudis, D., & Likothanassis, S. (1999). ARCHIMIDES: An intelligent agent for adaptive-personalized navigation within a Web server. In *Proceedings of the 32nd Annual Hawaii International Conference on System Science*, HICSS-32. Vol. 5.

Brusilovsky, P. (2001). Adaptive hypermedia. *User Modeling and User-Adapted Interaction*, 11: 87–110.

Brusilovsky, P., Eklund, J., & Schwarz, E. (1998). Web-based education for all: A tool for developing adaptive courseware. Computer Networks and ISDN Systems. In *Proceedings of the 7th International WWW Conference*, April 14–18, 30(1–7), 291–300.

Brusilovsky, P., & Nejdl, W. (2004). *Adaptive hypermedia and adaptive Web*, © 2004 CSC Press LLC.

Brusilovsky, P., & Peylo, C. (2003). Adaptive and intelligent Web-based educational systems. *International Journal of Artificial Intelligence in Education*, 13: 156–169.

Cassady, J. C. (2004). The influence of cognitive test anxiety across the learning–testing cycle. *Learning and Instruction*, 14(6): 569–592.

Cassady, J. C., & Johnson, R. E. (2002). Cognitive test anxiety and academic performance. *Contemporary Educational Psychology*, 27(2): 270–295.

Cassidy, S. (2004). Learning styles: An overview of theories, models, and measures. *Educational Psychology*, 24(4): 419–444.

De Bra, P., & Calvi, L. (1998). AHA! An open Adaptive Hypermedia Architecture. *New Review of Hypermedia and Multimedia*, 4: 115–139.

Demetriou, A., & Kazi, S. (2001). *Unity and modularity in the mind and the self: Studies on the relationships between self-awareness, personality, and intellectual development from childhood to adolescence.* London: Routledge.

Eklund, J., & Sinclair, K. (2000). An empirical appraisal of the effectiveness of adaptive interfaces of instructional systems. *Educational Technology and Society*, 3(4), ISSN 1436–4522.

Germanakos, P., Tsianos, N., Lekkas, Z., Mourlas, C., & Samaras, G. (2007a). Capturing essential intrinsic user behaviour values for the design of comprehensive Web-based personalized environments. *Computers in Human Behavior Journal*, Special Issue on Integration of Human Factors in Networked Computing, DOI: 10.1016/j.chb.2007.07.010.

Germanakos, P., Tsianos, N., Lekkas, Z., Mourlas, C., Belk, M., & Samaras, G. (2007b). An AdaptiveWeb system for integrating human factors in personalization of Web content. Demonstration in *Proceedings of the 11th International Conference on User Modeling (UM 2007)*, Corfu, Greece, June 25–29.

Germanakos, P., Tsianos, N., Lekkas, Z., Mourlas, C., Belk, M., & Samaras, G. (2007c). A semantic approach of an adaptive and personalized Web-based learning content: The case of AdaptiveWeb. In *Proceedings of the 2nd International Workshop on Semantic Media Adaptation and Personalization (SMAP 2007)*, pp. 68–73. London, December 17–18, 2007, IEEE Computer Society.

Germanakos, P., Tsianos, N., Lekkas, Z., Mourlas, C., & Samaras, G. (2008a). Realizing comprehensive user profiling as the core element of adaptive and personalized communication environments and systems. *Computer Journal*, Special Issue on Profiling Expertise and Behaviour, Oxford University Press, DOI: 10.1093/comjnl/bxn014.

Germanakos, P., Tsianos, N., Lekkas, Z., Mourlas, C., & Samaras, G. (2008b). The role of human factors in Web personalization environments. In *Encyclopedia of Information Science and Technology*, 2nd edition, IGI Global. (accepted).

Germanakos, P., Tsianos, N., Mourlas, C., & Samaras, G. (2005). New fundamental profiling characteristics for designing adaptive Web-based educational systems. In *Proceedings of the IADIS International Conference on Cognition and Exploratory Learning in Digital Age (CELDA 2005)*, pp. 10–17, Porto, December 14–16.

Goleman, D. 1995. *Emotional intelligence: Why it can matter more than IQ*. New York: Bantam Books.

Halberstadt, A. G. (2005). Emotional experience and expression: An issue overview. *Journal of Nonverbal Behavior*, 17(3): 139–143.

Kolb, A. Y., Kolb, D. A. (2005). The Kolb Learning Style Inventory, Version 3.1 2005, Technical Specifications, Experience-Based Learning Systems, Inc.

Korkea-aho, M. (2000). Context-aware applications survey. Paper presented at the Internetworking Seminar (Tik-110.551), Spring 2000, Helsinki University of Technology; http://www.hut.fi/~mkorkeaa/doc/context-aware.html.

Lankhorst, M. M., Kranenburg, S. A., & Peddemors, A. J. H. (2002). Enabling technology for personalizing mobile services. In *Proceedings of the 35th Annual Hawaii International Conference on System Sciences (HICSS-35 '02)*.

Lekkas, Z., Tsianos, N., Germanakos, P., & Mourlas, C. (2007). Integrating cognitive and emotional parameters into designing adaptive hypermedia environments. In *Proceedings of the 2nd European Cognitive Science Conference (EuroCogSci '07)*, Delphi, Hellas, May 23–27.

Lekkas, Z., Tsianos, N., Germanakos, P., Mourlas, C., & Samaras, G. (2008). The role of emotions in the design of personalized educational systems. In *Proceedings of the 8th IEEE International Conference on Advanced Learning Technologies (ICALT 2008)*, Santander, Cantabria, Spain, July 1–5, 2008, IEEE. (accepted).

Maglio, P., & Barret, R. (2000). Intermediaries personalize information streams. *Communications of the ACM*, 43(8): 96–101.

McKay, M. T., Fischler, I., & Dunn, B. R. (2003). Cognitive style and recall of text: An EEG analysis. *Learning and Individual Differences*, 14: 1–21.

Mobasher, B., Anand, S. S., & Kobsa, A. (2007). Intelligent techniques for Web personalization. In *Proceedings of the 5th Workshop ITWP 2007*, held in conjunction with the *22nd National Conference in Artificial Intelligence (AAAI 2007)*.

Mobasher, B., Dai, H., Luo, T., Nakagawa, M., & Wiltshire J. (2002). Discovery of aggregate usage profiles for Web personalization. *Data Mining and Knowledge Discovery*, 6(1): 61–82.

Mulvenna, M. D., Anand, S. S., & Buchner, A. G. (2000). Personalization on the Net using Web mining. *Communications of the ACM*, 43(8): 123–125.

MyersBriggs, I., McCaulley, M. H., Quenk, N. L., & Hammer, A. L. (1998). MBTI manual (*A guide to the development and use of the Myers Briggs type indicator*), 3rd edition. Palo Alto, CA: Consulting Psychologists Press.

Panayiotou, C., & Samaras, G. (2004). mPersona: Personalized portals for the wireless user: An agent approach. *Journal of ACM/Baltzer Mobile Networking and Applications (MONET)*, Special Issue on Mobile and Pervasive Commerce, (6): 663–677.

Papanikolaou, K. A., Grigoriadou, M., Kornilakis, H., & Magoulas, G. D. (2003). Personalizing the interaction in a Web-based educational hypermedia system: The case of INSPIRE. *User-Modeling and User-Adapted Interaction*, 13(3): 213–267.

Pazzani, J. M. (2005). A framework for collaborative, content-based and demographic filtering. *Artificial Intelligence Review*, 13(5–6): 393–408.

Riding, R. J., 2001. *Cognitive style analysis: Research administration*. Birmingham, New Zealand: Learning and Training Technology.

Rossi, G., Schwade, D., & Guimaraes, M. R. (2001). Designing personalized Web applications. ACM 1-58113-348-0/01/0005.

Sadler-Smith, E., & Riding, R. (1999). Cognitive style and instructional preferences. *Instructional Science*, 27(5): 355–371.

Spielberger, C. D. (1972). Conceptual and methodological issues in anxiety research. In C. D. Spielberger (Ed.), *Anxiety: Current trends in theory and research*, Vol. 2. New York: Academic Press.

Spielberger, C. D. (1983). *Manual for the State-Trait Anxiety Inventory (STAI)*. Palo Alto, CA: Consulting Psychologists Press.

Spielberger, C. D., & Vagg, P. R. (1995). Test anxiety: A transactional process model. In C. D. Spielberger and P. R. Vagg (Eds.), *Test anxiety: Theory, assessment, and treatment*, pp. 3–14. Washington, DC: Taylor & Francis.

Thomas, C., & Fischer, G. (1997). Using agents to personalize the Web. In *Proceedings of International Conference on Intelligent User Interfaces 1997, ACM IUI '97*, pp. 53–60, Orlando, Florida.

Tsianos, N., Germanakos, P., Lekkas, Z., Mourlas, C., & Samaras, G. (2007). Evaluating the significance of cognitive and emotional parameters in e-Learning adaptive environments. In *Proceedings of the IADIS International Conference on Cognition and Exploratory Learning in Digital Age (CELDA 2007)*, pp. 93–98, Algarve, Portugal, December 7–9.

Tsianos, N., Germanakos, P., Lekkas, Z., Mourlas, C., & Samaras, G. (2008a). An assessment of human factors in adaptive hypermedia environments. Chapter to appear in C. Mourlas, & P. Germanakos (Eds.), *Intelligent User Interfaces: Adaptation and Personalization Systems and Technologies*. Hershey, PA: IGI Global.

Tsianos, N., Germanakos, P., Lekkas, Z., Mourlas, C., & Samaras, G. (2008b). User-centered profiling on the basis of cognitive and emotional characteristics: An empirical study. In *Proceedings of the 5th International Conference on Adaptive Hypermedia and Adaptive Web-based Systems (AH 2008)*, Hannover, Germany, July 28–August 1, Springer Verlag. (accepted).

Weber, G., & Specht, M. (1997). User modeling and adaptive navigation support in WWW-based tutoring systems. In *Proceedings of User Modeling '97*, pp. 289–300.

Chapter 13

Image-Based Synthesis for Human Facial Expressions

Nikolaos Ersotelos and Feng Dong

13.1 Introduction

Recently, research in computer graphics and computer vision has focused on synthesizing the moods and emotions of human faces, which is one of the most difficult and highly applicable aspects of computer graphics since it can be used in important industry areas, such as games and entertainment, medical science, and telecommunications. Scientific efforts have already established many modeling and animation techniques that have resulted in creating realistic facial expressions in 2D or 3D formats. One of the major benefits of these techniques is synthesizing or capturing real-world illumination and graphic details and transferring them to the computer graphics area.

Facial characteristics such as creases and wrinkles can only be captured by the illumination changes during facial movement. Liu, Shan, and Zhang [1] presented an image-based approach that employs the expression ratio image (ERI). ERI is a method for capturing, transferring, and lighting illumination changes from two source images of the same person to a different person image.

Our current study aims to provide a novel approach to that existing technique, which will discover the limitations and provide new technique for better results. In this chapter, several approaches that are making a significant contribution in the computer vision area are presented, along with their advantages and disadvantages. The approach presented by Liu, Shan, and Zhang [1], on which our current study is based, is detailed. Its weaknesses are categorized, and corresponding improvements are proposed in order to provide realistic results in a faster and more automated way that requires minimum interaction from the user. In Section 13.4, some experimental results are presented, followed by a short discussion and proposals for future work.

13.1.1 Aim and Objectives

This chapter targets a novel approach that allows the synthesis of accurate facial expressions using a small set of input images. This research is motivated by the large amount of existing work in facial animation and modeling. The major goal is to be capable of generating different views and facial expressions of the human face, requiring limited interactions from users and limited input images. This goal can be achieved by a number of key techniques that are of great scientific interest:

- Facial animation and facial modeling
- Split process in small and fast sections
- Human facial geometrical expression deformation
- Image color transfer techniques to balance image colors

13.2 Previous Work

Since Parke's [2,3] innovative work on 3D facial model animation in 1970, several other approaches have been developed. Most of them are categorized as either facial modeling or facial animation [4]. Facial modeling includes all of the techniques regarding the synthesis of a high-quality 3D head. Facial animation concerns techniques that produce facial animation with high realism. Despite the different approaches developed in these two areas, several techniques have been based on their combined use [4].

The basic methodology for a 3D head construction is to use a triangle mesh. The triangle mesh describes the facial characteristics and consists of dots connected to each other by the common edges of the triangles. Another method for obtaining an accurate 3D head is to use a laser cylindrical scanner, such as those produced by Cyberware [13]. Lee, Terzopoulos, and Waters [5] presented a technique whereby the 3D head construction was established with the use of a Cyberware scanner. They created highly realistic models with facial expressions based on pseudo-muscles. The pseudo-muscles were constructed from several layers of triangles that described the skin, nerves, skull, and so on. By changing the settings of the triangle meshes (pseudo-muscles), new expressions can be synthesized.

A radically different approach is the performance-based animation in which measurements from real actors are used to drive synthetic characters [17–19].

DeCarlo [6] presented a technique for modeling a face based on anthropometric measurements. Anthropometry is a science that processes, collects, categorizes, and stores in libraries the statistical data regarding the race, gender, and age of real human heads. These data can be exploited in order to treat the facial characteristics of a 3D face model. The developed algorithm, using variational modeling, can synthesize the best surface that satisfies the geometric constraints imposed by the measurements.

Pighin, Szeliski, and Salesin [7] have presented a method for generating facial expressions based on photographs. The inputs of the process include a sufficient number of images of the faces, each one captured from a different angle, and an appropriate 3D model that is used as a base on which the digitized pictures are adjusted. To successfully match the 3D head with the facial pose of the pictures, the position, sizes, and facial characteristics are allocated on the pictures by manually placing several points as landmarks on them. The output of the process is a facial model that has been appropriately adjusted, as far as pose and facial characteristics are concerned, to the pictures. In order to create new facial expressions, 2D morphing techniques are combined with transformations.

Another face modeling technique was presented by Blanz and Vetter [8]. A face model can be created from a single picture. This technique requires a library of several 3D models. The final 3D model is based on a process that transforms the shape and texture of the example 3D model in a vector shape representation.

In a newer version of the Blanz approach, an algorithm was presented that allows us to change facial expressions in existing images and videos [9]. This study proposes a face exchange method that replaces the existing face of a 3D model with a new face from a 2D image. An algorithm can estimate a textured 3D face model from a 2D facial image. Moreover, by employing optimization methods, the 3D model is rendered with proper illumination and postures.

Another approach for creating a realistic facial expression was presented by Sifakis, Neverov, and Fedkiw [21], who used a 3D head consisting of 30,000 surface triangles. More analytically, the model consisted of 850,000 thresholds with 32 muscles. The 3D head is continuously controlled by the muscle activations and the kinematic bones' degrees of freedom. The 3D model is marked with different color landmarks that specify each muscle's identity, and the muscles are activated to generate the new expressions or even facial animations.

The morphable modeling method, which has been used for face modeling, is extended to cover facial expressions as well. The library of the system contains 3D head models with several expressions. The system, after isolating the neutral face from the photograph and synthesizing it as a 3D model, can change the expression and render it back to the original image or video.

Expressive expression mapping [1] is a technique for facial animation based on capturing the illumination alternances of one person's expressions and mapping them to another person's face. This technique was applied in the renewed film *Tony de Peltie* to animate facial expressions of the characters. This technique has also been employed and improved in our current work. The advantage of this method is that it is a low-cost process that produces realistic results and accurately preserves facial details. Several approaches have been introduced in the area of transferring illumination settings [14–16,20].

Zhang and colleagues [10] introduced a technique that automatically synthesizes the corresponding facial expression image, retaining photorealistic and natural-looking expression details. This method exploits the feature point positions of the facial characteristics and divides the face into 14 subregions. Those subdivisions are necessary for the system in order to change specific parts of the face according to the expression that is to be created. The system infers the feature points of expression from the subset of tracked points through an example-based approach. When the feature points change position, then geometric deformation is deployed to generate new facial expressions.

13.3 Existing Techniques and New Approach Implementations

Liu, Shan, and Zhang [1] presented an approach that generates facial expressions based on geometric deformation and facial illumination settings. This image-based approach employs the ERI, which allows for the capture of the illumination settings of a face. Those data are transferred between the source and the imported images.

The requisite inputs of the process are two source photographs of the same person, one in a neutral face position and the other with an expression. The positions of the features, such as the mouth, eyes, eyebrows, ears, and nose, and the shape of the head, are manually located by the user, who places dots to mark the positions.

The geometric deformation is produced by calculating the differences of the points' positions between the source images and transferring the differences to an imported image. Those dots are connected by triangles. The internal areas of the triangles are deformed according to the points' position changes and give the geometrically deformed facial expression (Figure 13.1).

Afterward, by aligning the source images with the deformed imported image (B') through image warping, the system can calculate the ratio image:

$$R(u,v) = A'(u,v)/A(u,v)$$

where R is the ratio image and A', A are the warped source images. Finally, by multiplying the $R(u,v)$ by B', the system can transfer the wrinkles of the source images onto the imported image. The above calculation only works if there is a match in the illumination settings of the source and the imported images. This process needs to be developed in order to produce results with more realistic graphic details.

Our current study aims to handle and improve the following issues:

The process requires the user to manually place a sufficient number of dots to specify the head shape and facial features. Taking into consideration that

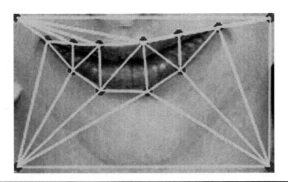

Figure 13.1 Dots are placed around the face, lips, nose, eyes, eyebrows, and other areas to describe the facial features. The dots are then connected by triangles. By moving the triangles, new deformed expressions can be generated.

a wrong placement of a dot will result in distorted geometric deformation, the accuracy with which the dots are placed is a crucial factor affecting the quality of the results. Moreover, the number of dots analogically increases the system requirements in terms of the system memory and processor capability; every additional dot inserted implies a considerable increase in the consequent calculations. Also, if the number of dots in the imported image is, for example, 100 dots, the same number of dots with the same order and position must be placed in the source images as well. Therefore, for each expression to be created, 300 dots need to be inserted manually.

All of the dots are connected with triangles. The larger the number of dots, the more triangles that will be produced. Because the triangles are connected to each other, the more there are in the images, the more distortion that will be generated on the final result. The distortion will be produced because the area covered by the triangles is deformed. The user cannot choose the number of triangles to be created.

The fact that the process is manual affects the duration of the procedure. The executable time for a facial expression synthesis is around 30 minutes, depending on the user's experience.

If the image warping process between the geometrically deformed imported image and the source images is generated with errors, those errors will be transferred later onto the imported image through ERI. According to Liu, Shan, and Zhang [1], there is no process that can remove that distortion from the final result.

The purpose of our research is to make this algorithm more functional by altering it to an automatic process, by modifying it to produce more accurate results through a faster procedure.

13.3.1 Divide a Face into Areas

In order to have the distortion on the geometric eliminated, the number and size of the produced triangles must be reduced. Consequently, the process has been focused on two isolated facial areas that primarily contribute to facial expressions: the areas around the mouth and eyebrows. These areas get extracted from the images as layers in order to be deformed separately (Figure 13.2). After the deformation of each individual area, the deformed result is imported to the images. The major advantage of this procedure is that by having a limited area to be deformed, the executable time is considerably reduced. Inserting dots to define areas such as the chin, ears, and hairline is no longer necessary to generate the new facial expression. The system can automatically detect and handle the areas of interest. At this stage of the study, there is an apparent limitation regarding the size of the imported image, which needs to be equal to the size of the source images.

13.3.2 Elimination of Geometrical Distortion

Another issue that must be addressed is the possibility that the geometrical deformation process will lead to geometrical distortion of the imported image. This effect particularly affects the shape of the face around the chin. More specifically, if the face in the source image has a big mouth, then the rectangle necessary to cover the mouth area must be of comparative size. The size of this rectangle may cover the chin or part of the contour of the face in the imported image. If a geometrical deformation process is then applied, it may insert significant distortion to the imported image. In order to avoid this distortion, the user can specify and copy the correctly deformed area, excluding the affected face contour or the other distorted parts, and place it on top of the imported image with the neutral expression. The correctly deformed area is defined by the placement of a sufficient number of dots. There is no restriction on the number of dots or on the shape of the area that these dots describe. The system adjusts and copies this user-defined area on the original imported image, constructing the deformed image with no distortion in the face's contour.

Figure 13.2 The first step of the process: the mouth has been extracted from the main image to be geometrically deformed and afterward pasted back on top of the original image.

13.3.3 Illumination Transfer

In order for the wrinkles of a facial expression to be calculated, transferred, and adjusted to the imported image, the method that Liu, Shan, and Zhang presented is analyzed and improved in this chapter so that better results are achieved regardless of the illumination conditions. As explained earlier, their algorithm uses a warping process to align source images with the imported deformed image. The next stage is the calculation of the ratio image A/A', by dividing the resultant warped source images (A for the neutral expression's pose and A' for the smiling expression's pose), and the multiplication of the ratio image with the imported deformed image. In this way, the illumination settings are transferred from the source image to the imported geometrically deformed image. The disadvantage of such a process is that the ratio image is affected by the color of the skin and by the illumination settings of the source images, which influence the wrinkle values that are eventually transferred to the imported deformed image. The resultant image can be further deteriorated if the source images are a bad quality because this will insert hard colors or artificial results in the wrinkle areas. In order to alleviate these distortions, Liu et al. propose the use of a filter, such as a Gaussian filter, which will normalize the specific areas.

In this chapter, the methodology has been changed to eliminate the above disadvantage. More specifically, the way that the ratio image is calculated has changed. Instead of dividing the source images by each other, each of them is divided by the imported deformed image. The purpose of this change is to keep the wrinkles of the source images but to also adjust them with the illumination and color skin settings of the imported image. The results are two new source images Bg/Ag and $Bg/A'g$, where Bg is the imported deformed image (Figure 13.3). The ratio image is then calculated by dividing these two resultant images. If the skin color of the source and imported images differs significantly, there is an option that allows the user to define a threshold in the percentage of wrinkle data that will be transferred to the final result.

13.3.4 Facial Expression Database

Models for several facial expressions of a specific face have been stored in a database along with the coordinates of the points that define all of the main facial characteristics. These data are available for the user as plain text and can be loaded any time that the user needs to accordingly modify the expression of the imported image. For each picture in the database, three types of datasets must be maintained in order to store the mouth perimeter, the eyes and eyebrows perimeter, and special characteristics such as wrinkles on the abovementioned areas that need to be described. This library eliminates the need for the manual placement of dots in order to define the facial characteristics. Moreover, a user-friendly interface can provide many options for facial expressions to be inserted in a source image for

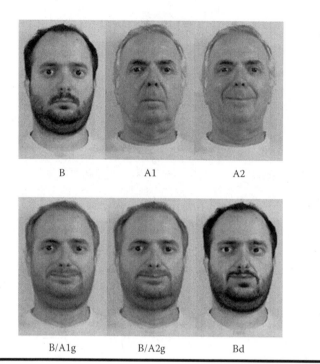

B   A1   A2

B/A1g   B/A2g   Bd

Figure 13.3   A new approach in the calculation of the ratio image.

future use. The main advantage of the previous process is that it is dependent only on the facial expressions because it is not affected by the image part surrounding the head, such as the ears, hair, neck, or clothes.

13.3.5 Copy Facial Area: Noise Reduction

Wrinkles processing comes after the geometrical deformation process. Details like wrinkles contribute (to a great extent) to the production of realistic results; therefore, it is important that they are copied and transferred from the source image. These fine details are normally captured by the illumination changes during facial movement. However, previous approaches have encountered difficulties in discriminating distortions caused by the hair, neck, and face shapes from wrinkles and useful details. In our present work, we examine the option of placing a rectangle on the face that covers and copies the mouth and eyes–eyebrows areas in order to isolate these specific areas and eliminate similar distortions. Facial expressions and overall picture quality can be improved by applying noise reduction techniques.

13.4 Results

Our new approach was applied to deform facial images and create synthesized facial expressions. The source images in Figure 13.4 were chosen because of their varied facial expressions and illumination settings. The images are grouped in pairs of a neutral and a nonneutral facial expressions.

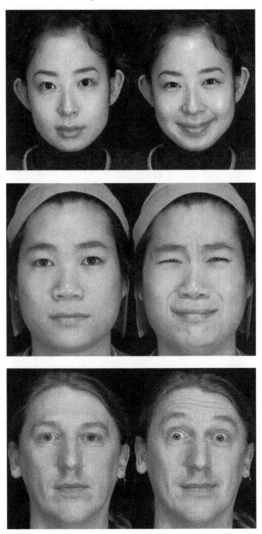

Figure 13.4 Source images that were used to synthesize new facial expressions. (From "Expressive Expression Mapping with Ratio Images" by Zicheng Liu, Ying Shan, and Zhengyou Zhang, 2001. In *Proceedings of the 28th Annual Conference on Computer Graphics and Interactive Techniques*, ACM SIGGRAPH, New York, pp. 271–276. With permission.)

Figure 13.5 Left: The imported image with a neutral expression. Right: The deformed image with a smiling expression and the corresponding wrinkles.

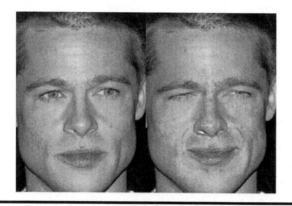

Figure 13.6 Left: An imported image with a neutral expression. Right: The deformed image with a sad expression and the corresponding wrinkles between the eyes and the mouth.

In Figure 13.5, the imported image and the resultant image after the deformation process are presented; the source images from the top row of Figure 13.4 were used. The wrinkles around the mouth contribute to a realistic result, providing a good level of physical details. Deformation has been applied only in the areas of the mouth and eyes. As can been seen from the result, the logic of dividing the face into areas does not deteriorate the naturalness of the facial expression. Even though the user applied no deformation to the area of the nose, it is deformed according to the geometrical deformation of the mouth. The width of the smile affects the area at the bottom of the nose, as can also be seen in the top row of Figure 13.4, which is an original image.

Figure 13.6 presents the imported and the deformed images of the process, using the pair of source images from the middle row of Figure 13.4. The wrinkles

Figure 13.7 **Left: An imported image with a neutral expression. Right: The deformed image with the raised-eyebrow expression and the appropriate wrinkles on the forehead.**

of the facial expression of the source image have been transferred to the deformed image by capturing the illumination settings (Figure 13.6). The difficulty in this example is encountered at the eyes' deformation. The fact that the eyes in the source image are almost closed introduces by itself a high level of distortion. However, the result illustrates that highly detailed graphics can be achieved, even though the face has been split into separate areas.

In Figure 13.7, the source image has been deformed according to the bottom row of Figure 13.4. What is interesting in this figure are the raised-eyebrows (surprised) expression and the resultant wrinkles in the forehead. In order to insert these wrinkles, the user has to include this area, by defining an appropriately sized rectangle, in the wrinkles calculation procedure, as described in Section 13.3.3.

13.5 Discussions and Future Plans

In this chapter, a process to deform images using warping and geometric deformation was presented. This process is not completely automatic because a user interactive process is deployed. The next step of this research is to make the procedure fully automated. To do so, the facial characteristics must be automatically identified, perhaps using an edge detection technique so that the system can detect facial characteristics, correctly place a sufficient number of dots around them, and proceed with the geometric deformation. In this way, the user does not interfere with the system, thus eliminating the possibility of human errors.

Furthermore, new approaches can be established to enable the system to detect and handle facial expressions that include an open mouth. This could fairly complicate the process because the system would need to generate teeth or a tongue by using the settings of the source images.

Future work could also include the creation of a 3D model that can be generated from a synthesized 2D facial expression, drawing from a library of 3D heads based on different anthropometric measurements. The 3D heads in the existing databases [11,12] are categorized by race, age, gender, and the size of the facial characteristics. The final deformed image would contain information about the position and the shape of the facial characteristics, defined by the landmarks and triangles, along with data about the illumination settings. Having this information as input, the system can search through the library, utilizing an efficient algorithm, to identify the 3D head that best matches the imported face. The system would continuously adjust the image on the 3D model. The same geometrical deformation of the 2D images must also take place on the 3D model in order to have the new expression fitted on the 3D head with no distortion. The advantage of this process is that it enables the user to have shots of the face from different angles.

13.6 Conclusion

In this chapter, several facial modeling and animation techniques were presented and comparatively analyzed according to their advantages and disadvantages. The main aim of this work was to introduce a new method for reproducing natural-looking human 2D or 3D facial expressions based on Liu, Shan, and Zhang's [1] approach.

This research intends to develop a novel technique to produce accurate, natural-looking facial expressions in a simple and fast way. For this purpose, facial expression mapping techniques have been investigated and used along with human face rendering. The technique was developed to effectively create 2D or 3D facial expressions, taking into consideration parameters such as distortion, interference, cost, and complexity, which need to be minimized.

The results presented in this chapter are accurately built with high graphic details. The distortion caused either by geometrical deformation or by transferring the illumination settings has been confined.

This method has a great potential for use. Possible applications include generating expressive characters for computer game design and movie animation. The method could also be useful for low-bandwidth telecommunications such as videoconferencing.

Nikolaos Ersotelos is a doctoral candidate in information systems and computing at Brunel University. He holds a BSc (1999) in music technology from Hertfordshire University, and an MSc in media production and distribution with distinction from Lancaster University. His research focuses on generating new algorithms for constructing new modeling and rendering techniques for facial synthesized expressions. He is a member of the Visual Computer Society, of the ACM, and the IEEE Computer Society.

Feng Dong is a professor of visual computing in the Department of Computing and Information Systems at University of Bedfordshire, Luton, United Kingdom. He received his PhD from Zhejiang University, China. His research includes 3D graphics rendering and image processing. He is currently a principal investigator for two EPSRC research projects on texture synthesis and human animation. He has also been involved in a number of other research projects on medical visualization and human modeling, and rendering. He has published over 30 research papers and a book. He was cochair for the IEEE Conference on Medical Information Visualization (Mediviz) in 2008.

References

1. Zicheng Liu, Ying Shan, and Zhengyou Zhang. 2001. Expressive expression mapping with ratio images. In *Proceedings of the 28th Annual Conference on Computer Graphics and Interactive Techniques*, ACM SIGGRAPH, New York, pp. 271–276.
2. F. Parke. 1972. Computer-generated animation of faces. In *Proceedings of the ACM Annual Conference*, ACM, Boston, pp. 451–457.
3. F. I. Parke. 1974. A parametric model for human faces. PhD Thesis, University of Utah, Salt Lake City. UTEC-CSc-75-047.
4. N. Ersotelos and F. Dong. 2007. Building highly realistic facial modeling and animation: A survey. *The Visual Computer: International Journal of Computer Graphics* (November): 13–30.
5. Y. Lee, D. Terzopoulos, and K. Waters. 1995. Realistic modeling for facial animation. In *Proceedings of the 22nd Annual Conference on Computer Graphics and Interactive Techniques*, ACM SIGGRAPH, New York.
6. D. DeCarlo, D. Metaxas, and M. Stone. 1998. An anthropometric face model using variational techniques. In *Proceedings of the 25th Annual Conference on Computer Graphics and Interactive Techniques*, ACM SIGGRAPH, New York, pp. 67–74.
7. F. Pighin, R. Szeliski, and D. Salesin. 1999. Resynthesizing facial animation through 3D model-based tracking. In *Proceedings of the 7th IEEE International Conference on Computer Vision*, Los Alamitos, CA: IEEE Computer Society, pp. 143–150.
8. V. Blanz and T. Vetter. 1999. A morphable model for the synthesis of 3D faces. In *Proceedings of the 26th Annual Conference on Computer Graphics and Interactive Techniques*, ACM SIGGRAPH, New York, pp. 187–194.
9. V. Blanz, K. Scherbaum, T. Vetter, and H.-P. Seidel. 2004. Exchanging faces in images. *Computer Graphics Forum*, 23(3): 669–676.
10. Q. Zhang, Z. Liu, B. Guo, and H. Shum. 2003. Geometry-driven photorealistic facial expression synthesis. In *Proceedings of the ACM Symposium on Computer Graphics*, ACM SIGGRAPH, San Diego, CA, pp. 48–60.
11. http://www.sic.rma.ac.be/~beumier/DB/3d_rma.html. 3D head model library database.
12. http://www.ee.surrey.ac.uk/Research/VSSP/xm2vtsdb. 3D head model library database.
13. Cyberware Laboratory, 3D Scanner with Color Digitizer, Monterey, California. 4020/RGB. 1990.
14. S. R. Marschner and D. P. Greenberg. 1997. Inverse lighting for photography. In *Proceedings of IS&T/SID 5th Color Imaging Conference*, Scottsdale, AZ, pp. 262–265.

15. P. E. Debevec. 1998. Rendering synthetic objects into real scenes: Bridging traditional and image-based graphics with global illumination and high dynamic range photography. In *Computer Graphics, Annual Conference Series*, SIGGRAPH, New York, pp. 189–198.

16. J. Chai, J. Xiao, and J. Hodgins. 2003. Vision-based control of 3D facial animation. In *Eurographics/SIGGRAPH Symposium on Computer Animation*, Eurographics Association, San Diego, CA, pp. 193–206.

17. P. Bergeron and P. Lachapelle. 1985. Controlling facial expressions and body movements in the computer-generated animated short "Tony De Peltrie." In *Advanced Computer Animation Seminar Notes*, SIGGRAPH '85, New York.

18. I. Essa, S. Basu, T. Darrell, and A. Pentland. 1996. Modeling, tracking and interactive animation of faces and heads using input from video. In *Computer Animation Conference*, Geneva, pp. 68–79.

19. L. Williams. 1990. Performance-driven facial animation. In *Conference Proceedings*, SIGGRAPH '90, v. 24, pp. 235–242.

20. P. Litwinowicz and L. Williams. 1990. Animating images with drawings. *Computer Graphics* (August): 235–242.

21. E. Sifakis, I. Neverov, and R. Fedkiw. 2005. Automatic determination of facial muscle activations from spare motion capture marker data. *ACM Transaction of Graphics* (July): 417–425.

Chapter 14

Image Retrieval Using Particle Swarm Optimization

Krishna Chandramouli and Ebroul Izquierdo

14.1 Introduction

Content-based image retrieval (CBIR) exploits visual content descriptions to index and search images from large-scale image databases. It has been an active and fast-advancing research field over the last decade. CBIR uses visual information extracted from an image, such as color, shape, and texture, to represent and index the database. In typical CBIR systems, the visual contents of the images in the database are extracted and described by multidimensional feature vectors. To retrieve images, users provide the retrieval system with example images. The system then changes these examples into its internal representation of feature vectors. The similarities and differences among the feature vectors are then calculated, and retrieval is performed with the aid of an indexing scheme. The indexing scheme provides an efficient way to search the image database. Recent retrieval systems have incorporated users' relevance feedback to adapt the retrieval process in order to generate perceptually and semantically more meaningful retrieval results.

Unlike textual information, which is human defined and precise in meaning, a picture has a hidden component of creative reasoning of the human brain. This gives the content an overall shape and meaning far beyond the capabilities of any language-based representation. Early approaches to image retrieval were based on keywords and manually annotated images inspired by information retrieval in text documents [1]. Although manual annotations were developed to preserve knowledge, they are burdensome and dependent on subjective interpretations of the professional annotator, thereby restricting the performance of the CBIR system. However, incorporating users' judgment on the similarity of some media items during a relevance feedback session is a consequence of the user's accumulated life experience and knowledge. Therefore, a level of this semantic information is transferred onto the similarity model in order to capture human notions of semantic similarity. Several researchers have worked on building a relational base of concepts and content through the use of iterative relevance feedback, as presented in La Cascia, Sethi, and Sclaroff [2] and Zhang and Su [3]. The objective of the system is to build a semantic network on top of the keyword association, leading to the enhanced deduction and utilization of semantic content. The conceptual framework common to most CBIR systems is depicted in Figure 14.1.

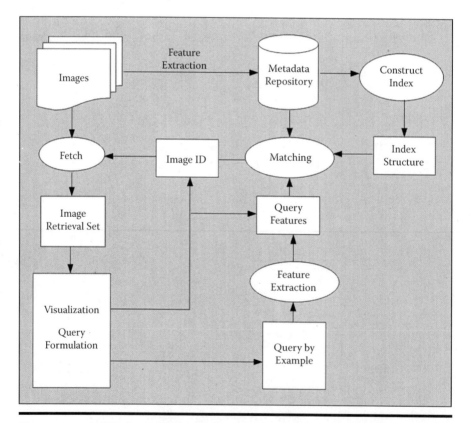

Figure 14.1   A CBIR framework. (From Survey on Image Content Analysis, Indexing and Retrieval Techniques and Status Report of MPEG-7, Zijun Yang and C.-C. Jay Kuo, 1999. *Tamkang Journal of Science and Engineering*, 2(3): 101–118.)

The user interface typically consists of a query formulation part and a result presentation part. The relevance feedback mechanism provides additional advantages for a retrieval system. The most significant advantages are as follows:

- It acts as a conceptual screen between the users and the query formulation mechanism, allowing the user to formulate effective queries without intimate or prior knowledge of the search process or the archive structure.
- It structures the search process by breaking the search operation into sequences of iterative steps designed to gradually approach the targeted relevant documents.
- It provides a controlled environment for query formulation and subsequent adaptation by allowing the user to emphasize relevant (and/or irrelevant) items and their features as required by the particular information needs of the users.

In designing a CBIR system, the first and most important assumption is that the discrimination between relevant and nonrelevant items is possible with the available features. Without this condition, satisfied relevance feedback is futile [1]. A relatively straightforward transformation between the topology of the feature space and the semantic characteristics of the items that the user wants to retrieve can be established. The distribution of documents relevant to the user forms a small part of the entire collection. If such items form the majority of the collection, the performance of the retrieval process might become limited, and sometimes inadequate feedback information is fed back by predominantly labeling positive items and, less often, negative items.

Over the last decade, a number of researchers have developed many machine learning algorithms for image clustering and classification and content retrieval. However, the effectiveness of these algorithms has been constrained by the performance of the optimization algorithm in solving the global minimization problem. Recent developments in applied and heuristic optimization have been strongly influenced and inspired by natural and biological systems. Biologically inspired optimization techniques are partially based on the observations of the sociobiologist E. O. Wilson, particularly by his statement: "In theory at least, individual members of the school can profit from discoveries and previous experience of all other members of the school during the search for food. This advantage can become decisive, outweighing the disadvantages of competition for food, whenever the resource is unpredictably distributed in patches" [5]. The advantages of modeling optimization problems using this sociobiologic paradigm are manifold: the model is less complex and performs inherently better in a multidimensional environment, and the convergence rate to the optimal solution is faster.

In this chapter, the investigation of one of the biologically inspired algorithms, the particle swarm optimization (PSO) algorithm for interactive CBIR, is presented. The machine learning algorithm for the user-relevance feedback system is based on a self-organizing map (SOM). The training of SOM network nodes is achieved by the PSO algorithm. The experimental results, using MPEG-7 visual descriptors, are on the Corel and Caltech databases and highlight the advantages of using the PSO algorithm for interactive image retrieval compared to existing algorithms.

The rest of the chapter is organized as follows. In Section 14.2, a brief outline of the PSO algorithm is presented, followed by a review of related work in Section 14.3. In Section 14.4, our proposed approach is presented. In Section 14.5, the experimental evaluation of the proposed approach is presented, followed by conclusions and future work suggestions in Section 14.6.

14.2 Particle Swarm Optimization

The study of optimization problems is currently being researched in three main research avenues [6]: genetic algorithms, evolution strategies, and evolutionary programming. Genetic algorithms focus on chromosomal operators; evolution strategies emphasize behavioral changes at the level of the individual; and evolutionary programming stresses behavioral change at the level of the species for natural evolution. Some of the algorithms based on such observations that have ties to artificial life (A-life) are ant colony optimization (ACO), introduced by Dorigo and colleagues [7]; PSO, introduced by Kennedy and Eberhart [8]; and artificial immune system-based optimization introduced by Dasgupta [9]. In the reminder of this section, a brief overview of the PSO algorithm is presented.

PSO is a class of evolutionary computation techniques [10]. It was originally inspired by the social behavior of a flock of birds. The initial studies on simulating social behavior of bird flocks and fish schools were conducted by Reynolds [11] and Heppner and Grenander [12]. Reynolds was intrigued by the aesthetics of bird flocking choreography, while Heppner and Grenander were interested in discovering the underlying rules that enable a large number of birds to flock synchronously, often changing direction. In PSO, the birds in a flock are symbolically represented as particles. These particles are considered to be flying through a problem space searching for the optimal solution. The location of the particles in a multidimensional environment represents a solution to the problem [13].

The particles at each time step are considered to be moving toward a particle's personal best *pbest* and the swarm's global best *gbest*. The motion is attributed to the velocity and position of each particle. Acceleration (or velocity) is weighted with individual parameters governing the acceleration being generated for *pbest* and *gbest*. The commonly used PSO versions are global and local versions of PSO. The two versions differ in the update of a particle's neighborhood, which is generally defined as the topology of knowledge sharing between particles in the swarm. In the local version of PSO, each particle's neighborhood includes a limited number of particles on its sides, while in the global version of PSO, the topology includes all of the particles in the population. The global version of PSO has a fast convergence rate, with a potential to converge to the local minimum rather than the global minimum, while the convergence rate of the local version of PSO is slow. The equations governing the velocity and position of each particle are presented in Equations 14.1 and 14.2.

$$v_{id}(t+1) = v_{id}(t+1) + c_1\left(pbest_i(t+1) - x_{id}(t+1)\right) + c_2\left(gbest_d(t+1) - x_{id}(t+1)\right) \quad (14.1)$$

$$x_{id}(t+1) = x_{id}(t+1) + v_{id}(t+1) \quad (14.2)$$

$v_{id}(t+1)$ represents the velocity of particle i in d – dimension at time $t+1$

$pbest_i(t+1)$ represents the personal best solution of particle i at time $t+1$

$gbest_d(t+1)$ represents the global best solution for d – dimension at time $t+1$

$x_{id}(t+1)$ represents the position of the particle i in d – dimension at time $t+1$

c_1, c_2 are constant parameters

The trajectory of each individual in the search space is adjusted by dynamically altering the velocity of each particle, according to a particle's own problem-solving experience and the problem-solving experience of other particles in the search space. The first part of Equation 14.1 represents the velocity at time $(t-1)$, which provides the necessary momentum for particles to move in the search space. During the initialization process, the term is set to 0 to symbolize that the particles begin the search process from rest. The second part is known as the *cognitive component* and represents the personal memory of an individual particle. The third term in the equation is the *social component* of the swarm, which represents the collaborative effort of the particles in achieving the global optimal solution. The social component always clusters the particles toward the global best solution determined at time t.

The advantages of the PSO over the genetic algorithm is that in PSO, interaction in the group enhances rather than detracts from progress toward the solution. Further, a particle swarm system has memory, while the genetic algorithm does not. Change in genetic populations results in destruction of previous knowledge of the problem, except when elitism is employed, in which case, usually one or a small number of individuals retain their identities. In PSO, individuals that fly past optima are tugged to return toward the optimal solution, and the knowledge of optimal solutions are retained by all particles and the swarm [13]. The PSO algorithm has been successfully implemented in various problem domains, such as in an ad hoc sensor network [14], in image classification [15,16], in gene-clustering

[17], in reconfigurable array design [18], to solve the traveling salesman problem [19,20], in recurrent network design [21], and as an effective learning tool for a neural network [22]. Binary PSO has been implemented in the field of distribution network reconfiguration for load balancing [23] and for unit commitment [24].

14.3 Related Work

Relevance feedback is regarded as an invaluable tool to improve CBIR systems for several reasons. Apart from providing a way to embrace the individuality of users, relevance feedback is indispensable for overcoming the *semantic gap* between low-level visual features and high-level semantic concepts. By prompting the user for relevance feedback, the initial estimation of relevant documents can be improved to steer the results in the direction that the user has in mind. Rather than trying to find better techniques and more enhanced image features in order to improve the performance of what has been referred to as "computer-centric" systems [25], it is more satisfactory to the user to exploit human–computer interaction to refine high-level queries for representations based on low-level features. This way, the subjectivity of human perception and the user's current context are automatically taken into account as well. Consequently, it is not surprising that there exist various techniques for using relevance feedback in CBIR. A comprehensive study of existing relevance feedback techniques for image retrieval can be found in Zhou and Huang [26]. In the remainder of this section, an overview of an existing neural network and a support vector machine (SVM)-based relevance feedback system is presented.

14.3.1 Neural Network-Based Relevance Feedback

One of the techniques for integrating learning approaches in relevance feedback is neural network training. The neural network-based relevance feedback is based on SOM.

- Bordogna and Pasi [27] have presented a relevance feedback model based on an associative neural network in which meaningful concepts to the users are accumulated at retrieval time by an interactive process. The network is regarded as a kind of personal thesaurus to the users. A rule-based superstructure is then defined to expand the query evaluation with the meaningful terms identified in the network.
- Zhou and Huang [26] proposed to control the order vector used in synergetic neural nets (SNNs) and use it as the basis of similarity function for shape-based retrieval. The use of self-attentive retrieval and a relevance feedback mechanism for similarity measure refinement is presented.
- The PicSOM system [28] is a CBIR system that uses SOM for indexing images with their low-level features. SOMs represent unsupervised, topologically ordered neural networks, which project a high-dimensional input space

(n-dimensional low-level feature vectors) into a low-dimensional lattice. The latter is usually a two-dimensional grid with n-dimensional neighbors connected in appropriately weighted nodes.

■ Wu and colleagues [29] have introduced a fuzzy relevance feedback approach in which the user provides a fuzzy judgment about the relevance of an image, unlike in a binary relevance system with a hard decision on relevance. A continuous fuzzy membership function is used to model the user's fuzzy feedback by weighting different image labels with different weights to simulate the user's perception. For learning users' preferences and visual content interpretation, a radian basis function (RBF) neural network is used.

14.3.2 Support Vector Machine (SVM)-
Based Relevance Feedback

SVM-based relevance feedback falls under the category of discriminative classification models, which describe not the classes but the boundaries separating these classes. This category also includes Fisher's discriminative analysis (FDA). Relevance feedback based on SVM provides a supervised learning method describing hyperplanes in feature space that separates classes [30,31].

■ Tian, Hong, and Huang [32] used a combination of weighted retrieval system with Mahalanobis distance as a similarity measure and the SVM for estimating the weight of relevant images in the covariance matrix. This approach is a combination of already exploited techniques and a new statistical learning algorithm (SVM). The overall similarity for a particular image in the database is obtained by linearly combining similarity measures for each feature.

■ Lee, Ma, and Zhang [33] exploited an unsupervised classification (clustering) to compute the updated correlation matrix between the query concepts and the clusters.

■ Gondra, Heisterkamp, and Peng [34] proposed a novel relevance feedback framework that uses the intraquery as well as the interquery information. Each query concept is modeled using one-class SVM from the retrieved results; it is stored in a concept database. This is a way to accumulate information about the interquery learning from previous relevance feedback queries. Fuzzy classification is used to merge all classifiers.

■ Djordjevic and Izquierdo [36] introduced an adaptive convolution kernel to handle relevance feedback in multifeature space. The positive definite property of the introduced kernel has been proven as an essential condition for uniqueness and optimality of the convex optimization in SVM.

The SVM-based relevance feedback system presented by Djordjevic and Izquierdo [36] is considered the reference system for evaluating the proposed approach.

14.4 Proposed Approach

To simulate human visual perception, multiple low-level features such as color, shape, and texture extracted from image content must be considered. The aim is to obtain information from different low-level visual cues at various levels of complexity and to jointly exploit that information to obtain higher levels of conceptual abstraction. Low-level descriptors are very useful to search for patterns of interest and similarities in the image database. The proposed framework, as shown in Figure 14.2, consists of two main subsystems. The first subsystem runs offline and embraces two processing steps. The aim of this step is to extract the different low-level features from the image dataset. The extracted features are stored in the metadata repository. The metadata repository is then further indexed based on the image IDs. The second subsystem involves online interaction with the user and comprises a number of processing steps. It consists of two online search modules: a visual search and an RF system, which are discussed in detail in the following subsections. The remainder of this section discusses the workflow of the framework.

The interaction is initialized by randomly presenting the user with equal distribution of images from the database. The user marks "only the relevant images" from the presented results. The first user interaction inputs are presented to the visual search module, which implicitly generates a model for irrelevant images and performs the retrieval. The objective of this step is to infer and predict the user preferences. From the set of results presented from the first iteration, the user selects

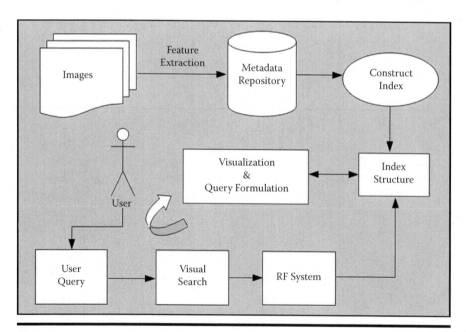

Figure 14.2   Proposed framework.

"both relevant and irrelevant images," and the input is presented to the RF system module. This step enhances the inference of the user preferences in order to improve the image retrieval. The user then iteratively interacts with the system until the user has retrieved all of the relevant documents or is satisfied with the retrieved results.

14.4.1 Visual Search System

Neural network-based clustering has been dominated by SOM [37]. In competitive neural networks, active neurons reinforce their neighborhood within certain regions while suppressing the activities of other neurons. This is called on-center/off-surround competition. The objective of SOM is to represent high-dimensional input patterns with prototype vectors that can be visualized in a usually two-dimensional lattice structure [38]. Each unit in the lattice is called a neuron, and adjacent neurons are connected to each other, which gives a clear topology of how the network fits itself to the input space. Input patterns are fully connected to all neurons via adaptable weights, and during the training process, neighboring input patterns are projected into the lattice, corresponding to the adjacent neurons. SOM enjoys the merit of input space density approximation and independence of the order to input patterns. Like the k-means algorithm, SOM needs to predefine the size of the lattice (i.e., the number of clusters). Each neuron represents an image with a dimension equal to the feature vector. In the basic SOM training algorithm, the prototype vectors are trained with Equation 14.3.

$$m_n(t+1) = m_n(t) + g_{cn}(t)\left[x - m_n(t)\right] \tag{14.3}$$

where m is the weight of the neurons in the SOM network, and $g_{cn}(t)$ is the neighborhood function as defined in Equation 14.4:

$$g_{cn}(t) = \alpha(t)\exp\left(\frac{\|r_c - r_n\|^2}{2\alpha^2(t)}\right) \tag{14.4}$$

where $\alpha(t)$ is the monotonically decreasing learning rate, and r represents the position of the corresponding neuron. The disadvantage of using a single-layer SOM is that the elimination of true negative images by the classifier is limited to those feature vectors represented by the term $x - m_n(t)$ in the training equation. Hence, a dual-layer SOM (DL-SOM) is used to improve the performance of the SOM. The structure is presented in Figure 14.3.

The second layer of the SOM is trained, based on Equation 14.5.

$$m_n(t+1) = m_n(t) + g_{cn}(t)\left[x + m_n(t)\right] \tag{14.5}$$

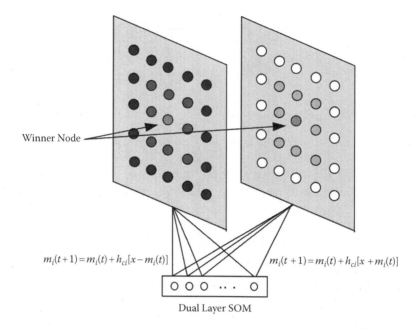

Figure 14.3   A dual-layer self-organizing map (DL-SOM) structure.

The pseudocode for training the DL-SOM mesh is as follows:

1. The square topology of the SOM is randomly initialized.
2. For each input training image feature vector:
    a.   The multidimensional feature vector x is presented to the network, forcing the central neuron as the winner node.
    b.   For each particle in each dimension, the $L1$ norm fitness function is evaluated:

$$D_{ij} = \sum_{l=1}^{k} |x_{nl} - x_{jl}|.$$

    c.   The personal best (*pbest*) and global best (*gbest*) of the particles are updated based on the contribution of the particle toward optimal solution.
    d.   Values for velocity and position are updated following Equations 14.1 and 14.2, respectively.
    e.   Repeat steps (a) through (d) for the second layer.

3. End of algorithm.

The output of the classifier is a measure of the visual dissimilarity from the classifier. The network is trained with limited (typically 1) image as positive, and the negative images models are implicitly generated by training the neighboring nodes based on Equations 14.3 and 14.5.

14.4.2 Relevance Feedback System

The relevance feedback system is implemented using a rectangular mesh structure trained with both positive and negative samples from the user preference input. The network structure is presented in Figure 14.4, where X is the input feature vector. The training of the network neurons is performed using the PSO algorithm. The input feature vector from the training model is presented to the network. The winner node based on the competitive learning is selected. The features from the selected winner node and the input training feature are presented to the PSO. The d – dimension optimization problem to be solved by the PSO is the $L1$ metric between the winner node feature vectors to the input feature vector. The particle swarm for each dimension of the input feature is randomly initialized. The evaluation function for each particle in each dimension is calculated, and the *pbest* and *gbest* values for the particle swarm are updated accordingly. The velocity and position of each particle in each dimension are updated. The iteration continues until the result of the evaluation function is less than the threshold e_{th}. The choice of the model selection parameters is discussed in Section 14.5.

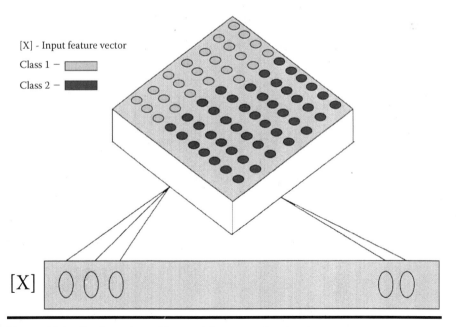

Figure 14.4   Rectangular self-organizing map structure.

The training of the algorithm is continued until all of the input patterns from the user inputs are exhausted. The features obtained from the metadata repository are presented to the trained network, and the label of the winner node is assigned to the corresponding image. The pseudocode for the algorithm is as follows:

1. The rectangular topology of the SOM is initialized with feature vectors $m_i(0)$, $I = 1, 2, \dots d$ randomly, where d is the length of the feature vector.
2. Input feature vector x is presented to the network; choose the winning node J that is closest to x, that is, $j = \arg_d \min \left\{ \| x - m_j \| \right\}$.
3. Initialize a population array of particles representing random solutions in $d-$ dimensions of the problem space.
4. For each particle, evaluate the $L1$ norm for x in the $d-$ dimensions.
5. Compare the particle's fitness evaluation with the particle's personal best *pbest*. Then set the *pbest* value equal to the current value and the *pbest* location equal to the current location in the $d-$ dimensional space.
6. Compare the fitness evaluation with the population's overall previous best. If current value reduces the global minima then update *gbest* value.
7. Update the velocity of the wind speed with the previously mentioned equation.
8. Update the velocity of the particles using Equation 14.1.
9. Update the position of the particles using Equation 14.2.

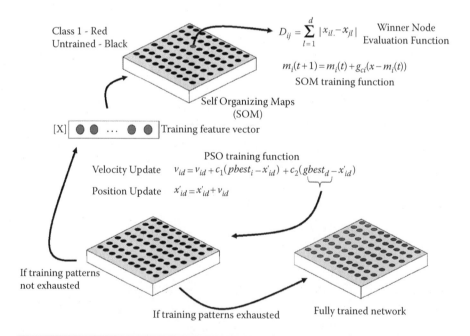

Figure 14.5 R-SOM training pseudocode flow diagram.

10. Loop to step 2 until the distance between $m_i(0)$ and x is greater than a threshold value e_{th}.
11. Repeat steps 2 through 10 until all of the input patterns for both positive and negative training models are exhausted.

In steps 2 through 10, the weights of the neuron in the SOM are trained to represent the input feature vector. The degree of closeness in pattern matching is determined by the value of e_{th}. The pseudocode flow diagram is presented in Figure 14.5. The classification algorithm produces the list of image IDs from the metadata repository and corresponding visual similarities. Hence, in the final step of processing, the image IDs are ranked in ascending order of the distance metric.

14.5 Experimental Results

14.5.1 Feature Set

The MPEG-7 visual descriptors color layout (CL) descriptor and edge histogram (EH) descriptor [39,40] are extracted for images in the following datasets. The CLD extracts color histograms over an 8 × 8 image layout. Its similarity measure is a weighted $L2$ metric with nonlinearly quantized discrete cosine transform (DCT) coefficients. The EHD builds on histograms of edges in different directions and scales. Detected edges in a number of directions are used as localized input for an edge histogram of 80 bins. Its distance is a sum of $L1$ distances over the original features, as well as global and semiglobal histogram values generated by various groupings of local image parts.

14.5.2 PSO Implementation

The PSO model that is implemented is a combination of cognitive and social behaviors. The structure of the PSO is fully connected, in which a change in a particle affects the velocity and position of other particles in the group; as opposed to partially connected, in which a change in a particle affects the limited number of neighborhoods in the group. Each dimension of the feature set is optimized with 50 particles. The size of the SOM network is prefixed with the maximum number of training samples to be used in the network. The stopping criteria threshold is experimentally determined to be 50.0.

14.5.3 Corel Dataset

The database used in the experiments was generated from the Corel dataset [36] and consisted of seven concepts: building, car, cloud, grass, elephant, lion, and tiger as shown in Figure 14.6, with the following number of ground truth images

Figure 14.6 Example images from Corel database. (From D. Djordjevic and E. Izquierdo, An object- and user-driven system for semantic-based image annotation and retrieval, *IEEE Transactions on Circuits and Systems for Video Technology*, March 2007, 17(3): 313–23.)

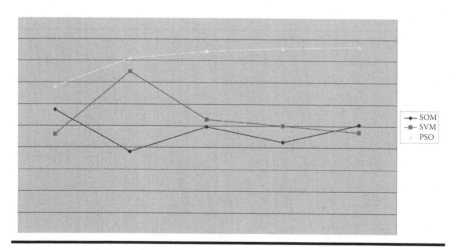

Figure 14.7 Retrieval precision for building.

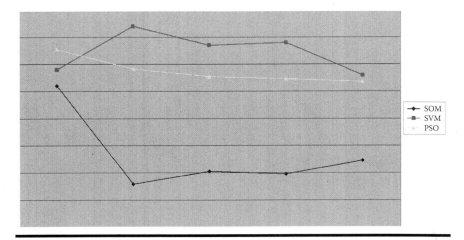

Figure 14.8   Retrieval precision for car.

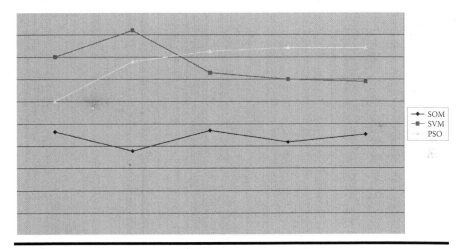

Figure 14.9   Retrieval precision for cloud.

per concept: 100, 100, 141, 100, 100, 264 and 279 respectively. The Corel database was specifically modeled for the seven concepts, and although it is small, it consists of natural images with a variety of background elements with overlapping concepts that make the dataset complex. The results of the visual search module are presented in Table 14.1 using a single image as training sample. The results of different algorithms are compared in Figures 14.7 through 14.13 for the seven selected concepts C, with precision and recall as performance measures. Precision is the ratio of the number of relevant images retrieved to the total number of retrieved images; and recall is the ratio of the number of relevant images retrieved to the size of the relevant class.

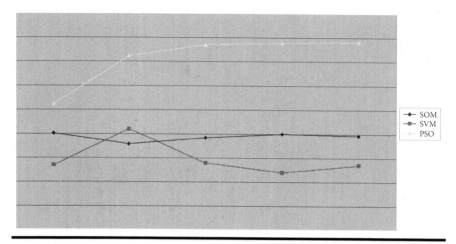

Figure 14.10 Retrieval precision for grass.

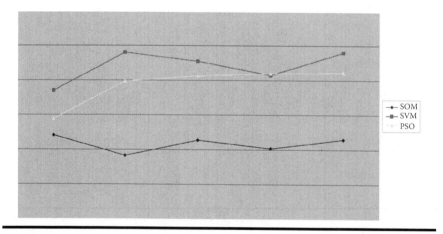

Figure 14.11 Retrieval precision for elephant.

However, in order to show the improvement of performance for different algorithms, the ratio between the relevant retrieved images and the size of the relevant class was kept constant. In the experimental results, the ratio is maintained as one. Therefore, both precision and recall can reach the value of one in the ideal case. The training set for each iteration was limited to 15% of the total image database.

The results presented in Figures 14.7 through 14.13, show that the PSO-based machine learning algorithm performs better in most cases. The evaluation of the system was carried out by a set of users $u \in \{1, 2, \ldots, U\}$, where U represents the total number of users and is set to 10. Each individual user u selected one concept from the set of concepts C and interacted with the system for UI times. Although

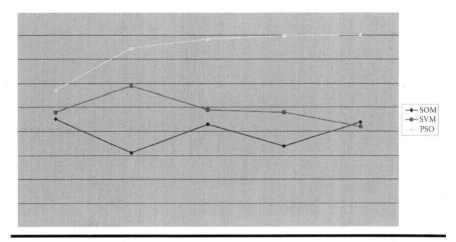

Figure 14.12   Retrieval precision for lion.

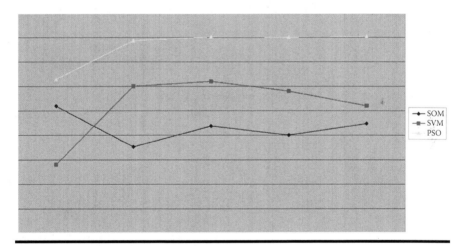

Figure 14.13   Retrieval precision for tiger.

the users could interact with the system without any predefined value, for experimental evaluation, the user interaction with the system was set to 5. Thus, each individual user interacted five times with the system for seven concepts, providing a total of 35 interactions. Thus, the values presented for SOM/PSO were obtained as an average of 350 user interactions for seven different concepts. In order to have a fair evaluation, each individual user was presented with a set of random images from the database to initiate the process of relevance feedback. In Table 14.2, the standard deviation for each concept is presented against each user interaction. The

Table 14.1 Visual Search Module Result

Concept	DL-SOM (%)
Building	12
Car	15
Cloud	17
Grass	12
Elephant	22
Lion	12
Tiger	16

Table 14.2 Standard Deviation Results for SOM and PSO Learning

Concept/User Interaction	1	2	3	4	5
Building_SD_SOM	5.81	5	5.8	5.8	5.5
Building_SD_PSO	7.2	3.4	4.5	3.5	2.7
Car_SD_SOM	6.1	3.2	3	2.5	3.6
Csr_SD_PSO	5.6	4.7	4.8	4.1	4.6
Cloud_SD_SOM	7.4	6	3.33	2.9	4.2
Cloud_SD_PSO	9.1	2.4	3.6	4.1	4
Grass_SD_SOM	4.9	3.2	4.37	2.5	4.27
Grass_SD_PSO	5.1	3	3.7	3.4	3.8
Elephant_SD_SOM	8	5.3	4.7	4.9	7
Elephant_SD_PSO	7.07	3.9	4.1	4.8	5.1
Lion_SD_SOM	4.4	3.1	2.5	4.4	3.67
Lion_SD_PSO	4	2.2	2.4	2.3	3
Tiger_SD_SOM	4.65	4.1	4.2	4.2	5.6
Tiger_SD_PSO	5.34	1.7	2.2	2.37	2.27

results indicate a large variation for user interaction 1 and subsequently settle to a lower standard deviation. The large variation for interaction 1 can be attributed to the sensitivity of the machine learning algorithm to the changes in the training dataset. However, as the user interaction increased, the proposed approach was able to generate a meaningful retrieval set in accordance with the user's requirement. This is noted by the drop in the value of the standard deviation.

14.5.4 Caltech Dataset

The Caltech dataset [41] consists of objects belonging to 101 different categories. Each category contains 30 to 800 images. Hence, a subset of the database is selected to maintain a relative distribution of images from different classes and consists of 6852 images. Similar to the previous experiment, to facilitate a fair evaluation of the proposed system, three different users participated in system evaluation, providing feedback for 10 interactions with the system. Each individual user was assigned the task of retrieving the most relevant document for a particular concept; concepts included Airplanes, Bonsai, Car_side, Faces, Faces_easy, Hawksbill, and Ketch. The training set was limited to 1% to 2% of the total image database (see Figure 14.14). The concepts Car_side and Faces_easy provided better results than Bonsai and Hawksbill. The performance of the other concepts was reasonable. As opposed to the experimental setup of the Corel dataset, the experiment on the Caltech database did not include the visual search module because of the low performance of the module. Hence, the user interaction was started by randomly presenting images from the databases for each concept. However, as in the previous experiment, different sets of images were presented to the user.

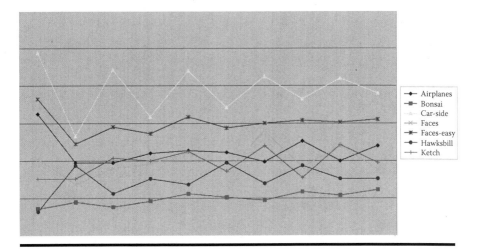

Figure 14.14   Average retrieval precision for Caltech database.

14.6 Conclusions and Future Work

One of the most important aspects of today's interactive multimedia system is the ability to retrieve visual information related to a given query, preferably formulated in semantic terms. Unfortunately, the semantic gap is formidable enough to restrict the performance of the CBIR systems. Thus, this chapter presented a CBIR framework that revolves around user relevance feedback using PSO. The evaluation of the proposed system presented on the Corel and Caltech databases quantifies the effectiveness of the machine learning algorithm for modeling user preferences when subjectively retrieving relevant documents. Future work will consider developing data mining techniques based on the user interaction logs in order to improve the performance of relevant documents. The problem of overlapping concepts will also be studied.

Acknowledgment

The research work leading to this chapter was supported by the European Commission under the IST Research Network of Excellence K-Space FP6-027026 of the 6th Framework Programme.

Krishna Chandramouli received a bachelor of engineering in instrumentation and control systems from the University of Madras, India in 2003, and subsequently received a master of technology in very large-scale integration design from the SRM Institute of Science and Technology, India in 2005. He is currently pursuing a PhD in multimedia and vision research from Queen Mary, University of London. His research findings have been published in several conference publications including some hosted by IEEE. His research interests include biologically inspired optimization techniques, machine learning, semantic retrieval of multimedia content, and summarization of video content. He is a member of IEEE and the IEEE Computer Society.

Ebroul Izquierdo is a professor and head of the Multimedia and Vision Group at Queen Mary, University of London. He received the Doctor Rerun Naturalium (PhD) from the Berlin Humboldt University in 1993. From 1990 to 1992, he was a teaching assistant in the Department of Applied Mathematics, Technical University, Berlin. From 1993 to 1997, he was with the Berlin Heinrich-Hertz Institute for Communication Technology as an associate researcher. From 1998 to 1999, he was with the Department of Electronic Systems Engineering at the University of Essex as a senior research officer. Since 2000, he has been with the electronic engineering department at Queen Mary. He is an associate editor of the *IEEE Transactions on Circuits and Systems for Video Technology* (*TCSVT*) and the EURASIP journal on image and video processing. Professor Izquierdo is a chartered engineer, a fellow of the IET, chairman of the executive group of the IET Visual Engineering Professional Network, a senior member of the IEEE, a member of the British Machine Vision Association, and a member of the steering board of the Networked Audiovisual Media technology platform of the European Union. He is a member of the program committee of the IEEE Conference on Information Visualization, the international program committee of EURASIP, the IEEE Conference on Video Processing and Multimedia Communication, and the European Workshop on Image Analysis for Multimedia Interactive Services. He coordinated the EU IST project BUSMAN on video annotation and retrieval. He is a main contributor to the IST integrated projects aceMedia and MESH on the convergence of knowledge, semantics, and content for user-centered intelligent media services. Professor Izquierdo coordinates the European project Cost292 and the FP6 network of excellence on semantic inference for automatic annotation and retrieval of multimedia content, K-Space.

References

1. C. J. Van Rijsbergen. *Information Retrieval*, 2nd ed. London: Butterworths, 1979.
2. M. La Cascia, S. Sethi, and S. Sclaroff. Combining textual and visual cues for content-based image retrieval on the World Wide Web. *IEEE Workshop on Content-Based Access of Image and Video Libraries*, pp. 24–28, 1998.
3. H.-J. Zhang and Z. Su. Improving CBIR by semantic propagation and cross-mode query expansion. *Proceedings of the International Workshop on Multimedia Content-Based Indexing and Retrieval*, pp. 83–86, 2001.
4. Z. Yang and C.-C. J. Kuo. Survey on image content analysis, indexing and retrieval techniques and status report of MPEG-7. *Tamkang Journal of Science and Engineering*, 1999, 2(3): 101–118.
5. E. O. Wilson. *Sociobiology: The new synthesis*. Cambridge, MA: Belknap Press of Harvard University Press, 1975.
6. L. Davis, Ed. *Handbook of genetic algorithms*. New York: Van Nostrand Reinhold, 1991.
7. M. Dorigo, V. Maniezzo, A. Colorni, F. Maffioli, G. Righini, and M. Trubian. Heuristics from nature for hard combinatorial optimization problems. *International Transactions on Operational Research*, 1996, 3(1): 1–21.
8. R. C. Eberhart and J. Kennedy. A new optimizer using particle swarm theory. *Proceedings of the 6th International Symposium on Micro Machine and Human Science*, pp. 39–43, October 1995.
9. D. Dasgupta, Ed. *Artificial immune systems and their applications*. Heidelberg: Springer, 1999.
10. R. C. Eberhart and Y. Shi. Tracking and optimizing dynamic systems with particle swarm. *Proceedings of the IEEE Congress on Evolutionary Computation*, pp. 94–97, 2001.
11. C. W. Reynolds. Flocks, herds and schools: A distributed behavioural model. *Computer Graphics*, 1987, 21(4): 25–34.
12. F. Heppner and U. Grenander. A Stochastic nonlinear model for coordinated bird flocks. In S. Krasner, Ed., *The ubiquity of chaos*. Washington DC: AAAS Publications, 1990.

13. M. Birattari. The problem of tuning metaheuristics as seen from a machine learning perspective. Ph.D. dissertation, Université Libre de Bruxelles, Brussels, Belgium, 2004.

14. P. Yuan, C. Ji, Y. Zhang, and Y. Wang. Optimal multicast routing in wireless ad hoc sensor networks. *IEEE International Conference on Networking Sensing and Control*, Vol. 1, pp. 367–371, March 2004.

15. K. Chandramouli and E. Izquierdo. Image classification using self-organizing feature maps and particle swarm optimization. *7th International Workshop on Image Analysis for Multimedia Interactive Services (WIAMIS 2006)*, pp. 313–316, April 2006.

16. K. Chandramouli. Particle swarm optimisation and self-organising maps based image classifier. *2nd International Workshop on Semantic Media Adaptation and Personalization*, pp. 225–228, December 2007.

17. X. Xiao, E. R. Dow, R. Eberhart, Z. B. Miled, and R. J. Oppelt. Gene clustering using self-organizing maps and particle swarm optimization. *Proceedings of the International Parallel and Distributed Processing Symposium*, April 2003.

18. D. Gies and Y. Rahmat-Samii. Reconfigurable array design using parallel particle swarm optimization. *IEEE International Symposium on Antennas and Propagation*, pp. 177–180, June 2003.

19. K.-P. Wang, L. Huang, C.-G. Zhou, and W. Pang. Particle swarm optimization for travelling salesman problem. *International Conference on Machine Learning and Cybernetics*, Vol. 3, pp. 1583–1585, November 2003.

20. X. H. Zhi, X. L. Xing, Q. X. Wang, L. H. Zhang, X. W. Yang, C. G. Zhou, and Y. C. Liang. A discrete PSO method for generalized TSP problem. *Proceedings of International Conference on Machine Learning and Cybernetics*, Vol. 4, pp. 689–94, August 2004.

21. C. F. Juang. A hybrid of genetic algorithm and particle swarm optimization for recurrent network design. *IEEE Transactions on Systems, Machines and Cybernetics*, April 2004, 34(2): 997–1006.

22. H. B. Liu, Y.-Y. Tang, J. Meng, and Y. Ji. Neural networks learning using VBEST model particle swarm optimization. *Proceedings of the 3rd International Conference on Machine Learning and Cybernetics*, pp. 3157–3159, August 2004.

23. X. Jin, J. Zhao, Y. Sun, K. Li, and B. Zhang. Distribution network reconfiguration for load balancing using binary particle swarm optimization. *International Conference on Power System Technology (PowerCon 2004)*, Vol. 1, pp. 507–510.

24. Z.-L. Giang. Discrete particle swarm optimization algorithm for unit commitment. *IEEE Power Engineering Society*, July 2003, 1: 13–17.

25. Y. Rui, T. S. Huang, M. Ortega, and S. Mehrotra. Relevance feedback: A power tool for interactive content based image retrieval. *IEEE Transactions on Circuits and Systems for Video Technology*, September 1998 (Special Issue on Segmentation, Description and Retrieval of Video Content); 8(5): 644–655.

26. X. S. Zhou and T. Huang. Relevance feedback in image retrieval: A comprehensive review. *ACM Multimedia Systems Journal*, 2003 (Special Issue on CBIR); 8(6): 536–544.

27. G. Bordogna and G. Pasi. A user-adaptive neural network supporting a rule-based relevance feedback. *Fuzzy Sets and Systems*, September 1996, 82(9): 201–211.

28. M. Koskela, J. Laaksonen, and E. Oja. User of image subsets in image retrieval with self-organizing maps. *Proceedings of the International Conference on Image and Video Retrieval (CIVR)*, pp. 508–516, 2004.

29. P. Wu, W. Y. Ma, B. S. Manjunath, H. Shin, and Y. Choi. Texture descriptor. ISO/IEC/JTCI/SC29/WG11, p. 77. Lancaster, U.K., February 1999.

30. S. R. Gunn. Support vector machines for classification and regression technical report. Image Speech and Intelligent Systems Research Group, University of Southampton, 1997.
31. Y. Chen, X. S. Zhou, and T. S. Huang. One-class SVM for learning in image retrieval. *International Conference for Image Processing*, Thessaloniki, Greece, October 7–10, 2001.
32. Q. Tian, P. Hong, and T. S. Huang. Update relevant image weights for content-based image retrieval using support vector machines. *IEEE International Conference on Multimedia and Expo*, New York, July 30–August 2, 2000.
33. C. Lee, W. Y. Ma, and H. J. Zhang. Information embedding based on users' relevance feedback for image retrieval. *SPIE International Conference on Multimedia Storage and Archiving System IV*, Boston, September 1999.
34. I. Gondra, D. R. Heisterkamp, and J. Peng. Improving image retrieval performance by inter-query learning with one-class support vector machines. *Neural Computing and Applications*, 2004, 13(2): 130–139.
35. L. Zhang, F. Qian, M. Li, and H. Zhang. An efficient memorization scheme for relevance feedback in image retrieval. *IEEE International Conference on Multimedia Expo (ICME)*, 2003.
36. D. Djordjevic and E. Izquierdo. An object- and user-driven system for semantic-based image annotation and retrieval. *IEEE Transactions on Circuits and Systems for Video Technology*, March 2007, 17(3): 313–323.
37. R. Xu and D. Wunch II. Survey of clustering algorithm. *IEEE Transactions on Neural Networks*, May 2005, 6(3): 645–678.
38. T. Kohonen. The self-organizing map. *Proceedings of IEEE*, September 1990, 78(4): 1464–1480.
39. B. S. Manjunath, J.-R. Ohm, V. V. Vinod, and A. Yamada. Color and texture descriptors. *IEEE Transactions on Circuits and Systems for Video Technology*, June 2001 (Special Issue on MPEG-7); 11(6): 703–715.
40. B. S. Manjunath, P. Salembier, and T. Sikora. *Introduction to MPEG-7: Multimedia content description interface*. New York: Wiley, 2003.
41. L. Fei-Fei, R. Fergus, and P. Perona. Learning generative visual models from few training examples: An incremental Bayesian approach tested on 101 object categories. *IEEE Conference on Computer Vision and Pattern Recognition (CVPR 2004), Workshop on Generative-Model Based Vision*, 2004.

Chapter 15

Image Description Using Scale-Space Edge Pixel Directions Histogram

António M. G. Pinheiro

15.1 Introduction

The huge amount of multimedia information stored in digital format and distributed over different systems connected through the World Wide Web requires reliable and efficient accessing methods. Nowadays, access to multimedia content is essentially based on text annotations that describe the image semantics. Apart from the practical problems related to the different meanings that the same images have for different people, manual annotation is very expensive for large image/multimedia databases. The need for automatic methods for semantic annotation that allow the recognition and semantic characterization of multimedia information is becoming increasingly important. However, the technological knowledge is still quite limited, and automatic systems are in general not reliable. This fact is easily recognized considering the large number of initiatives related to multimedia semantic analysis for high-level annotation and retrieval, such as the TREC video retrieval evaluation [21] and the European Union action COST 292 [18]. Also, new standardization efforts are focused on effective solutions for multimedia organization and efficient access. An example is the Multimedia Content Description Interface MPEG-7 standard

[3,15], which defines a set of low-level image descriptors that describe and measure the physical properties (color composition, structure, textures, and shapes) of images and videos. The ISO/IEC JPEG commission is also developing a project, JPSearch, that aims to create a standard framework for searching large image collections [19].

Considering a human interface, a higher level approach is needed that allows an automatic semantic annotation of the multimedia information. A possible scheme to derive a semantic annotation can be based on a general low-level description. Using classification techniques, some descriptors might allow for the extraction of the multimedia semantic annotation. Many classification techniques can be found, such as clustering techniques, the Bayesian decision [5], neural networks [10], the k-nearest neighbor (kNN) algorithm [4], and support vector machines [16]. Figure 15.1 represents a possible scheme, where color, texture/shape, and faces are considered for low-level descriptions. These descriptors should be carefully selected. They must allow a description that results in an image comparison based on the human visual perception. With low-level descriptors, a high-level annotation based in semantic concepts

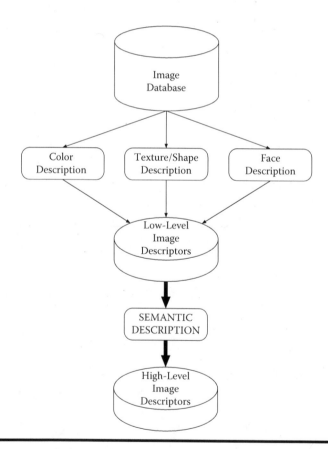

Figure 15.1 Description model.

can be extracted using classification methods. Using a set of training examples, pattern recognition systems can be trained to make decisions based on the low-level descriptors. These methods will allow the automatic detection of semantic concepts, resulting in a high-level annotation of images and other multimedia information.

Edge description seems to be close to image content description [9]. Edges are related to two of the most important image features: textures and shapes. Edge description combined with color description provides very reliable image description based on low-level features [8,13]. Furthermore, in opposition to color descriptors, edge descriptors are more robust to light or illumination variations. For the description model shown in Figure 15.1, a color structure histogram descriptor similar to the one defined in the MPEG-7 standard [11,1] might be a good choice for color description.

A face descriptor scheme based on the characteristic distances between the eyes, nose, and mouth would allow an automatic high-level description of pictures/videos with faces, relating them with people's identification. Those descriptors could be used together with an edge pixel directions histogram, resulting in a robust and reliable image description. However, solutions integrating several low-level descriptors require a multimodal analysis that is not the aim of this work. In this chapter, a scale-space edge pixel directions histogram representing textures and shapes is defined. Histograms have been widely used for image analysis, recognition, and characterization applications [7]. MPEG-7 methods also define an edge histogram direction (EHD) descriptor [1,11]. In this work, to achieve a closer approach to the human visual perception of shapes and textures, edges are detected in scale space. Edges are extracted with the Canny method [2] in two different scales. In the lower scale, no edge thresholding is applied, and the resulting edges are mainly representative of textures. In the higher scale, edges are selected by hysteresis thresholding, and the main shapes of the images result [6].

The reliability of the description method will be tested using retrieving techniques such as query by example, classification using the nearest class mean, neural networks, and the kNN algorithm. The results obtained will also be compared with the ones achieved using the edge description in the low scale only.

This chapter is organized as follows. Section 15.2 describes the scale-space edge pixel directions histogram extraction. In Section 15.3, the scale-space edge pixel directions histograms are classified using different methods. The ability of this descriptor to define different semantic concepts is tested using 242 higher resolution images of the texture database available from the MIT Media Lab [20]. A private image database with 437 key-frames of TV sequences is also used. Concluding remarks are given in Section 15.4.

15.2 Scale-Space Edge Pixel Directions Histogram

Edges are detected with the Canny algorithm [2] in two different scales. Before edge extraction, a linear diffusion of the image (Gaussian filtering) is applied in the

Canny method. It results in a dependence of a scale t ($\sigma = \sqrt{2t}$) that is proportional to the inverse of the bandwidth of the Gaussian filter given by

$$G_\sigma = \left(\frac{1}{2\pi\sigma^2} \right)^2 \exp\left(-\frac{x^2 + y^2}{2\sigma^2} \right)$$

The local maxima of the gradient of the filtered image will be selected as possible edge points. Those points are selected using a hysteresis thresholding, considering the gradient magnitude. In the lower scale, no hysteresis thresholding is done (high threshold and low threshold are equal to zero), and all of the edge points are used to define the descriptor. For this reason, the resulting edges represent the image textures. In the higher scale, textures and noise tend to be removed [17]. Additionally, edges are selected by hysteresis thresholding, resulting in a selection of the image edges of the main shapes.

The image descriptor will be derived from the edge directions. Edge directions are perpendicular to gradient directions, and it is straightforward to compute them. Those edges will be described in four directions (Figure 15.2a). The histogram of the edge pixel directions will count the number of times the edge pixels have in any of the four directions. In the lower scale, the image is divided into 16 subimages (4×4), and a descriptor with 64 bins (16×4) results. With this image division, the local influence of the edge pixel directions is measured (Figure 15.2b). In the higher scale, no image division is done because only the most important image features will be present. Only four bins result. A total of 68 bins are used to describe the image based on the two scales' edge pixel directions. The scale $t = 4$ was used ($\sigma = \sqrt{2t}$ is the Gaussian filter parameter) as the lower scale, and the scale $t = 8$ (double scale) was used for the higher scale. In this chapter, all of the image edges in the higher scale have been computed with the hysteresis high-thresholding

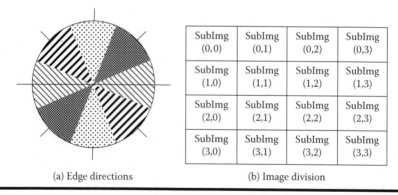

(a) Edge directions   (b) Image division

Figure 15.2   Edge pixel directions histogram computation.

parameter 80% and the low-threshold parameter 20%. An example of the resulting edges can be seen in Figure 15.3. The lower scale edge image (Figure 15.3b) is rich in textures, although the main edges have a strong definition. The higher scale edge image (Figure 15.3c) is composed of the main shapes' edges. Almost all of the texture edges have been removed.

(a) Original image

(b) Low-scale edges with no thresholding

(c) High-scale edges after hysteresis thresholding

Figure 15.3 **Edges in the two scales used to compute the scale-space edge pixel directions histogram.**

15.3 Image Classification Using Scale-Space Edge Pixel Directions Histogram

The reliability of the developed scale-space edge pixel directions histogram is tested using several retrieval models. In this work, a simple distance computation (the Minkowski distance of order one) is used to compare and compute the similarity measure between images. This method results in a low-level understanding of the image content because it does not use any prior knowledge of the system. After this simple image comparison, the defined scale-space descriptors will be tested using the nearest class mean method. The level of annotation is higher, because the access to the image database is made based on multiple examples. The two previous methods together also allow a feedback of the user to a first database access.

To enrich the level of semantic annotation, pattern recognition methods based on a training set can provide a high-level image description. In this work, neural networks and the kNN algorithm [5] have been used.

The three methods are representative of three different solutions for image database access:

- Query by example
- Retrieval refinement
- Query using semantic concepts

15.3.1 Image Comparison

A simple image comparison based on the Minkowski distance of order one (also known as the Manhattan distance) between the two image scale-space edge pixel directions histograms is given by

$$d(\mathrm{Img}_1, \mathrm{Img}_2) = \sum_{i=0}^{67} \left| h_1[i] - h_2[i] \right|$$

which results in a similarity measure between images, where h_i are the histograms representative of the two compared images. In general, the use of the scale-space description results in an improvement of the similarity measure when compared with the description of the low-scale histogram only. As an example, Figure 15.4 shows the results of image retrieval for the 242 database images when the image of Figure 15.3 is the query, with the scale-space edge pixel directions histogram description. Figure 15.5 shows the same result considering the histogram in the low scale only. Several experiments using the described method have been done. In general, the robustness of the similarity measure was improved by using the scale-space description, and the number of negative matches is reduced. The distance between histograms also reflects from the human perception perspective a better measure of the difference between images.

(a) $d(\text{Qry}; \text{1stRtr}) = 0.145$

(b) $d(\text{Qry}; \text{2ndRtr}) = 0.539$

(c) $d(\text{Qry}; \text{3rdRtr}) = 0.550$

(d) $d(\text{Qry}; \text{4thRtr}) = 0.555$

(e) $d(\text{Qry}; \text{5thRtr}) = 0.576$

(f) $d(\text{Qry}; \text{6thRtr}) = 0.597$

Figure 15.4   Example of image retrieval using the defined scale-space edge pixel directions histogram descriptor.

(a) d(Qry; 1stRtr) = 0.156

(b) d(Qry; 2ndRtr) = 0.577

(c) d(Qry; 3rdRtr) = 0.598

(d) d(Qry; 4thRtr) = 0.610

(e) d(Qry; 5thRtr) = 0.611

(f) d(Qry; 6thRtr) = 0.616

Figure 15.5   Example of image retrieval using the defined edge pixel directions histogram descriptor without the higher scale information.

15.3.2 Classification Using the Nearest Class Mean

Improved classification can be achieved by using two or more training images to define a class. In the classification using the nearest class mean method [14], the mean of the training images histograms is computed. The proximity to that mean histogram establishes how close an image represented by its histogram is to an image class. This classifying method was also used to test the reliability of the scale-space edge pixel directions histogram. In general, this method results in better classification and retrieval results than using just one image histogram, as in the previous section [14]. Instead of computing the similarity to a query image, the similarity to the mean histogram of the training images histograms is computed. Using Figures 15.3a and 15.4c, the false positive of Figure 15.4d is suppressed. Figure 15.6 shows an example of image retrieval using this classification method. Figures 15.6a, 15.6g, and 15.6i were used as the training images. The results show 8 positive matches out of 12. This is a very good result considering that only edge pixel directions histogram distance is used for the classification. The same sets of experiments have been realized with histograms without the extraction of the four bins in the higher scale (histograms with the lower scale 64 bins). In that case, the experiment of Figure 15.6 results in 5 matches out of 12 (Figures 15.6g, 15.6h, and 15.6k are not retrieved in the first 12). This is a typical situation in the different experiments that were done. The number of true positives that result from the retrieval is always larger when the scale-space descriptor is used. In general, using the scale-space 68 bins descriptor improves the classification and almost doubles the number of true positives when compared with the use of the low-scale 64 bins histogram. In practical applications, this classification method can be useful, because after a first query, a user can select one or two of the retrieved images to improve a second query to the system.

(a) d(Qry; 1stRtr) = 0.292

(b) d(Qry; 2ndRtr) = 0.311

Figure 15.6 Example of image classification with the nearest class means using the defined scale-space edge pixel directions histogram descriptor.

(c) d(Qry; 3rdRtr) = 0.326

(d) d(Qry; 4thRtr) = 0.354

(e) d(Qry; 5thRtr) = 0.379

(f) d(Qry; 6thRtr) = 0.381

(g) d(Qry; 7thRtr) = 0.408

(h) d(Qry; 8thRtr) = 0.415

Figure 15.6   (continued)

(j) d(Qry; 10thRtr) = 0.423

(i) d(Qry; 9thRtr) = 0.419

(l) d(Qry; 12thRtr) = 0.433

(k) d(Qry; 11thRtr) = 0.426

Figure 15.6   (continued)

15.3.3 *High-Level Annotation of Images*

The previous method results in a higher semantic level of image classification when compared with the simple comparison of an image. However, the method cannot be defined as a high-level feature annotation method. In this section, two classification methods are used for high-level feature annotation:

1. A neural network is trained to detect semantic concepts and features of the images.
2. A kNN algorithm is used for image classification.

The scale-space edge pixel directions histograms are used as the characteristic vectors representing the images. Those results will be compared with the ones that result from using the histogram without higher scale information. Previous work of neural network classification using a edge pixel directions histogram in one scale can only be found in Pinheiro [12].

Several experiments were conducted to test the method. In general, a better classification results by using the scale-space description. In particular, the three images used for computing the mean histogram of Figure 15.6 were used as a training set to detect urban scenes. Five extra images representing negative classification examples were also used for training. The testing database has 20 images that might be considered as having urban scenes. Considering the urban scenes presented in the images of Figures 15.6a, 15.6b, 15.6d, 15.6e, 15.6g, 15.6h, 15.6i, and 15.6k, 12 extra pictures representing the remaining urban scenes are shown in Figure 15.7. The neural network used has 68 input nodes, 68 hidden nodes, and 1 output node. For the neural network training, the output one was considered for positive classification images and zero for the negative classification images. Results considering the decision threshold in the middle of the defined training values (0.5) are shown in Table 15.1 and Figure 15.8. For the neural network training that provides the best results, Table 15.1 shows the number of false negatives when 19, 18, and 17 true positives were obtained for the scale-space descriptor and for the descriptor with the low-scale information only. The figure numbers of the false-negative images are also shown for 19 and 18 true-positive images. It was possible to classify urban scenes in 19 of the 20 images in the database, in both cases. However, classifying 19 images results in a high number of false positives. In the experiments where 18 images were classified as urban scenes, the number of false positives dropped to acceptable values (37) when the scale-space description was used.

However, if the low-scale 64 bins descriptors (without the high-scale information) were used, it was not possible to have acceptable values of false positives. This

(a)

(b)

Figure 15.7   Remaining 12 images with urban scenes.

(c)

(d)

(e)

(f)

Figure 15.7 (continued)

is an example representative of several experiments realized during the testing of the described technique. The scale-space information is very valuable for the neural network decision process, reducing the number of false positives (see the best results in Figure 15.8 for the urban classification). The graphic shows the number of false-positive detections versus the number of true positives.

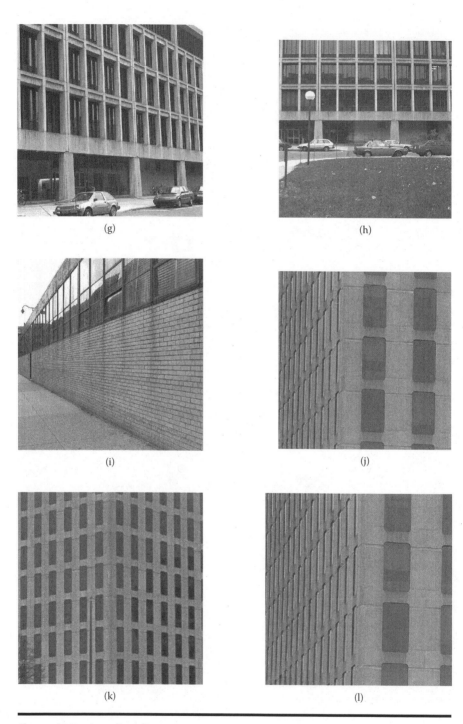

Figure 15.7 (continued)

Table 15.1 Classification as Urban Images

	Scale Space			Low Scale Only	
True Positives	False Positives	Wrong Decisions		False Positives	Wrong Decisions
19	70	Figure 15.6b		75	Figure 15.7b
18	37	Figures 15.7d, 15.7e		75	Figures 15.6b, 15.7a
17	35			57	

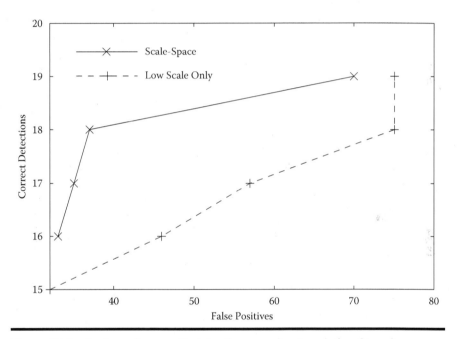

Figure 15.8 Best results provided by the neural network for the urban scene classification.

Figure 15.9 represents the receiver operating characteristic (ROC) of the neural network recognition performance and also represents the points that result with the kNN algorithm. This figure was obtained varying the decision threshold from zero to one. In the case of the kNN algorithm, a confidence interval $IC \in (0,1)$ was obtained using $IC = N_{Pk}/K$. N_{Pk} as the number of description histograms belonging to the positive training set obtained within the closer K description histograms. The distance is measured with the Minkowski distance of order one. The different ROC points were obtained for different decision threshold values of the confidence interval IC. For comparison purposes, the training set is exactly the same as for the neural network. As this training set has only three positive elements, a K of three

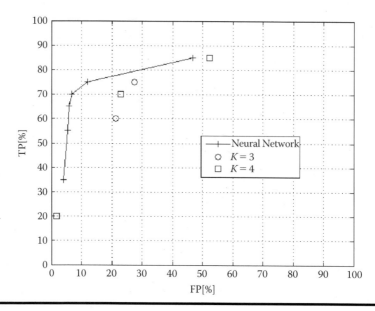

Figure 15.9   ROC provided by the neural network and kNN algorithm for the urban scene classification of the VisTex database.

(circle points) and four (square points) were used. However, a larger training set would be desirable for improved classification.

In order to obtain a more general testing of the classification method, a private testing database was also used. This database contained a set of 388 key-frames of TV sequences with natural and urban images. Many of these images included people, and some of them were studio images. A set of 20 key-frame images with urban scenes and a set of 29 key-frame images with nonurban scenes were also used as training sets. One of the results provided by the neural network (each neural network training produces different results) for this key-frames testing database is represented in the ROC of Figure 15.10. The results of the kNN classification algorithm are also shown for $K = 7$ using the same training set. Changing the value of K produces only slight changes in the results. The ROC resulting from the kNN classification when the descriptor is computed in low scale only (squares) is also presented in Figure 15.10. The previous graphs were obtained with descriptors represented by floating-point values. If quantized integer descriptors with four bits are used instead of the floating point, a very similar curve is obtained, as can be seen in the graph (represented with ◊←). In general, better results are obtained using the scale-space description instead of a description in one scale only. For comparison purposes, the results obtained when the images are represented with the EHD of MPEG-7 [1,11] are also shown. In this case, the classification is also achieved by the kNN algorithm with $K = 7$. Usually, the EHD is quantized nonuniformly with three bits. However, to allow a direct comparison, the EHD descriptors have

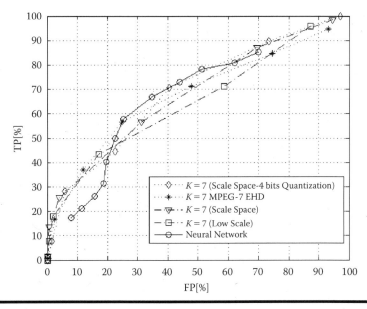

Figure 15.10   ROC provided by the neural network and kNN algorithm for the urban scene classification of the key-frames testing database.

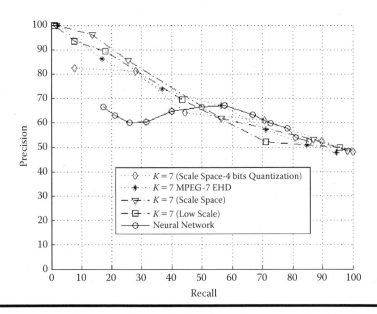

Figure 15.11   Precision-recall graphic for the urban scene classification of the key-frames testing database.

also been quantized with four bits. As can be seen, the developed multiresolution method provides a better relation between true-positive and false-positive classifications than does the EHD. The precision-recall graphic is represented in Figure 15.11. For recall values close to 100%, it is possible to have precisions of 50%.

15.4 Final Remarks and Future Work

The direction of the edges detected with the Canny algorithm are used for image description. Edges are detected in two different scales, resulting in a scale-space descriptor, where texture and main shapes are represented.

This work shows that describing edges in the two chosen scales improves the recognition provided by the descriptor when compared with the description extracted in the low scale only. This is an expected result because the scale-space detection is closer to the human image understanding. It allows an automatic separation between local image features and global image features. Scale-space description also results in a more stable training of the neural network. The use of the low-scale description produces less stable training of the neural network, creating a higher dependency on the training, while the scale-space descriptor reduces that dependency. The use of the extra four bins of high-scale information provides a general improvement of the classification using the tested methods.

The scale-space edge pixel directions histogram is a reliable descriptor that allows for improved image retrieval based on similarity. A high-level semantic annotation can be achieved using classification techniques. In this work, a neural network and the kNN algorithm were used separately to study the ability of the descriptor in achieving a high-level semantic annotation. In several situations, the neural networks provided a more accurate classification. However, the results are highly dependent on the training process. By contrast, the kNN algorithm results in very stable solutions that are not dependent on parameters like K or on the number of bits used to represent the descriptor. These scale-space descriptors also provide a better semantic image analysis than those provided by the EHDs of MPEG-7.

Several semantic concepts were tested. While only the results related to the urban semantic concept are reported here, other semantic concepts, such as flowers and plants, have been tested with reliable classification results too.

For future work, new methods of classification will be used to improve the semantic annotation level. A color descriptor will be added to the decision process, and a multimodal classification will be researched. It is expected that a higher level of annotation reliability will be reached.

António M. G. Pinheiro received a BSc in electrical and computer engineering from Instituto Superior Técnico, Lisbon, Portugal, in 1988, and a PhD from University of Essex, United Kingdom, in 2002. He is currently an assistant professor at Universidade da Beira Interior, Portugal. He is a member of the IEEE and a Portuguese representative of the EU action COST-292.

References

1. M. Bober. MPEG-7 visual shape descriptors. *IEEE Transactions on Circuits and Systems for Video Technology*, 11(6): 716–719, June 2001.
2. J. Canny. A computational approach to edge detection. *IEEE Transactions on Pattern Analysis and Machine Intelligence, PAMI*, 8(6): 679–698, November 1986.
3. S. Chang, T. Sikora, and A. Puri. Overview of the MPEG-7 standard. *IEEE Transactions on Circuits and Systems for Video Technology*, 11(6): 688–695, June 2001.
4. Dasarathy, B. V. *Nearest neighbor (NN) norms: NN pattern classification techniques.* Los Alamitos, CA: IEEE Computer Society Press, 1990.
5. R. O. Duda, P. E. Hart, and D. G. Stork. *Pattern Classification*, 2nd ed. New York: Wiley, 2000.
6. M. Ferreira, S. Kiranyaz, and M. Gabbouj. Multi-space edge detection and object extraction for image retrieval. In *ICASSP 2006*, Toulouse, France, May 2006.
7. E. Hadjidemetriou, M. D. Grossberg, and S. K. Nayar. Multiresolution histograms and their use for recognition. *IEEE Transactions on Pattern Analysis and Machine Intelligence*, 26(7): 831–847, July 2004.
8. Q. Iqbal and J. K. Aggarwal. Image retrieval via isotropic and anisotropic mappings. *Pattern Recognition Journal*, 35(12): 2673–2686, December 2002.
9. D. Lowe. Distinctive image features from scale-invariant keypoints. *International Journal of Computer Vision*, 60(2): 91–110, 2004.
10. D. J. C. MacKay. *Information theory, inference, and learning algorithms.* Cambridge, U.K.: Cambridge University Press, 2003.
11. B. S. Manjunath, J.-R. Ohm, V. V. Vasudevan, and A. Yamada. Colour and texture descriptors. *IEEE Transactions on Circuits and Systems for Video Technology*, 11(6): 703–715, June 2001.
12. A. M. G. Pinheiro. Edge pixel histograms characterization with neural networks for an improved semantic description. In *WIAMIS 2007*, Santorini, Greece, June 2007.
13. Y. Rubner, C. Tomasi, and L. J. Guibas. The earth mover's distance as a metric for image retrieval. *International Journal of Computer Vision*, 40(2): 99–121, 2000.
14. L. G. Shapiro and G. C. Stockman. *Computer Vision.* Upper Saddle River, NJ: Prentice Hall, 2001.
15. T. Sikora. The MPEG-7 visual standard for content description: An overview. *IEEE Transactions on Circuits and Systems for Video Technology*, 11(6): 696–702, June 2001.
16. V. Vapnik. *The nature of statistical learning theory.* New York: Springer, 1995.
17. A. Witkin. Scale-space filtering. In *International Joint Conference on Artificial Intelligence*, pp. 16–22, Karlsruhe, West Germany, 1983.
18. Cost 292 home page, semantic multimodal analysis of digital media. http://www.cost292.org/.
19. JPEG committee home page. http://www.jpeg.org/.
20. MIT Media Lab, Vision and Modelling Group. http://vismod.media.mit.edu/pub/VisTex/.
21. TREC Video Retrieval Evaluation home page. http://wwwnlpir.nist.gov/projects/trecvid/.

Chapter 16

Semantic Language for Description and Detection of Visual Events

Ahmed Azough, Alexandre Delteil,
Fabien De Marchi, and Mohand-Saïd Hacid

16.1 Introduction

A picture is worth a thousand words—better still, multimedia documents simulate reality. Multimedia is the combination of text, videos, animations, and sound in a single document to present information in a more enriched and comprehensive way. Produced previously by analog devices, audiovisual documents gained more importance in daily use after the introduction of digital technologies. In many domains, such as medicine, news, sports, and video surveillance, the video is a main resource of information. Multimedia documents have become an important part of many Web activities with the rise of affordable digital devices and the growth of Web 2.0 and social-site audiences. Nevertheless, the numerous media collections and the large diversity of research interests make exploitation of video clips difficult and the access to them nontrivial. Most videos are published as raw data with poor semantic information. And even for structured data, the information structure is guided by supply, not by demand. While most multimedia resources suppliers fail to efficiently annotate and structure their documents, the unsuitable existing retrieval techniques, often keyword-based, do not enable efficient access [13]. For example, the large collection of sport videos presents a big challenge for video analysts. Although the digitization of multimedia documents and the rapid advance in computer technologies allow powerful processing and analysis of videos, only the important highlights and actions within such resources have gained the interest of researchers [5,8,22,25,27]. Most existing methods of sport video analysis are designed for the needs of a large audience, but few approaches focus on other users, such as trainers and players, who are interested in specific and personalized event and action detection. The main reason sport video analysis is broad rather than specialized is that most methods of analysis use elements such as emotions and camera motion to characterize and detect important highlights rather than constituting the complete model of the event. While this method enables relatively rapid responses to event recognition, it may also cause excessive false alarms [7]. In addition, existing approaches usually summarize extracted events and present them without the ability for users to request changes or further information [28]. Many studies [18] assert that the perception of "event" varies widely among people and among use cases. Even if users are not motivated to annotate their multimedia documents, they are usually willing to spend time describing their retrieval queries as clearly as possible to get a restricted number of responses and the most efficient results. The best way, then, to provide efficient access to the right information would be to conceive advanced retrieval systems that offer users the further ability to specify the events they want to detect through the video streams. While most users express their requests with high-level concepts, only low-level features can be extracted in a reliable way. Thus, such retrieval systems should narrow the semantic gap and provide bridges between the different levels of semantic abstraction.

Our objective in this work is to conceive a semantic representation language that enables complete specification and modeling of visual events. These event models can then be used to automatically retrieve the visual events from a video database or in a real-time video broadcast. This modeling language is also used for the validation of the MPEG-7-based description of video sequences. In addition to the expression of spatial and temporal constraints, this language takes into consideration uncertainty, offers different levels of granularity in description, and is independent from storage format in order to assure interoperability between description systems. Based on finite automata formalism, the language allows the description of state sequences. Each state is associated with a situation occurring within the event, and each situation is characterized using fuzzy conceptual graphs to describe its spatial composition. By enabling the description of complex concepts, this formalism can be used, for example, to monitor behaviors in a video-surveillance context, to detect important highlights in a sport context, and to validate MPEG-7-based descriptions.

This chapter is organized as follows. After a brief survey of the work carried out in the domain of semantic description and high-level detection of visual events (Section 16.2), we will explain our contributions and the requirements that should be fulfilled by our multimedia resources description language (Section 16.3). The language dedicated to describing visual events is presented in Section 16.4, and then its applications to automatic event detection (Section 16.5), video-guided monitoring (Section 16.6), and semantic validation of MPEG-7-based visual descriptions (Section 16.7) are presented.

16.2 Related Work

The number of works carried out in semantic description and high-level detection of visual events is so huge that it becomes difficult to summarize them. Nevertheless, general observations can be derived from a survey of these works. Generally speaking, approaches aiming to fill the semantic gap between the semantic-level descriptions and low-level features of video content can be divided into two categories. The knowledge-based approaches, conceived by the community of Semantic Web and artificial intelligence, aim to adapt description languages and techniques to image and video context using top-down methods. The processing-based approaches, conceived by the image and video indexing community, aim to connect the low-level features in video documents in order to infer high-level semantic descriptions in a bottom-up way. Some interesting approaches are cited in the following.

16.2.1 Semantic Description of Multimedia Resources

Description logics is a family of knowledge representation formalisms descended from semantic networks and the frame language KL-ONE [4]. These formalisms allow the description of a given domain in terms of concepts (classes), roles (properties, relationships), and individuals. They offer a formal semantics constructed from decidable fragments of first-order logic and related to propositional modal and dynamic logics. They are also equipped with decidable inference algorithms services allowing decisions to be made about key problems such as satisfiability and subsumption. Straccia [20] extended the simple description logic ALC with fuzzy logic in order to support reasoning about imprecise concepts. A concept C of the fuzzy description logic is interpreted as a fuzzy set, and the assertions associating an individual with a concept or a couple of individuals with a role are given a truth value in [0, 1], representing a degree of membership. SHOIN(D) description logic [15] is a powerful language that allows reasoning with concrete data types such as strings and integers using so-called concrete domains. Straccia [21] presents an extension of the SHOIN(D) with fuzzy logics. It provides further capabilities, especially by using fuzzy sets of concrete domains and fuzzy modifiers and by allowing values from the interval [0, 1] for subsumption and entailment relationships. Linckels and Meinel [14] presented an application of ALC description logic in the multimedia context. This application aims to ameliorate semantic search of multimedia resources in the eLearning tool Computer History Expert System (CHEST). It takes as input a question about computer history expressed in natural language, translates it into a formal description logic expression, and returns as output the list of multimedia clips whose description is subsumed by the formal query.

Conceptual graphs are very useful formalisms for representing structured knowledge. However, simple conceptual graphs (that correspond to positive, conjunctive, and existential formulas) are not suitable for matching images because they contain only exact facts. Mulhem, Leow, and Lee [16] presented a new variation of fuzzy conceptual graphs (fCGs) more suited to image matching. This variant differentiates between a model graph that describes a known scene and an image graph that describes an input image. A new measurement is defined to measure how well a model graph matches an image graph. A fuzzy graph-matching algorithm is developed based on error-tolerant subgraph isomorphism. Test results show that the matching algorithm gives very good results for matching images to predefined scene models. Another interesting approach in this sense is the work presented by Isaac and Troncy [11], an experimentation concerning the description of audiovisual documents used in medicine and based on relational indexing schemas. This description rests on the concept of patterns of indexing based on existing usage scenario and exploit technologies resulting from the Semantic Web. The authors show that the combination of several ontologies and rules of inference allows for a more completely structured and pertinent description base of descriptions that can be increased by additional facts according to the knowledge contained in the ontologies.

16.2.2 *Detection of Events and High-Level Concepts in Videos*

Automatic recognition of multimedia document content, particularly soccer videos, has been studied in several works. There are plenty of proposed approaches but only those dealing with low level detections are mature (see [19]). Assfalg and colleagues [3] presented a system that performs automatic annotation of the principal highlights in a soccer video, suited for both production and posterity logging. The knowledge of the soccer domain is encoded into a set of finite state machines (FSMs), each of which models a specific highlight. Highlight detection exploits visual cues that are estimated from the video stream, and particularly ball motion, the currently framed playfield zone, player positions, and colors of the player uniforms. Authors use highlight models that are checked against the current observations using a model-checking algorithm. Video annotations include the description of the most relevant highlights and other in-depth information. Highlights are modeled using FSMs, and each highlight is described by a directed graph: $G^h = <S^h, E^h>$, where S^h is the set of nodes representing the states, and E^h is the set of edges representing the events. Bonzanini, Leonardi, and Migliorati [6] and Leonardi and Migliorati [12] have presented a semantic video indexing algorithm based on FSMs and low-level motion indices extracted from the MPEG-compressed bitstream. The proposed algorithm is an example of a solution to finding a semantically relevant event (e.g., scoring of a goal in a soccer game) in the case of specific categories of audiovisual programs. To face the semantic indexing problem, an automatic system operates in two steps: first, some low-level indices are extracted to represent low-level information in a compact way, and then a decision-making algorithm is used to extract a semantic index from the low-level indices.

A similar approach is the one proposed by Ekin, Tekalp, and Mehrotra [8]. They propose an automatic framework for analysis and summarization of soccer videos using cinematic and object-based features. Based on some *low-level* soccer video–processing algorithms, such as dominant color region detection, robust shot boundary detection, and shot classification, and on some *higher level* algorithms such as goal detection, referee detection, and penalty-box detection, the system can output three types of summaries: all slow-motion segments in a game, all goals in a game, and slow-motion segments classified according to object-based features.

Tovinkere and Qian [22] have presented a new method for detecting semantic events that may happen in a soccer game. They differentiate between events defined as semantically significant actions and consequences and actions as simple physical motions. They divide events into observed events, which are independent and can be readily observed, and interpreted events, which are annotations of an observed event. The semantic events are represented by entity relationship diagrams, and then an algorithm of detection takes place in two steps: the detection of basic actions and then the detection of complex events.

16.3 Our Contribution

Many of the problems with existing approaches remain unsolvable. Inconsistencies can easily be observed between detection and description techniques. While detection techniques are based directly on the image and video processing, heavy description formalisms stay far from concrete situations. The adoption of a unified intermediate level for description and detection techniques enables the merge of manual and automatic techniques for video content recognition. On the other hand, most high-level event detections in videos are dependent on the context in which they were developed. Detection software programs are provided as prefabricated black boxes with few possibilities of interaction or modification of parameters and recognition process. In our approach, the user would be able to conceive his or her own methods of event detection, combining two or more existing low-level detectors to produce personalized and robust detectors.

Geurts, van Ossenbrugen, and Hardman [9] proposed a set of requirements that language of multimedia content description should fulfill for an efficient annotation. The language should:

■ Be lightweight and extensible
■ Reuse existing vocabularies
■ Relate concept to media asset
■ Provide structured annotations

- Offer unrestricted fair use
- Provide functional specification of media assets

In addition to these requirements, our language that is conceived for visual events modeling aims to fulfill recommendations for event-centric video analysis as mentioned in Westermann and Jain [26]:

- Express spatial and temporal constraints
- Take into consideration uncertainty
- Offer different levels of granularity in description
- Be independent of storage format
- Satisfy interoperability between description systems

16.4 Modeling Visual Events

16.4.1 Video Semantic Structure

Content descriptions are needed for different levels of abstraction. The use of processable schemas to explicitly define the structure of video content is indispensable for generic multimedia description languages. To this end, some notions for structuring content semantics within videos were proposed:

Basic object: Elementary item representing low-level and midlevel concepts that can be expressed either using image processing detectors or by manual annotations (car, person, Zidane, . . .)

Complex object: A semantic entity composed of connected objects using spatial or logical relations (occupied car, empty zone, . . .)

Situation: Set of objects related spatially or logically to describe a situation that can remain true during many consecutive frames (ball in penalty zone, . . .)

Event: A set of situations regrouped by temporal relations to represent the different possible states during the occurrence of an event (penalty, goal, car theft, . . .)

Figure 16.1 depicts our adopted semantic structure to describe the video.

16.4.2 Formal Model Language

This section introduces the formalism to represent the semantic descriptions of a video's content. This language is based on the combination of deterministic FSMs and fCGs. Let C be a set of object types and R a set of topological and spatial binary relations. A basic object (the lowest semantic component) is represented by a referent f and an object type o from the C set. Complex objects and situations are represented by a referent f, a set O of

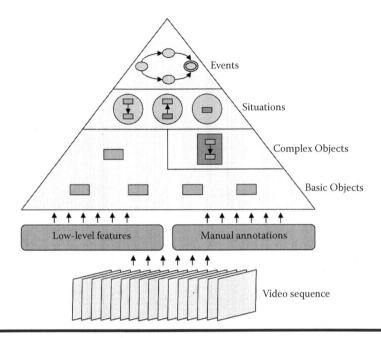

Figure 16.1 **General semantic structure of video contents.**

basic objects composing the complex object, and a graph $G = \{(o_1, o_2, r)|(o_1, o_2) \in O^2,$ $r \in R)\}$ describing the spatial and logical links between the composing objects. An event is described by a model M, which is defined as $M = (P, G)$, where P is a temporal FSM, and G is the set of fCGs, each associated with the states of P states. The event is described as connected states of automata, each associated with a situation occurring within the execution of the event. Each situation is characterized using an fCG to describe its spatial composition (Figure 16.2). In addition to their flexibility and power to represent qualitative and uncertain information, fCGs were chosen to express spatial constraints due to their adaptability to build graph structures, which better express spatial positioning of video contents. In contrast, an event can occur following different sequences of states, and FSM are the most adequate means to describe them.

16.4.2.1 Fuzzy Conceptual Graphs

Spatial situations are described fCGs [16]. $G(C, R, A)$ is a directed graph formed using three types of components: fuzzy concepts, fuzzy relations, and fuzzy relation attributes, grouped respectively in the sets C, R, and A. They are defined as follows:

■ *Fuzzy concept*: $[T, e, f]$, where e is a referent, $T = t_0, \ldots, t_n$ is a sequence of concepts, and $0 " f(t_i) " 1. f(t_i)$ indicates the probability that the referent e belongs to concept t_i. A crisp concept is a unique concept such that $f(t) = 1$.

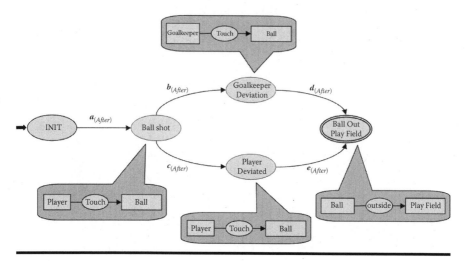

Figure 16.2 Example of an event model.

- *Fuzzy relation*: (t, v), where t is a relation type, and $0 "v" 1$ indicates its probability of occurrence. A crisp relation is a relation where $v = 1$.
- *Fuzzy relation attribute*: $[t, e, f]$, where t is a relation attribute type, e is a referent, and $0 "f(e)" 1$. f indicates the probability that the value of the attribute t is e.

16.4.2.2 Temporal Finite State Machine

The used FSM [2] is defined as $P = (S, s_0, F, M, R)$, where S is the set of spatial states (each one described by an fCG); s_0 is the initial state; F is the set of final states; M is the set of transition labels having the form $after_{(MinSec, MaxSec)}$, where $_{MinSec}$ and $_{MaxSec}$ are the minimum and the maximum duration in seconds separating the occurrence of the two states; and $R = \{(s_i, s_j, m) | s_i \in S, s_j \in S, m \in M\}$ is the set of all possible transitions between states.

16.4.3 Hierarchical Description

The representation language defined previously is conceived to construct bridges between different levels of semantic abstraction and to combine different descriptors and concepts to express complex events. In fact, the composition of different descriptions from different levels allows for the creation of a superposition of concepts and events organized in a hierarchical model (Figure 16.3). This concept is very beneficial during the conception of high-level detectors: rather than expressing the event using the low-level features (color, shape, etc.), midlevel concepts (composing objects) can be used to describe concepts. This also helps to satisfy interoperability between description systems and to keep the definition of the event correct

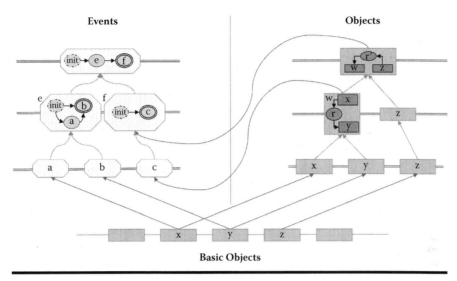

Figure 16.3   Hierarchic description of complex objects and events.

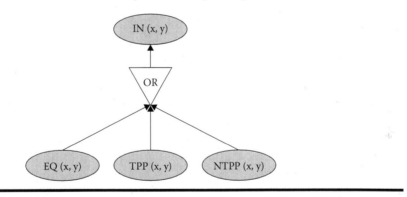

Figure 16.4   Example of a hierarchic description of a complex relation.

in all conditions. Logical and spatial relations relying on objects to form a situation can be defined in a hierarchical way too. While the relations in the lower level should be related to algorithms dealing with visual features and enabling their verification within a frame, complex relations should be defined using logical operators. Figure 16.4 depicts the definition of the relation *IN* based on the basic relations *EQ* (equal), *TPP* (tangential proper part), and *NTPP* (nontangential proper part) in a 2D vision context. These binary relations are parts of the well-known system of spatial relations RCC8 [17]. We can write:

$$IN(x, y) = EQ(x, y) \cap TPP(x, y) \cap NTPP(x, y)$$

where x and y are the objects concerned with the relation *IN*.

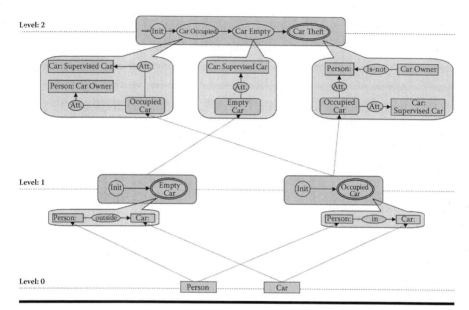

Figure 16.5   Example of a hierarchic representation of a complex visual event.

Figure 16.5 depicts a hierarchic definition of the event *Car theft*, which is pretty difficult to automatically detect. Using only the two objects *Car* and *Person* (partially easy to detect on videos), the detection of this complex event becomes easier. For this aim, we define an intermediate level containing the two opposed events *Empty Car* and *Occupied Car*. Using these two events and the basic objects, we define the *Car theft* event model. The model expresses the fact that the *Car theft* event occurs when the supervised car becomes empty of its owner, and then a different person occupies the car.

16.5 High-Level Events Detection

This language is conceived in order to bridge the gap between the high- and low-level visual concepts and to facilitate recognition of complex events in video clips based on low-level objects and relations. Figure 16.6 shows the correspondence between the event model *Goal* and a real video sequence. The used event models can be conceived either by domain experts or by nonexpert users aiming to describe and detect their typical events on video clips. This is done via appropriate interactive interfaces.

16.5.1 Detection Framework

While detection frameworks of visual events usually summarize the extracted events and present them with no ability for users to request additional information,

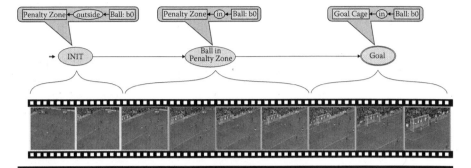

Figure 16.6   Detecting the event *Goal* in a soccer video.

our detection framework is more adaptable to users' needs. Using this framework, users can express precisely the structure of the events they want to retrieve from a video collection. The detection framework can be used in two different application scenarios. The first scenario is the real-time event detection within video streams. In this case, an interface is provided to configure the capture of a video stream and to specify the event model, the detection strategy, and the associated alerts. The event detector runs directly on the live video stream. The second scenario corresponds to the event retrieval within a collection of video documents. In this case, the event detector is launched offline on each video within the collection, and videos are indexed by the events they contain. The user interacts online with a search engine that provides a query interface and exploits the indexes to compute the answer to the query. The developed detection framework (Figure 16.7) is composed of three major packages: a model editor, video annotator, and event detector.

16.5.1.1 Model Editor

Instead of limiting the user to selecting only the desired retrieved event, this module of the framework allows the user to describe exactly the event that he or she wants to retrieve. Using some midlevel concepts provided by the framework, the user composes the structure of the event by drawing automata and then associates the adapted fCG to each state, which is also drawn in a separate screen. The constructed model is then stored in an event models base.

16.5.1.2 Video Annotator

While modeling the events, the user may need some additional descriptors that are not provided by the framework. This module enables the user to annotate some regions of the video with a specific descriptor name. Based on the low-level features of this annotation (e.g., color, shape), the system builds the midlevel concept

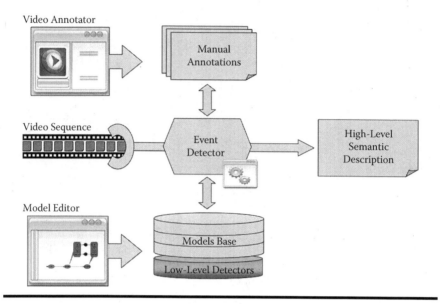

Figure 16.7   Detection framework architecture.

detector. This concept can then be used in the modeling and detection of events. This module is also used to directly annotate videos using the objects and the events contained in the model's base. These manual annotations are then used in the detection of more complex events within the annotated video.

16.5.1.3 Event Detector

This module is the heart of the framework. It takes as input a model describing the event structure and the video to analyze, and then it returns a report about the occurrences of the specified event in the explored video.

16.5.2 Detection Algorithms

Let $V = \{f_0, f_1, f_2, ..., f_n\}$ be the analyzed video (sequence of frames) and $M = (P, G)$ the model of the tracked event within this video. The detection of the event in the video is done using three major algorithms.

16.5.2.1 ModelOccurrence

The algorithm *ModelOccurrence* (Algorithm 1) is recursive. At each step it takes as input the current frame f_i, the current state s, the number of unrecognized frames during event occurrence unF, and the frame where the event starts at each occurrence *start-Frame*. It returns the list of all of the occurrences of the event M in V. The algorithm starts by ($i = 0$). If the frame f_i matches the state s with a degree higher than the satisfaction match threshold sTh, the algorithm initializes *startFrame* if s is initial and checks the next frame unless s is final. If f_i does not match s, the algorithm tries to match the f_i with all the successors of s in P. If no successor of s matches f_i, the algorithm increases unF if the event has begun. The algorithm then checks the next frame f_{i+1}, but only if unF is lower than a toleration threshold uTh. The algorithm continues frame by frame until the end of the video and returns the list of correct occurrences of the event M in the video.

16.5.2.2 objectInstances

The algorithm objectInstances (Algorithm 2) also is recursive. It aims to extract all instances of a set of objects G in a specified video frame f. It begins by extracting all the stored manual annotations of the frame f and verifies the occurrence of objects of G in these annotations. Then for each o in G, if o is a basic object, it applies the detection algorithms on the frame f; otherwise (if o is a complex object), it extracts the set of the object composing o and calls *objectInstances* on this set.

16.5.2.3 Matching

The algorithm *Matching* (Algorithm 3) computes the degree of satisfaction of the visual graph associated to a state in an event model s by the object instances of a video frame f (Figure 16.8). It takes as input a set of instances I and a state s of an event model. The algorithm computes the best combination of instances that returns the higher certainty coefficient of satisfaction of the relations in the graph of s based on the responses of low-level features algorithms.

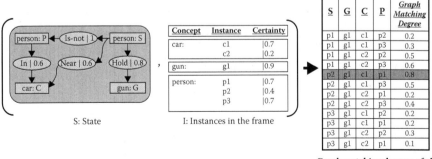

S	G	C	P	Graph Matching Degree
p1	g1	c1	p2	0.2
p1	g1	c1	p3	0.3
p1	g1	c2	p2	0.5
p1	g1	c2	p3	0.6
p2	g1	c1	p1	0.8
p2	g1	c1	p3	0.5
p2	g1	c2	p1	0.2
p2	g1	c2	p3	0.4
p3	g1	c1	p2	0.2
p3	g1	c1	p1	0.2
p3	g1	c2	p2	0.3
p3	g1	c2	p1	0.1

Concept	Instance	Certainty
car:	c1	0.7
	c2	0.2
gun:	g1	0.9
person:	p1	0.7
	p2	0.4
	p3	0.7

S: State

I: Instances in the frame

Graph matching degrees of all combinations of instances

Figure 16.8 Matching object instances of a video frame to an event state.

16.6 Video-Guided Monitoring of Behavior

Our method is also conceived for real-time behavior monitoring within a video broadcast. This application requires the complete description of the monitored behavior and the use of fast low-level detection algorithms. All of the spatial and temporal constraints should be expressed using the formalism, taking into consideration all possible behavior cases. Automata are extended by modules for the definition of alerts, strategies, and decisions that have to be launched depending on the current state.

Algorithm 1 ModelOccurrence(s, f_i, unF, startFrame)
Require:
$V = \{f_0, f_1, f_2, ..., f_n\}$
$P = (S, s_0, F, M, R)$
$\text{succ}(s) = \{s \in S | \exists m \in M, (s, s, m) \in R\}$
sTh: Acceptance threshold for matching a frame to a state
unF: Number of unrecognized frames
uTH: Authorized number of unrecognized frames during the event occurrence checking
startFrame: Frame where the event starts within the video (null at the beginning)
occList: Occurrence List
Ensure:
ModelOccurrence(s, f_i, unF, startFrame)
if $i \neq n$ **then**
if Matching(s, f_i) > sTh **then**
if $s = s_0$ **then**
startFrame $\leftarrow f_i$
end if
if $s \in F$ **then**
if startFrame $\neq$ null **then**
$i \leftarrow i + 1$
while Matching(s, f_i) and $i \neq n$ **do**
$i \leftarrow i + 1$
end while
occList $\leftarrow$ occList $\cup$ {eventName, startFrame, f_i}
end if
else
occList $\leftarrow$ occList $\cup$ ModelOccurrence(s, f_{i+1}, unF, startFrame)
end if
else
matchNextState $\leftarrow$ false
for each $s \in \text{succ}(s)$ **do**
if Matching(s, f_i) > sTh **then**

matchNextState ← true
occList ← occList ∪ ModelOccurrence(s, f_i, unF, startFrame)
end if
end for
If matchNextState ← false **then**
if startFrame = null **then**
occList ← occList ∪ ModelOccurrence(s, f_i+1, unF, startFrame)
else
unF ← unF + 1
if unF <= uTH **then**
occList ← occList ∪ ModelOccurrence(s, f_i+1, unF, startFrame)
end if
end if
end if
end if
end if
return occList

Algorithm 2 *objectInstances(G, f)*
Require:
M(f) ← ManualAnnotations(f)
I: Object instances List
Ensure: objectInstances(G,f)
I ← empty
for each c ∈ G **do**
I ← instances of c in M(f)
if c is *basic object* **then**
I ← I ∪ BasicDetection(c,f)
else
T ← graph of objects of c
I ← I ∪ objectInstances(T,f)
end if
end for
return I

Algorithm 3 *Matching(s, I)*
Require:
G ← set of objects composing the state graph
Cb ← getAllCombinations(G,I)
R ← relations(s)
Ensure: Matching(s,I)
maxCoef ← 0
for all combin ∈ Cb **do**

matchCoef ← 0
for all rel ∈ R **do**
if verify(rel, combin) **then**
matchCoef ← matchCoef +1
end if
end for
matchCoef ← matchCoef /size(G)
if maxCoef < matchCoef **then**
maxCoef ← matchCoef
end if
end for
return maxCoef

16.6.1 *Monitoring Protocol Construction*

Monitoring behaviors via real-time broadcast allows for video surveillance of limited zones using fixed cameras. The behavior is described by constituting the model and describing it in a semiautomated way (Figure 16.9), following these steps:

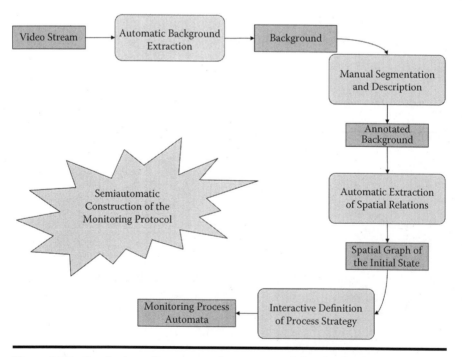

Figure 16.9 Semiautomatic construction process of the monitoring protocol.

- *Automatic background extraction*: The system automatically extracts the background of the monitored area.
- *Manual segmentation and description*: The user segments the background into regions and annotates them using predefined domain ontology. The actors entering in the execution of the behavior are also added to the description model. Low-level features (shape, texture, color) related to regions and to the added actors are also extracted.
- *Automatic extraction of spatial relations*: Spatial relations between determined annotated segments are extracted automatically. This results in a conceptual graph representing the initial state of the monitored behavior or process.
- *Interactive definition of process strategy*: The system performs an interactive process for the specification of the automata representing the monitoring strategy. The user is assisted in specifying the important states that compose the process, in identifying the corresponding conceptual graphs for each state, and in associating the adequate decisions to be made and the alerts to be launched in each state.

At the end of this operation, the monitoring protocol is complete and ready to use.

16.6.2 Monitoring Behavior for Video Surveillance

After producing the *Monitoring Protocol*, the real-time video-guided behavior monitoring is performed by the *Event Detector* module of the framework (Figure 16.10).

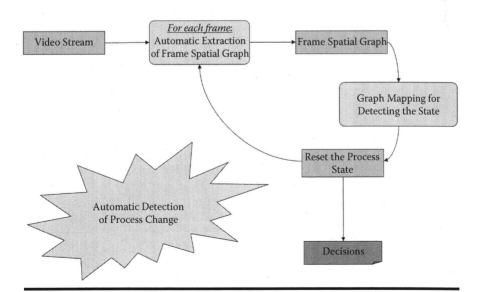

Figure 16.10 Process of automatic monitoring of behavior.

■ At the beginning, the monitoring index used to indicate the current state of behavior is set on the initial state.
■ Then, frame by frame, and for each successive state, the detector extracts the content graph and applies low-level detectors to extract the instances of the objects.
■ The produced instances lists are then mapped to the automata states using the matching algorithm (Algorithm 3).
■ The algorithm selects the state returning the higher matching degree, updates the monitoring index to the current state, and launches the appropriate alert associated with the new state.

Automatic referring and video surveillance are appropriate fields in which to apply this process.

16.6.3 Use Case: Car Theft

To illustrate our approach, a monitoring protocol related to the use case of *Car theft* is conceived and used to detect the event of the theft of a car in a real-time video stream. The monitoring protocol in Figure 16.11 describes the main ways that a car theft is likely to occur. Using simple objects like Car, Person, and Gun, the protocol describes three scenarios: the path P1 = {INIT, a Occupied car, f, Stranger

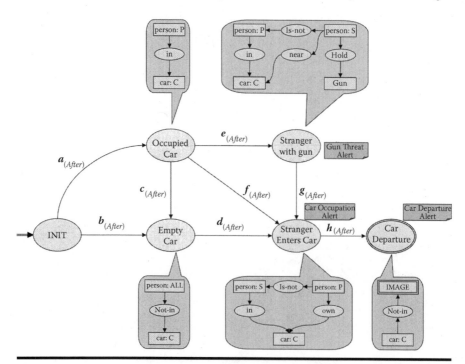

Figure 16.11   Car theft monitoring protocol.

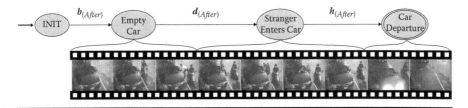

Figure 16.12   Car theft detection in real-time video stream.

enters car, *h*, car departure} that describes a forced car theft, the path P2 = {INIT, a Occupied car, *e*, Stranger with gun, *g*, Stranger enters car, *h*, car departure} that describes a forced car theft where the thief uses a gun, and the path P3 = {INIT, *b*, Empty-Car, *d*, Stranger-With-Gun, *g*, Stranger-Enters-Car, *h*, car departure} that describes a stranger who steals the car when it is empty. Figure 16.12 shows the result of a performed *car theft* detection using the monitoring protocol and the detection framework.

16.7 MPEG-7 Annotation Validation

MPEG-7 is a description standard used to create complex and comprehensive metadata descriptions of multimedia content [1]. Unfortunately, XML Schema, used by MPEG-7, is a language for constraining syntactic structures, not for describing semantics. High-level visual concepts and events can be described in multiple ways, which profoundly affect the interoperability and automatic use of MPEG-7-based descriptions. Many works have focused on the structural and syntactical validations of MPEG-7-based video descriptions [10]. Other works have focused on reducing the semantic variability by using the MPEG-7 profiles subsets [23].

However, few works have focused on semantic validation of specific events. Consider a goal event in a soccer game: it should begin with the ball being shot and then the same ball entering the goal box. Verifying the sequence of occurrences within an event inside an MPEG-7 description is very difficult with existing approaches. In our system, we enable semantic validation of the spatiotemporal structure of events in MPEG-7-based descriptions. Considering an event modeled using the description language defined previously (Section 16.4), each MPEG-7 file describing the occurrence of such an event is mapped to the model of this event to validate its spatiotemporal decomposition (Figure 16.13). The process of MPEG-7 description validation is defined as follows:

■ Execution paths are extracted from the event model. Each execution path represents a possible way that the event can occur within a video. It represents a correct chronological decomposition of this event. Since each event is associated with an automata, where the states are the spatial situations happening during the execution of the event, the execution path then corresponds to a sequence of states that starts from the initial state of the automata and ends with its final state. The set of such paths is defined as $E_M = \{e = s_0.s_1 \ldots s_n | s_n \in F(M), s_0 = initState(M)\}$, where M is the event model. In Figure 16.14, $E_M = \{A.B.D, A.C.D, A, B, C, D\}$ where $S_M = \{A, B, C, D\}$.

■ Spatial structure corresponding to each state in the automata is extracted. Each state is associated with an fCG that describes the spatial objects occurring in the situation and the spatial relations regrouping them. The set of such structure is defined as $Ss_M = \{(C, R, A) | \exists s \in S(M), (C, R, A) = graph(s)\}$ (see Section 16.4).

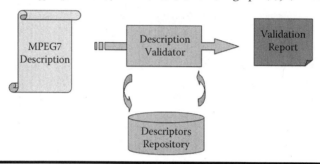

Figure 16.13   Semantic validation framework architecture.

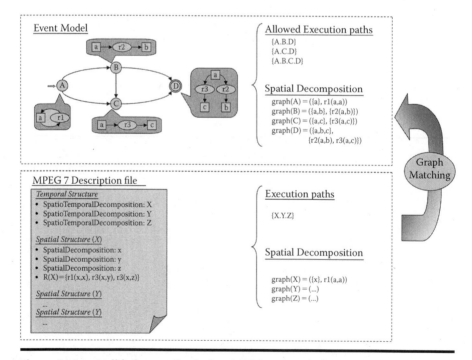

Figure 16.14   Validation method of an MPEG-7 description.

In Figure 16.14, $Ss_M = \{ graph\ (A) = (a,\ r1(a,\ a),\ \phi),\ graph\ (B) = (a,\ b,\ r2(a,\ b),\ \phi),$ $graph\ (C) = (a,\ c,\ r3(a,\ c),\ \phi),\ graph\ (D) = (a,\ b,\ c,\ r2(a,\ b),\ r3(a,\ c),\ \phi)\}.$

■ The spatial and temporal structures of the MPEG-7 visual description are extracted. This information is contained in the *Location* and *Basic Elements* descriptors, which represent the region locator, the spatiotemporal locator, and the spatial 2D coordinates [24] of the described resource. From the description file, we extract the temporal segments of the event, and then for each segment we extract the still regions composing it. Then we compute the relations among the regions based on their 2D coordinates. In the same example, the description is decomposed into the temporal sequences *X, Y, Z*, where the state *X* is decomposed into regions *x, y,* and *z*, and regrouped between them by the relations $R(X) = \{r1(x,\ x),\ r3(x,\ y),\ r3(x,\ z)\}$. Figure 16.15 depicts the MPEG-7-based description from which the information was extracted.

```
<MPEG7 type="complete" xmlns="http://www.mpeg7.org/2001/MPEG-7_Schema"
        xmlns:xsi="http://www.w3.org/2000/10/XMLSchema-instance"
        xsi:schemaLocation="http://www.mpeg7.org/2001/MPEG-7_Schema">
    <ContentDescription xsi:type="ContentEntityType">
        <MultimediaContent xsi:type="VideoType">
            <Video>
                <TemporalDecomposition gap="false" overlap="false">
                    <VideoSegment>
                        <MediaTime>
                            <MediaTimePoint> T00:00:00 </MediaTimePoint>
                            <MediaDuration> PT0M15S </MediaDuration>
                        </MediaTime>
                        <TextAnnotation type="scene description" relevance="1" confidence="1">
                            <FreeTextAnnotation> Event M </FreeTextAnnotation>
                        </TextAnnotation>
                        <SpatioTemporalDecomposition>
                            <TextAnnotation type="scene description" relevance="1" confidence="1">
                                <FreeTextAnnotation> X </FreeTextAnnotation>
                            </TextAnnotation>
                            <StillRegion>
                                <MediaIncrTimePoint timeUnit="PT1N30F"> 421 </MediaIncrTimePoint>
                                <SpatialDecomposition>
                                    <StillRegion>
                                        <TextAnnotation>
                                            <FreeTextAnnotation> x </FreeTextAnnotation>
                                        </TextAnnotation>
                                        <SpatialLocator>
                                            <Poly>
                                                <Coordsl> 41 135 290 135 290 230 41 230 </Coordsl>
                                            </Poly>
                                        </SpatialLocator>
                                    </StillRegion>
                                </SpatialDecomposition>

                                <SpatialDecomposition>

                                            <FreeTextAnnotation> y </FreeTextAnnotation>

                                </SpatialDecomposition>

                                </SpatialDecomposition>

                                            <FreeTextAnnotation> z </FreeTextAnnotation>

                                </SpatialDecomposition>

                        </SpatioTemporalDecomposition>
                        <SpatioTemporalDecomposition>

                                    <FreeTextAnnotation> Y </FreeTextAnnotation>

                        </SpatioTemporalDecomposition>
                        <SpatioTemporalDecomposition>

                                    <FreeTextAnnotation> Z </FreeTextAnnotation>

                        </SpatioTemporalDecomposition>
                    </VideoSegment>
                </TemporalDecomposition>
            </Video>
        </MultimediaContent>
    </ContentDescription>
</MPEG7>
```

Figure 16.15   Example of an MPEG-7 video segment description.

■ Finally, the matching algorithm (Algorithm 3) is used to verify whether the spatiotemporal decomposition $\{X, Y, Z\}$ of the event in the MPEG-7 file can be mapped to an allowed possible execution path in the event model.

16.8 Conclusion and Perspectives

In this chapter, we introduced a new generic language of semantic representation of video content. This language is based on two formalisms, finite state machine and fuzzy conceptual graphs, to represent respectively temporal and spatial structures of visual events and to recognize them using a detection framework. This formalism enables high-level semantic descriptions and bridges the gap between the different abstraction levels. In addition to automatically extracting events from a video database, the framework allows the monitoring of behavior in a video-surveillance setting and validating MPEG-7-based descriptions. Future works will be directed toward using more expressive formalisms, such as description logic, to fit with the real requirements of the description of complex visual concepts and to introduce audio and text processing into the description model and the detection framework.

Ahmed Azough (http://liris.cnrs.fr/~aazough/) is a PhD candidate in computer sciences at the University Claude Bernard Lyon, in collaboration with France Telecom R&D. He is a member of the Department of Data, Knowledge and Services of the Lyon Research Center for Images and Information Systems (LIRIS CNRS UMR 5205, http://liris.cnrs.fr/). He holds a master's degree in computer sciences from the National Institute of Applied Sciences, Lyon, France. His research is focused on the semantic interpretation and representation of complex events within video sequences.

Alexandre Delteil is a researcher at Orange Labs, France. He holds a PhD in computer sciences from INRIA and Nice Sophia Antipolis University. His research interests include multimedia analysis and understanding, multimedia multimodal fusion, and the Semantic Web.

Fabien De Marchi is an associate professor at the University of Lyon, France. He holds a PhD in computer sciences from University of Clermont-Ferrand, France (2003). His research interests include databases and data mining, and the current main application fields are Web services monitoring and multimedia content retrieval. He is involved in the European Union project COMPAS (FP-7, 2008–2011) and the EU Network of Excellence S-Cube (2008–2012).

Mohand-Saïd Hacid (http://www710.univ-lyon1.fr/~mshacid) is a professor in the Department of Computer Sciences at the University Claude Bernard Lyon 1,

France. He is leading the Department of Data, Knowledge and Services of the Lyon Research Center for Images and Information Systems (LIRIS CNRS UMR 5205) and the Lyon Center for Higher Education. His research interests include multimedia databases, Web services, and the Semantic Web.

References

1. MPEG-7: Overview of MPEG-7 description tools, part 2. *IEEE MultiMedia*, 9(3): 83–93, 2002.
2. R. Alur and D. L. Dill. A theory of timed automata. *Theoretical Computer Science*, 126(2): 183–235, 1994.
3. J. Assfalg, M. Bertini, C. Colombo, A. D. Bimbo, and W. Nunziati. Semantic annotation of soccer videos: automatic highlights identification. *Computer Vision and Image Understanding*, 92(2–3): 285–305, 2003.
4. F. Baader, D. Calvanese, D. L. McGuinness, D. Nardi, and P. F. Patel-Schneider, editors. *The Description Logic Handbook: Theory, Implementation, and Applications*. Cambridge, U.K.: Cambridge University Press, 2003.
5. M. Bertini, A. D. Bimbo, and W. Nunziati. Model checking for detection of sport highlights. In *MIR '03: Proceedings of the 5th ACM SIGMM International Workshop on Multimedia Information Retrieval*, pp. 215–222. New York: ACM Press, 2003.
6. A. Bonzanini, R. Leonardi, and P. Migliorati. Event recognition in sport programs using low-level motion indices. In *Proceedings of IEEE International Conference on Multimedia and Expo (ICME)*, 255, 2001.
7. C.-Y. Chen, J.-C. Wang, J.-F. Wang, and Y.-H. Hu. Event-based segmentation of sports video using motion entropy. In *ISM '07: Proceedings of the 9th IEEE International Symposium on Multimedia*, pp. 107–111. Washington, DC: IEEE Computer Society, 2007.
8. A. Ekin, A. M. Tekalp, and R. Mehrotra. Automatic soccer video analysis and summarization. *IEEE Transactions on Image Processing*, 12(7): 796–807, 2003.
9. J. Geurts, J. van Ossenbrugen, and L. Hardman. Requirements for practical multimedia annotation. In *Multimedia and the Semantic Web, 2nd European Semantic Web Conference*, 2005.
10. J. Hunter and F. Nack. An overview of the MPEG-7 description definition language (ddl) proposals. *Signal Processing: Image Communication*, 16(1–2): 271–293, September 2000.
11. A. Isaac and R. Troncy. Using several ontologies for describing audiovisual documents: A case study in the medical domain. *Workshop on Multimedia and the Semantic Web, 2nd European Semantic Web Conference (ESWC 2005)*, Heraklion, Crete.
12. R. Leonardi and P. Migliorati. Semantic indexing of multimedia documents. *IEEE MultiMedia*, 9(2): 44–51, 2002.
13. M. S. Lew, N. Sebe, C. Djeraba, and R. Jain. Content-based multimedia information retrieval: State of the art and challenges. *ACM Transactions on Multimedia Computing, Communications, and Applications*, 2(1): 1–19, 2006.
14. S. Linckels and C. Meinel. A simple application of description logics for a semantic search engine. In N. Guimares and P. T. Isaas, editors, *Proceedings of the IADIS International Conference of Applied Computing 2005 (IADIS AC2005)*, pp. 306–311. IADIS, 2005.

15. C. Lutz, C. Areces, I. Horrocks, and U. Sattler. Keys, nominals, and concrete domains. In G. Gottlob and T. Walsh, editors, *Proceedings of the 18th International Joint Conference on Artificial Intelligence (IJCAI)*, pp. 349–354. San Francisco: Morgan Kaufmann, 2003.

16. P. Mulhem, W. K. Leow, and Y. K. Lee. Fuzzy conceptual graphs for matching images of natural scenes. In B. Nebel, editor, *Proceedings of the 16th International Joint Conference on Artificial Intelligence (IJCAI)*, pp. 1397–1404. San Francisco: Morgan Kaufmann, 2001.

17. J. Renz and B. Nebel. On the complexity of qualitative spatial reasoning: a maximal tractable fragment of the region connection calculus. *Artificial Intelligence*, 108(1–2): 69–123, 1999.

18. K. Rodden, K. R. Wood, and K. R. Wood. How do people manage their digital photographs? In *CHI '03: Proceedings of the SIGCHI Conference on Human Factors in Computing Systems*, pp. 409–416. New York: ACM Press, 2003.

19. A. F. Smeaton, P. Over, and W. Kraaij. Evaluation campaigns and TRECVID. In *MIR '06: Proceedings of the 8th ACM International Workshop on Multimedia Information Retrieval*, pp. 321–330. New York: ACM Press, 2006.

20. U. Straccia. Reasoning within fuzzy description logics. *Journal of Artificial Intelligence Research (JAIR)*, 14: 137–166, 2001.

21. U. Straccia. A fuzzy description logic for the semantic web. In *Capturing Intelligence: Fuzzy Logic and the Semantic Web*. New York: Elsevier, 2005.

22. V. Tovinkere and R. J. Qian. Detecting semantic events in soccer games: Towards a complete solution. In *Proceedings of IEEE International Conference on Multimedia and Expo (ICME)*, 00: 212, 2001.

23. R. Troncy, W. Bailer, M. Hausenblas, and M. Höffernig. VAMP: Semantic validation for MPEG-7 profile descriptions. Technical Report INS-E0705, CWI and JRS, April 2007.

24. B. L. Tseng, C.-Y. Lin, and J. R. Smith. Using MPEG-7 and MPEG-21 for personalizing video. *IEEE MultiMedia*, 11(1): 42–53, 2004.

25. J. Wang, C. Xu, E. Chng, K. Wah, and Q. Tian. Automatic replay generation for soccer video broadcasting. In *Multimedia '04: Proceedings of the 12th Annual ACM International Conference on Multimedia*, pp. 32–39. New York: ACM Press, 2004.

26. U. Westermann and R. Jain. Toward a common event model for multimedia applications. *IEEE MultiMedia*, 14(1): 19–29, 2007.

27. C. Xu, J. Wang, K. Wan, Y. Li, and L. Duan. Live sports event detection based on broadcast video and web-casting text. In *Multimedia '06: Proceedings of the 14th Annual ACM International Conference on Multimedia*, pp. 221–230. New York: ACM Press, 2006.

28. G. Zhu, Q. Huang, C. Xu, Y. Rui, S. Jiang, W. Gao, and H. Yao. Trajectory-based event tactics analysis in broadcast sports video. In *Multimedia '07: Proceedings of the 15th International Conference on Multimedia*, pp. 58–67. New York: ACM Press, 2007.

Chapter 17

MPEG-7-Based Semantic Indexing of Film Heritage Audiovisual Content

Yolanda Cobos, María Teresa Linaza, Cristina Sarasua, Ander García, and Isabel Torre

17.1 Introduction

MPEG-7 is an excellent choice for describing audiovisual content in many applications, mainly because of its comprehensiveness and flexibility. Because it is designed for a broad range of applications and thus employs very general and widely applicable concepts, the standard comprises a large set of tools for diverse types of annotations on different semantic levels.

The flexibility of the MPEG-7 standard makes it appropriate for many application areas without imposing strict constraints on the metadata models of these sectors. Its flexibility relies strongly on the structuring tools and allows the description to be modular and on different levels of abstraction. MPEG-7 supports fine-grained descriptions, allowing the attachment of descriptors to arbitrary segments in any level of detail.

Two main problems arise in the practical use of MPEG-7: complexity and limited interoperability. The former results from the use of generic concepts, which allow deep hierarchical structures; the high number of different descriptors (D) and description schemes (DS); and their flexible inner structure. As a result, learning MPEG-7 is time consuming, so developers may hesitate to use this standard in products. Their hesitance may be compounded by the difficulty in implementing tools for working with MPEG-7 and the consequent lack of tools and implementations.

On the other hand, films are unquestionably part of our heritage. Current systems for accessing contents related to film objects include the following limitations: distributed sources that store huge amounts of information; different content formats, ranging from traditional ones such as paper to advanced multimedia objects; and, more crucial for content providers, a lack of systems that support users' needs, such as enriched content, interaction with the information, usability, and exchange of experiences with other users.

This chapter presents the implementation of a user-friendly tool for MPEG-7-based semantic indexing so that nonexpert users from some European cities with a strong connection with the film sector can index their audiovisual content in a simple and accessible way. Section 17.2 summarizes some other projects and tools related to this work. The CINeSPACE project is outlined in Section 17.3 as the application scenario for the implemented tool. Section 17.4 explains the reasons for selecting MPEG-7 as the standard to perform this task, including the selection of the main descriptors. In Section 17.5, the CINeSPACE annotation tool is described. Then, Section 17.6 outlines the results obtained with the annotation tool. Finally, Section 17.7 presents conclusions and future work.

17.2 Related Work

17.2.1 Description of the MPEG-7 Standard

MPEG-7, the Multimedia Content Description Interface, is an ISO/IEC standard developed by the Moving Pictures Expert Group (MPEG) (MPEG-7, ISO/IEC JTC1/SC29/WG11). This standard (Gagnon 2005) is harmonized with other standards that have been successful and accepted in both traditional media and new media business (e.g., W3C as XML and XML Schema; IETF as URI, URN, and URL; Dublin Core; SMPTE Metadata Dictionary; TV Anytime; EBU P/Meta).

MPEG-7 allows different granularity in its descriptions, offering the possibility of different levels of discrimination. If the example of visual material is analyzed, a lower abstraction level would be a description of color, movement (trajectory), or final device (pocket PC or magnifiers) and language, mood, or tempo changes in the case of audio material.

This standard includes three main elements, as depicted in Figure 17.1: Description Tools, Description Definition Language (DDL), and System Tools. The Descriptions Tools include two main components: the Descriptors, which define the syntax and the semantics of each feature (metadata element), and the Description Schemes that specify the structure and semantics of the relationships among their components, which may be both Descriptors and Description Schemes.

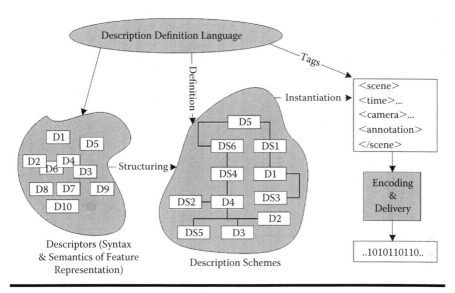

Figure 17.1   MPEG-7 main elements.

The DDL defines the syntax of the MPEG-7 description tools and allows for the creation of new description schemes and possibly descriptors as well as extending and modifying existing description schemes.

The system tools support binary-coded representation for efficient storage and transmission, transmission mechanisms (both for textual and binary formats), multiplexation of descriptions, synchronization of descriptions with content, or management and protection of intellectual property in MPEG-7 descriptions.

The MPEG-7 standard is used for describing audiovisual content data that supports some degree of interpretation of the meaning of the information. This description allows indexing, searching, and retrieving information about the described contents in both real-time and virtual-time environments. However, the standard neither includes the (automatic) extraction of descriptions/features nor specifies the search engine (or any other program) that can make use of the description.

MPEG-7 does not target any application in particular; rather, the elements that MPEG-7 standardizes support as broad a range of applications as possible. There are many applications and application domains that will benefit from the MPEG-7 standard; for example,

■ Digital libraries (image catalog, musical dictionary)
■ Biomedical applications
■ Shopping (e.g., searching for preferred clothes)
■ Multimedia directory services (e.g., yellow pages)
■ Broadcast media selection (radio channel, TV channel)
■ Multimedia editing (personalized electronic news service, media authoring)

Potential applications are spread over the following application domains: education, journalism (e.g., searching speeches of a certain politician using his or her name, voice, or face), tourist information, cultural services (history museums, art galleries, etc.), entertainment (e.g., searching a game, karaoke), geographical information systems (GIS), architecture, real estate, interior design, social (e.g., dating services), film, video and radio archives, and so on.

17.2.2 Annotation Tools Based on MPEG-7

Although products like ACDSee Google, Picasa, and Adobe Photoshop Album allow the annotation of photos using keywords or self-defined tags, which are visually attached to the image, these commercial products do not use the MPEG-7 standard. Nevertheless, there are also numerous annotation tools available for the creation of MPEG-7 documents.

Caliph, a "Common and Lightweight Interactive Photo" annotation tool (Lux, Becker, & Krottmaier 2003; Lux & Granitzer 2005), allows the creation of MPEG-7 descriptions for digital photos. It is implemented using Java SDK 1.4; JRE 1.4 and higher versions are also supported as a runtime environment. Besides the ability to describe the content of the photos textually, an editor for semantic descriptions based on the MPEG-7 Semantic Description Scheme has been integrated. The editor uses the metaphor of "drawing a concept" graph with semantic objects as nodes and semantic relations as arcs. Nodes can be reused because they are stored in a node catalog. Some of the annotations have to be made manually, while others are automatically extracted such as MPEG-7 Descriptors Scalable Color, Color Layout, and Edge Histogram, as well as the Exchangeable Image File Format (EXIF) and International Press Telecommunications Council (IPTC) metadata encoded in image files.

Plenty of tools exist for working with video annotation based on the MPEG-7 standard. IBM's MPEG-7 Annotation Tool, for example, supports both MPEG-1 and MPEG-2 files as well as region annotations. It has a customizable lexicon restricted to three default categories (event, static scene, and key objects), although free text keywords can also be added. IBM's system does not support hierarchical video segmentation but focuses on the extraction of high-level metadata, extracting up to 200 different semantic concepts automatically from video streams.

The Intelligent Multimedia Database (IMB) (Klieber et al. 2003) supports the annotation and retrieval of semantic descriptions, focusing on video data and including a visual annotation and query creation tool. Annotations in IMB are based on a specific domain ontology. Therefore, the system only uses a single domain ontology, restricting the possibilities of the MPEG-7 Semantic Description Scheme. Moreover, the retrieval mechanism supports only exact matches based on existing instances of semantic objects, not supporting partial matching or relevance calculation along with common information and knowledge retrieval features like relevance feedback or user models.

Another representative project is Mecca (Lux, Granitzer, & Klieber 2004), a hypermedia capturing of collaborative scientific discourses about movies, which supports the annotation of videos based on a growing and evolving ontology for collaborative knowledge creation. Despite dealing with semantic knowledge about video assets, MPEG-7 descriptors for semantic annotations are not used. The Mecca navigation panel allows accessing classified multimedia artifacts. Therefore, the community's core ontology for browsing artifacts is stored in the MPEG-7-compliant XML database management system eXist (Meier 2002) connected via an Apache Web server to enable remote collaboration.

The video annotation system MovieTool, developed by Ricoh, supports hierarchical segmentation within a timeline-based representation of the video. Although the tool is the most mature and complete of the systems, the user interface is too difficult because it is closely tied to the MPEG-7 specifications. The user has to have a good knowledge of the large and complex XML Schema definition of MPEG-7 in order to browse over it using the MPEG-7 Editor.

ZGDV's VIDETO video description tool was developed as a research tool to generate video metadata or to test a video server and its retrieval module. It is a video annotation system that hides the complexity of MPEG-7: the description properties are based on a simple description template mapped to the standard using XSLT. Domain-specific description templates together with their corresponding XSLT mappings are generated.

OntoMat-Annotizer (Carsten et al. 2006) is another representative tool developed within the aceMedia project. A user-friendly tool for semantic annotation of images and videos for multimedia analysis and retrieval has been implemented, supporting the initialization and linking of Resource Description Framework (RDF) domain ontologies with low-level MPEG-7 visual descriptors. The tool is based on the CREAM framework, which has been extended in order to allow low-level multimedia feature annotation. It extracts the MPEG-7 descriptors calling a Feature Extraction Toolbox developed inside the project that saves the extracted MPEG-7 descriptors in XML format.

MuViNo (2004) is an MPEG-7 video annotation tool consisting of an embedded video player based on the open source ViTooKi Video Tool Kit and on an XML tree view allowing navigation through an MPEG-7 document. It was developed within the DAHL project (Taschwer, Muller, & Boszormenyi 2005). A video clip can be divided temporally into a hierarchy of semantic sections, so that the tool helps in the creation and annotation of MPEG-7 VideoSegment descriptions.

Finally, there are other Web-based video annotation systems, such as CSIRO's Continuous Media Web Browser, which generates a proprietary HTML-format (Annodex) file, and Microsoft's Research Annotation System (MRAS) (Bargeron et al. 1999), which enables students to asynchronously annotate Web-based lecture videos and to share their annotations.

Regarding the use of the MPEG-7 standard, the LogCreator tool of the Content-Oriented Audiovisual Library Access (COALA) project supports video descriptions, providing automatic shot detection and an interface for hierarchical segmentation of videos that can be uploaded to the server, where it is saved as MPEG-7 in a native XML database. However, it is a domain-specific tool developed specifically for TV news documents with a predefined structure. The descriptors that are used to annotate the different video segments are predefined as well.

17.2.3 Projects Based on the MPEG-7 Standard

Many MPEG-7-related projects are being undertaken within commercial enterprises, particularly broadcasting and digital imaging companies, which involve the adoption of MPEG-7 conformance, some of which are described below.

The Harmony Project is an International Digital Libraries Initiative project that aims at developing a framework to describe networked collections of highly complex and mixed-media digital objects. The approach brings together research approaches on the RDF, XML, Dublin Core, MPEG-7, and INDECS standards. The project also focuses on allowing multiple communities of expertise (e.g., library, education, rights management) to define overlapping descriptive vocabularies for annotating audiovisual content.

The objective of the DICEMAN Project is to provide an end-to-end framework for indexing, storage, search, and trading of audiovisual content. The technical work will focus on MPEG-7 indexing through a content provider's application (COPA), the use of Foundation for Intelligent Physical Agents (FIPAs) to search and locate the best content, and support for electronic commerce and rights management.

The purpose of the A4SM project (Nack & Putz 2001) is to seamlessly integrate a framework into the production process—that is, preproduction (e.g., script development, story boarding), production (e.g., collection of media data by using an MPEG-2/7 camera), and postproduction (support of nonlinear editing). In collaboration with TV reporters, cameramen, and editors, an MPEG-7 camera has been designed combining a mobile annotation device for the reporter and a mobile editing suite suitable for generating news clips.

Finally, the MISTRAL research project (Manuel, Barrios, & Gütl 2006) aims at implementing smart, semiautomatic solutions for semantic annotation and enrichment of multimodal data from meeting recordings and meeting-related documents. MPEG-7 represents a standardized bridge between the MISTRAL units, serving as a basic metadata source for applications in the Semantic Application Unit (SemAU). Moreover, the standard enables a standardized exchangeability of semantic annotations with other systems or research groups.

17.2.4 MPEG-7 and Cultural Heritage

Concerning existing applications for the cultural and film heritage sector, there are very few examples that have implemented MPEG-7-based standardization techniques. The SIMIPE-Ciné (Gouaillier et al. 2005) project was designed as a Web-enabled software prototype to search through geographical and visual content criteria. Various types of data about the site have been integrated into the database: annotations, photos, panoramic views, audio clips, maps, and geometric information. The system assists location managers in retrieving the sites more efficiently, fulfilling visual and logistical requirements of a particular film shooting. Since an important part of the metadata concerns the description of photographs, working within the MPEG-7 framework appeared for this project to be a good choice.

MultiMatch: Multilingual/Multimedia Access to Cultural Heritage (Amato et al. 2007) is a research project aimed at developing a multilingual search engine specifically designed for the access, organization, and personalized presentation of cultural heritage content. Different types of documents—text, audio, image, video, and mixed content—will be indexed. Regarding the use of generic standards, MPEG-7 has been used, incorporating audiovisual content and metadata in a single semistructured document.

The MILOS multimedia content management system (Maurer et al. 2000) offers specialized functionality to support multimedia digital library applications. It can be seen as the equivalent of a database system for document-intensive applications (like digital library applications). Within the three basic functionalities offered by MILOS (management of arbitrary XML-encoded metadata, transparent management of document storage strategies, and metadata mapping), MPEG-7 visual descriptors have been added to their XML-encoded metadata in order to allow similarity search queries.

Finally, the aim of the Afghan Community Information System for Cultural Heritage Management (ACIS) (Klamma, Spaniol, & Cao 2006) project is to provide a networked community with a cheap, long-lasting, and flexible environment that allows them to rebuild the disaster-struck area without requiring the users to be on site. It hosts an intercultural, generational, and disciplinary community from all over the world in order to preserve the cultural sites and monuments in Afghanistan.

The generated prototype within the project is a system based on a Microsoft Access database designed to support learning communities in the area of cultural heritage. The learning process was disrupted by the civil war and the Taliban regime in Afghanistan (Klamma et al. 2006). Various multimedia formats, such as photos, panoramic views, maps, and geographic information, have been described using the MPEG-7 standard. Thus, the user interface employs MPEG-7 for the input of content. In ACIS, MPEG-7 was chosen to be the solution to enhance multimedia information retrieval and exchange.

17.3 Application Scenario: The CINeSPACE Project

17.3.1 Main Objectives of the Project

The CINeSPACE project (Santos et al. 2007) aims at designing and implementing a mobile rich-media collaborative information exchange platform, scalable, and accessible through a wide variety of networks. Therefore, the final platform is an interoperable and location-based for the promotion of Film Heritage, going beyond the current state of the art.

CINeSPACE will enable users to interact with location-based audiovisual content while navigating a city (Figure 17.2). Audiovisual content will be delivered through a small, low-cost wireless head-mounted display with a high-definition screen situated near the eye and with audio phones. CINeSPACE also includes a camera that is able to record or send what the user is "seeing." This information can be uploaded to a database through a wireless local area network hot spot or a 3G connection in order to create collaborative experiences with other end users.

The system will address three target users: film tourists who choose a tourist destination due to its relationship with cinema (film-induced tourism); cinema professionals and film producers who search for possible locations and film

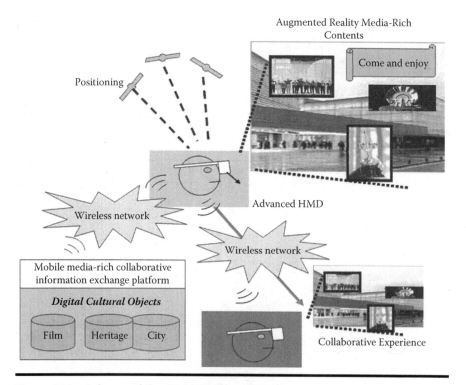

Figure 17.2 Schema of the CINeSPACE prototype.

facilities in some urban environments; and citizens who have stories to tell in order to enhance their community memory.

17.3.2 Architecture of the Content Management System

Figure 17.3 shows the architecture of the CINeSPACE Content Management System (Cobos et al. 2007). The system is designed to be client and platform independent. Taking into account these requirements, a Web Service interface was chosen for the system because it provides interoperability between different platforms and programming languages. Moreover, client libraries are available for most Web Services.

Starting from the top of the architecture, the Application Level is in charge of delivering the content, that is, managing the queries from the users. The first time a user logs into the system, his or her profile is loaded or, if it does not exist, created. This level manages the state of each user, tracking the audiovisual content that has been required and visualized, managing the relationships among users, and asking for the content to be delivered. User profiles are used to include personalization functionalities into the system. Although georeference information is the key factor to retrieve the content, other aspects of the personalization include language, device, and areas of interest.

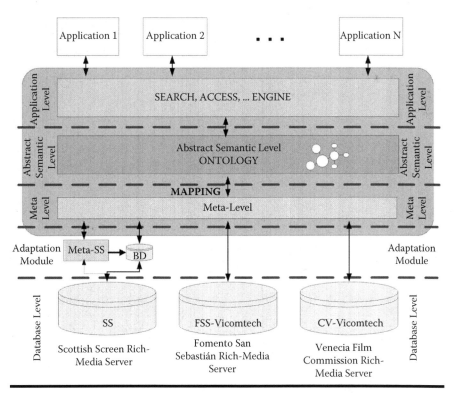

Figure 17.3   Architecture of the CINeSPACE Content Management System.

Second, the Abstract Semantic Level, or translation level, includes the ontology of the system. Using the search engine, users may query the multimedia information through this level, which translates the queries to a language understood by the Meta-Level. In order to define a concrete ontology for the CINeSPACE project, some existing ontologies have been mapped to the MPEG-7-compliant ontology CIDOC Conceptual Reference Model (CIDOC CRM) (Crofts et al. 2007) and International Federation of Information Technology and Travel and Tourism (IFITT) ontologies. Therefore, MPEG-7 is used for describing the features of audiovisual content (audio-video records, shooting shorts, interviews), CIDOC-CRM as a domain ontology for cultural heritage information, and IFFIT RMSIG as a reference model for modeling electronic tourism markets (gastronomy, accommodations).

Third, the Meta-Level manages the connection between metadata and the multimedia resources stored in the distributed databases. Metadata has a key role in audiovisual content management through media content life cycle (create, manage, and distribute/transact). Moreover, it is critical for describing essential aspects of audiovisual content, including main topics, author, language, events, scenes, objects, times, places, rights, packaging, access control, content adaptation, and so forth (Development of a European Service for Information on Research and Education 1997). Some requirements must be taken into account when defining the metadata, such as localization, user preferences, and some technical aspects related to visualization devices.

Finally, audiovisual content is stored in a rich-media server in each city (Glasgow, Venice, and San Sebastian). Although not focused specifically on optimizing annotation, CINeSPACE will provide the cities with tools to manually index the audiovisual content that will be available for the prototype. Once the content is indexed with the CINeSPACE annotation tool, the metadata will be used to query the system.

A uniform Meta-Level among three databases and a Semantic Level are needed, as the multimedia repository of Glasgow already has a Meta-Level defined for its database. Therefore, an Adaptation Level between the Meta-Level and the Semantic Level has been defined to support this particular situation. In the case of San Sebastian and Venice, a database in MySQL 5.0 was created. Therefore, the translation between the Meta-Level and all of the databases is straightforward.

17.3.3 Performance of the Annotation and Retrieval CINeSPACE System

Regarding the performance of the CINeSPACE indexing and retrieval system (Figure 17.4), first, geographical description is needed as a basic metadata. Then, low-level features for the audiovisual content, including structural and semantic aspects, are indexed. Some MPEG-7 files describe all multimedia information in such a way.

On the other hand, the user of the system will retrieve information on the basis of three main parameters: the geographical location of the user, user personalization

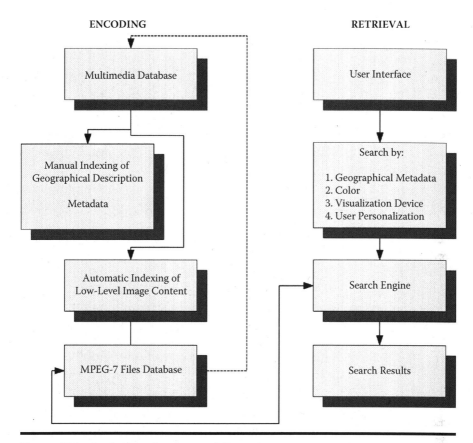

Figure 17.4 Logical performance of the system.

parameters, and other features of the content such as color or visualization devices. This information is taken into account when searching in order to retrieve audiovisual content that best fits the query.

17.4 CINeSPACE and MPEG-7

17.4.1 Motivation for Using MPEG-7

One of the major challenges of the CINeSPACE project is the design of a suitable data and metadata structure that supports semantic queries using content-based retrieval tools. Moreover, the metadata schema should include mechanisms to link all of the audiovisual material related to a city (tourist attractions, cultural heritage, and locations for film shooting).

Since an important part of the CINeSPACE metadata concerns the description of audiovisual content (pictures, videos), working within the MPEG-7 framework appears to be a good approach. In fact, the standard comprises predefined descriptors and description schemes specifically tailored for describing both structural and semantic aspects of audiovisual content, as requested by CINeSPACE. It also provides constructs for classification schemes that define sets of controlled terms forming vocabularies for particular domains or applications. Furthermore, the MPEG-7's DDL offers all the XML advantages, such as platform independence and human readability. Thus, we have chosen to explore the usability of the MPEG-7 schema for this application.

17.4.2 Requirements for the CINeSPACE Metadata

Although the location of the user of the CINeSPACE prototype is the first query to retrieve georeference content to be delivered within the system, other aspects of the content retrieval include content personalization depending on the profile of the user and visual appearance of the content in relation to color (black and white or color) and the final visualization device (PDA or binoculars).

Information search results will depend on the exact location of the user of the CINeSPACE prototype (Glasgow, San Sebastian, or Venice). For instance, when the visitor is in San Sebastian, he or she will be unable to access the information from Glasgow or Venice. Moreover, some visitors may not want to view a certain image or video more than once. Therefore, the usage history of the user must be recorded.

User personalization of the content refers to the type of information that will be provided to the final user depending on his or her profile. Therefore, a taxonomy of user profiles is being defined so content provided to a profile is personalized, taking into account some demographical and sociological aspects. Thus, personalization parameters will include the preferred language so that audiovisual content will be indexed and only retrieved when the corresponding language is selected.

Finally, basic low-level features will be used, as audiovisual content may be black and white (such as historical film content in Glasgow) or color (in the other two cities). Moreover, audiovisual content will be available for two types of visualization devices (PDA or binoculars). Therefore, the CINeSPACE approach should include some additional descriptors to take this issue into account.

17.4.3 MPEG-7 Descriptors for CINeSPACE Metadata

According to the MPEG-7 philosophy, all metadata can be represented by means of descriptors. Because many types of metadata can be associated with a given content, there are many types of MPEG-7 descriptors available. Considering the CINeSPACE project, three types of descriptions can be considered: structural description (structural information given by the audiovisual content such as visual descriptors or creation and production information), classification description

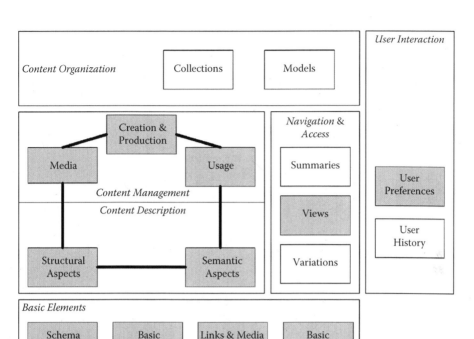

Figure 17.5   Overview of the MPEG-7 Multimedia Description Scheme (MDS); the tools selected for CINeSPACE are highlighted.

(characteristic keywords given in a certain domain); and semantic description (a set of related semantic entities limited to a certain abstraction level).

This section presents a brief summary of the data and metadata that have been identified for the task of indexing audiovisual content in CINeSPACE and their relation with MPEG-7 descriptors (Figure 17.5).

17.4.3.1 Basic Elements

The basic elements deal with the essentials of audiovisual content description, including time, linking and media localization, annotation, and a definition of description vocabularies. Unlike the other parts of MPEG-7, which are organized around different aspects of audiovisual content description, the basic elements are a library of common description tools (Figure 17.5).

The description of audiovisual content using natural language text is called text annotation. The practice of using text annotations to search, catalog, and index audiovisual content is both long-standing and widespread. MPEG-7 supports this practice with the TextAnnotation data type that allows free text, keywords, and structured and dependency structure annotations.

MPEG-7 provides a tool for structured textual annotation by including specific fields corresponding to questions such as Who? Where? When? What Action? that are used for the CINeSPACE metadata. These data describe the creation and classification of the audiovisual content, such as the director, title, date, and location.

17.4.3.2 User Preferences

Gaining information about target users of the content is very important within the CINeSPACE project. Descriptors to describe user preferences and usage history related to the consumption of the audiovisual content have been selected from the user interaction description tool, mainly the UserPreference description scheme.

The CreationPreferences description scheme is used to specify users' preferences related to keywords or to the period when the content was created. The ClassificationPreferences description scheme is used to specify users' preferences related to their favorite genre, subject, or keyword.

17.4.3.3 Visual Descriptors

Low-level image analysis aspects can also be used to infer information about the subjects of a picture or a movie shot. First, the edge histogram descriptor (EdgeHistogram) represents the local-edge distribution in the image. Specifically, dividing the image space into 4×4 subimages, the local-edge distribution for each subimage can be represented by a histogram.

Second, the dominant color descriptor (DominantColor) allows for the specification of a small number of dominant color values as well as their statistical properties such as distribution and variance. Its purpose is to provide an effective, compact, and intuitive representation of colors presented in a region or image. This feature could be very interesting for film professionals who search for locations.

Third, the color layout descriptor (ColorLayout) captures the spatial layout of the representative colors on a grid that are superimposed on a region or image. Representation is based on coefficients of the discrete cosine transform.

Finally, the scalable color descriptor (ScalableColor) is derived from a color histogram defined in the Hue-Saturation-Value color space with fixed color space quantization.

17.4.3.4 Semantic Features

Conceptual information of the reality captured by the content enables defining semantic relationships among people, places, objects, and interactions between objects. Regarding the CINeSPACE scenario, the SemanticBase description scheme includes a number of specialized description schemes that describe those specific types of semantic entities (AgentObject, Event, SemanticTime, SemanticPlace).

17.4.3.5 Camera Metadata

EXIF and IPTC Information Interchange Model (IIM) metadata record the parameters of the camera at the point that a photograph was taken, including aperture setting, focal length of the lens, exposure time, time of photo, flash information, camera orientation (portrait/landscape), and focal distance. Some of the main descriptors selected for such metadata are CreationTool and CreationCoordinates. It must be mentioned that these metadata will only be applied to images within the project.

17.4.3.6 Global Positioning Data

GPS data can be recorded live in EXIF, or alternatively, GPS track logs can be used to determine the location accurately. The coordinates of the creation moment descriptor (CreationCoordinates) provide information related to the place where the content was created.

17.5 CINeSPACE Annotation Tool

An additional CINeSPACE annotation tool has been implemented so that nonexpert users from the cities can index the content themselves. The MPEG-7 metadata is saved in XML files.

After analyzing the state of the art, it was decided that Caliph best serves as the basis for the work developed within CINeSPACE (Santos et al. 2007). Besides the ability to textually describe the information within the audiovisual content (pictures, video), it integrates an editor for semantic descriptions based on the MPEG-7 semantic description scheme. The editor uses the metaphor of "drawing" a concept graph with semantic objects as nodes and semantic relations as arcs. This section presents the adaptation process of the tool to the CINeSPACE requirements.

As mentioned earlier, this open source tool developed by the University of Klagenfurt allows for the creation of MPEG-7 descriptions for digital photos. Therefore, the basic software has been extended so that other types of multimedia formats, especially video shots, can be indexed within the same framework.

Caliph was implemented using Java SDK 1.4; JRE 1.4 and higher versions are also supported as runtime environment.

Based on the graphical interface of Caliph, the CINeSPACE annotation tool includes the following panels to describe, both semantically and structurally, the content:

- The Image Information panel, displays the EXIF tags and values and holds the creator of the image.
- The Semantics panel for defining semantic relationships among people, places, objects, and interactions between them.

- The User Preferences panel describes user preferences pertaining to the consumption of the audiovisual content.
- The Shape panel and Visuals panel create ColorLayout and ScalableColor descriptors, which are extracted from the image on first loading.

If the user selects video content to annotate, the Shape and Visuals panels will be disabled.

Although Caliph supports the preannotation of sets of images using the so-called autopilot, the indexation process will be manually carried out within CINeSPACE. It is very important that the cities providing the content have overall control over the descriptors in order to efficiently retrieve the content. Once the audiovisual content has been fully described, each annotation of the audiovisual content can be saved as an MPEG-7 XML file.

17.5.1 Image Information Panel

Figure 17.6 shows the graphical interface of the extended Image Information panel. In order to select the content that is going to be indexed, the user can navigate

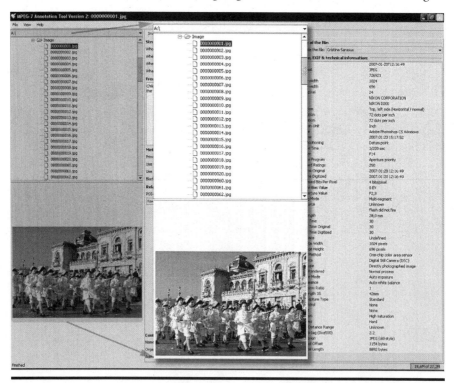

Figure 17.6   The Image Information panel of the CINeSPACE annotation tool for image content.

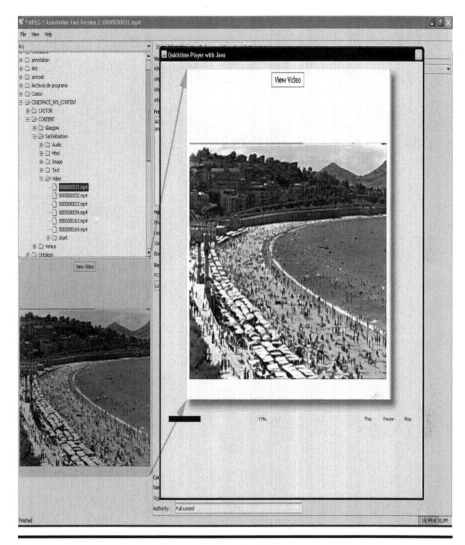

Figure 17.7   The Image Information panel of the CINeSPACE annotation tool for video content.

through a tree structure on the top left of the interface to find the desired files (images, video shots).

If the selected file is an image, it will be prerendered at the bottom of the tree structure. If the selected file is a video, its thumbnail will be shown at the bottom of the tree structure, and a button to play the video will also appear, as depicted in Figure 17.7.

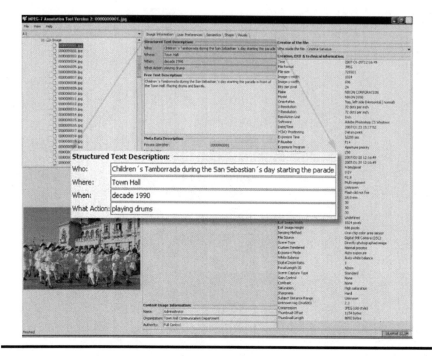

Figure 17.8   The StructuredText descriptor from the Image Information panel.

In the middle column of the interface (Figure 17.8), the StructuredText descriptor has been reduced to four categories:

- *Who*: description of the people or animals of the audiovisual content selected
- *Where*: location of the image or the places shown in the audiovisual content selected
- *When*: date when the audiovisual content selected was recorded
- *What Action*: events, actions, and so on, displayed in the audiovisual content selected

The same information can also be typed just under the StructureText description, in a free text description area, as shown in Figure 17.9.

One of the main extensions of the CINeSPACE tool includes the addition of new metadata related to the requirements of the project, such as a descriptor for the color of the audiovisual content (black and white or color) and a further descriptor for the appropriate CINeSPACE device that will render the content (Figure 17.10). The user should activate each checkbox (use for PDA, use for binoculars, B and W contents) depending on the final use of the file. Moreover, a unique private identifier has been defined to classify each audiovisual content in an MySQL database.

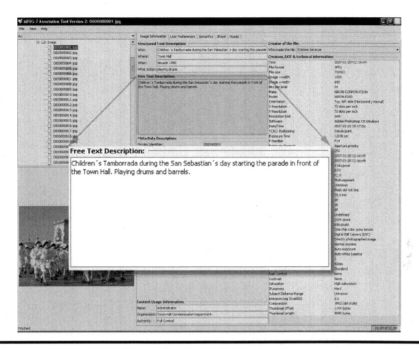

Figure 17.9   The FreeText descriptor from the Image Information panel.

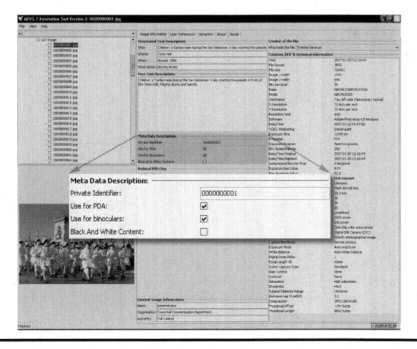

Figure 17.10   The MetaData descriptors from the Image Information panel.

A further section called Related POI-City is also an extension of the CINeSPACE project. A Point of Interest (POI) can be considered as any part of the city with some tourist and/or cultural heritage attractions (Figure 17.11), such as La Concha beach in San Sebastian or Piazza San Marco in Venice.

Because CINeSPACE content has been provided by several distributed institutions, partners and nonpartners of the consortium, one of the main problems that arose related to sharing the content was the digital rights management associated with each piece of content. Therefore, a specific MPEG-7 ContentUsage descriptor was added to the annotation tool to specify the usage rights, as shown in Figure 17.12. In this index, the user can specify the rights of the content owners.

On the right-hand side, the user can define the person who recorded the audio-visual content. If it is available, the EXIF information (Figure 17.13) is extracted and converted into MPEG-7 descriptors. Although Caliph is able to automatically extract existing EXIF and IPTC IIM annotations from images and convert them into valid MPEG-7 descriptors, this functionality has not been fully exploited because of the historical origin of the content that is used in the CINeSPACE project.

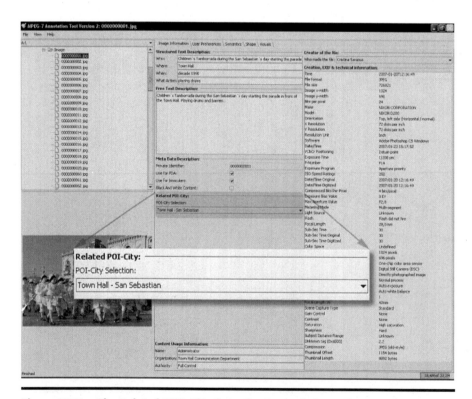

Figure 17.11   The Related POI-City from the Image Information panel.

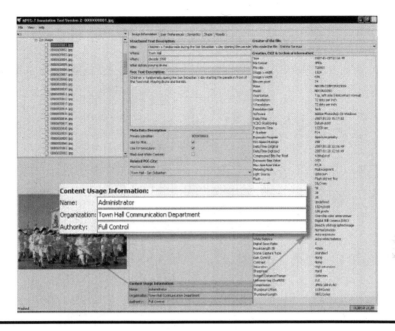

Figure 17.12   The Content Usage Information from the Image Information panel.

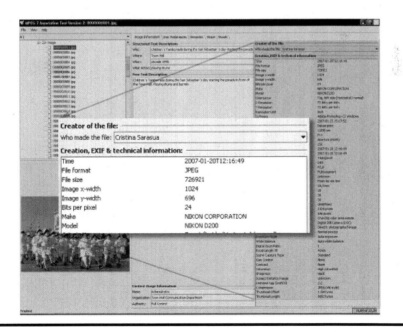

Figure 17.13   The Creation, EXIF, and Technical Information from the Image Information panel.

This additional information is crucial for two tasks: to extract all of the audiovisual content related to one concrete POI in the retrieval information system and to contribute more information for the location-based system. Therefore, the user retrieves audiovisual content based on the georeference information (latitude and longitude) and the name of the POI.

17.5.2 User Preferences Panel

A new User Preferences panel dedicated to user preferences metadata has been added to the Caliph basic editor (Figure 17.14). From the UserPreferences description scheme, the CreationPreferences description scheme and the Classification Preferences description scheme were selected. The period when the content was created (e.g., during the 1920s), keywords or georeference data (longitude and latitude) were selected from the CreationPreferences description scheme. The definition of the genre (comedy, documentary, etc.), the subject (military, religion, etc.) and in the case of video content, the language (English, Spanish, Italian, etc.) was made using descriptors from the ClassificationPreferences description scheme. The defined metadata will allow information retrieval based mainly on the geographical location of the user of the CINeSPACE device and his or her interests.

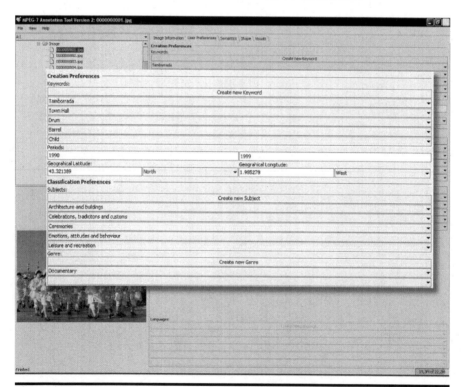

Figure 17.14   The User Preferences panel of the CINeSPACE annotation tool.

In the CreationPreferences, the user can write up to five keywords related to the file selected as favorite news or documentary topics, as shown in Figure 17.15. While the Periods index temporally locates the file (1950s, 1960s, etc.), the location information (geographical latitude and longitude) is necessary to locate geographically the audiovisual content selected. This information can be extracted from Google Earth, for example.

Regarding the ClassificationPreferences, several indexes (subjects and genre) have been added to select classification preferences information, which will be used later in the retrieval process. A simplified use case related to the ClassificationPreferences features of the system is the following:

- The user defines in the preferences of the audiovisual content that which is related to the *comedy* genre in his or her profile.
- The Application Layer receives a query in which the user wants to retrieve all of the audiovisual content related to her or his genre profile. The system checks the profile of the user and his or her georeference position.
- The Application Layer retrieves all of the audiovisual content around his or her georeference position and that which is related to the *comedy* genre.

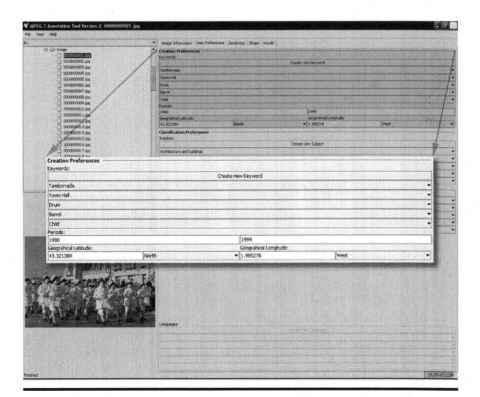

Figure 17.15   The CreationPreferences from the User Preferences panel.

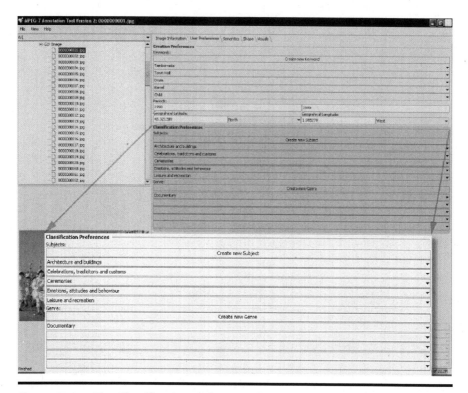

Figure 17.16   The ClassificationPreferences from the User Preferences panel.

It must be mentioned that it is mandatory to complete each of the fields shown in Figure 17.16.

17.5.3 Semantics Panel

One of the main panels of the CINeSPACE annotation tool is the Semantics panel, which allows the defining of semantic objects like agents, places, events, and times. The objects are saved for subsequent reuse. These semantic objects can also be imported from an existing MPEG-7 file to allow the exchange of objects among users and the edition and creation of those objects in a user-preferred tool. Semantic objects can be used for creating the description by dragging and dropping them onto the blue panel with the mouse, as shown in Figure 17.17.

Once the required semantic objects are placed onto the blue panel, the user can interconnect the objects by drawing relations among them using the middle mouse button. The graph is saved as part of the MPEG-7 description.

This panel includes three main subsections: Persons; Events; and Places, Times and Objects. The concept of Persons is related to all of the people, animals, or living objects in the audiovisual content (Figure 17.18). In order to add a new Person

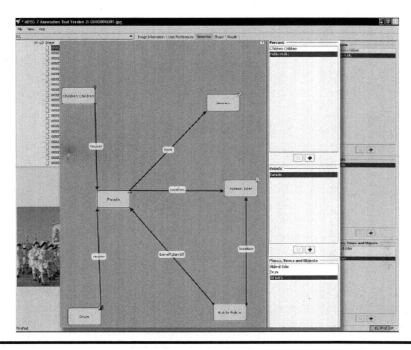

Figure 17.17   The Semantics panel of the CINeSPACE annotation tool.

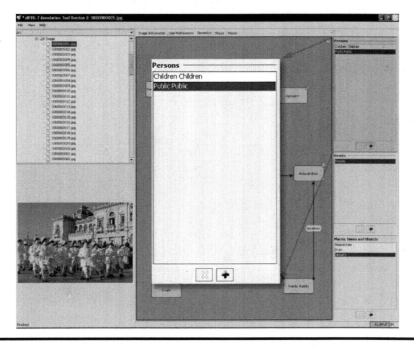

Figure 17.18   The Persons subsection of the Semantics panel.

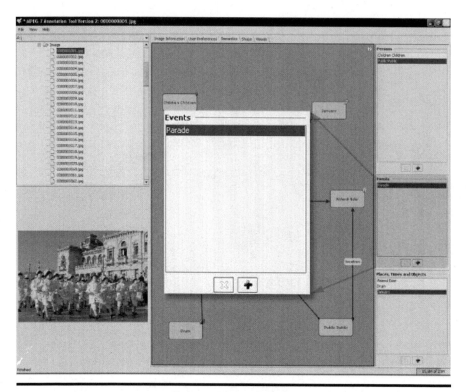

Figure 17.19   The Events subsection of the Semantics panel.

object, two fields must be filled: the name and the surname of the person. For other living objects, these two fields can contain the same name or text.

The Events concept is related to the actions, meetings, movements, and so on, of the audiovisual content (Figure 17.19). For each new event object, the user should define the name of the event, the date when the event was created within the CINe-SPACE annotation tool, the location of the event, and the address of the location.

The Places, Times, and Objects concepts are necessary to provide a temporal and local context to the audiovisual content. Places are related to all of the different locations displayed in the audiovisual content, as shown in Figure 17.20. Their annotation should include the name of the place and its address. Times is related to the date when each of the events was created. To create time information, the following aspects should be annotated: the name of the historical period (e.g., Medieval Age) and the century. Finally, Objects are the items that interact with the people in the audiovisual content. Only the name of the object is necessary.

Once all of the semantic data have been created, it is enough to drag and drop them onto the drawing panel (the blue one in the center) and create relations, starting in the source object and drawing a line into the target. The dialog of Figure 17.21 will pop up in order to select a relation to associate one semantic concept with the other.

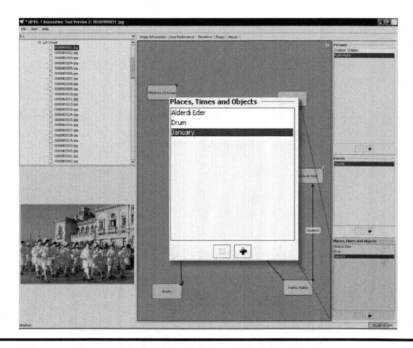

Figure 17.20   The Places, Times, and Objects subsection of the Semantics panel.

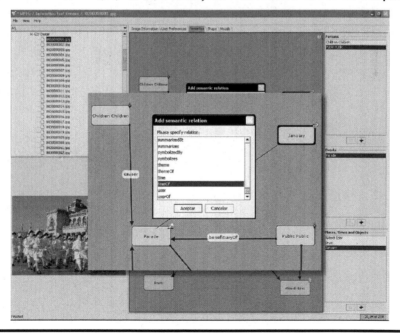

Figure 17.21   Adding semantic relationships for an object in the Places, Times, and Objects subsection of the Semantics panel.

17.5.4 Shape Panel and Visuals Panel

The Shape panel and Visuals panel are limited to a smaller number of descriptors, such as the EdgeHistogram (edginess), the DominantColor (dominant colors), the ColorLayout (color distribution in an image), or the ScalableColor (basically a color histogram), because the CINeSPACE project does not focus on low-level descriptors (Figures 17.22 and 17.23). These descriptors are extracted automatically by the original Caliph tool.

17.6 Results

The CINeSPACE annotation tool has been tested with the audiovisual content (image and video) of the CINeSPACE project. Content providers are located in the three cities that take part in the project: San Sebastian, Venice, and Glasgow. Regarding the content of the city of San Sebastian, the annotation tool indexed 10 clips (each 30 seconds or shorter) from the Basque Film Archive (Filmoteca Vasca), 65 photographs provided by the Fototeca Kutxa, and 26 pictures provided by the Town Hall Press Department.

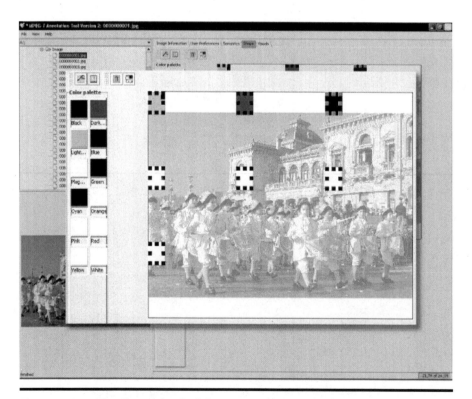

Figure 17.22   The Shape panel of the CINeSPACE annotation tool.

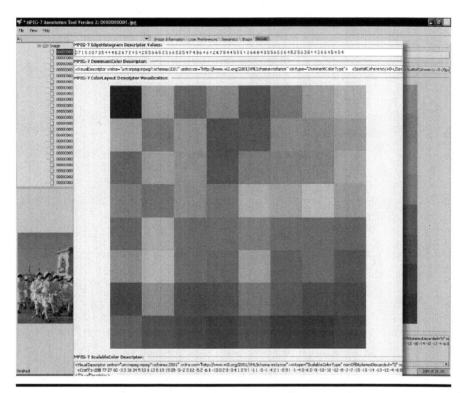

Figure 17.23   The Visuals panel of the CINeSPACE annotation tool.

Content providers from Venice are Videoteca Pasinetti, from which 24 images and 25 clips were annotated. Videoteca Pasinetti is a video library owned by the City of Venice and founded in 1991, dedicated to the memory of Francesco Pasinetti (1911–1949), who is widely considered to be the greatest Venetian cinematographer. Fondo Filippi is a collection of audiovisual content produced by the Venetian photographer Tomaso Filippi (1852–1948). Eight images from this collection were also annotated.

Finally, Scottish Screen Archive provides the content for Glasgow. It is the national development agency for the screen industries in Scotland. Twelve clips of around 30 seconds duration were used to test the developed tool. This archive has many films from several decades that provide an historical overview of the Scottish city.

Because of their historical origin, the images and videos vary significantly in quality and resolution. There are grayscale and color images and videos, and some of the videos also have audio. The topics of the audiovisual content are related to film heritage, but also include sport, cultural, social, and political aspects of life in those cities.

The CINeSPACE annotation tool was flexible enough to index all of the audio-visual content provided by the cities.

17.7 Conclusions and Future Work

This chapter described the implementation of the CINeSPACE semantic-based annotation tool, which enables semantic and structural annotations of audiovisual content for film heritage. Since an important part of the CINeSPACE metadata concerns the description of audiovisual content, the MPEG-7 standard was selected as the development framework. Three types of descriptions were considered: structural description, classification description, and semantic description.

After analyzing the existing approaches for multimedia annotation, the open source tool called Caliph was selected as the basis for the work developed within the project. The annotation process is manually carried out within CINeSPACE, because it is very important that the cities providing the content have overall control over the descriptors in order to be able to efficiently retrieve the content.

Regarding the annotation tool, several extensions were added to the basic Caliph software. First, new metadata related to the requirements of the project were added, such as a descriptor for the color, a unique private identifier to classify each audiovisual content in a MySQL database, and a further descriptor for the appropriate CINeSPACE device that will display the content. Moreover, a specific MPEG-7 descriptor named ContentUsage was added to the annotation tool to take into account the rights of the content owners. Finally, a new panel dedicated to user preferences metadata was added to the Caliph basic editor.

Concerning future work, the CINeSPACE annotation tool has been distributed and tested among the final users of the project, analyzing the viability of such tools in order to annotate audiovisual content databases. Although the tool has not been widely used by nonexperts from the cities, initial feedback is quite positive toward the new tool. Moreover, the tool will be extended to be used in other sectors, such as tourism or cultural heritage, that deal with large multimedia digital libraries.

Yolanda Cobos received a BS in computer science in 2004 from the University of the Basque Country, Spain. From 2001 to 2004, she worked at the Hypermedia and Multimedia Group of the University. From December 2004 to June 2005, she worked as a senior computer technician in Irún, Spain. From July 2005 to July 2006, she worked in research and development at Onity S.L., an electronic locks company. In late 2006, she started as a researcher with the Tourism, Cultural Heritage and Creativity Department of VICOMTech. She is currently a PhD student at the University of the Basque Country in the computer engineering program with a concentration in communications, control, and artificial intelligence.

María Teresa Linaza obtained her degree in electrical engineering in 1996, and a PhD in industrial engineering in 2001, from the University of Navarra, Spain. From September 1996 to December 2001, she was a member of the research and development team in electronics and communications at the CEIT Research 1 Center in San Sebastian, Spain. She has been a member of the VICOMTech research and development team since January 2002, heading the Department of Tourism, Heritage and Creativity. Linaza also participates in teaching and training activities at the University of Navarra, Spain, and has worked as an associate professor at the University of the Basque Country.

Cristina Sarasua received a bachelor's degree in computer science from the University of the Basque Country in 2006. She is currently a PhD student at that University. She has also worked in the Industrial Engineering Department at Echesa S.A. Since October 2007, she has been a researcher in the Tourism, Cultural Heritage and Creativity area of the VICOMTech research center.

Ander García studied telecommunications engineering at the University of the Basque Country, Spain. He is currently finishing his PhD program in computer science with a focus on communications, control, and artificial intelligence at that university. Since 2003, he has worked at VICOMTech as a researcher for the Tourism, Heritage and Creativity Department. He has been an associate professor of computer science language and systems at the University of the Basque Country since 2005.

Isabel Torre studied telecommunications engineering at Deusto University in Bilbao, Spain. She is currently a PhD student at the University of Basque Country. Since October 2006, she has been a researcher in the Tourism, Cultural Heritage and Creativity Department of the VICOMTech research center.

References

ACDSee Google. http://www.acdsystems.com.

Adobe Photoshop Album. http://www.adobe.com.

Amato, G., Cigarrán, J., Gonzalo, J. et al. 2007. MultiMatch-Multilingual/Multimedia Access to Cultural Heritage. *Proceedings of the ECDL*, pp. 505–508.

Bargeron, D., Gupta, A., Grudin, J. et al. 1999. Annotations for streaming video on the Web: System design and usage studies. *International Journal of Computer and Telecommunications Networking*, 31: 1139–1153. http://www.research.microsoft.com/ research/coet/MRAS/WWW8/paper.htm.

Carsten, N., Timmerman, S., Kosmas, D. et al. 2006. M-Onto-MatAnnotizer: Linking ontologies with multimedia low-level features for automatic image annotation. *Proceedings of 3rd European Semantic Web Conference*, Budva, Montenegro, LNCS 4253, pp. 633–640.

Cobos, Y., Linaza, M.T., García, A. et al. 2007. Applicability of MPEG-7 descriptors to film heritage. *Proceedings of SMAP 2007*, Uxbridge, Middlesex, U.K., pp. 205–210.

Content-Oriented Audiovisual Library Access: LogCreator. Swiss Federal Institute of Technology (EPFL). http://coala.epfl.ch/demos/demosFrameset.html.

Crofts, N., Doerr, M., Gill, T. et al. 2007. Version 4.2.2 of the reference document, *Definition of the CIDOC Conceptual Reference Model*. http://cidoc.ics.forth.gr/index.html.

CSIRO. The Continuous Media Web (CMWeb). http://www.cmis.csiro.au/cmweb/.

Development of a European Service for Information on Research and Education (DESIRE). 1997. Deliverable Number: D3.2, Specification for resource description methods. Part 1. A review of metadata: a survey of current resource description formats.

DICEMAN Project. http://www.teltec.dcu.ie/diceman/_vti_bin/shtml.exe/index.html/map.

Filmoteca Vasca. http://www.filmotecavasca.com/index.php/es.

Fondo Filippi. http://www.tomasofilippi.it.

Gagnon, L. 2005. R&D status of ERIC-7 and MADIS: Two systems for MPEG-7 indexing/ search of audio-visual content. *Proceedings of SPIE*, Vol. 6015, 601511, Boston, MA.

Gouaillier, V., Gagnon, L., Paquette, S. et al. 2005. Use of the MPEG-7 standard as metadata framework for a location scouting system: An evaluation study. *Proceedings of Dublin Core Conference*.

Harmony Project. http://metadata.net/harmony/.

IBM MPEG-7 Annotation Tool. http://www.alphaworks.ibm.com/tech/videoannex.

International Federation for IT and Travel & Tourism (IFITT). http://www.ifitt.org/.

Klamma, R., Spaniol, M., Cao, Y. 2006. MPEG-7-compliant community hosting. *Journal of Universal Knowledge Management*, pp. 36–44.

Klamma, R., Spaniol, M., Jarke, M. et al. 2006. A hypermedia Afghan sites and monuments database. Lecture notes in *Geoinformation and Cartography*, Berlin: Springer, pp. 189–209.

Klieber, W., Tochtermann, K., Lux, M. et al. 2003. *IMB: Ein XML-basiertes retrieval framework für digitales audio und video.* Berlin: Berliner XML Tage.

Lux, M., Becker, J., Krottmaier, H. 2003. Semantic annotation and retrieval of digital photos. *Proceedings CAiSE 03 Forum Information Systems for a Connected Society.* http://ftp. informatik.rwth-aachen.de/Publications/CEURWS/.

Lux, M., Granitzer, M. 2005. Retrieval of MPEG-7-based semantic descriptions. *BTW-Workshop WebDB Meets IR*, University of Karlsruhe, Germany. http://caliph-emir. sourceforge.net/docs.html#publications.

Lux, M., Granitzer, M., Klieber, W. 2004. Caliph & Emir: Semantics in multimedia retrieval and annotation. *Proceedings of the 19th International CODATA Conference*, Berlin.

Manuel, V., Barrios, G., Gütl, C. 2006. Exploitation of MPEG-7 descriptions on multimodal meeting data: First results within MISTRAL project. *Journal of Universal Knowledge Management*.

Maurer, F., Dellen, B., Bendeck, F. et al. 2000. Merging project planning and Web-enabled dynamic workflow technologies. *Internet Computing*, pp. 65–74.

Meier, W. 2002. eXist: An open source native XML database. *Lecture Notes in Computer Science*, Vol. 2593/2008, pp. 169–183.

MPEG-7, ISO/IEC JTC1/SC29/WG11 Coding of moving pictures and audio. http://www. chiariglione.org/mpeg/standards/mpeg-7/mpeg-7.htm.

MuViNo, an MPEG-7 video annotation tool. 2004. http://vitooki.sourceforge.net/components/ muvino/.

Nack, F., Putz, W. 2001. Designing annotation before it's needed. *Proceedings of the 9th ACM International Conference on Multimedia*, Ontario, Canada, pp. 261–269.

Picasa. http://www.picasa.com.

Santos, P., Stork, A., Linaza, M. T. et al. 2007. CINeSPACE: Interactive Access to Cultural Heritage While On-The-Move. *HCI International*, Beijing, pp. 435–444.

Scottish Screen Archive. http://www.scottishscreen.com/.

Ricoh MovieTool. http://www.ricoh.co.jp/src/multimedia/MovieTool/.

Taschwer, M., Muller, A., Boszormenyi, L. 2005. Integrating semantic search and adaptive streaming of video segments. Klagenfurt, Technical Reports of the Institute of Information Technology, (TR/ITEC/05/2.04), pp. 34.

Videoteca Pasinetti. http://www.comune.venezia.it/flex/cm/pages/ServeBLOB.php/L/EN/IDPagina/2033.

VIDETO, video description tool. Zentrum fuer Graphische Datenverarbeitung e.V. (ZGDV). http://www.rostock.zgdv.de/ZGDV/Abteilungen/zr2/Produkte/videto/index_html_en.

Chapter 18

Automatic Feature Extraction to an MPEG-7 Content Model

M. J. Parmar and M. C. Angelides

18.1 Introduction

Automatic content modeling (also called high-level feature extraction or concept detection) of video or video segments is essential for content-based video searching and filtering. Multimedia content has no abstract connection between the grammatical medium of the content and the higher level concepts portrayed within. This detachment between the form of the content and the meaning of the content makes it difficult to find methods that can search the content directly with any success or accuracy in a timely manner. A translation layer between the syntax of the content and the higher semantics is needed to tie the underlying concepts to the physical structure of the content itself. This mapping, or content modeling, allows the concepts to be tied directly to the physical structure of the content in a pragmatic approach; that is, scenes, shots, and objects can be mapped to the physical structure. Such mapping allows users to search the content in a content-centric fashion [1] (as opposed to searching the bit-centric physical structure) that is directly related to the way they perceive the content. The effectiveness of an indexing scheme depends on the effectiveness of attributes in content representation. However, we cannot map extractable video features (e.g., color, texture, shape, structure, layout, motion) easily into semantic concepts (e.g., indoor and outdoor, people, or car-racing scenes). In the audio domain, features (e.g., pitch, energy, bandwidth) can enable audio segmentation and classification. Although visual content is a major source of information in a video program, an effective strategy in video-content analysis is to use attributes that are extractable from multimedia sources. Much valuable information is also carried in other media components, such as text (super-imposed on the images or included as closed captions), audio, and speech, that accompany the pictorial component. A combined and cooperative analysis of these components would be far more effective in characterizing video programs for both consumer and professional applications.

Video semantic feature extraction frequently encounters two interrelated problems:

1. When users query multimedia content, they approach it from a perspective related to an abstract task that is the motivation for the search. This abstraction must be considered along with the low-level features of the content to make sure that the users' queries are adequately addressed. If not, the results that are returned will not match the users' representation of what he or she required, but they will match from an analytical sense based on low-level features. The way users perceive the meaning of content is not easily translatable to the way that the content is portrayed. This problem is called the semantic gap [2].

2. Feature selection should not be restricted to what should be extracted to represent the content; it should also include how it should be extracted and modeled for the users' information needs.

Feature selection that supports the reduction of the semantic gap means being able to model content from a multiperspective view that enables granular descriptions [3]. This allows users to query the content from different points of view and be able to extract all of the pertinent information and to disregard information that does not fit his or her needs.

In this chapter, we will look at how to reduce the semantic gap problem by select-ing appropriate features that allow the querying of the content from multiple per-spectives. In extracting the features, we model them based on the user's view of the content, thereby providing more accurate results to queries. A content model scheme is produced that takes advantage of the rich granular description of the multimedia content.

Before we look at what features to select, we introduce the concept of multi-media indexing. We perceive video content structure in much the same manner as the structure of a text document. Video indexing should be analogous to text document indexing, where we perform a structural analysis to decompose a docu-ment into paragraphs, sentences, and words before building indices [4]. Therefore, one of the core research tasks in content modeling is to develop technologies to automatically parse content into a meaningful composition structure that represents the content in a multifaceted perspective that can accommodate the rich set of features available in multimedia. Books have a table of contents and an index to allow readers to obtain the information they require without manually having to search through each page. Using this paradigm, we should segment video into meaningful structural components such as scenes and shots as content headings and subheadings, respectively. Using another paradigm, but this time from the world of scriptwriting, we can garner a richer set of feature analogies. The scenes are like acts and depict an occurrence of an event, while shots are like scenes from a play and depict a group of actions. Within these scenes and shots are actors and props, which are objects.

The main building blocks for the content model are scenes, shots, and objects which provide a systematic way of accessing the content in a rich but granular manner. To access the content from a particular viewpoint, however, this model is inadequate because the interactions and structuring of the content on an interlevel and intralevel are not clearly defined or described. To provide such multifaceted perspectives, the spatial and temporal relationships between the content features must be described in a systematic fashion. Spatial and temporal relationships are the key to reducing the semantic gap by ensuring the user's perspective is taken into account when formulating the query.

The rest of the chapter is organized as follows. The next section describes related work in extracting features. We then explain the framework of the application used to extract the feature set. It will present the algorithms that are used for feature extraction and how the process facilitates the production of a multifaceted, rich, granular description of the content. We then discuss how the features are modeled using MPEG-7 and explain how the tools are integrated to produce the content model with the aforementioned qualities.

18.2 Related Work

We mentioned the importance of selecting the correct feature set to model content in a multifaceted and richly detailed manner. These features can be extracted using a multitude of algorithms that provide a solution for different problems associated with feature extraction. Following is a summary of recent research performed in this area.

18.2.1 Shots/Actions

The first feature to be extracted is shots. Shots are actual physical basic layers in video, the boundaries of which are determined by editing points or points at which the camera switches on or off. They usually represent a minor incident or action. Fortunately, analogous to words or sentences in text documents, shots are a good choice as the basic unit for video-content indexing, and they provide the basis for constructing a video table of contents. Shots are basic spatiotemporal building blocks not only for content modeling but also for creating video abstracts and summaries [1]. Shot boundary detection algorithms that rely only on visual information can segment the video into shots with contiguous visual content. These visually exclusive algorithms have been well researched; they are quite robust and precise and have very good results for identifying shot boundaries [2]. Color Histogram Difference (CHD) is a popular method for shot segmentation, but problems in detecting shot changes occur where two contiguous shots have a CHD below the boundary threshold or a shot has a sharp CHD change registering a false shot. To address CHD detection problems, researchers have combined other visual features to complement shots. For example, Angelides [3] used Motion Vector Filtration (MVF) to eliminate two types of errors found in CHD detection: (1) missed shots arising from two different perspective shots of the same scenario and (2) false shots being detected because of fast camera pans, both familiar to sports videos. Features other than color can be used for shot detection; pixel intensity, for instance, is used in linear transition detection [4]. Pixel intensity values are exploited in that the mean and variance of pixel intensity during the transition have both linear and quadratic behavior. Therefore, the criterion used to determine the presence of a transition is that the ratio of the second derivative of the variance curve to the first derivative of the mean curve should be a constant. Shot segmentation can be performed using nonaudiovisual features to segment the video. Using compressed data, Discrete Cosine Transform (DCT) coefficients are used to detect regions of change and global changes that signify a shot boundary [5]; this is achieved by applying a pairwise comparison technique to DCT coefficients of corresponding blocks of adjacent video frames. Another method that operates in the compressed domain uses a supervised classification technique that uses feature vectors consisting of six parameters per frame from all frames in a temporal window [6]. Using a multiclass classifier with fusion of three Support Vector Machine (SVM) binary classifiers, they group all of the frames into three categories: cut change, gradual change, and nonchange. Researchers are going further back in the compressed domain and operating in the entropy-decoding stage, which is the very first stage in the entire decoding process [7]. Using H.264/AVC bitstreams, the partitioning for macroblocks is used to determine whether or not there is a shot change. In the same shot, the macroblocks are coded uniformly because there is little noise or entropy change, but when a new shot begins, the coding scheme changes dramatically as homogeneous areas, shapes, contours, noise, and so on, change significantly. Using a weighted value, called Partition Histogram Difference (PHD), they calculate how much the partitioning scheme changes between two consecutive frames.

18.2.2 Scenes/Events

Shots describe actions or self-contained events that do not have much focus until they are put together to describe a larger story unit, commonly called a scene. The parsing of video segments into scenes or "logical units" is an important step in the process of a well-defined video structure [8]. From a narrative point of view, a scene consists of a series of consecutive shots grouped together because they are shot in the same location or because they share some thematic content, usually an event. The process of detecting these video scenes is analogous to paragraphing in text document parsing, but it requires a higher level of content analysis. There are two approaches for automatically recognizing program sequences: one based on film production rules [9] and the other based on a priori program models [10]. Both have had limited success because scenes or stories in video are only logical layers of representation based on subjective semantics, and no universal definition and rigid structure exist for scenes and stories. Researchers have tried to overcome the definition problem by providing feedback to the process. One proposed method is semantic-based video scene retrieval [11] that uses 12 low-level features extracted from a video clip, which are represented as genetic chromosomes. Users' target videos are retrieved by the interactive genetic algorithm through feedback itera- tion. Using high-level semantic relevance between retrieved videos, the algorithm estimates a semantic relevance matrix and semantic frequency matrix, which are produced for all iterations. The matrices are combined with an automatic feature weight update scheme to retrieve more target videos at the next iteration.

Some genres have low-level features that remain constant. They have visual and/or audio characteristics that can be used to identify the start of scenes. One approach employs transitions, which directors use between shots to demarcate the boundary between scenes [12]. Cuts, dissolves, fades, and wipes are devices in film grammar used to structure video. The video can then be segmented into scenes by exploiting three film grammar rules: (1) The selection of key-frames for shot similarity measurement should take the position of gradual shot transitions into account. (2) Gradual shot transitions have a separating effect, and this local cue can be used to improve the global structuring into logical units. (3) Gradual shot transitions also have a merging effect on shots in their temporal proximity. Weng, Chu, and Wu [13] have used low-level features to initially segment the video using a global k-means clustering algorithm that extracts shots and key-frames to repre- sent each shot. Then a spectral clustering method is applied to cluster the shots into groups based on visual similarity, and a label is assigned to each shot according to the group to which it belongs. Next, a method for segmenting the sequence of shot labels is applied, providing the final scene segmentation result.

Some researchers have used other features combined with shots to help iden- tify scene boundaries. A graph-based multilevel temporal segmentation method for scripted content videos [14] makes use of a priori knowledge of the scripts produced by the content creators. In each level of the segmentation, a similarity matrix of frame strings, which are a series of consecutive video frames, is constructed by using temporal and spatial contents of frame strings. A strength factor is estimated for each frame string by comparing it against the scripted content. According to the similarity matrix that is reevaluated from a strength function derived by the strength factors, a weighted undirected graph structure is implemented. The graph is partitioned into clusters, which represent segments of a video. The resulting structure defines a hierarchically segmented video tree. Audio cues have been combined with visual features to provide a robust method of scene detection [15]. An enhanced set of Eigen-audio frames is created that is related to an audio signal subspace. This subspace can help detect audio background changes quite easily. Visual information is used to align audio scene-change indications with neighboring video shot changes and, accordingly, to reduce the false alarm rate of the audio-only scene-change detection. Moreover, video fade effects are identified and used independently to track scene changes. The false alarm rate is reduced further by extracting acoustic features to verify that the scene-change indications are valid.

18.2.3 Objects

Scenes and shots alone do not adequately describe the inner dynamics of the semantic content held in the media. To provide a granular view of events and actions, we need to describe the objects and the interactions between them. In order to do this and provide more efficient content-based functionalities for video applications, it is necessary to extract meaningful video objects from scenes to enable object-based representation of video content. Petersohn [16] developed a family of hierarchical generative models for objects, the parts composing them, and the scenes surrounding them. This work focuses on the basic level of recognition of visually identifiable categories rather than on the differentiation of object instances. The models share information between object categories in three distinct ways. First, parts define distributions over a common low-level feature vocabulary, leading to computational savings when analyzing new images. Then, objects are defined using a common set of parts. This structure leads to the discovery of parts with interesting semantic interpretations and can improve performance when few training examples are available. Finally, object appearance information is shared between the many scenes in which that object is found. We not only need the objects but the spatial relationships and temporal relationships among them to accurately dissect each event and action. Such a technique is described by Chasanis, Likas, and Galatsanos [17] for the automatic detection and tracking of salient objects and the derivation of spatiotemporal relations among them in video. The system aims to significantly reduce the work of manual selection and labeling: because it detects and tracks salient objects, the label for each object needs to be entered only once within each shot instead of being specified for each object in every frame in which it appears. It covers a scalable architecture for video processing and stages of shot boundary detection, salient object detection and tracking, and knowledge-based construction for effective spatiotemporal object querying. To get more accurate categorization, more acute methods of feature extraction and selection must be used. To recognize an object, the user must have some a priori knowledge of the category to which that object belongs (e.g., a cow comes from the category *animal*). Using a set of learned features from each object category, called a codebook, it is possible to match them to an object in a candidate image and identify what type of object it is [18]. This is done by extracting local features around interest points and comparing them to the codebooks' entries of object categories. Matching patches then cast probabilistic votes, which lead to object hypotheses that can optionally be refined by sampling more features. Based on the back-projected hypotheses, Sakarya and Telatar [18]can compute a category-specific segmentation. Object extraction and recognition can be based on a hybrid of features that may or may not be present in the media itself. For instance, cast indexing is an important video mining technique that allows users to efficiently retrieve scenes, events, and stories from a long video by querying using a cast list of the actors [19]. This is done by recognizing actors from the provided cast list with the associated image of the cast member. The system first uses face tracker to group face images in each shot into face sets, and then it extracts local Scale-Invariant Feature Transform (SIFT) features. There are two key problems for cast indexing. One is finding an optimal partition to cluster face sets into a main cast. The other is exploiting the latent relationships among characters to provide a more accurate cast ranking. For the first problem, Kyperountas, Kotropoulos, and Pitas [19] modeled each face set as a graph node and adopt Normalized Graph Cuts (NCuts) to realize an optimal graph partition. A local neighborhood distance algorithm is used to measure the distance between face sets for NCuts, which is robust to outliers. For the second problem, they build a relation graph for characters by their cooccurrence information and then adopt the PageRank algorithm to estimate the Important Factor (IF) of each character. The PageRank IF is fused with the content-based retrieval score for final ranking.

Another difficulty in object extraction is the recognition of real-world objects in complex 3D scenes. A similar motion search and retrieval system has been developed, but it is for 3D video and is based on a modified shape distribution algorithm [20]. A 3D video is a sequence of 3D models made for real-world objects. The most significant feature in 3D video is that each frame is generated regardless of its neighboring frames. This is because of the nonrigid nature of the human body and clothes. Therefore, the number of vertices and topology differ frame by frame, which makes it very difficult to search the correspondent vertices or patches among frames. Using a shape distribution histogram, Sudderth et al. [20] sampled a number of points (e.g., 1024) that make up the vertices of the 3D model surface and calculate the distance between all of the possible combinations of points. A histogram of distance distribution is then generated as a feature vector to express the shape characteristics of a 3D model. Then, using a motion segmentation algorithm, they conduct an extraction of feature vectors by analyzing the degree of motion.

Object extraction is a very computationally expensive exercise because the video has to be decoded frame by frame and then analyzed pixel by pixel. Recent work by Sevilmis et al. [21] on MPEG movies tried to minimize this expense by detecting objects in the compressed domain, thereby reducing the amount of resources dedicated to decoding. First, using temporal scaling, they eliminated redundant frames and only kept the motion information of the P-frames to detect the objects. Then the DCT coefficients from the I-frames were extracted; these coefficients included the DC (Discrete Cosine) and AC (Arithmetic Coding). The DCT coefficients were passed into a module to calculate the energy values texture of each frame. The texture information values were propagated into P-frames. The texturally filtered motion vectors were then passed into an object-extraction algorithm to get a set of detected objects in each frame.

18.2.4 Spatial and Temporal Relations

As described previously, in order to provide a multiview perspective of events, actions, and objects, we must describe the temporal and spatial relationships among them. Spatial–temporal relationships among events, actions, and objects from a new area of research in terms of how to effectively query such relationships using nonproprietary, standardized methods such as MPEG-7 [22]. Present research is currently looking at spatial–temporal relationships in the context of feature extraction for other feature sets. For example, Yong et al. [23] employed a framework to model the temporal information of a video sequence in a universal parametric space for primarily shot boundary detection and then shot classification and key-frame extraction. If such a model could be learned either from the data or from the physics of the actual scenario, it would help significantly in problems such as identifying and synthesizing video sequences. They employed a time-series parametric model—the AutoRegressive Moving Average (ARMA) model—not relying on a specific distribution but reflecting the underlying temporal relation of frame sequences. With the great ability to present the temporal relation in the frame's spatial feature sequence, the framework is applied to several applications in video content analysis. Yamasaki and Aizawa [24] proposed a framework for matching video sequences using the spatiotemporal segmentation of videos. Instead of using appearance features for region correspondence across frames, they used interest point trajectories to generate video volumes. Point trajectories, which are generated using the SIFT operator, are clustered to form motion segments by analyzing their motion and spatial properties. The temporal correspondence between the estimated motion segments is then established based on the most common SIFT correspondences. A two-pass correspondence algorithm is used to handle splitting and merging regions. Spatiotemporal volumes are extracted using the consistently tracked motion segments. Next, a set of features, including color, texture, motion, and SIFT descriptors, is extracted to represent a volume. They employed an EarthMover's Distance (EMD)-based approach for the comparison of volume features. Given two videos, a bipartite graph is constructed by modeling the volumes as vertices and their similarities as edge weights. Maximum matching of the graph produces volume correspondences between the videos, and these volume matching scores are used to compute the final video matching score.

18.3 Feature Extraction Framework

In Figure 18.1, we present the MPEG-7 content modeler. The decoded video stream is first split into shots by the shot detector. Two types of shots are identified by two different shot detecting processes: (1) cut shots are detected by CHD, while (2) transition shots (fade in/out and dissolves) are detected by Edge Change Ratio (ECR). These two algorithms are optimized and best suited to finding the types of shots they have been assigned, negating the disadvantages of both techniques if used to identify both types of shots. Once the shots are extracted, they are sent to the temporal relationship processor and the object extraction processor. The temporal relationship processor models the temporal relationships of the shots into the MPEG-7 content model. The object processor extracts objects on a per-shot basis. The object processor uses a multistage technique of edge detection and then interconnected color regions to detect objects. Extracted objects are sent to the spatial relationship processor before going on to the temporal relationship processor. Once the spatial and temporal relationships are formulated, they are embedded into the MPEG-7 content model along with the earlier shots that were modeled. The scene processor takes the object results as well as the input shot data that was used to process. The scene processor uses genetic programming to determine where the scene boundaries are, depending on evolved rules based on the feature sets that have already been processed. After the scenes are determined, they are processed by the temporal relationship processor. The temporal relationships with the scenes are modeled and combined with shots and objects and their relationships; the next step is the events/action annotation stage. Finally, the events and actions are annotated for the scenes, shots, and objects and combined with their spatial–temporal relationships for the final MPEG-7 content model. At any of the three stages of shot, object, or scene extraction, the process can be halted. This allows users to determine the granularity and feature sets required for their own personal information needs.

18.3.1 Shot Processor

Color histogram difference is used to identify abrupt shot changes using a frame-by-frame comparison method that reduces the RGB values of two consecutive frames and computes the differences between them. If that value is above a certain threshold, then a cut shot is detected. This method is robust against global motion and most large object motion if used only for cut shot detection. The formula for CHD is given in Equation 18.1.

$$CHD_i = \frac{1}{N} \sum_{r=0}^{2^B-1} \sum_{g=0}^{2^B-1} \sum_{b=0}^{2^B-1} \left| p_i(r,g,b) - p_{i-1}(r,g,b) \right| \qquad (18.1)$$

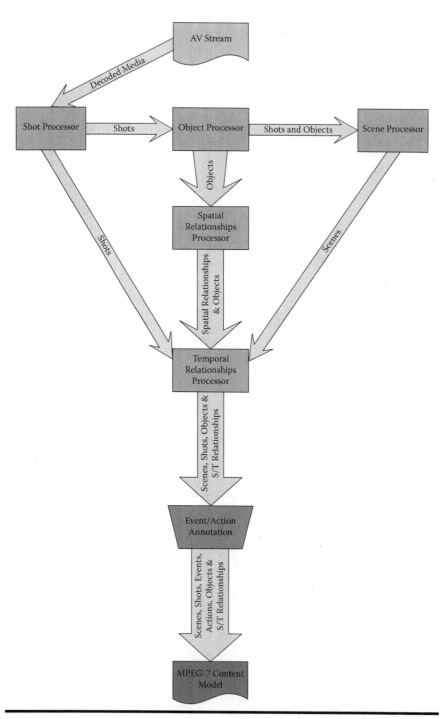

Figure 18.1   Framework for extracting features to an MPEG-7 content model.

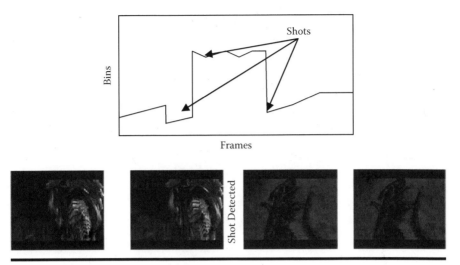

Figure 18.2 CHD shot detection.

Figure 18.2 shows a cut shot detection graph indicating where the rapid changes occur that indicate a shot change. Below that is a pictorial representation of one of these shot changes.

Gradual transitions are detected using the edge ratio technique to produce graphs that describe the type of gradual transition. The ECR is given by Equation 18.2.

$$ECR_n = max\left(X_n^{in} / \sigma_n, \; X_{n-1}^{out} / \sigma_{n-1} \right), \qquad (18.2)$$

Edge transition graphs compare the contrast of object boundaries and number of edge points within n consecutive frames over time. In fade shots, the amount of hard edges of objects increases from zero or decreases to zero over time. With fade-in, the amount of edges that are visible increases, leading to a positive-sloped graph. Fade-outs have decreasing edges as the shot gradually fades to black, creating a negative-sloped graph. Dissolve shots, on the other hand, produce a concave hyperbolic graph as the predissolve edges dissolve and the postdissolve edges form. Figure 18.3 presents two graphs that correspond to different transition shots.

18.3.2 Object Processor

Object extraction is a three-stage process: (1) defining the edges of all of the potential objects depicted in a frame, (2) identifying the color change between two object boundaries, and (3) tracking the object for the remaining frames of the shot.

The first stage of finding the edges of potential objects is performed by the Canny edge detection algorithm [25]. Canny edge detection combined with pixel-by-pixel–based color edge contrast is used to identify objects. The edges are found

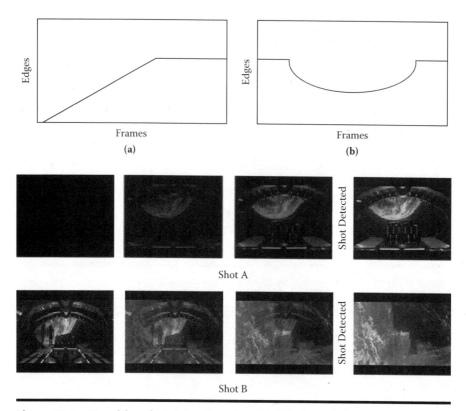

Figure 18.3   Transition shot detection: shot (A) fade-in and shot (B) dissolve.

by the Canny edge detection algorithm to provide a silhouette of the object. The Canny edge detection algorithm, also known as the optimal edge detector, follows a list of criteria to improve edge detection over other similar methods [26]. The first and most obvious is that it produces a low error rate. It is important that edges that occur in images not be missed and that there be no responses to non-edges. The second criterion is that the edge points should be well localized. In other words, the distance between the edge pixels as found by the detector and the actual edge should be at a minimum. A third criterion is to have only one response to a single edge. This was implemented because the first two criteria were not substantial enough to completely eliminate the possibility of multiple responses to an edge.

The second stage is to identify objects by color classification. We found interconnected regions of color in the HS (Hue, Saturation) color space. This color space is used because it has a high tolerance against color changes caused by shadows and change of lighting. We found objects by comparing edge boundaries that are adjacent to each other to see if they have the same color. They are then grouped together and marked as either foreground, background, or unknown objects based on their color distribution of interconnected color regions. Then the SIOX algorithm [27] is used, it works on separating the foreground from the background based on color characteristics.

The tracking of objects is achieved by pattern recognition of the color contours of the object on a block-by-block basis and measuring the block motion estimation (local) against the cumulative motion of all of the pixels (global). Objects within a shot are automatically labeled with arbitrary labels that are unique to the video sequence and other objects are extracted from different shots.

18.3.3 Scene Processor

The scene boundary detection is a semiautomatic process that detects boundaries by using a trained Genetic Programming (GP) algorithm to identify low-level feature combinations that identify boundary edges. Because scene boundaries are a high-level feature (i.e., semantic), they are abstract in their precise classification. Therefore, a user must train the GP algorithm with a small clip of video of identified scene boundaries. The algorithm then formulates rules that identify certain feature sets (e.g., objects, shot transitions cuts, shot durations common to the scene boundaries in the training clip).

The GP algorithm makes an initial population of rules and then tests them against a precision/recall fitness function based on the training clip input. It evolves the rules that have the highest fitness into the next generation. It keeps on doing this until either a greater than 98% fitness is achieved or the maximum number of generations is completed, in which case the rule with the highest fitness is used. The fitness function for scene boundary detection is given in Equation 18.3:

$$f = \frac{Nc}{Nt} \tag{18.3}$$

where Nc is the number of correctly identified scene boundaries and Nt is the total number of shots.

18.3.4 Spatial Relationships Processor

The spatial processor identifies spatial relationships among objects within a shot. The spatial relations are predefined in a classification scheme that identifies all the relations and inverse relations, which are shown in Table 18.1.

To establish the spatial relationship between two objects, it is necessary to locate the center of mass, or centroid, for each object. The centroid must be known because the boundaries of two objects may extend to different geometric positions around each other, leading to inconclusive estimations to their relative positioning. The centroid of each object is calculated using the formula given in Equation 18.4.

Table 18.1 Spatial Relations

Relation	Inverse Relation
South	North
West	East
Northwest	Southeast
Southwest	Northeast
Left	Right
Right	Left
Below	Above
Over	Under

$$c_x = \frac{1}{6A} \sum_{i=0}^{N-1} (x_i + x_{i+1})(x_i y_{i+1} - x_{i+1} y_i)$$

$$c_y = \frac{1}{6A} \sum_{i=0}^{N-1} (y_i + y_{i+1})(x_i y_{i+1} - x_{i+1} y_i) \tag{18.4}$$

where x,y are the Cartesian coordinates of the boundaries of the object. Once the centroid of each object is found, the spatial relationship between them can be defined. It is determined by splitting the area around one of the objects into nine blocks with the object in the center. The relationship between objects depends on where the other objects' center lies in the surrounding nine blocks.

18.3.5 Temporal Relationship Processor

The temporal relationships among scenes, shots, and objects are determined between each feature's own results and against other feature sets. This provides querying between temporal relationships between feature sets and permits a multifaceted dimension to temporal querying. The temporal processor uses timestamps from the decoded media to determine the temporal relationship between each feature. The temporal relationships are defined using Allen's temporal relationships [32] and the MPEG-7 extended temporal relationships. The supported temporal relations are shown in Table 18.2.

18.3.6 Content Modeler

Once the features are extracted, they are modeled into an MPEG-7 content model using Java Architecture for XML Binding (JAXB), which encapsulates the

Table 18.2   Temporal Relations

Binary	Inverse Binary	N-ary
Precedes	Follows	Contiguous
Cooccurs	Cooccurs	Sequential
Meets	Met by	Cobeing
Overlaps	Overlapped by	Coend
Strict during	Strict contains	Parallel
Starts	Started by	Overlapping
Finishes	Finished by	—
Contains	During	—

native Java data structures of the separate extracted features and binds them into a unified MPEG-7 content model that embeds and links all the features to each other. Using Cartesian coordinates, the spatial relationships are extracted for the objects. The timestamps of the shots and scenes are processed to provide the temporal relationships.

18.4 Modeling Content in MPEG-7

From the features identified earlier, certain physical or abstract attributes determine which description schemes will be used to create the MPEG-7 content model. MPEG-7 provides myriad tools that offer broad functionality and can be assimilated and configured in different ways. The following sections outline how to incorporate the features and relationships into an MPEG-7 content model. We will describe what MPEG-7 tools are used to describe the features. We will also describe the integration of these features into a unified content model that is granular and is rich in descriptions of both the features and the relationships among them. We integrate both semantic and syntactic features where it is beneficial to the user.

18.4.1 Scene and Shot Descriptions

For describing the scenes and shots, we used the VideoSegment description scheme (DS) (Figure 18.4). Scenes and shots are similar because they have the same physical attributes (e.g., start time and duration), so temporally they are treated the same in the modeling process. Scenes are described using the VideoSegment DS and are given an ID to uniquely identify them. The physical location of the media is defined by the MediaLocator DS and can locate media from either a local or a remote source using the MediaUri descriptor. The physical media is then given a unique ID using the Video DS tag.

Scenes are created using the VideoSegmentTemporalDecompositionType DS to segment the scenes temporally. A scene is embedded into the root of the Video DS using the VideoSegmentTemporalDecompositionType DS. Using the MediaTime DS within the VideoSegment DS, the start of the scene is stated by its timestamp and its duration using the MediaTimepoint descriptor and MediaDuration descriptor, respectively. A unique ID is given to the scene in the VideoSegment DS. Shots are created using the AnalyticEditingTemporalDecomposition DS to segment the shots temporally. The shots are embedded in the scene using the Shot DS and GlobalTransition DS. The GlobalTransition DS comes before the Shot DS and describes the edit of the shot boundary, that is, whether it is a cut or a transition. The GlobalTransition DS has an EvolutionReliability attribute that shows the confidence in the transition state.

For video segment identification, we use the VisualDescriptor DS (Figure 18.5). We set the type of the VisualDescriptor Ds to GoFGoPColorType, which aggregates the color distribution across a number of frames in a shot. We then use the

```
<Video id="Alien Vs Predator">
        <MediaLocator>
                <MediaUri>AVP.mpg</MediaUri>
        </MediaLocator>
        <MediaTime>
                <MediaTimePoint>T00:00:00</MediaTimePoint>
                <MediaDuration>PT1H48M00S</MediaDuration>
        </MediaTime>
        <VideoSegmentTemporalDecomposition>
                <VideoSegment id="AVP-V-VS73">
                        <MediaTime>
                                <MediaTimePoint>T01:25:00</MediaTimePoint>
                                <MediaDuration>PT0M30S</MediaDuration>
                        </MediaTime>
                        <AnalyticEditingTemporalDecomposition>
                                <GlobalTransition evolutionReliability="0.975084">
                                        <MediaTime>
                                                <MediaTimePoint>T01:25:00</MediaTimePoint>
                                                <MediaDuration>PT0S</MediaDuration>
                                        </MediaTime>
                                <EvolutionType href="urn:mpeg7:cs:EvolutionTypeCS:2001:Cut"/>
                                </GlobalTransition>
                                <Shot id="AVP-V-VS73-S1">
                                        <MediaLocator xsi:type="TemporalSegmentLocatorType">
                                        </MediaLocator>
                                                <MediaTime>
                                                        <MediaTimePoint>T01:25:00</MediaTime...
                                                        <MediaDuration>PT0M15S</MediaDuration>
                                                </MediaTime>
                                </Shot>
                                <GlobalTransition evolutionReliability="0.786786">
                                        <MediaTime>
                                                <MediaTimePoint>T01:40:00</MediaTimePoint>
                                                <MediaDuration>PT3S</MediaDuration>
                                        </MediaTime>
```

Figure 18.4   Code example of scenes and shots.

```
<VisualDescriptor xsi:type="GoFGoPColorType" aggregation="Average">
        <ScalableColor numOfCoeff="16" numOfBitplanesDiscarded="0">
                <Coeff> 1 2 3 4 5 6 7 8 6 0 1 2 3 4 5 …
        </ScalableColor>
</VisualDescriptor>
```

Figure 18.5   Code example of a visual descriptor.

ScalableColorDescriptor DS to model the color distribution. This can then be used to locate shot segments based on cinematography or on query-by-example.

To classify the events and actions within the scenes and shots, in a way that describes the scenes and shots from a semantic perspective, we have the Event DS. It is used to group one or more events with the Semantic DS. Using a TermUse DS tag, we can define the event to a standardized ontology. The TermUse DS uses terms defined by the Term DS in the ClassificationScheme CS. This enables the creator/user of the content to create a standardized set of terms for a particular domain (e.g., action movies that are standardized, comprehensive, and expandable). An example of a ClassificationScheme CS is given in Figure 18.6.

The event is referenced to scenes using the MediaOccurrence DS (Figure 18.7). The MediaInformationRef DS references the corresponding ID from the VideoSegment DS. We then reference the objects tied to this event by using the SemanticBase DS and typecasting it AgentObjectType. The SemanticBase DS uses the unique ID of the object in question and then gives it a name using the Label DS.

The events are defined by typecasting the SemanticBase DS to EventType (Figure 18.8). The event is given a unique identifier through the ID attribute tag in the SemanticBase DS. Using the TermUse DS, we can add additional event information to the main event that can be used to fine tune searches based on secondary events within the main one. An optional Definition DS tag can be used to add free annotated text that describes the scene/event. The Relations DS is used

```
<Description xsi:type="ClassificationSchemeDescriptionType">
        <ClassificationScheme uri="avpevents">
                <Term termid="fight">
                        <Name>fights</Name>
                                <Term termid="wrestle">
                                        <Name>wrestles</Name>
                                </Term>
                                <Term termid="shoot">
                                        <Name>shoots</Name>
                                </Term>
                </Term>
                <Term termid="jump">
                        <Name>jumps</Name>
                </Term>
        </ClassificationScheme>
</Description>
```

Figure 18.6   Code example of a classification scheme.

```
<MediaOccurrence>
        <MediaInformationRef idref="AVP-V-VS73" />
</MediaOccurrence>
<SemanticBase xsi:type="AgentObjectType" id="Alien-03">
        <Label>
                <Name> Alien </Name>
        </Label>
</SemanticBase>
```

Figure 18.7   Code example of a visual descriptor.

```
<SemanticBase xsi:type="EventType" id="AVP-EV73">
        <TermUse href="=" urn:avp:cs:avpevents:jump"/>
        <TermUse href="=" urn:avp:cs:avpevents:trapped"/>
        <Definition>
                <FreeTextAnnotation>
                        An Alien fights with Alexa.
                </FreeTextAnnotation>
        </Definition>
        <Relation type="urn:mpeg:mpeg7:cs:SemanticRelationCS:2001:agent" target="#Alien-O3"/>
        <Relation type="urn:mpeg:mpeg7:cs:SemanticRelationCS:2001:accompanier" target="#Alexa-O"/>
</SemanticBase>
```

Figure 18.8   Code example of an event.

to show the relationships hierarchically among the actors in terms of importance to the event.

Actions are structured similarly to events, mirroring the structure between the scenes and shots. Using the SemanticBase DS rooted inside of the event, actions are tied to individual shots. The actions use the same classification schemes as the events and can also use additional ones that are action specific. Each action is referenced to its accompanying shot using the MediaOccurrence DS in the same way as shown earlier.

18.4.2 Object Representation

Objects are described by modeling them using the Semantics DS tool. A unique ID is given to the object using the attribute tag in the Semantics DS (Figures 18.9 and 18.10). The Label DS tag is used to describe the object.

The SemanticBase DS is typecast to the AgentObjectType to create the MPEG-7 object for a person (Figure 18.10). The Graph DS and ClassificationScheme CS are used to identify the person from multiple perspectives. We can specify this by using the "depictedby" relation in the SemanticRelation CS.

The object is then referenced to the scenes and shots using the MediaOccurrence DS in a similar manner to the events and actions referenced to them (Figure 18.11). The difference is that a Mask DS typecast to a SpatialMaskType is used to outline the object boundary in the first frame of the scene or shot where the object appears. A SubRegion DS is used to demarcate the boundaries; in this instance, it is demarcated using the Polygon descriptor with its coordinate values expressed using the Coords descriptor. Shots are similarly referenced employing the same mechanism. All instances of the object are temporally referenced in the MediaOccurrence DS.

The objects are referenced to the events and actions by using the Relation DS and the SemanticRelation CS as pointers to the events and actions that the object is involved with (Figure 18.12). The SemanticRelation CS, which is part of the MPEG-7 standard, specifies semantic relationships that apply to the entities that have semantic information. In this particular instance, the SemanticRelation CS describes the relationship between the object and the events and actions, referenced by their unique IDs as an AgentOf relationship. The object is an agent of

```
<Description xsi:type="SemanticDescriptionType">
        <Semantics id="Alexa-SEM">
                <Label>
                        <Name>Alexa Woods</Name>
                </Label>
```

Figure 18.9   Code example of Semantics DS.

```
<SemanticBase xsi:type="AgentObjectType" id="Alexa-O">
        <Graph>
                        <Relation type="urn:mpeg:mpeg7:cs:SemanticRelationCS:2001:depictedby" source="#Alexa-O" target="
urn:avp:cs:AVPCharacters:Alexa Woods "/>
                        <Relation type="urn:mpeg:mpeg7:cs:SemanticRelationCS:2001:depictedby" source="#Alexa-O" target="
urn:avp:cs:AVPCast:Sanaa Lathan "/>
                </Graph>
```

Figure 18.10   Code example defining object classification through the Graph DS.

```
<MediaOccurrence>
        <MediaInformationRef idref="AVP-V-VS73"/>
        <Mask xsi:type="SpatialMaskType">
                <SubRegion>
                        <Polygon>
                                <Coords mpeg7:dim="2 5"> 5 25 10 20 …
                        </Polygon>
                </SubRegion>
        </Mask>
</MediaOccurrence>
```

Figure 18.11   Code example for defining the outer boundary of an object.

```
<Relation type="urn:mpeg:mpeg7:cs:SemanticRelationCS:2001:agentOf" target="#AVP-EV73"/>
<Relation type="urn:mpeg:mpeg7:cs:SemanticRelationCS:2001:agentOf" target="#AVP-EV73-A2"/>
```

Figure 18.12   Code example of a relationship with events for an object.

```
<Object id="Alexa-O-Face">
        <MediaInformationRef idref="AVP-V-VS73"/>
        <Mask xsi:type="SpatialMaskType">

                <SubRegion>
                        <Polygon>
                                <Coords mpeg7:dim="2 5"> 5 3 7 8 6 …
                        </Polygon>
                </SubRegion>
        </Mask>
</Object>
```

Figure 18.13   Code example for masking the outer boundary for a part of an object.

the event or action if the object is the agent of or performs or initiates the event or action [29].

The object can be split anatomically to identify semantically meaningful parts using the Object DS (Figure 18.13) in a manner similar to the way Mask DS is used

```
<SemanticBase xsi:type="SemanticStateType" id="Alexa-O-Physical-Attributes">
        <AttributeValuePair>
                <Attribute>
                        <Name>Height</Name>
                </Attribute>
                <Unit>
                        <Name>cm</Name>
                </Unit>
                <IntegerValue>170</IntegerValue>
        </AttributeValuePair>
        <AttributeValuePair>
                <Attribute>
                        <Name>Eye Colour</Name>
                </Attribute>
                <StringValue>Brown</StringValue>
        </AttributeValuePair>
</SemanticBase>
```

Figure 18.14   Code example of physical attributes for an object.

```
<Semantics id="Object-Hierarchy">
        <Label>
                <Name>Object Hierarchy</Name>
        </Label>
        <Graph>
                <Relation type="urn:mpeg:mpeg7:cs:SemanticRelationCS:2001:specializes" source="#Alexa-O"
target="#Human-O"/>
                <Relation type="urn:mpeg:mpeg7:cs:SemanticRelationCS:2001:specializes" source="#Alien-O3"
target="#BadAlien-O"/>
                <Relation type="urn:mpeg:mpeg7:cs:SemanticRelationCS:2001:specializes" source="#Predator-O3"
target="#GoodAlien-O"/>
                <Relation type="urn:mpeg:mpeg7:cs:SemanticRelationCS:2001:specializes" source="# BadAlien-O "
target="#Alien-O"/>
                <Relation type="urn:mpeg:mpeg7:cs:SemanticRelationCS:2001:specializes" source="# GoodAlien-O "
target="#Alien-O"/>
        </Graph>
</Semantics>
```

Figure 18.15   Code example of object hierarchy.

to outline the object boundary in the same frame as the earlier demarcation of the object. The MediaInformationRef DS is used to link the Object DS to its particular temporal instance reference.

The physical attributes of the object are addressed using the SemanticBase DS typecast to SemanticStateType (Figure 18.14). This allows us to declare attribute value pairs, using the AttributeValuePair DS, which can be used to describe the important physical attributes of the object. We can declare an attribute and value and also an attribute, unit, and value for measurements.

Object hierarchy is provided by the Graph DS and the Relation DS (Figure 18.15). The object hierarchy is stated in the ID attribute of the Semantic DS and named in the Label DS. In the Relation DS, the SemanticRelation CS describes the relationship as "specializes," which means that A is a subcategory of B. In the example given above, we see that the Alexa object is a subcategory of the Human object. Multiple relations can be stated within the Graph DS.

18.4.3 Spatial Relationships

The spatial relations are modeled using the SpatialRelation CS (Figure 18.16). Typecasting the Description DS to the SemanticDescriptionType allows us to

```
<Description xsi:type="SemanticDescriptionType">
        <Semantics>
            <Label>
                    <Name>Spatial Relations</Name>
            </Label>
            <SemanticBase xsi:type="ObjectType" id="Alien-O3">
                    <Label>
                            <Name> Alien#3 </Name>
                    </Label>
            </SemanticBase>
            <SemanticBase xsi:type="ObjectType" id="Alexa-O">
                    <Label>
                            <Name> Alexa </Name>
                    </Label>
            </SemanticBase>
            <Graph>
                    <Node id="nodeA" href="#Alien-O3"/>
                    <Node id="nodeB" href="#Alexa-O"/>
                    <Relation type="urn:mpeg:mpeg7:cs:SpatialRelationCS:2001:left" source="#nodeA"
target="#nodeB"/>
                    <Relation type="urn:mpeg:mpeg7:cs:SpatialRelationCS:2001:right" source="#nodeB"
target="#nodeA"/>
            </Graph>
        </Semantics>
</Description>
```

Figure 18.16   Code example for spatial relations.

```
<Semantics>
        <Label>
                <Name>Temporal Relations</Name>
        </Label>
        <Graph>
                <Node id="nodeA" href="##AVP-EV73-A1"/>
                <Node id="nodeB" href="##AVP-EV73-A2"/>
                <Node id="nodeC" href="##AVP-V-VS73-S1"/>
                <Node id="nodeD" href="#Alexa-O "/>
                <Relation type="urn:mpeg:mpeg7:cs:TemporalRelationCS:2001:precedes" source="#nodeA" target="#nodeB"/>
                <Relation type="urn:mpeg:mpeg7:cs:TemporalRelationCS:2001:precedes" source="#nodeC" target="#nodeD"/>
                <Relation type="urn:mpeg:mpeg7:cs:TemporalRelationCS:2001:co-occurs" source="#nodeA" target="#nodeC"/>
                <Relation type="urn:mpeg:mpeg7:cs:TemporalRelationCS:2001:co-occurs" source="#nodeB" target="#nodeD"/>
        </Graph>
</Semantics>
```

Figure 18.17   Code example for temporal relations.

describe the spatial relations among objects. Using the Semantics DS, we can state objects and then describe the spatial relationships among them. We also name the spatial relations graph using the Label DS within this element. Objects are stated by using the SemanticBase DS typecast to the ObjectType and the ID attribute set to the object's unique identifier. This references it back to instances in the object, scenes/shots, and events/actions descriptions described earlier. They are also named using the Label DS. The Graph DS is then used to describe the spatial relationships among those objects. Each object is created into a node using the Node DS to reference the object. The SpatialRelation CS is then used within the Relation DS to describe the spatial relationship between the nodes. The node structuring allows for a flexible and clearer way of describing relationships rather than stating them directly.

18.4.4 Temporal Relationships

Temporal relationships are grouped in the same way as spatial relations in the Semantic DS (Figure 18.17), where Temporal-Relationships is the ID and Label. It uses the same graph node structure as described in the spatial relationship graph description but has noticeable differences. We do not expressly state the entities involved but directly reference them within the Node DS for all entities. This is because the entities are multimodal (e.g., objects and events have no physical attributes in common). Using the TemporalRelation CS, we can then state the temporal relationships among the nodes.

18.5 Conclusion

The multifaceted, multiperspective MPEG-7 content model we have described greatly enhances the interaction between the user and the multimedia content by allowing the user to search and filter the information contained in an acute and precise fashion. The content model is structured to provide efficient and effective access to both semantic and structural elements of the content as well as the ability to view them from different contexts by applying relationships both temporally and spatially. The content model is structured using MPEG-7 semantic concepts that are widely adhered to in the industry, making it accessible to all information providers, and it is proprietary free.

The approach in this chapter was to automatically extract features from audiovisual content and model this content in a granular and rich manner using MPEG-7 tools so that any filtering application adopting the MPEG-7 standard may fully utilize its feature set of both semantic and syntactic details.

The automatic extraction of low-level visual cues and characteristics makes publishing a MPEG-7 content model more appealing because the obstacles of time and manual labor are negated. This approach could help the wide-scale adoption of content models because multimedia authors would find it easier to publish. The features extracted are familiar, standardized features common to both publishers and consumers of multimedia content. This approach facilitates a more coherent way to devise different applications for different environments for information filtering and retrieval. The application of genetic programming allows the content model itself to be personalized to a user's perception of the structure of the content semantically. Therefore, when the content is filtered or retrieved, the results obtained should be more directly pertinent to the user's information requirements than results obtained using other methods that do not involve the user in the content model creation process.

These low-level syntactical elements are tied to the higher level semantic concepts in a methodical and systematic manner. This encourages the use of the content model for searching both the physical attributes of the content and the meaning of the content either individually or in a combined manner.

M. J. Parmar is a doctoral candidate in information systems and computing at Brunel University, United Kingdom. He holds a BSc in multimedia computing (2000) from the University of Westminster, United Kingdom, and an MSc in multimedia information systems (2002) from Brunel University. His research interests include image processing, multimedia content modeling, multimedia content filtering and retrieval, and the application of MPEG standards. His research findings have been published in journals and edited books and his work has been presented at several conferences including several hosted by IEEE. He is a member of the British Computer Society, the ACM, and the IEEE Computer Society.

M. C. Angelides is a professor of computing at Brunel University, United Kingdom, a chartered fellow of the British Computer Society, and a chartered engineer. He has been researching multimedia for two decades and the application of MPEG standards through evolutionary computing for the last 8 years. In the last 6 years, the EPSRC has funded his research work on MPEG standards and evolutionary computing through several projects. Project results have been published extensively in relevant journals. The peer group that evolved from the funded research has led to the foundation of the IEEE group on Semantic Media Adaptation and Personalization (SMAP) whose membership has witnessed exponential growth. He holds a BSc and a PhD, both from the London School of Economics.

References

1. Sebe, N., and Q. Tian. Personalized multimedia retrieval: The new trend? *Proceedings of the International Workshop on Workshop on Multimedia Information Retrieval*, 2007, pp. 299–306.
2. Vasconcelos, N. From pixels to semantic spaces: Advances in content-based image retrieval. *Computer*, 2007, 40(7): 20–26.
3. Angelides, M. C. Multimedia content modeling and personalization. *IEEE Multimedia*, 2003, 10(4): 12–15.
4. Dimitrova, N. et al. Applications of video-content analysis and retrieval. *IEEE Multimedia*, 2002, 9(3): 42–55.
5. Money, A. G., and H. Agius. Video summarisation: A conceptual framework and survey of the state of the art. *Journal of Visual Communication and Image Representation*, 2008, 19(2): 121–143.
6. Lefèvre, S., J. Holler, and N. Vincent. A review of real-time segmentation of uncompressed video sequences for content-based search and retrieval. *Real-Time Imaging*, 2003, 9(1): 73–98.
7. Hu, Y. et al. Enhanced shot change detection using motion features for soccer video analysis. In *IEEE International Conference on Multimedia and Expo*, 2007: 1555–1558.
8. Grana, C., and R. Cucchiara. Linear transition detection as a unified shot detection approach. *IEEE Transactions on Circuits and Systems for Video Technology*, 2007, 17(4): 483–489.
9. Primechaev, S., A. Frolov, and B. Simak. Scene change detection using DCT features in transform domain video indexing. In *Systems, Signals and Image Processing*, 2007, and *6th EURASIP Conference Focused on Speech and Image Processing, 14th International Workshop on Multimedia Communications and Services*, 2007: 369–372.
10. Cao, J., and A. Cai. A robust shot transition detection method based on a support vector machine in compressed domain. *Pattern Recognition Letters*, 2007, 28(12): 1534–1540.

11. Schöffmann, K., and L. Böszörmenyi. Fast segmentation of H.264/AVC bitstreams for on-demand video summarization. In *Advances in Multimedia Modeling*, 2008, p. 265–276.

12. Petersohn, C. Logical unit and scene detection: A comparative survey. In *Proceedings of SPIE*, 2008, 6820: 17 pages.

13. Weng, C.-Y., W.-T. Chu, and J.-L. Wu. Movie analysis based on roles' social network. In *IEEE International Conference on Multimedia and Expo*, 2007: 1403–1406.

14. De Santo, M. et al. Segmentation of news videos based on audio-video information. *Pattern Analysis & Applications*, 2007, 10(2): 135–145.

15. Yoo, H. W. Retrieval of movie scenes by semantic matrix and automatic feature weight update. *Expert Systems with Applications*, 2008, 34(4): 2382–2395.

16. Petersohn, C. Improving scene detection by using gradual shot transitions as cues from film grammar. *Proceedings of SPIE*, 2008, 6820: 11 pages.

17. Chasanis, V., A. Likas, and N. Galatsanos. Scene detection in videos using shot clustering and symbolic sequence segmentation. In *IEEE 9th Workshop on Multimedia Signal Processing*, 2007: 187–190.

18. Sakarya, U., and Z. Telatar. Graph-based multilevel temporal segmentation of scripted content videos. In *Graph-Based Representations in Pattern Recognition*, 2007, pp. 168–179.

19. Kyperountas, M., C. Kotropoulos, and I. Pitas. Enhanced eigen-audioframes for audiovisual scene change detection. *IEEE Transactions on Multimedia*, 2007, 9(4): 785–797.

20. Sudderth, E. B. et al., Describing visual scenes using transformed objects and parts. *International Journal of Computer Vision*, 2008, 77(1): 291–330.

21. Sevilmis, T. et al. Automatic detection of salient objects and spatial relations in videos for a video database system. *Image and Vision Computing*, 2008, 26(10): 1384–1396.

22. Leibe, B., A. Leonardis, and B. Schiele. Robust object detection with interleaved categorization and segmentation. *International Journal of Computer Vision*, 2008. 77(1): 259–289.

23. Yong, G. et al. Cast indexing for videos by NCuts and page ranking. In *Proceedings of the 6th ACM International Conference on Image and Video Retrieval*, 2007. Amsterdam: ACM Press, 441–447.

24. Yamasaki, T., and K. Aizawa. Motion segmentation and retrieval for 3D video based on modified shape distribution. *EURASIP Journal on Applied Signal Processing*, 2007, 2007(1): 11 pages.

25. Ahmad, A. M. A., and S. Y. Lee. Fast and robust object-extraction framework for object-based streaming system. *International Journal of Virtual Technology and Multimedia*, 2008, 1(1): 39.

26. Adistambha, K. et al. The MPEG-7 query format: A new standard in progress for multimedia query by content. In *International Symposium on Communications and Information Technologies 2007 (ISCIT '07)*, 2007: 479–484.

27. Chen, W., and Y.-J. Zhang. Parametric model for video content analysis. *Pattern Recognition Letters*, 2008, 29(3): 181–191.

28. Basharat, A., Y. Zhai, and M. Shah. Content-based video matching using spatiotemporal volumes. *Computer Vision and Image Understanding*, 2008, 110(3): 360–377.

29. Canny, J. A computational approach to edge detection. *IEEE Transactions on Pattern Analysis and Machine Intelligence*, 1986, 8(6): 679–698.

30. Pratt, W. K. Digital image processing. 4th Edition. 2007. John Wiley and Sons: New York.

31. Gerald, F. et al. A practical approach to boundary accurate multi-object extraction from still images and videos. In *8th IEEE International Symposium on Multimedia 2006 (ISM '06)*, 2006: 307–316.

32. Allen, J. F. Maintaining knowledge about temporal intervals. *Communications of the ACM*, 1983, 26(11): 832–843.

33. Salembier, P., and J. R. Smith. MPEG-7 multimedia description schemes. *IEEE Transactions on Circuits and Systems for Video Technology*, 2001, 11(6): 748–759.

Index

A

Abstract semantic level, 374
Active entertainment services, 97
Active facets, 190
Active facets selection, 197
Adaptation
    classification of operations, 34
    concepts for, 33
    of content, 33
    decision-taking component, 38
    knowledge-based multimedia, 35
    process, 56–58, 256–266
    runtime UI, 56–59
    user-centered, 43
    utility-based multimedia, 35
    video, 68
Adaptation engine, 58
Adaptation modes, experimental results for, 197
Adaptation space, 33
Adaptation targets, 26
Adaptive hypermedia *vs.* web personalization, 249–250
AdaptiveInteliWeb (AIWeb), 255, 263
    component, 263
    environment, 263–266
Adaptive multimedia retrieval systems, simulation framework, 120
Adaptive video retrieval model, research framework, 120–122
AdaptiveWeb system
    architecture, 255–256
    comprehensive user profile in, 250–253, 267
AdaptiveWeb user interface, 255, 263
Advanced video coding (AVC), 69
Afghan Community Information System (ACIS), 371
ALC description logic, application of, 343

Algorithm matching, 353, 355–356, 362
Annotation, 138, 191, 231
Annotation CINeSPACE system, performance of, 374–375
Annotation tools, *see also* CINeSPACE annotation tool
    based on MPEG-7, 368–370
    Caliph, 368, 379, 394
Ant colony optimization (ACO), 300
Anthropometry, 284
Apache Cocoon, 193
APML, *see* Attention Profiling Markup Language
Application layer, 387
Application level, 373
ARMA model, *see* Autoregressive moving average model
A4SM project, 370
ASR, *see* Automatic speech recognition
Asynchronous JavaScript and XML (AJAX), 4, 122
Attention Profiling Markup Language (APML), 232, 238
AttributeValuePair DS, 418
Audio cues, 404
Audio/video on-demand systems, 97
Audiovisual content, 212, 372, 374
Automatic background extraction, 357
Automatic content modeling, 399–400, 402
Automatic extraction of spatial relations, 357
Automatic feature extraction to MPEG-7 content model 399–420
Automatic monitoring of behavior, 357
Automatic speech recognition (ASR), 116, 124–125, 234
Autoregressive moving average (ARMA) model, 406

425